ACCOUNTING FOR MANAGERIAL DECISIONS (MANAGEMENT ACCOUNTING)

Accounting for Managerial Decisions (Management Accounting)

[For B.Com./M.Com., and other Management Courses of All Universities]

By
Ved Prakash

ANMOL PUBLICATIONS PVT. LTD.
NEW DELHI - 110 002 (INDIA)

ANMOL PUBLICATIONS PVT. LTD.
4374/4B, Ansari Road, Daryaganj
New Delhi - 110 002
Ph.: 23261597, 23278000
Visit us at: www.anmolpublications.com

Accounting for Managerial Decisions (Management Accounting)

First Published, 2005

[Responsibility for the facts stated, opinions expressed, conclusions reached and plagiarism, if any, in this volume is entirely that of the Author. The Publishers bear no responsibility for them, whatsoever.]

PRINTED IN INDIA

Published by J.L. Kumar for Anmol Publications Pvt. Ltd., New Delhi - 110 002 and Printed at Mehra Offset Press, Delhi.

Contents

Preface

Accounting For Managerial Decisions as a paper is being taught at the graduate and post graduate level in B.Com., M.Com. and other Management courses syllabus in almost all the Indian Universities and Institutions. The various courses conducted by management institutions at the Central and State level too have been considered in respect of their syllabus, course contents and requirements. Thus the material presented here would be of interest as well as great use to the students of B.Com., M.Com. and other Management Courses. This book will provide complete knowledge of different accounting activities, budgeting in managerial decision, standard and capital costing, trends and other issues in management accounting for getting bettere knowledge in managerial decisions.

The major topics dealt in this book are—Accounting for Management; Accounting Activities and Responsibility Centres; Budgeting in Managerial Decisions; Standard Costing; Capital Budgeting; Marginal Costing; Emerging Trends in Management Accounting; Application of Marginal Costing; Ratio Analysis; Fund Flow and Cash Flow Analysis; Reporting to Management; Contemporary Issues in Management Accounting

Ved Prakash

1

Accounting for Management

In order to understand this, it is appropriate to analyse a more traditional but commonly accepted definition of accounting given in the *Accounting Terminology Bulletin No.1 of the American Institute of Certified Public Accountants, viz*:

"Accounting is the art of recording, classifying and summarising in a significant manner and in terms of money, transactions and events, which are in part at least, of a financial changes and interpreting the results thereof."

Explanation

(A) Transactions. Recordable happenings or events (usually exchanges) that affect the assets, liabilities, capital, revenues or expenses of an entity.

(B) Event. A process or a part of a process having a particular moment and place of occurrence. A typical event is a transaction with an outsider.

Thus the accounting must be viewed in its fundamental processes of recording classifying and reporting the transactions and interpreting the financial data, thereof. It aims at revealing the financial conditions of an organisation and financial changes which take place in it from time to time. Following basic features of are accounting function may be explained as under:

1. Recording. It means that the transactions of financial character must be written down reasonably soon after occurrence in the books of the organisation *e.g.*, cash book, sales and purchase books, journals, and so on, so that a complete record is available about different phases of business activities of the organisation. In addition, it must also be made certain that all of financial transactions are recorded in an orderly manner that is under appropriate account titles. Such records would be of great assistance for presentation and interpretation of business results, that is, the extent to which the business is successful or whether its finances are in good order. Timely and orderly recording of transactions makes it possible to obtain whatever information which is necessary.

2. Summarising. The art of summarising in a significant manner involves the preparation of statements such as income statement, balance sheet and other reports from the classified data in a manner useful to the internal management and external users of accounting information. In this way all important and material accounting information is disclosed.

3. Classifying. It is concerned with the systematic analysis of the recorded data so that the items of same type or like nature are grouped under appropriate accounts. This accounting classification is accomplished in an orderly fashion by maintaining ledgers with individual account heads under which all financial transactions of similar nature are collected. For example, all transactions relating to cash/bank would be recorded in the cash book while the credit purchases and sales in the purchases and sales books respectively and so on.

4. Interpreting. Finally, the accountants are required to interpret the contents of their statements and reports in a manner beneficial to the users and enable them to make meaningful judgements about the operational efficiency or and financial position of the business enterprises. "The emergence of mechanised and electronic data processing devices has freed accountants from the routine aspects of recording and classifying data, enabling them to concentrate more on the analytical and interpretation aspects of the accounting function. These are the areas most affected by the new demands for accounting function."

Interpretation may involve explanation of the uses, meaning and limitations of 'accounting information. The past figures are important for future guidance. "Consequently the accountant must be able to .explain not only what did happen but also why it happened and most important what is likely to happen under certain conditions in future". He must be able to interpret correctly the meaning of data recorded so as to use the same for future projections. Comparison of past and present statements and reports, use of ratio analysis and long term trends are the important tools for this purpose. His very largely the ability to weave a living, dynamic pattern from a mass of inert figures that makes the accountant worth his salt.

NATURE OF ACCOUNTING

The definition of accounting includes such important phrases as: "in a significant manner" and "transactions and events". These phrases raise important questions like 'significant for whom?' and what son of transactions and events?' Though the definition clarifies that the recording is carried out in terms of money, a layman can hardly appreciate the nature and scope of accounting in this manner. While accounting is many things to many people, its nature is essentially described as follows:

1. **An Intellectual Discipline.** The commonly recognised fields of specialised study are philosophy, physics, chemistry, mathematics, political science, economics and biology, space research etc. These are often called intellectual disciplines or simply disciplines. Most people agree that accounting is a separate discipline. It is in a way a dynamic discipline in which new procedures and principles are constantly evolving. Other disciplines are also concerned with measurements and information. Thus the boundaries of accounting merge readily and significantly with the boundaries of economics, engineering, psychology, law, statistics etc. When accounting is related to and combined with other disciplines, it tends to be more useful than when it stands alone. The many practical uses to which accounting knowledge can be put serve as a 'primary attraction to the field.

2. **A Social Force.** A third pan of accounting is its thrust as a social force. The expansion of large scale modern business

or public organisations would have been impossible without an adequate financial information system. The separation of ownership and management, a characteristic feature of corporate form of business organisation, is feasible only if reliable periodic financial upon are supplied by professional managers to the owners. In a sense, accounting facilitates ownership by remote control. Accounting information is also helpful in the fields of price determination of products monopoly and restrictive trade practices legislation, the regulation of stock markets, the fixation of rates in public utilities and lot of other similar issues. Accounting information directly influences decisions in these areas. This influence arises from the way in which the accounting records the transactions, classifies and summarises them and later reports to various interested users.

3. **A Profession.** Although modem accounting dates back to 1494 when an Italian monk named Fr. Luca Paciolo described a double-entry accounting procedure that forms the basis for accounting practice today, the development of accounting as a profession is relatively new. It was stimulated primarily by new forms of economic activity resulting from industrial revolution. The development of the corporation form of business organisation, the product of industrial revolution, also created a new social need—the need for an independent audit to provide some assurance that management's financial representations were reliable. In fact this audit function, often referred to as the "attest function" was chiefly responsible for the development of accounting as a profession. Other functions are management consultants and tax services. Professional accountants are recognised by different names in different countries of the world *e.g.* Chartered Accountants in India, Certified Public Accountants in D.S.A. The phenomenal growth in commerce education and rapid increase in the number of chartered accountants, cost and works accountants etc.,

provide an adequate evidence for the growth of accounting as a profession.

4. **A Tool of Social Welfare.** The nature of accounting should not be analysed in a way that it is confined only to private use of information which has limited scope and which is concerned with the effect of accounting information on the welfare of individuals as such. The social welfare concept of accounting is related to the impact of information on all the individuals making the society. As we shall discuss later that accounting information is used by a number of groups having vested interest in the activities of the business enterprise *e.g.*, managers, owners, creditors, employees etc. It is clear that the supply of information to one group may give them unfair advantage over the other groups in the decisions which they subsequently make, resulting in the changes in the allocation of social benefits. "The social welfare theory of accounting requires that the interests of employees, trade unions and consumers ought to be taken into account and the traditional imbalance existing in the supply of information should be corrected.

OBJECTIVES OF ACCOUNTING

1. Resource Allocation Decisions And Accounting Information. One of the central economic problems of every economy is the allocation of limited resources among competing alternative uses. Considering it at the micro level, this problem affects the decisions of business entities, individuals and even the Government. The primary purpose of any business activity is to earn profit. Due to scarcity of almost every type of resources, the business entities must decide whether to invest in stock of goods (or raw materials) plant and machinery, advertising, research and development or other alternatives. Managers of these entities are responsible for obtaining maximum advantage from the use of resources placed at their disposal. Thus they need accounting it formation to help them make decisions regarding the use of firm's limited resources. For example, a business enterprise engaged in the production of more than one kind of product must be aware of the cost of producing each type of product. The financial information would enable the management to decide whether or not certain products should be continued or whether certain products should be manufactured in greater quantities. Management can also determine from financial information when certain machinery is to be replaced; whether additional labour force be employed or some employees should be dismissed. In addition to business firms, individuals and non-profit entities tend to use accounting information for decisions concerning the investment of their limited funds. An investor attempts to analyse the accounting information to determine which company best meets his investment goals. The utilisation of financial information in allocation of limited funds from the point of various segments of society may be explained as under:

(i) A supplier of goods will decide whether or not to sell goods on credit and will determine the total amount of credit that should be provided?

(ii) The grantors of loans such as banks or specialised financial institutions will decide whether or not loans should be advanced for the existing or future projects.

(iii) An owner will decide whether or not he should continue or increase his investments in the company.

(iv) Labour unions are assisted in negotiating working conditions and wage agreements.

(v) A prospective investor will make a decision between different investment opportunities.

Even the Governments use accounting information to decide whether the resources should be allocated to defence, construction of infrastructure, welfare programmes, space research, etc.

2. Accounting As The Basis of Decision-Making. Accounting is a service activity. It's purpose is to provide quantitative Information about economic entities. The information is primarily financial in nature and is intended to be useful in making economic decisions in making reasoned choices among alternative courses of actions. In fact the accounting information is used as an input to the decision-making process. Decision-making is a unique human capability. One of the main distinctions between the human being and other forms of animal life is the ability to make conscious decisions. If the entity for which the accounting information is provided is a business, the information is used by its management to make decisions some of which are listed below:

3. Identification of Economic Information. There is a wide variety of information which may be collected and used in the decision making process. Accounting, is one source of information for decisions. The ascertainment of information which is to be included in accounting relies on the criteria of relevance and quantifiability. This is the basic characteristic of the accounting information since if information is not relevant it is useless. To be relevant to a decision, the information must be available on a sufficiently timely basis to influence the decision. The accountant is faced with the problem of selecting from the mass of data those things which are most likely to meet the needs of different goals. For example, the information required by bankers or some security analysists is not necessarily the same as required by small investors or internal managements. The accountant must analyse the needs of various users (known and unknown) and determine which information is common and relevant to all existing and potential decision-makers.

4. The Accounting Process. One of the most important tasks of modem accounting is, therefore, to assist different users in making decisions outlined above. In order to adequately serve this task accounting is concerned with the processes of:

(A) identifying;

(B) measuring; and

(C) communicating useful economic information to permit informed Judgments and decisions by users of the information.

The accounting processes of identification, measurement and communication involve financial transactions about business entities the primary motive of which is to earn profits. As noted earlier, resources are assumed to be limited; therefore choices must be made.

5. An Aid in Resource Management. To a man in the street, the accounting is a study of commercial or profit-making activities. Even an ordinary individual with some academic background relates the role of accountant to prepare the tax-returns or as an adviser on the financial to of business or investments. But these misconceptions about the role of accounting can be cleared to a great extent when we find in practice that individuals, both in private business and in public bodies, engage in transactions which may be recorded classified and summarised yet which may have no profit motive. The point is that the accountant may serve any social unit, large or small, private or public, profit seeking or not. He serves it by recording the resources at its disposal, who owns these resources and any change which occurs in the amounts held. The accountancy has constantly changed to meet the different requirements of society.

FINANCIAL ACCOUNTING PROCEDURE

Financial Accounting is the traditional form of accounting which is mainly concerned with the recording of business transactions. Under the system of accounting, business transactions are first recorded in the books of original entry then classified into ledger and finally summarized by preparing trial balance. From trial balance the profit and loss a/c is prepared to ascertain the periodic profit or loss. The profit and loss a/c or Income statement shows the operating results of the business done during the accounting period. The B/S is prepared which is, as a matter of fact, position, statement of the business. It shows the financial position of the business as at the end of the accounting period. This whole system of financial accounting is of historic nature. It is static in character. During the initial stages of business development, the financial accounting has served the business world very well but with the growing complex business organisations the limitations of financial accounting have become obvious. Though, nobody can deny with the utility of the two basic financial statements - income statement and position statement, but there are certain important limitations and deficiencies too in this system. In short, financial statements of system of financial accounting suffers from the following deficiencies:

1. **Financial Accounts are of Historic Nature.** Financial accounts are of historic nature. They record the net effect of events which take place in the business, *i.e.* expenses are recorded when they have actually been spent. Such recording of past facts does not help the management in planning for future and decision-making. Profit and loss a/c shows the amount of profit or loss earned during the last accounting period but it cannot analyse the causes for low profits. It cannot suggest anything to increase the profits in future. This work is "done by management accounting. Management accounting analyses the past records and presents the relevant facts in a suitable manner before the management so he may take decision for the future.

2. **Incomplete Knowledge of Costs.** From the costing point of view also the financial accounts are incomplete. In trading and profit and loss a/c all expenses are debited to one account only. The existence of profits in a particular period is taken as an index of efficiency of business under financial system of accounting. But product wise or job wise cost of production can not be determined on their basis. Information regarding wastages and losses is very difficult to get from financial accounts. Prices cannot be fixed on the basis of information given by these accounts because they deal with total expenditure arid not with expenditure incurred on even product or unit of service. These accounts cannot indicate the exact remunerative price which may be quoted in periods of difficulties.

These all deficiencies of financial accounts have been over-come by management accounting as it makes intensive use of most accounting. Cost accounting records the costs product, process or job wise as necessary. It can throw a good deal of light on unnecessary losses and wastage. A good system of cost Accounting affects an independent and most reliable check on the accuracy of final accounts too.

3. **No help in Decision Making.** Financial accounts do not help in decision making also. Due to the historic nature of accounting data available from financial accounts is not of much help to the management. Management accounting presents this data in a suitable form and useful manner and helps the management in selecting a profitable alternative on the basis of that information. Management accounting is very dynamic and forward looking in this respect.

4. **Financial Accounting is a Technical Subject.** It is also a serious limitation of financial accounting that it is highly technical in nature. People possessing adequate knowledge of accounting concepts and principles, well conversant in the practice of accountancy can prepare and interpret the financial accounts. Management accounting is not technical. It presents the accounting information in a simple, easy, non-technical and intelligible manner. It does not follow any set format for the presentation of data. Various statements in management accounting are prepared according to the needs of the business and its management. Any educated man can understand them easily.

5. **Recording of Actual Cost.** In financial accounts assets and properties are shown at their cost acquisition. No effect of changes in their value is recorded in the books after their acquisitic data. Generally, assets are shown at going concern value which has nothing to do with the realisable value or replacement value of the assets. This limitation of financial accounts reduces their utility. This financial accounts report about the profitability of the assets as a whole.

6. **No Evaluation of Business Policies and Plans.** Financial accounts do not provide for evaluation of business policies and plans. They do not throw any light on the implementation of programmes and policies of the Management. They do not make any study of variances in the performance and possible reasons for it. On the other hand, Management Accounting does not help only in me formulation of the policies; it is intimately concerned with their implementation also. Budgetary control system is a unique device to carry on the programmes in the desired direction.

7. **Financial Accounts do not Provide for Cost Control.** Cost can not be controlled through financial accounting. Its main reasons are as follows:
   - (i) Here expenses are recorded after when they have actually been spent. Hence they provided no change to take corrective action.
   - (ii) Financial accounts do not have any technique to check the reasonableness of any expenditure.
   - (iii) Financial accounts do not fix definite responsibility on any authority for wastage or excessive expenditure.

Management accounting makes intensive use of standard costing, marginal costing, cost-volume-profit analysis, etc. Responsibility accounting is also an important aspect of management accounting. The various tools and techniques of management accounting help the management in exercising effective control on the cost and revenues.

Thus, we see that Financial Accounting serves only general purpose. In spite of the accounting devices, improved techniques and elaborate subsidiary records, financial accounting is of limited use to the management due to the above said obvious limitations of them. The Management Accounting which has -grown out of traditional accounting, is the most dynamic aspect of accounting. The main purpose and function of management accounting is to help management in planning and controlling the operation of a business. It is a service function. It aids management in doing better management. But, however, Financial Accounting and Management Accounting are not conflicting. The both are complementary and co-operative in character. The advent of management accounting has added strength and vitality to the main stream of accounting.

MEANING OF MANAGEMENT ACCOUNTING

Till recently accountant's role was as one of book-keepers and his duties ended with the, balancing of accounts for a given period. The growing complexities of the business and the awareness that the figures can unfold the behaviour of production and distribution have enhanced the demand for accountant's work. The characteristic feature of modem business is the tendency to large size. The gulf between management and ownership has widened, thus raising the problem of 'control'. Moreover, the stiff competition has necessitated the need to raise productivity and shorn off wastes. Such problems cannot be solved through the there procedural financial accounting. Truly speaking, the resultant effects of World War I, the great' depression of thirties and subsequent World War II attacked the thoughts of businessmen to devise the ways and means by which efficiency, that is, productivity, could be stepped up and control achieved with the aid of organisational methods. Management became conscious of the accountants contribution and the term Movement accounting began to acquire universal status.

Management accounting has been defined by the Anglo-American Council on Productivity as "the presentation of accounting information in such a way as to assist the management in the creation of policy and operation of day-to-day undertaking". It is, therefore, the provision, analysis, reporting and discussion of accounting information as a guide to management in the day-to-day running and future planning of the business, as distinguished from the recording part of the accounting function for historical and statutory purposes. The accountant does not furnish only routine figures to the management but renders a well-designed service and advice and management can work on the principle of reporting by exception whereby only items calling for special attention are brought to the notice of senior management and not a multitude routine.

There is a general misconception that the management accounting is something new and complex and requires an expensive system capable of comprehension only by experts. This contention is not true. A reference to the accounting literature would reveal that even in the past, the accountant went beyond figure work and discussed with his management the implications of events and trends in broad financial terms and that is what the management accounting does. It is the role of the accountant as an adviser or helper, instead of the "accountant" who feels his task done when the results are ready. The accountant is a partner in the management team though this feeling has been realised now because the accountant is a '**Johny come lately**' to the team management accounting system works on simple lines in that management must be provided with the relevant figures in a 'well presented' manner. It is not always necessary to seek the assistance of expensive electronic data though the utility of the same cannot be discounted. Even if the amount spent is considerable the benefits derived in the long run would outweigh the costs.

In nutshell, management accounting serves the information requirement of the insiders-directors, managers and employees. When it issues reports, it need not adhere to specified accounting principles. The number, frequency and content of reports can be determined at the discretion of management.

FUNCTIONS OF MANAGEMENT ACCOUNTING

An efficient management strives to raise productivity by utilising the available resources. Management, therefore, has to make important decisions from time to time. Management accounting plays an important role in this connection. Accounting is opinion expressed in numbers and since decisions are based on opinions, accounting is one of the most useful tools for decision-making. With sound data to base its decisions, management can operate more efficiently, more economically and more profitably. Managerial function of planning, co-ordinating and control etc. are assisted by facts, figures and their interpretation provided by originating and control etc. are assisted by facts, figures and their interpretation provided by management accounting. The following is the description of managerial functions:

(A) Planning. Management has to plan the activities well in advance to cope with the prevailing dynamic conditions. Planning offsets uncertainty, focuses attention of objectives, obtains economical operations and facilitates control. Plans have to be based upon detailed information and must be flexible and for longer terms, if the business is to survive.

An important plank is the forecasting which is preliminary to business planning. The success in forecasting is achieved when the past events are related to the future and to this extent the alert management is guided by the accounting data from the historical reports and therefore the coming events can be accurately predicated.

Planning is the selection from among alternatives for the organisation as a whole and each part within it. In business, financial factors are involved. The accountant has the past data of the firm and relevant information of other enterprises as well from the published records. An analysis and interpretation of such information is of material help to management in choosing between alternatives.

The formal outcome of forecasting and plans are put in budget which as a plan is a statement of expected results expressed in numerical terms. The budget, in fact, is sheet-anchor of management accounting and it covers all phases of business ranging from the production function to the marketing of the products.

The accountant participates in the preparation of various types of budgets, by providing past data so as to work out the future changes. The accountant must organise the process of budgeting for optimum benefits. The sales budget is only one budget and the real problem, as a part of planning, is to find out the plan which provides for sales which give the lowest cost or production, the lowest employment of funds in working capital, and lower requirement for new capital investment. It is not 'merely putting the figures together; the management accountant will have to make intelligible conclusions and a firm commitment to the plans. The accountant, therefore, assists management planning as:

(a) By presenting and analysing the results of the enterprise in terms of income and expenses.

(b) By converting technical details in terms of money.

(c) By estimating the future figures of profits and the overall general financial position.

It is imperative to underline that the accountant can be a good partner in management planning function only if he is fully aware of the objectives of the Chief Executive and realises that he is a member of the planning team.

(B) Controlling. Control function is best studied in three parts: Motivating, Checking and Restraining.

Motivational aspect of the control function entails to induce people to work as they are able and trained to do. Inducement comes from pecuniary and non pecuniary benefits. Accountant is required to assist management in framing schemes regarding pecuniary benefits and report the cost of benefits like incentives, wage plans, fringe benefits (*i.e.* holidays with pay, premium plans and so on) etc.

The vital contribution to control function is found in the 'checking aspect.' As **Fayol** puts it: 'In an undertaking, control consists in verifying whether everything occurs in conformity with the plans adopted.' The accounting reports, made to different levels, are used to compare the actual performance with the scientifically laid standards, the details of which are contained in the reports. A clear revelation should be made in the reports regarding the success of the plan objectives; the reasons for difference, if any, must be clearly stated.

Leadership and persuasion are the necessary elements of the restraint aspect of control for desired results. What is required is the fixation of realistic standards and well established uniform procedures to be followed by inspection and review of results. The accounting reports should be drawn to make this review feasible.

Controlling is, therefore, related to the determination of success in planning and the best control corrects deviations from plans before they occur. It is rightly held that 'management control seeks to compel events to conform to plans'. Management must ensure that the existing devices of control are adequate and used by the individuals concerned. The activity of 'internal auditing' is an effective tool to provide this help. An internal audit is a review of operations and records and the internal auditor, an employee of the firm, assures the management of the effectiveness of the policies and procedures in carrying out the aims of management. Summing up the control function, the management is aided by budgeting, methods, procedures and internal audit-the facets of management accounting."

(C) Developing New Products and Capital Projects. The development of new products and the projects requires the estimates of the expenditure and the returns thereof. It is the balancing of these two factors which is necessary for decision-making. Management accounting does the job by taking help from such disciplines as cost accounting. In a talk delivered under the auspices of the Forum of Free Enterprise, Bombay, Shri P.L. Tandon, the then Chairman of Hindustan Lever Limited pointed out, "Our accounts department offers much services in the field of development of new packs, new products and new projects. Whenever our management thinks of something new, they turn to the accountants to study the financial implications. This, in short, is where the accountants and our general management together look ahead to make sure that a change or new development will produce healthy results. It should be underlined that it is not the accountants who dictate the managers' policy. Managers must make their own decisions, based upon the information they receive. And they may decide for other perfectly valid reasons to go ahead with the project which has a longer pay-back period and lower yield: it may have broader economic or social objectives; but management must know where they stand and what they base their decisions on. This is where the accountant can help them."

(D) Co-oridinating. Co-ordination, the essence of the management functions, aims at achieving harmony of individual effort towards the accomplishment of the enterprise goals. The best co-ordination occurs when individuals see how their jobs contribute to the dominant goals of the enterprise, that is, achieving maximum benefits with minimum of expenses. The accountant can bring about complete co-ordination in the organisational structure by spelling in details the responsibilities of each function and its relationship with other positions. Accounting records must be drawn in terms of the costs and accomplishment. It may be emphasised here that the accountant must be conversant with 'the organisation hierarchy' and be alert to the changes if he is to prove his abilities in co-ordinating business activities.

SCOPE OF MANAGEMENT ACCOUNTING

Management accounting has a very wide scope. It embraces within its ambit not only financial accounting and cost accounting but tax accounting, auditing, reporting and office services also. The following are the different fields which are covered under management accounting:

(1) Financial accounting provides the basic information for analysis for managerial use. The historical data, records and accounting details help management to plan for the future. Management accounting is futuristic but future trends and tendencies are always based on the past; hence the need for financial accounting first.

(2) Management accounting techniques are primarily cost accounting techniques. The techniques of marginal costing, budgetary control and standard costing which are techniques of cost control are important tools of control in the hands of management. The costs of different cost centres and cost units are calculated under cost accounting which are relevant for decision-making by the management. The concepts of controllable and uncontrollable costs, relevant and irrelevant costs, opportunity costs, differential costs-all are used in management accounting.

(3) Auditing, of course, internal, is another field which has been plunged into the arena of management accounting of late. Internal audit has become so important these days that management relies heavily on it for fixing responsibilities

and taking action against individuals. The system is used as a basis for performance appraisal.

(4) For planning business affairs, forecasting and budgeting both are very significant. Forecasts provide the basis for budgets. Predetermined targets help people in business to perform tasks accordingly and if there are deviations, corrective steps can be taken by management.

(5) Financial analysis is a part of management accounting. Through analysis of financial statements, interpretations can be made about the profit-ability, solvency and liquidity positions of an enterprise. Financial appraisal can be made and after assessing the short-term and long-term financial position by applying various techniques of financial analysis, decisions can be taken regarding several issues to improve the financial position and to increase the profitability of the business.

(6) Management accounting lays out its hands on different control procedures and methods. As a matter of fact, the basic objective is to use various resources available the most economical, effective and efficient manner and this can be fulfilled when different techniques of control are adopted and implemented successfully.

(7) Reporting is another significant aspect of management accounting. Prompt and timely reporting is essential for quick and timely action. Reports are prepared at lower managerial levels and submitted to middle-level management and by middle-level management to top management. Both routine and special reports are prepared. The reports may take the shape of statements, graphs, charts, diagrams, tables, accounts, narratives etc.

(8) Tax has become an important part of business life. How can such a crucial burden on the funds of the enterprise be left ignored by management accounting. Large amount of liabilities is required to be paid by business and it has

necessitated tax planning by every management. Proper tax planning and tax management save business from the clutches of this monster to a very great extent.

LIMITATIONS OF MANAGEMENT ACCOUNTING

Despite the fact that the development of an effective discipline in managerial accounting is one of the most significant steps to improve managerial performance, the new discipline has to face conditions which limit the effectiveness of management through accounting. Such conditions are:

1. Though the main contribution of management accounting has been the elimination of intuitive management, there is always a temptation to take an easy course of arriving at decisions by intuition rather than taking the tortuous path of scientific decision-making.
2. Adoption of a system of management accounting brings about a radical change in the established pattern of the activity of management personnel. It calls for a rearrangement of personnel as well as their activities. This is bound to encounter opposition from some quarter or the other.
3. As the emergence of management accounting has been the result of fusion of a number of subjects like statistics, accounting, management theory, economics, engineering, etc. an inadequate grounding on the part of management in anyone or more of these subjects is bound to have an unfavourable effect on the consideration and solution of problems relating to management performance.
4. The installation of a system of management accounting requires a very elaborate organization and a very large number of rules and regulations with the consequence that the entire proposition becomes quite costly and can, there-fore, be adopted only by very big concerns.
5. Comparatively, management accounting is a new discipline and is still very much in a state of evolution. Therefore, it

comes across the same impediments as a relatively new discipline has to face - sharpening of analytical tools, improvements of techniques and fluidity of concepts creating uncertainty about their applications.

6. The ambitious nature of the objective, which management accounting seeks to serve, and the extremely wide scope of the subject-matter dealt with by it create many difficulties. Thus, it is one thing to record, interpret and evaluate an objective historical event convened into money figures while it is something quite different to perform the same function in respect of past possibilities, future opportunities and unquantifiable situation.

SIGNIFICANCE OF MANAGEMENT ACCOUNTING

The Management Accountant's services are invaluable management in all their functions. Indeed, the Management Accountant may be said to act as the eyes and ears of management. All the necessary information and data are provided by him to the management. He also gives his suggestions and recommendations as to where and when management should exercise vigilance and control and what course of action should be pursued in any given situation. It is through the timely submission of accounting reports by the management accountant that the attention of operational managers and supervisors is drawn to adverse trends and thus precautions and correctives can be applied in time.

Management accounting is the blending of all processes connected with financial and cost accounting and is also concerned with the establishment and operation of internal controls. The shaping, timing and circulation of resulting information constitute, so to speak, the premise on which management functions are carried out. But for the informational materials supplied by the management accountant, planning, control and operating activities would have been lacking in objectivity and teeth.

The significance of management accounting has increased very rapidly in recent times due to the improvement in analytical and problem-solving techniques and the availability of more efficient data processing equipment. With the help of these techniques and apparatus, the management accountant is able to process data and satisfy the management's informational needs for assessing the causes and effects of cost and revenue changes, the cost implications of making and buying a component, whether it would be profitable to process a by-product beyond the split off or to sell it without further, processing, whether output should be expanded beyond the existing level, and similar other matters.

Management accounting involves a process of selective and discriminating reporting of data. It emphasises and highlights the relevant facts, out of the mass of data-facts which would be useful in the solution of problems at hand. Thus it aids and facilitates prompt decision-making by the management.

In the large, complex organisations of today, it is hardly possible for managers particularly at higher levels to maintain adequate contact with all operations on a continuous basis. It is thorough systematic meaningful reports that efficient management of operation can be secured in the modern enterprises. Moreover, the management accountant consolidates all relevant information about which activities are clearly related to the principal objectives.

OBJECTIVE OF MANAGEMENT ACCOUNTING

Decision making in any business concern is the primary function of management Technological developments and data processing by computers have left traditional accounting far behind in its ability to serve the decisional needs of management. Traditional accounting very well served the purpose under simple conditions of business but the tremendous expansion of the scale of production has brought out its inadequacy in grappling with the new business conditions. The two key elements in the success of an undertaking are accounting control and management capacity. These two are fully met by management Accounting through the harnessing of accounting for the purpose of management.

The evolution of management accounting has given a new dimension to the function of accounting. The basic objective of management accounting is to help the management in their functions of formulating policies, making decisions, planning activities and controlling business operations. The manner in which management accounting satisfies the diverse needs of management for arriving at proper business decisions are the modification of accounting data and the analysis and interpretation of this data. It does not restrict itself only to financial data but also draws upon sources, other than accounting, for such information as is not capable of being convertible into monetary terms. Management accounting processes accounting data in a way that yields concise information covering the entire field of business activities as to serve the top management.

The main objective of Management Accounting can be summarised as follows:

(1) Business success very much depends upon proper planning which is the primary function of management. It includes analysing properly the available data and forecast on the basis of available information. When the data is put in a proper prospective it helps the management in effective planning. The financial accountant presents the relative figures of the past and estimates of the future. These assist the management in determining courses of action and deciding on the programme of activities to be undertaken by the concern. Management accounting provides costing and statistical data to be utilised in setting goals and framing policies. Management accounting assists in planning for a specific purpose as well as over all planning for the organisation.

(2) Accounting is the language for communicating the financial facts about the organisation and its activities to those who have an interest in making their proper use by interpreting them. It improves the efficiency of the concern and assist the management in its task of maximising profits or minimising losses. Management accounting provides a means of communicating management plans through the

organisation. It is an important part of the company's management information system.

(3) Assistance in the interpretation of financial information. Management accounting is concerned with the analysis and the interpretation of such data which has opened up new directions. It is concerned with records of past achievements, maintenance of values, fixation of responsibilities and basis for assisting the future development. The financial accountant maintains detailed record of transactions affecting assets of the organisation, creditor's claims, owner's equity, revenues and costs etc. The management may not find time to go through all this information provided in the law form. Management accounting presents accounting information in an intelligible form that will enable business executives, investors and creditors in analysing and interpreting the various financial statements.

(4) Decision making is primarily a function of management. Management accounting helps the management in making sound decisions. These decisions may relate to expansion of the business or contraction or diversification of an existing business or it may be in question of starting a new line, the management accounting helps in solving all such questions. Management accounting uses the available accounting figures in solution of the various management problems. Its function is to provide necessary data and not decisions. It only informs the management and leaves the task of decision making with them. It provides and presents the alternative plans in a comparative manner and gives an insight into the implication on the future of the organisation. With the help of the available information placed by management accounting, it is up to the management to choose the best course of action. Its useful techniques regarding marginal costing, cost volume profit analysis, standard costing and capital budgeting assist the management

in arriving at rational and sound decisions. Anthony has described Management Accounting as "the use of accounting figures in recognition or solution of management problems.

(5) Marketing management emphasises on budgetary control, marginal costing, standard costing, funds flow analysis, internal financial control etc. All this requires an intensive study Of the organisational structure of the organisation. It helps in rationalising the organisational structure of the business concern more efficiently.

(6) Management accounting facilitates management in controlling the destiny of the organisation. Standards for performance are maintained and any deviation from them is measured and estimated. Measuring actual performance against approved operating plans, standards and budgets are interpreted and reported to the heads of the departments at higher levels. All these help the management in controlling the overall performance of the organisation. Cost control techniques and functional control enables the management to delegate the authority easily and successfully.

(7) The setting of goals, proper planning, employment of economical course of action, measuring the performance go a long way in improving and increasing the effectiveness of the organisation. Thus management accounting helps the management in motivating their employees.

(8) Management accounting is concerned with the efficiency of the various phases of management. It helps in overall control and proper coordination of business operations. Budgets serve as the best means of coordination. The various plans are based on budget which is a statement of plans in financial terms. Planning is followed by directing the planed operations coordinating the activities of different departments and units and controlling the operations so as to achieve the desired goals.

TOOLS AND TECHNIQUES USED IN MANAGEMENT ACCOUNTING

The presentation of accounting information in such a way as to assist management in the creation of policy and in the day-to-day operation of an undertaking In order to discharge its duty of helping the management sincerely and faithfully in the various managerial functions planning, co-ordination, control and appraisal of activities management accounting uses the following tools and techniques:

(1) **Historical Costing Accounting.** Cost accounting is an integral part of the accounting process which provides management with cost data relating to products, processes, jobs and operations. The statement of actual costs after they have been actually incurred is called historical cost accounting. These are based on recorded costs and can be easily verified with the help of evidences regarding are transactions involved. These costs are accumulated continuously over time and summarised at the end of each accounting period so that a comparison can be made with the standard costs.

(2) **Funds Flow Statements.** Preparation of funds flow statements is also an important tool of management accounting. A Funds Statement is technical device designed to analyse the changes in the financial condition of a business enterprise between two dates. In other words, it describes the sources from which additional funds were derived and the uses to which these funds were put. Funds-flow statements help a lot in financial analysis and control, future guidance and comparative studies.

(3) **Marginal Costing.** Marginal costing is also known as opportunity costing or costing for alternatives. It is an important tool of managerial decision-making. Marginal cost is the increase or decrease in total cost which results from producing or selling certain additional or fewer units of a product or from a change in the method of production or distribution Marginal costing includes the discussion of

cost-volume-profit analysis and break-even analysis also. An integrated application of these techniques help the management in taking sound production and distribution decisions.

(4) **Analysis of Financial Statement.** Analysis of financial statements is the second important tool of management accounting. In the words of Kennedy and MC Multer, "The analysis and interpretation of financial statements are an attempt to determine the significance and meaning of the financial statement data so that a forecast may be made of the prospects for future earnings, ability to pay interest and debt maturates and probability of a sound dividend policy." The preparation of comparative financial statements, trend analysis, funds-flow techniques and ratio analysis are some important techniques of financial analysis. The analysis and interpretation of financial statements results in the presentation of information that will aid to business executives, investors and creditors.

(5) **Budgetary Control.** One of the essential features of modern management is planning and control. There are a number of devices which help in controlling. The most widely used device for managerial control is 'budget'. A 'budget' is a quantitative expression of plan of action. It is an estimate of future needs arranged according to an orderly basis, covering some or all of the activities of an enterprise for definite period of time. 'Budgeting' is the process of preparing budgets and budgetary control is the technique of managerial control through budgets. It is an important technique of directing business operations in a desired direction, *i.e.*, a satisfaction return on investment.

(6) **Financial Planning.**Planning is always concerned with the future course of action. Financial planning is the act of deciding in advance the financial activities that are necessary if the firm is to achieve its primary goal. It involves three fundamental steps: *(a)* determining both long-term and short-term financial objectives of the firm; *(b)* formulating

financial policies and *(c)* developing the financial procedures to achieve the objectives. A business firm's ultimate objective is to make the optimum use of all factors of production in order to maximise the return of' investors. Financial policies act as a guide to the firm achieving this goal. The determination of the following financial policies is important in this connection:

(i) Policies that determine the optimum level of investment in various current and fixed assets.

(ii) Policies that govern the determination and distribution of income.

(iii) Policies that act as a guide in the use of debt and equity capital.

(iv) Policies that determine the amount of capital required for the firm, and policies that determine the sources of funds.

(7) Standard Costing. Standard costs are pre-determined costs, *i.e.* estimates of what costs should be under best possible conditions. They provide a yardstick for measuring actual performance. Standard costing is the preparation and use of standard costs, their comparison with actual costs and the analysis of variances to their causes and points of incidence. Thus standard costing is an important tool of cost control which is one of the main objectives of management accounting.

(8) Decision Accounting. Decision making is the primary function of top management. It is a process of selecting the one best alternative for doing a work. The increasing complexity of organisational problems requires that improved methods of decision.

(9) Others

(a) Reporting

(b) Statistical & Graphical Techniques

(c) Revaluation Accounting.

MANAGEMENT ACCOUNTING PRINCIPLES

Besides the basic accounting principles, which are accepted generally throughout the accounting profession, the following are the additional conventions/principles which are now generally regarded as essential part of management accounting.

(1) A profit cannot be said to be earned unless capital is maintained intact in real terms.

This convention recognises that the monetary unit is not stable attempts to overcome the effects of changes in the value of money have been made via revaluation accounting, but as yet there is no general acceptance of the theory. However, there is strong evidence that more and more accountants are modifying their views to meet the dynamic state of business and the economy.

(2) Costs are best controlled at the points at which they are incurred "Control-at-source accounting".

Recognition of this convention is acknowledged through the preparation of departmental operating statements and the design of costing system which control individual workers, material issues; and the usage of services. The inculcation of cost consciousness is also an essential part of this convention.

(3) The "principle of management by exception" is followed when presenting information to management.

This assumes that plans are predetermined and then actual results are compared with expected results. If there are no deviations there is no necessity to report. When there are variations from predetermined place management is informed precisely of what is going wrong. In this way, the information presented to management is kept to the minimum, yet at the same time all important fads are being revealed. What is more, management has less to read and study and, therefore, should have more time to take action.

(4) Accounting information, records, reports, statements, and other evidence of past, present, or future results should be designed and compiled to meet the needs of the particular business and/or specific problem.

This implies a certain flexibility of system. When a particular problem is to be solved the system should be capable of producing the relevant data. If necessary, there must be departure from double-entry principles. Accounting and operational-research principles should be linked together. Information should be accumulated and then presented to solve problems. The accounting information should be modified and adapted to meet each need whenever possible. However, it is important to remember that if this principle is carried too far, the cost of the management accountancy system may become excessive. It is partly for this reason that a systematic, rather than an ad hoc method, is used for accumulating costing data.

(5) Management accountancy should endeavour to show whether or not the resources of the business are being utilised in the most effective manner.

(6) Personal contact with departmental managers, foremen, and others cannot be replaced entirely by reports and statements.

(7) There should be integration of all management information so that fullest use is made of the facts available and at the same time, the accounting service should be provided at minimum cost.

(8) Management accounting systems and related forms should be used only as long as they serve a useful purpose.

This normally implies that mechanisation should be adopted as much as possible. It does not mean that every business should employee a computer. The machines selected should be of a size and, type that can economically be employed by the particular concern to deal with its own problems. If there is insufficient work for a computer, then clearly this should not be required.

(9) Return on capital employed is used as the criterion for measuring the efficiency of the business. For this purpose the capital employed should be calculated by reference to current replacement values.

(10) The most appropriate means of accumulating, recording and presenting the accountancy information should be selected.

(11) Management accountancy should seek to anticipate problems and prevent them. There should be a forward-looking approach and actual costs should be employed only as measures of achievements realised. This principle recognises the importance of budgetary control and standard costing.

(12) Overhead cost should be apportioned to cost centres and absorbed to products on the basis of benefits received for fixed costs or responsibilities incurred for variable costs. The method or methods selected should bring about the desired results of recovering the overheads in the most equitable manner. However, this is subject to what is stated on this matter in the chapter on Marginal Costing.

(13) When tracing responsibility a clear distinction should be made between those costs which are controllable and those which are uncontrollable by the management of the business or department concerned.

The above list of conventions is fairly long. However it is not exhaustive on account of the subject of management according to being a growing one. It may be possible that in the times to come many more suitable convention may be developed by the management accountants all over the world which may take the form of universally acceptable management accounting principles.

ESSENTIALS FOR SUCCESS OF MANAGEMENT ACCOUNTING

1. Reporting to management in time is necessary so that management can take timely action. The management should observe the 'principle of exception' for control purposes.
2. Proper systems of performance evaluation should be in operation. Actual performances should regularly be compared with those budgeted and pre-determined on the basis of standards. Quick and constant comparisons will help management to remain alert about off-standard performances.
3. Looking 'ahead' is a must for the management. The management must be competent enough to look into the future so that effective planning may be possible through forecasting and budgeting.
4. Human factor must be recognised by the management. Proper incentives, both pecuniary and non-pecuniary should be provided to people in the concern.
5. Sound financial and cost accounting systems must exist.
6. It is essential that the people with whom management accountant has to work have faith in management accounting.
7. The objectives and basic policies of the business should be made clear to everyone in the organisation.
8. There must be a team spirit among all members of the organisation. Management must objectively criticise the functioning of a department and the departmental heads should also take it sportingly. They should work in the interest of the concern as a whole rather than of their own department alone.

MANAGEMENT ACCOUNTING IN THE INDIAN CONTEXT

With the increasing tempo of industrial growth and product development which started with the second five year plan, there has been a phenomenal change in the business methods and systems in India. Management of large and medium scale industries has become increasingly more complex and difficult partly due to the adoption of modem technology and partly due to the necessity of tackling multifarious problems in the operational and financial fields. Under these conditions, the professional manager's need for information and data which have been discreetly selected, organised and interpreted has become all the more greater.

On the other hand, the scope of using quantitative techniques and analytical tools has been increasing rapidly with greater opportunities of management education and training. The usefulness of management accounting techniques like standard costing, budgetary control, marginal costing, cash flow and funds flow analysis, inventory control techniques, probability estimates, operations research and others have been recognised more consistently in the process. Indeed, the Management Accountant is now regarded as an important member of top management in many companies.

A special feature of Indian economic development since independence is the rapid growth of the public sector as a direct consequence of the objective of working towards the realisation of a socialist pattern of society. The significance of management accounting in public enterprises can hardly be overemphasised. The necessity of successful management of large undertakings has posed a new challenge to the public sector. Advance planning and control have as much importance in public enterprises as in the private sector. Planning is a pre-condition of success as it provides the basis for organisation, assembling resources, direction and control. It has been observed by the Planning Commission that the preparation of advance costs, operation and capital budgets greatly reduces the need for making references to the administrative Ministry and straining then the autonomy and flexibility of the enterprises. Besides, advance planning provides an opportunity for seeing that each part fits in with the other and is directed towards the overall purpose. Setting up of specific goals and subgoals is an inseparable part of the whole planning process. A wide variety of operating standards and 'norms' need also to be set up to express the anticipated results of the detailed plans. Comparable data from other similar plants in the country and outside are often found to be of great value in this connection for administrative control. Continuous appraisal of results is equally vital. Availability of necessary information and data for planning, decision-making and control is thus of prime importance. The role of management accounting in that context can make or mar the success of the whole enterprise.

When public enterprises run efficiently and follow proper price policy for their goods and services, the results of their operations must be reflected in larger earnings and surpluses. In a developing economy, these constitute a ready and increasingly important source for financing investment it is therefore incumbent on public enterprises to produce efficiently and to accumulate surpluses which should be earmarked for further development. As an aid to management providing meaningfully arranged data with objective analysis and interpretation, management accounting can go a long way in making public enterprises efficient and productive.

The role of the Financial Adviser who performs the role of Management Accountant as well in the public undertaking has often caused serious misgivings. However, the Planning Commission it made the position clear as early as 1961. The Financial Adviser is expected to function subject to the authority of the General Manager. In case of difference of opinion, it should be quite open to the General manager to overrule the advice of the Financial Adviser, but there should be a convention that such cases should be brought to the notice of the Board by the General manager at the next Board meeting. According to the Planning Commission, the Financial Adviser of any public undertaking should concern himself with problems of financial management rather than devote exclusive attention to the control of expenditure.

ACCOUNTING AND BOOK-KEEPING

There is some confusion over the distinction between accounting and book-keeping and some people took upon them as one and the same. Although the two are clossly related and there is no universally accepted line of separation. Yet, book-keeping is only a part of accounting *i.e.* the record making part and the book-keeper is one who records the transactions. Much of the work of the book-keeper is clerical in nature and is increasingly being accomplished through the use of mechanical and electronic equipment.

Accounting is primarily concerned with the design of the system by which business transactions are to be recorded by a book-keeper. An accountant may supervise the work of the book-keeper; he may prepare reports based on the recorded data and interpret the reports. Although the work of the book-keeper is more routine, it is difficult to draw a line where the book-keeper's work ends and the accountant's begins. The work of the accountants at the beginning levels may possibly include some book-keeping. "In any event the accountant must possess a much higher level of knowledge conceptual understanding and analytical skill than is required of the book-keeper". Simply stated the confusion over the difference between the book-keeping and accounting therefore is understandable because of following reasons:

(A) Even in education, the inclusion of accounting as a subject in the courses of studies at the stage of secondary education is of recent origin; the major thrust earlier was on book-keeping.

(B) Record keeping as a trade is ancient, that is many centuries old; accounting is yet to make its impact felt.

(C) It is very common to find some financial records almost in every type of business. Only few are aware of the problems of analysis and interpretation involved in dealing with large mass of financial data in commercial transactions.

(D) The first part of the definition-recording, classifying and summarising is the major source of confusion between book-keeping and accounting, the former is only one aspect of the latter.

General Considerations

It is relevant to mention that in its book-keeping aspect the accounting proceeds on the following general considerations:

(i) **Only Cost is The Basis of Record.** The assets are recorded in the books only at their cost, that is, the actual price paid or incurred for them. To this price we may add the incidental charges incurred-on their acquisition.

(ii) **Money-As A Unit of Measurement.** It means that for the purpose of recording transactions, only the items capable of being expressed in money values are considered. No attempt is made to record the general efficiency or health of the executive or employees of the organisation. For instance, business records are concerned only with the payment of salary in terms of money to the purchase manager and not his efficiency in effecting the economy in purchases which would be recorded in terms of total amount spent for the same.

(iii) **Historical Facts.** Only those transactions which have really taken place are recorded. There is no scope to record that will happen in future. Thus the buildings would be recorded as an asset only when they are actually purchased and similar treatment would be given to the sale of different items when they are actually sold. There is no such thing as the possibility or likelihood of sale or purchase of any item in the accounting records.

(iv) **Cost Accounting & Management Accounting.** Cost Accounting is the process of accounting for costs. It embraces the accounting procedures relating to recording of all income and expenditure and the preparation of periodical statements and reports with the object of ascertaining and controlling costs. It is, thus, the formal mechanism by means of which the costs of products or services are ascertained and controlled. On the other hand, management accounting involves collecting, analysing, interpreting and presenting all accounting information which is useful to the management. It is by associated with management control which comprises planning, execut measuring and evaluating the performance of an organisation. Thus, management accounting draws heavily on cost data and other information derived from cost accounting. Today cost accounting is generally indistinguishable from the so called management accounting of internal accounting use it serves multiple purposes.

However, management accounting can be distinguished from cost accounting in one important respect. Management accounting has a underscope compared to cost accounting. Cost accounting deals primarily with cost data while management accounting involves the considerations of both cost and revenue. Management accounting is an all inclusive accounting information item which covers financial accounting cost accounting and all aspects of financial management. But it is not a substitute for other accounting functions involves a continuous process of reporting cost, financial and other relevant to in an analytical and informative way to management.

We should not be very much concerned with the boundaries of cost counting and management accounting since they are complementary in nature. In the absence of a suitable system of cost accounting management will it be in a position to have detailed cost information and their function is bound to lose significance. On the other hand, the management cannot effectively use cost data unless it has been reported to them in a meaningful and informative form.

❐

2

Accounting Activities and Responsibility Centres

KINDS OF ACCOUNTING ACTIVITIES

1. Kinds of Accounting Activities—'One of the major accounting accounting activities relates to *financial accounting* which is concerned with recording and summarizing financial transactions and preparing statements relating to the business in accordance with generally accepted accounting principles enunciated by the accounting profession. These reports on the financial condition and profitability of business enterprise essentially relate to the accountability of the managers of the business to its owners and, therefore, this accounting process is a part of management accounting

2. Management accounting (or Management control systems as it is often called) relates to the use of financial and cost data for purposes of evaluating the performance of the business as a whole and the various departments comprising it in relation to predetermined targets. It also aids in reviewing existing policies or making decisions about new policies, and in forward planning. In contrast with financial or cost accounting, there are no set procedures for management accounting since the classification, summarization and interpretation of data for managerial purposes must essentially be related to the specific needs of the management of individual enterprises.

3. Income tax accounting involves preparing records and reports necessary for filling tax returns to local, state and central governments. Tax regulations often differ from concepts underlying financial accounting and, moreover, they are in a state of continuous change. This results in the expenditure of considerable specialised effort by

company accountants to comply with prevailing regulations and yet minimise the tax burden by choosing appropriate accounting techniques (permissible under the law).

4. Cost accounting is basically concerned with the determination of the aggregate costs (as well as the various components of such cost) of the goods and services manufactured or offered by the business. The cost accounting process is again based on data recorded for purposes of financial accounting, though the classification, summarization and interpretation of Such data are essentially governed by the need to determine and report costs relating to the various activities of the business to be aggregated for purposes of determination of cost of the goods or services produced by the company.

5. National Accounting.

6. Social Accounting.

Significance

A businessman starts business for earning profits. He is, thus naturally interested in knowing answers to the following questions:

1. The types and amounts of earnings.
2. The types and amount of expenses.
3. The amount of loss, if any.
4. The amount of capital and size and causes of increase or decrease.
5. The nature and value of liabilities.
6. Customers who owe to the business and the amount in each case.
7. The nature and value of assets possessed by the business.
8. Suppliers to whom the business has to make payments and the amounts in each case.
9. Other facts for filing various returns for external use, *e.g.*, income-tax return.

A systematic accounting procedure is the only answer to these questions. Without developing a good system of accounting a businessman will not be able to find out any fact about the business and it will float like an abandoned boat in the sea.

Significance of accounting can also be justified by following users who are using accounting information.

(A) It is not difficult to conclude that the internal people who would be most interested are the owners of the business. The owners are proprietors in proprietary concerns and the partners in partnership businesses, while in the case of a company (or corporation, as it is sometimes caned) the legal owners of the company are the shareholders. Shares may be held by individuals or companies or corporations or even the Government. Clearly the owners would like to know:

(i) whether its costs are in line with the volume of sales and norms of costs in similar enterprises elsewhere.

(ii) whether the growth of its sales are in line with the expectations of the shareholders;

(iii) whether these operations are profitable in terms of return on funds invested or return on assets, profits per rupee of sales, gross-margin per unit of sales, etc.;

(iv) whether the financial condition of the enterprise is sound as reflected in its capital to retained earnings ratio, current assets to current liabilities ratio, funds flow statement, etc.;

(v) whether the enterprise made any profit during the period reported and if so, what the dividend prospects are;

There might be individual shareholders who are interested in greater financial details relating to the operations of a company, but the average shareholder would expect to find answers to the questions set out above in the balance sheet and the income statement prepared by the enterprise for purposes of external reporting.

However, the owners are not the only persons within the company or the internal group who are interested in the various aspects of the operations of a business. With the separation of management and ownership.

(B) Managers at various levels beginning from shop floor superintendent to the Chairman and Chief Executive, are also interested in the business. Some of their needs for accounting information relate to:

(i) taking remedial action for overcoming such shortfalls;

(ii) highlighting the areas of shortfalls from planned performance;

(iii) evaluating the performance in relation to the targets set up;

(iv) measuring the performance of the various units of the business as also the enterprise as a whole; and

(v) setting up targets for future periods, usually the next financial year.

Most of this information would be financial in nature and would essentially be prepared from the accounting records. However, it would require special knowledge and skill to assemble the data and to present them in meaningful terms for resolution of the managerial problems outlined above.

(C) The last category of persons belonging to the internal group who are interested in ascertaining the financial condition of the companies for the resolution of their problems are the employees of the business.

(D) In order to understand the communication process, we might ask ourselves who are the people interested in the operations of a business enterprise. There are several entities outside the business (or in other words external to it), which are interested in its operations because of their business dealings with the enterprise. There are individuals or organisations who have economic transactions with the business, *e.g.* suppliers of goods and services on credit, banks or financial institutions lending money either for a short or a long period, buyers of goods and services produced by the enterprise on the basis of stipulated targets, contractors who have undertaken to build plants and buildings and other facilities for the business. They are all interested in varying degrees in the operations of the businesses with which they deal in order to determine whether the enterprise is credit worthy and the terms under which credit can be extended, *i.e.* the amount of goods or services that can be sold on credit (or the loans that can be advanced), the period of such credit and the likelihood that the debt arising out of the transactions would be repaid in time.

(E) The external group is by no means limited to such individuals or organisations who have economic transactions with the business. Government departments or other agencies who are charged with the responsibility for regulating general business activity or particular types of business are also naturally interested in the operations of the business. Some of the Government departments having general interest, in the Indian context, are the Company Law Board, Registrar of Companies, Income Tax Department, Ministry of Industrial Development, Ministry of Foreign Trade, etc. Government organisations looking after particular product groups are Ministry of Health as also officials and bodies designated for overseeing particular activities like Drugs Controller, Cost and Prices Bureau, Tariff Commission, etc. Some of the Government departments are specifically charged by law to regulate the operations of a particular group of companies, *e.g.* the State Electricity Boards. The interest of the regulatory agencies is essentially to ensure that the enterprise complies with the requirements of the law relating to financial transactions, *e.g.* it pays the required amount of tax, does not over trade on its capital, pays dividends to its shareholders out of the profits, provides depreciation according to prescribed norms, and

(i) provides data relating to its borrowings (and the assets charged or mortgaged for raising such loans) so that future lenders are provided with the required information regarding the present level of borrowings and the state of the security provided by the assets, etc.

(ii) discloses its capital, retained earnings, profits, sales and costs to the public at large so as to submit its activities to public scrutiny.

Obviously, the balance sheet and the income statement prepared in consonance with the requirements of the disclosure provided in the law would be of great help to the regulatory agencies in these matters.

(F) The next category of external users consists of those who have neither any economic transactions nor are concerned with regulation of business activities but are interested in the operations of the business on behalf of constituents which they represent, *i.e.*, *as representatives of external interests.* In this category can be included labour unions, stock brokers, chambers of commerce, trade associations, export agencies, etc. These bodies would like to ensure that their members or clients interests are safeguarded in terms of the required degree of financial viability of the enterprise with which they deal or that the revenue costs and profits of the enterprises are disclosed fairly so as to enable their members of clients to determine accurately, in financial terms, the quantum of economic transactions, for instance, bonus to be paid to the members of a trade union or dividends to be paid to investors.

(G) The external group would include, on the one hand, the *auditor* of the business who is required by law to certify the accounts and, on the other, the: *prospective shareholders* who wish to subscribe for shares of a business entèrprise or want to buy an already-issued share from another shareholder. Other persons who would be interested in the business, even though they may not be directly concerned, are the business economists analysing the business enterprise's success or the *financial press* providing information to their readers regarding the operations of the business world.

(H) In other circumstances, a person or a body might be interested in the results of the operations of a business for determination of claims or resolution of disputes, *e.g.* a court deciding upon the ownership of shares as between two claimants or judging the merits of a claim against a business in liquidation, an arbitrator settling a dispute between a business organisation and the suppliers of goods and services to that business or a tax tribunal assessing a claim of a business enterprise for income tax relief.

RESPONSIBILITY CENTRE

Responsibility accounting focuses on responsibility centres. A responsibility centre is a sub-unit of an organisation under the control of a manager who is responsible for the activities of that responsibility centre. A small firm can possibly be managed by an individual or a small group of individuals. However, for effective control a large firm is divided into meaningful segments/departments. Each sub-unit has certain activities to perform and its manager is assigned the responsibility/authority to carry out those activities. These sub-units of an enterprise for the purpose of control are called responsibility centres/division centres. As observed in the introductory part of this chapter, the responsibility centre can be a big unit, such as a production department or division, or a small unit such as the cash section of the accounting department. The important criterion for creating a responsibility centre is that the unit of the organisation should be separable and identifiable, for operating purposes and its performance measurement should be possible.

TYPES OF RESPONSIBILITY CENTRES

For purposes of measuring financial performance the divisions of a firm may be classified according to the type of financial data used in the measurement of performance. Three basic classes of divisions can be identified on these grounds: profit centres, cost centres and investment centres. Detail account of each of these is' given below:

I. Profit Centres

"A profit centre is a responsibility centre in which inputs are measured in terms of expenses and outputs are measured in terms of revenues." Both the elements of accounting information cost and revenues are considered. In other words, in a profit centre the measure of performance is broader than in an expense centre because in an expense centre the accounting system measures only one element, whereas in a profit centre both the elements (cost as well as revenue) are measured in monetary terms. The difference between revenues and costs is profit. Stated operationally, the profit centre is a division or sub-unit of an organisation in which financial performance is measured on the basis of profit. While the cost figures are the same as used in expense centres, the term "revenue" with reference to responsibility accounting is used in a different sense. It may be recalled that the generally accepted principle of accounting is to recognise revenue only when sales are made to outside customers. For purposes of profit centre performance, revenue represents a monetary measure of the output of a profit centre in a given accounting period whether or not the firms actually realise the revenue in that period. *The test is that a department has output which are amenable to monetary measurement.*

Since in profit centre there are financial measures of the output as well as of the input, it is possible to measure the effectiveness and efficiency of performance in financial terms. Profit analysis can be used as a basis for evaluating the performance of a division as an entity and/or for evaluating the performance of a divisional manager. A profit centre requires all of the data needed in an expense centre as well as additional data regarding revenues. Therefore, management can determine whether the division was efficient in the utilisation of resources and, further, whether the division was effective in attaining its objectives. This objective is presumably to earn a satisfactory "profit". The criterion for a satisfactory profit may be budgeted profit/past profit in the division/profits of other similar divisions/ some combination of two or more of these. "Profit" as a performance measure, is based on revenues and expenses directly traceable to the division and avoidable if the division were closed down. This concept of divisional profit is referred to as "profit contribution" as it is the amount of profit contributed directly by the division. It might also be described as "incremental profit" or the additional profit earned solely as a result of operations of the division. Further, divisional profits are before taxes, the reason being that taxes are assessed on the basis of the income of the entire company and they may be regarded as similar to common costs and excluded from the calculation of the divisional profit.

Another element in the computation of profit as performance measurement for a profit centre. This relates to the types of profit centres. A profit centre, *e.g.* a product division, uses inputs and produces output. Such a profit centre is very like an independent firm. It is called a "natural profit centre." The alternative to the natural profit centre is the "constructive profit centre." It is not a natural profit centre but it may be made to appear as one. An example is the computer centre or data processing department. It makes use of inputs but it produces no revenues as it renders computer services to other departments and does not sell its products/services. This is logically an expense centre. However, the management has an alternative to owning and operating a computer: to purchase computer time from a data processing service. The management will compare the two alternatives and select one which involves a lower cost. *The cost avoided is the revenue to the firm by owning a computer. This is constructive profit. Divisional profit data can be used to evaluate the performance of the division/divisional manager in the case of natural profit centres alone.*

In brief, the relevant profit to form the basis of performance measurement of a profit centre is the before tax incremental contribution profit margin of a natural profit centre. The profits of all the divisions thus calculated will not necessarily be equal to the profit of the entire firm. The divergence would arise from the fact that costs not attributable to any single division are excluded from the computation of divisional profits but they are considered in determining the profit of the organisation as a whole. It may, therefore, be concluded *that divisional profit is a unique concept, designed to serve specific managerial needs.*

Advantages

A profit centre, as a responsibility centre, is of considerable significance in measuring the performance divisions divisional managers. Three aspects deserve special mention.

(A) Profit, defined, as the difference between revenues and costs is a combined measure of both effectiveness and efficiency. It provides a powerful tool for measuring how well the profit centre/manager of the profit centre has performed.

(B) The profit centre is closely related to the organisational principle of decentralistion; profit centres make decentralised organisation possible. Top Management can safely delegate the authority to the divisional managers because the profit centre reports/provide adequate information about how well the operating managers are doing their jobs. In brief, profit centres provide a broader and more inclusive measurement of performance than the expense centres. If managers are responsible for both revenue and expense aspects of performance (profit centre), the contribution of each manager to the goal of the entire organisation is easier to measure than when no single manager is responsible for both revenues and expenses (expense centres).

(C) A profit centre resembles a business in miniature. Like a separate firm its profit are calculated. The performance of the managers is measured by profit. Therefore, they will be motivated to take decisions about inputs and outputs in such a way that the profit of a profit centre is maximised. In other words, managers can he expected to behave as if they were running their own business. For this reason, the profit centre is a good training ground for general management responsibility.

Problem

The profit centre approach also encounters certain problems. These relate to *(A)* transfer prices, *(B)* criteria for profit centres, and *(C)* measurement of expenses.

(A) Transfer Price. The measurement of profit in a profit centre type of responsibility accounting is also complicated by the problem of transfer prices. A transfer price is a price used to measure the value of goods/services furnished by a profit centre to other responsibility centres within a company. In other words, when internal exchange of goods and services take place between the different divisions of a firm, they have to be expressed in monetary terms. *The monetary amount for these inter-divisional exchanges/ transfers is called the transfer price.* The determination of an appropriate transfer price is one of the major problems of profit centres. The implication of the transfer price is that for the selling division (the division whose goods/services are being transferred) it will be a source of revenue, whereas for the buying division (the division which is receiving/acquiring the goods/services) it is an element of cost. It will, therefore, have a significant bearing on the revenues, costs and profits of responsibility centres. Hence the need for correct determination of transfer prices. The determination is, however, complicated because a wide variety of alternative methods are available. We therefore first discuss the basic types of transfer prices. Transfer price policies to indicate the circumstances in which different types of transfer prices are suitable are also examined.

(B) Criteria for Profit Centres. One problem with profit centre is that it cannot be used for all responsibility centres. The criteria to use a profit centre for a responsibility centre includes the consideration of the following points: *(a)* (Extra record-keeping is involved to measure input and output in monetary terms. *(b)* When a responsibility centre is required by management to provide service to other responsibility centres, the service department (*e.g.* internal audit) should not be a profit department. *(c)* Unless the divisional managers of responsibility centres have reasonable authority to decide on the quality/quantity of outputs or on the relation of output to costs, a profit centre will be of little use as a control device. *(d)* If the output of a product/division is fairly homogeneous (*e.g.* cement), a profit centre may not offer substantial advantage; however, an expense centre may do so. *(e)* There may be friction between profit centres due to the spirit of intense competition. Moreover it may generate too much interest in short run profit to the detriment of long-term results. The operational implication is that unless these problems are overcome, the profit centre technique would not serve its purpose and should therefore not be used.

(C) Measurement of Expenses. Another problem with profit centres may relate to the measurement of certain types of expenses which have to be included in the computation of profit centres. There is scope for difference of opinion relating to the treatment of those expenses which relate to the organisation as a whole. In view of the special nature of divisional profits, such expenses should not be considered since they are not the responsibility of the division/ divisional manager. That such expenses are not the responsibility of the division is another way of saying that they cannot be traceable/ attributable to it and should be ignored in working out the profit of the division as a profit centre.

II. Cost Centres

Cost centre is a responsibility centre in which inputs, but not outputs, are measured in monetary terms. It has been pointed out earlier that responsibility accounting is based on financial information relating to cost and outputs. In an expense centre of responsibility the accounting system records only the cost incurred in by the centre/ unit but the revenues earned are excluded. Stated differently, an expense centre is a segment whose financial performance is measured in terms of cost. Since the performance of an expense centre is measured by the financial measure of cost only, an essential requirement is that the cost of operating the division be directly traceable to it. This means the relevant costs are the *avoidable cost* of operating that division. The incremental cost would include both variable and fixed costs but would exclude costs common to several divisions and allocated among them on some arbitrary basis. From the viewpoint of the measurement of performance of the divisional manager, the implication of the expense centre is that his performance will be judged on the basis of the cost incurred in his division; what is done in the division (output) will be of no consequence. The analysis of performance is restricted to the consumption of resources in the division and there is no reference to what the division has achieved as a consequence of consuming those resources.

What is the suitability of *cost* as an index of performance? The expense centre can be employed in three situations. *(a)* In several cases, the output of a responsibility centre cannot be reliably measured in financial terms. Included in this category are centres such as legal departments, accounting departments, public relations departments and the personnel departments. Each of these centres/

divisions has a conceptually identifiable output-legal advice, good public relations (public relations department), reliable accounting reports (accounting departments) and better qualified personnel (personnel department). Their outputs cannot obviously be expressed in monetary terms. The only measurable performance measure is their efficiency in the use of inputs. Thus, such divisions can be evaluated only as expense centres. In brief, *cost is a suitable measure of performance in staff units/divisions. (b)* If a production centre/unit/segment is producing one single product, its performance can be measured as expense centre in terms of *efficiency and effectiveness.* Although, the output cannot be expressed in monetary terms, the number of units produced can reasonably represent output. The cost per unit of the product would be indicative of the efficiency of the department. A comparison of the actual number of units produced of a single product with the units produced in some previous period would measure divisional effectiveness (c) An expense centre can also be suitably employed to measure performance if the responsibility of the departmental manager is to produce a stated quantity of outputs at the lowest feasible cost.

However, in general, an expense centre is not a useful basis of measuring performance of responsibility centres. This is mainly because it ignores output measured in financial terms. A common feature of production departments is that they are much product units. There must be some common basis to aggregate the dissimilar products to arrive at the overall output of the responsibility centre. If this is not done, the efficiency and effectiveness of the responsibility centre cannot be measured. Monetary measure represents the common denominator to measure the overall output of the responsibility centre producing multi-products. The implication is that to arrive at the overall output the different products have to be expressed in financial terms. This is a limitation of the expense centre. The profit centre provides a solution to this problem.

III. Investment Centres

The third type of responsibility centre is an investment centre. It is defined as a responsibility centre in which inputs are measured in terms of cost-expenses and outputs are measured in terms of revenues and in which assets employed are also measured. In other words, investment centres consider not only cost and revenues but also the assets used in the division. As a responsibility centre, the performance of a unit would be measured in relation to the revenues/profits and the assets employed in a division. The essence of investment centre analysis is the relationship between the profits and the assets that are used to generate those profits. It may, therefore, be said to be an extension of the profit centre in that it covers all the elements relevant to the measurement of the overall performance of its various divisions. In point of fact, an investment centre is essentially a profit centre. It is for this reason that it is sometimes said that there is no distinction between investment centres and profit centres, and the term "profit centre" is used to apply to both. Since, however, the investment centre is one step above a profit centre in terms of the additional financial data (assets), it should best be treated as a separate responsibility centre.

The investment centre analysis can be used as a basis for evaluating the contribution of a division as an entity as also the performance of a divisional manager. The measure of performance in an investment centre is based on the relationship between the profits/income and the amount of assets employed in generating the profits. There are two ways to relate income to assets:

(A) Residual Income. An alternative measure of financial performance in an investment centre is *residual income.* The preceding discussion clearly shows that the ROI suffers from serious limitations. Essentially it is a relative measure, *i.e.* a ratio or rate of return. This is so because net profit is related to investments which encounter several problems. The residual income alternative to measure divisional performance avoids some of the problems associated with the ROI analysis.

Residual income is the amount that remains after deducting an "implied" interest charge from operating income. The implied interest charge reflects an opportunity cost. The basis of the interest charge is the amount of assets in each investment centre. The rate of interest charge is equal to the minimum rate on investment specified by top management as part of the corporate strategic plan. Operationally, the management of the firm lays down an amount of interest charge as a compensation for providing the original investment to a division. The difference between the actual operating income and the required/expected income is residual income.

The residual income approach has some merits. A principal advantage is that it encourages capital investment any time a divisional manager can earn more than the required rate/cut-off rate. The amount of residual income indicates the investment centre's ability to earn more than a normal profit on the amount of capital that it uses. Any new investment will increase the residual income if it yields an income higher than the required/cut-off percentage. A second advantage is that it allows different rates of return for different divisions/assets, *e.g.* higher rates for risky and lower for less risky/certain. Thus, the performance measure can be made consistent with the decision criterion employed in capital budgeting.

Residual income as a performance measure overcomes some of the shortcomings of ROI analysis. But it is not a perfect measure it has certain limitations. First, most of the problems in measuring the divisional income and divisional investment base are also present in the measurement of residual income. There is an additional problem of selecting/specifying a fair and equitable measure of the required/cut-off percentage.

(B) Return on Investment (ROI). A widely used device for reporting performance in an investment centre type of responsibility accounting is the rate of return on investment in assets or simply return on investment. The ROI is the ratio of net income to total assets.

There are two components to the return on investments calculations. Alternatively, the ROI is composed of two supplementary measures of divisional activity. These are: *(i)* profit margin on sales; and *(ii)* asset/investment turnover. Therefore, ROI is a product of two elements:

Profit margin on sales means profit as a percentage of sales (net income divided by sales). The asset turnover measures the velocity of utilisation of assets (sales divided by investment in assets). Therefore, clearly, the ROI can be computed in any of the above mentioned three ways, the three-step method, shows more detailed information that may be particularly useful in individual industries. The ROI may be increased by increasing the profit margin, by increasing the asset turnover, or by some combination of the two. Planning and evaluation of operations is more effective if each of these components is examined separately. For instance, in a retail grocery business the profit margin is usually low but the assets turnover is high/ rapid. In contrast, in a heavy industry, the profit margin on sales is high but the asset turnover is low. Therefore, three-step method has more analytical value in assessing divisional performance measurement.

There are several advantages in using ROI to measure divisional performance. In the first place, ROI is the generally accepted measure of overall performance. As a measure of divisional performance, it is consistent with a firm-wise rate of return analysis. It is also compatible with the common-sense view that investments are made to achieve the goal of a desired rate of return. Secondly, ROI analysis is a relative and not absolute measure. It is, in fact, a ratio/percentage. It, therefore, serves as a common denominator so that a comparison can be made between the performance of different divisions. By enabling an inter-divisional comparison, ROI is of great practical significance. Thirdly, ROI is conceptually easy to understand and interpret. Finally, ROI analysis can provide incentive for utilisation of the assets of a firm. In operational terms, it encourages divisional managers to obtain/retain assets that provide satisfactory return on investment and to discard/dispose off assets that are not giving acceptable returns.

Thus, the ROI analysis is conceptually sound and appealing, as a performance measure. Nevertheless, it suffers from certain operational limitations. Some of these are outlined below.

One operational problem with the ROI analysis relates to the determination of the investment base. One significant element in the ROI analysis is the assets in the generation of net income. The determination/measurement of the value of investments is referred to as "investment base". The measurement of the divisional investment base requires *(1)* a precise definition of all elements that should be included, and *(2)* the value that should be assigned to them. There are, however, operational problems in respect of each of these aspects in that there are alternatives available which imply different practices. This is so because the measurement of assets is not standardised.

The problems of measuring investment in assets in connection with the investment centre analysis fall into two categories: *(a)* problems of allocation/ apportionment and *(b)* problems of valuation.

Allocation Problems. These arise out of the possibility of different treatment of assets that are pooled/shared among the different divisions. The most common of such assets are cash receivables and inventories. How should such assets be allocated among different divisions? One alternative is to ignore them while working out the investment base of a division, the underlying principle being that only those assets which are exclusively used traceable to a division should be included. Alternatively, the common share assets should be allocated to the benefiting divisions for the proper measurement of their individual investments. Apart from the theoretical differences as to whether, such assets should be allocated or not, there is the more difficult problem of identification of assets with separate divisions and reasonable allocation.

The second aspect of the allocational problem relates to the treatment of assets that are currently idle. If such assets are excluded as they presumably do not generate income, the ROI would be actually a return on capital employed rather than on the total investments available invested capital. This approach would tend to raise the ROI. This will not however, reveal how efficiently assets have been used the basic objective of ROI analysis. The presence of ideal assets is suggestive of inefficient utilisation of resources. Its inclusion/exclusion would affect the ROI.

Valuation Problems. Apart from the problem of allocation/ traceability of items of assets, the measurement of investment base is complicated by the difficulty of assigning values to the assets of a division. There are a variety of methods to value assets for purposes of ROI analysis. They include *(i)* book value, *(ii)* gross book value (original costs), *(iii)* current replacement cost.

Book value, the most readily available method of valuation of assets defined as the original cost less accumulated depreciation, is probably the least useful measure owing to an inherent weakness. Due to the declining investment base as a result of depreciation charges, the carrying value of assets decline. If the net income of the division remains constant or does not decline as rapidly as the book value of the division's assets, the divisional ROI would show improving performance as the assets become more worn out and obsolete. Since continued use of obsolete resources due to a low investment base would inflate ROI, the division's productive capacity would ultimately decline.

Gross book value which is the original cost without any deduction for depreciation, provides a partial solution to the defect in ROI analysis based on book values. If earnings are constant, this approach will give a constant ROI over the years. A variation of this approach is to use a method of depreciation with increasing charges over the life of the asset. It will result in a constant ROI as each year a lower income is related to a smaller asset base. While this approach thus avoids the problem of meaningless rise in the ROI as time passes, it is not a measure of the current economic value of the assets involved.

The replacement cost basis provides the best measure of current performance. Its weakness, however, is that replacement cost is difficult to determine and may require subjective assessment.

In brief, in arriving at the value of the assets that generate income for ROI analysis several alternative approaches/practices are available possible. That several approaches can be adopted is another way of saying that the measurement of the investment base is problematic.

Net Income

The second element in the computation of ROI is the net income/profit of a responsibility centre. The determination of divisional net income also involves some problems.

First, as an extension of the profit centre, *the investment centre analysis encounters all the problems of the profit centre analysis.*

In addition there are some special problems of income measurement as a rate of return is to be calculated. These relate to the treatment of (a) tax. (b) interest. These items are outside the control of the divisional managers. Should they be considered in calculating the divisional income? According to the incremental approach, since these items do not fall in the areas of responsibility of a division. *i.e.* they are not controllable by the division they are to be excluded. Further, should depreciation be based on historical cost or replacement cost? If replacement cost is the basis of asset value on depreciation should also be based upon replacement cost. Moreover since ROI measures current operating performance non-recurring items such as extraordinary gains and losses should be excluded. Thus, items having a bearing on net income can be treated in different ways. This creates problems in the measurement of net income for ROI analysis.

To conclude responsibility accounting is relevant to divisional performance measurement. Of the three types of responsibility centres the measure of managerial performance is broader in the profit centre as compared to the expense centre. The investment centre type of responsibility centre permits even a broader measure than the profit centre. The investment centre is, in a way the ultimate extension of the responsibility centre idea because it encompasses all the elements that are involved in the overall goal of a firm to earn a satisfactory return on investments.

TRANSFER PRICING

Transfer pricing becomes necessary when there are internal transfers of goods or services and it is required to appraise the separate performances of the divisions or departments involved. This chapter reviews the objectives which any system of transfer pricing should try to meet and analyses the theoretical background to transfer pricing using relevant aspects of economic theory. This includes the setting of optimum transfer prices the determination of output levels and the apportionment of company profits between the supplying and buying divisions. The problems involved in setting transfer prices in practice are then discussed and market based, cost based and negotiated pricing are described.

Why Necessity of Transfer Pricing?

Transfer pricing is the process of determining the price at which goods are transferred from one profit centre to another profit centre within the same company. Such internal trading is more prevalent within horizontally and vertically integrated companies than conglomerate operations with their heterogeneous groupings.

It profit centres are to be used, transfer prices become necessary in order to determine the separate performances of both the 'buying' and 'selling' profit centres. If transfer prices are set too high, the selling centre will be favoured whereas if set too low the buying centre will receive an unwarranted proportion of the profits.

In general terms, transfer pricing is purely an internal, bookkeeping exercise which does not affect the overall profitability of the firm. However, in certain circumstances, transfer pricing may have an indirect effect on overall company profitability by influencing the decisions made at divisional level. For example, based on the proposed transfer price, a divisional manager may decide to purchase an item externally rather than accept the internal transfer even though such a decision may reduce overall company profitability.

Objectives of Transfer Prices

Ideally, transfer prices should be set in a manner and at a level which fulfil three objectives:

(a) ***Divisional Autonomy.*** The prices should seek to maintain the maximum divisional autonomy so that the benefits of decentralistion (motivation, better decision making, initiative, etc.) are maintained. The profits of one division should not be dependent on the actions of other divisions.

(b) ***Goal Congruence.*** The prices should be set so that the divisional management's desire to maximise divisional earnings is consistent with the objectives of the company as a whole. The transfer prices should not encourage sub-optimal decision making.

(c) ***Performance Appraisal.*** The prices should enable reliable assessments to be made of divisional performance. The prices form part of information which should.

(i) evaluate the contribution made by the division to overall company profits

(ii) guide decision making

(iii) appraise managerial performance

In practice there are extreme difficulties in establishing prices which meet all these objectives. If prices are set centrally at levels where overall company objectives are met, then the autonomy of divisions is jeopardized, motivation may diminish and some of the benefits of decentralistion will be lost. Alternatively, where divisions act autonomously and freely set transfer prices, sub optimal decision making is hard to avoid. There is no completely satisfactory solution to this problem but research studies suggest that companies are prepared to accept a certain level of sub-optimal decision making on the part of divisions in order to gain the more than compensating advantages which they perceive arise from decentralisation.

TRANSFER PRICE POLICIES

Transfer price policies refer to the selection of policies that would govern the calculations of such prices under various circumstances. The concern of transfer price policies is with developing a transfer pricing system that *(i)* allows a measure of performance to reflect the use of resources by a division, and *(ii)* allows the optional allocation of the firms resources. In other words, suitable transfer prices should be related to *(A)* decision optimisation, and *(B)* management performance assessment.

Decision Optimisation. The ideal transfer price for management decision-making is the price that would be used by a firm if it were not divided into units/ divisions. In other words, for decision-making purposes, the transfer price should reflect the opportunity cost of the goods/services transferred between divisions. This is so because an optional allocation of resources take place only if the goods/service's are priced on transfer at the opportunity cost that would be incurred to obtain the goods/services elsewhere when they are needed. The best measure of opportunity cost is the open-market price, if available. In case market prices are not readily available, the top management may prescribe a transfer price. Alternatively, a negotiated price between divisions with arbitration, if necessary, by top management, reflecting the corporate objectives and coordination of the activities of all the divisions, may be taken to be the opportunity cost. One widely used approach treats the incremental cost of the selling division as the transfer price. The advantage of this is that if price standard costs are used, the inefficiency of the selling division will not be also facto passed on to the buying division.

Management Performance. The best transfer price of measuring management performance is the one that reflects the price in an open, competitive market. These market prices are the best measure of revenue for the selling division, and of cost for the purchasing division. For market prices to have maximum effectiveness in management performance measurement, both the buying and the selling divisions must be bale to act independently, *i.e.*, the selling division must have a choice of suppliers.

If, however, a market price for the goods/services is not readily available, negotiated prices may be used to determine the transferrer price. This price is negotiated between the buying and the selling units.

In circumstances where there are no competitive market prices and a negotiated transfer price cannot be established, the firm cannot set up profit centres. It can use cost centres for management performance measurement. By using standard cost as the transfer prices for cost centres, the selling divisions are encouraged to have good control.

To conclude, the question of appropriate transfer prices for the two functions of management-performance measurement and decision optimisation-does not have any easy answer. There is no single measure of transfer price that can fit all circumstances. The firm must give serious consideration to its goals and objectives in using transfer prices before adopting a particular measure.

TYPES OF TRANSFER PRICES

There are two general approaches to the determination of a transfer price: *(l)* market-based; and *(2)* cost based.

Market Price. One approach to transfer pricing is the market price-based approach. There are three ways to arrive at the market price. First, through the prevailing market price if there is an active market for the goods/services transferred between divisions. The prevailing price would require adjustment for discounts as well as for certain selling costs that are not involved in inter-divisional exchange. The merits of this basis of transfer price are: *(A)* market prices represent the alternatives to the divisions. That is to say, if the selling division sells the goods to outside customers or if the buying division purchases the goods from outside suppliers, the market price will be the basis. *(B)* They are neither arbitrary nor artificial, rather they reflect the collective values of several buyers/sellers. In operational terms, a market price-based approach implies that the selling division will receive equal to what it would get by selling the goods to outside customers while the purchasing division will pay what it would pay to outside suppliers. Yet both the selling and the buying divisions would derive some special benefits. The advantages to the selling division include *(1)* no risk of bad debt on sales to sister divisions, and *(2)* no direct promotional expenses on sale to a sister division. The special benefit to the buying department will be in the form of assured delivery schedules and full customer service. Therefore, where divisions have the alternative to buy/sell to/from the open market, they would prefer to buy from/sell to the sister division.

Secondly, in situations in which market price is not readily available bids from several different manufacturers can form the basis. The low bid may be taken as the market price and used for internal transfer pricing. This alternative of market price suffers from two limitations: either spurious bids would be submitted by the bidders or bids will not be submitted. This is likely because the bidders would come to know that the firm does not intend buying the goods but will only use the bid for internal pricing.

Finally, in cases where easily identified market prices are not available, costs plus a normal profit margin can be a reasonable approximation of the market price.

Based on these, there are five basic types of transfer prices:

(A) Incremental Cost. Yet another basis of transfer prices is the incremental cost in the selling division. Depending upon the circumstances, incremental cost can be computed in two ways. The first situation may be such that the entire production of the selling division is transferred to the sister divisions and there are no independent outside customers for the goods. In that case, incremental cost includes all variable costs plus any fixed costs directly and exclusively attributable to the internal transfer/inter-divisional transfer. Transfer pricing at incremental cost defined in this sense is inconsistent with the objective of measuring divisional profit as performance measurement.

An alternative market situation arises when there may be outside customers for the goods and the division is unable to produce the full demand (from the outside customers as well as sister divisions). The incremental cost to the selling division in that case would be the revenue lost on sales to outside customers that must be foregone to make the internal transfer to a sister division. Then, the incremental cost would equal the market price for those goods services. This version of the incremental cost data would be useful for profit centre analysis. The incremental cost data related to the internal production costs is not of much analytical value.

(B) Cost Price. According to this, transfer price is equal to the cost price. This means the goods/services transferred will be priced on the basis of the selling division's unit cost of production. The cost could be either actual cost of production or, where available, standard cost of production. The merit of this method is simplicity and convenience because all the required information is available in the cost accounting records. But it is inappropriate for profit centre analysis. The reason is that transfer prices based on cost would distort the profit figures. For the selling division the profit figure would be an under estimate as it will not earn any profit on goods/services sold to the sister divisions. The profit figures for the purchasing decision would be inflated to the extent the cost of purchases of goods would be lower because there is no element of profit for the selling divisions. If profit figures are distorted, the profit centre analysis would not be of much value.

(C) Cost Plus a Normal Mark-up. This type of transfer price is an improvement over the first category. It includes besides unit cost of production, some profit margin of normal mark-up. Thus, the price received/paid by the selling and the purchasing decisions respectively will contain an element of profit. There are two ways in which the normal mark-up/profit margin is determined. First, the management of the firm may set a target profit alternatively, the normal mark up may be equivalent to the profit margin that a competing firm might reasonably be expected to realise. If the second basis is adopted, the transfer price will approximate a market value. Depending upon its closeness to the real market value, it may be useful for profit centre analysis. But if the basis is the managerial pre-determined target, the mark-up is an artificial margin dictated by policy. Therefore, its validity as performance measurement of a division/divisional manager is open to question. On the whole, therefore, this type of transfer price has no unique value of its own for profit centre analysis.

(D) Negotiated Transfer Pricing. As an alternative to setting prices based rules or formulae, transfer prices could be set by negotiation between the buying and selling divisions. This would be appropriate if it could be assumed that such negotiations would result in decisions which were in the interests of the firm as a whole and which were acceptable to the parties concerned.

However, there are difficulties in this approach because it is unlikely that the parties concerned have equal bargaining power and protracted negotiations may be time consuming and divert management energies away nom their primary tasks. Disagreements, which are all too likely; will require some form of arbitration by central management which itself undermines the autonomy of divisions and may cause resentment. It must be remembered that the objective of divisionalisation is to enhance the overall efficiency of the organisation so that care must be taken not to nullify any benefits through inter-divisional wrangling transfer prices.

RESPONSIBILITY ACCOUNTING

Responsibility accounting is a responsibility set-up for cost control purposes. It is an approach to cost control that relies on the performance of persons responsible for the implementation of decisions. It is an accounting system designed to control costs by relating executives responsible for their incurrence. Tied closely to the control over costs, this concept emphasises "personalisation of costs by putting questions as to where the cost was incurred and who was responsible for it. The technique seeks to control costs at their starting point by fixing responsibility. Broadly speaking, responsibility accounting is designing the accounting system according to answer ability of the managers. The accumulation, classification, measurement and reporting of financial data is so arranged that it promotes the fixing of precise responsibility on the persons within the managerial hierarchy. Horngren says "Responsibility accounting is a system which is tailored to an organisation so that costs are accumulated and reported by levels of responsibility within the organisation. That is, it focuses attention on people, not things, shifts emphasis from product costing to responsibility accounting. The obvious hypothesis is that since all activities in an enterprise and all items of income, operating costs, other expense and capital expenditures are the responsibility of some manager, none should be left unassigned. The concept is structured around functional activities for which specific individuals are responsible. One can, therefore, dare say that responsibility accounting as the process of matching the costs and benefits with the unit whose activities led to their achievement.

Insofar as accounting is a financial information system, responsibility accounting could be interpreted as an information system resting with the theory that costs and revenues should be assigned to the manager most responsible for making decisions about them. Higgins makes the point clear when he writes. "In effect, the system personalizes the accounting statements by saying, 'Joe, this is what you originally budgeted and this is how you performed for the period with actual operations as compared against your budget" By definition it is a system of accounting which is tailored to an organisation so that costs are accumulated and reported by levels of responsibility within the organisation. Each supervisory area in the organisation is charged only with cost for which it is responsibility and over which it has control. Thus, the focal point of responsibility accounting is that it looks at each major category of expense and attempts to establish relationship between specific actions and the incurring of costs. Naturally, it extends beyond the normal responsibility and authority of financial management. While a cost accounting system assigns costs primarily for product costing purposes, the main thrust of responsibility accounting is the control of costs at different echelkons of management. Within his own area of responsibility; each manager is supreme such that he could make decisions, spend money, investigate the causes of divergence and take whatever corrective action seemed necessary. In view of its reliance on controllability of costs, which commonly are marginal costs, the system is also called as "Attributable costing", "Combined marginal/absorption costing", "Partial absorption costing", "Hybrid direct costing", and by way of commendation as "productivity-oriented accounting".

The aforesaid techniques of responsibility accounting apply to all enter-prises-big and small, centralized or decentralized, business, non-profit, or governmental. But the system will differ from organisation to organisation because no two organisations can be expected to delegate responsibilities for decision-implementation the same way. The "law of situation" will dictate how the principles should be implemented.

The principles governing the responsibility accounting system may be explained as under:

(1) Costs should be Traced Directly to the Department. An example would indicate the point clear. Two production departments may incur transportation costs jointly, but the manager of one production department may have the power to decide about incurrence of the cost. Here, the burden to be shared by the other production department in respect of transportation costs may be unfair. A suitable mechanism of transfer pricing should be evolved so as to charge the other production department, reasonably treating it as an external customer.

(2) **Variances from Budget and Comparisons Between Budget and Actual Results must be Grounded Firmly in a Discernibly Uniform and Clearly Comparable System of Budgeting and Reporting.** The responsibility for adhering to standards and the responsibility for any deviations from those standards should also be clearly distinguished. There should be uniformity in preparation and presentation of budgetary and actual data for the sake of comparison.

(3) A clear cut guideline as to the declaration of responsibility is a pre-requisite, otherwise one departmental manager may shrug off the responsibility by passing it over to the other. Confusion as to the shouldering of the responsibility cannot lead in any decisive action by the management.

TECHNIQUES AND ESSENTIALS OF RESPONSIBILITY ACCOUNTING

So many varied techniques have begun to be practised now-under the banner of responsibility accounting that really it has become synonymous with management accounting. It ties accounting, reporting and budgeting to management organisation and responsibilities. The programme engulfs all operating management for which the accounting, cost or budget divisions provide technical assistance. However, there are some points of principles or fundamental aspects of responsibility accounting which are often called its techniques or phases. The four concepts which are basic to the initiation and maintenance of a responsibility accounting system are the following:

I. Once the responsibility centres of a business have been established, the costs and revenues under the control of each responsibility centre must he identified. Only those costs and revenues over which the manager has a definite control can be used in setting standards for his performance. Responsibility accounting has an appeal because it specifies a boundary of operations and distinguishes between controllable and uncontrollable costs. Thus, instead of classifying costs by functions-manufacturing, selling and administrative or as product and period costs, the viewpoint of division here is controllability. The attention is direct toward the individual or the group, and the basic question is who spent the money rather than what the money was spent on. The question 'who did it' is more important than what it was expended upon. A cost is deemed controllable if the head of the responsibility centre under consideration possesses the power to change it by his actions. He exerts spending authority over it such that he can affect (decrease, and possibly increase) the amount there of. The manager of a machinery department does influence by his action indirect labour and manufacturing supplies used in his department, but not also salary or the salary of higher executives. Generally, variable costs are charged to a department which are controllable by its manager. In fact, responsibility accounting is married with the technique of direct costing which should better be referred to as variable costing. Such costs as direct materials and direct labour may be easiest to identify as controllable costs. Others such as sales commission and salaries, office costs, and certain elements of manufacturing overhead may also be controllable by the manager. On the other hand, fixed expenses are not controllable, at least, in the short run, by the departmental manager and price, not charged to the responsibility centre. In this connection, the following guidelines should be noted which are available in deciding the appropriate costs to be charged to a person:

1. Even if the person cannot significantly influence the amount of cost through his own direct action, he may be charged with those elements with which the management desires him to be concerned, so that he will help to influence those who are responsible.
2. If the person has authority over both the acquisition and the use of the services, he should be charged with the cost of such services. That is, he should have both the acquisition right and the use right over the cost, and

3. If the person can significantly influence the amount of cost through his own action, he may be charged with such costs.

II. Control is centered on performance reports, called here responsibility reports, prepared for each responsibility unit. Performance reports constitute the control mechanism, not because they help rectify past mistakes, but because they spur managerial action that prevents future mistakes. The report to each unit shows its expenses, income and capital expenditures in the headings appearing in the account classification, statistics such as volume of work, costs per unit and perhaps man-hour data and number of employees. The questions to be resolved for a report are how often it is to be made, the amount of detail to be presented and the format. In general terms, at successively higher levels in the organisational chain, less and less time is devoted to control and more and more to planning.

Performance reports are feedback reports to assure the follow-through and therewith the ultimate success of the programme. These are addressed to the particular manager who delegated the responsibility. Reports should be simple, attractive and couched in terms understood by the recipients. Presentation can be in the form of statements, graphs, charts or tables. If there is machine-processing, it may force a uniform format for reports turned out in volume. These feedback reports show only the budgeted amount and the variance. This places focus on the variances and management by exception which means that the executive's attention is concentrated on the important deviations from budgeted items. In this way, managers do not waste time on those parts of the reports that reflect the smoothly running phases of operations. Variances identify the deviations of actual performance from the planned or prior performance that is being used as the reference point. Each manager should be informed of deviations within his own area of responsibility so that he can look into the causes and take appropriate action. In essence, a communication system which is designed to aid an enterprise in achieving its cost and profit goals is what is called responsibility accounting. The fact of the matter is that control reports are always comparative, that is, they embody or facilitate comparisons between observed performance and some reference point. In some cases, the comparison may be with a prior time period, in others, the current budgetary plan provides the point of reference. About the extent of details, the guideline is that the factors and variables having a significant impact on decision must be incorporated. But there should be no information overload; too much information cannot be used, it may rather confuse the manager.

III. Flexible Budgeting

Budgeting is the key technique, the cornerstone of cost control procedures. If pre-planning is the heart of the control providing an opportunity for corrective, action, budget is its principal instrument. Fitted to various areas of responsibility, operating budgets express the plans in figures. It is through budgets that responsibility for implementing the decisions made at each level of management is communicated. However, effective responsibility accounting may require more sophisticated budgeting than was previously use. Each manager heading a responsibility centre should prepare or, at least, participate in preparing his budget since he will be held accountable for achieving it. Without a good budget, there is no point in trying to use it as a yardstick. The budget must be based on carefully set objectives and operating plans, not as someone aptly put it, on past history eloquently defended. But it is important that individual's budget is considered an integral part of the overall company budget.

Fixed budgets, flexible budgets and profit planning can all be incorporated into an overall system of responsibility accounting. Fixed budgets offer a medium for overall planning and expression of objectives, and sometimes responsibility reports include comparisons only with fixed budgets. Where it is hard to predetermine volume and changes happen quickly, fixed budgets should be supplemented by flexible budgets or standard costs if a manager cannot control the volume of his work, fixed budget can positively be misleading. It is fallacious to compare results at one activity level with a budget predicted on another level. Flexible budgeting permits comparison of actual costs with budgeted costs that have been geared to changes in production volume. In the context of responsibility reporting, flexible budgets provide greater accountability for performance in that budgets remain realistic regardless of activity levels.

IV. Establishing Responsibility Centres

Responsibility accounting is founded upon responsibility centres. Fixing responsibility for control requires the establishment of definite lines of authority. The organisation chart presents the structure, and following these lines of authority, allows the assignment of cost control responsibility to specific individuals. It is imperative, therefore, that clear-cut lines of authority are drawn by establishing responsibility centres. Responsibility centres represent the sphere of authority or points where decisions have to be implemented. These are generally operating departments or smaller sub-divisions used solely for costing. The subdivisions are appropriate for an operating department containing basically different kinds of sub-sections, some using expensive machinery and other not. This naturally requires an organisation structure where no doubt responsibility for deciding has been decentralized but it has also been specifically fixed for each organisational unit. In fact, an accounting system should parallel the organisation and provide financial and statistical data to evaluate actual results of each supervisor responsible for a function. Costs should be recorded and traced to the individual in the organisation who shoulders primary decision responsibility for an item. The organisation structure should clearly spell out the duties, authority and responsibilities of various managers, foremen, supervisors, departmental and divisional managers, vice-presidents, etc. Hence before installing a system of responsibility accounting, first an attempt is made to determine the decision-points within an organisation, and then the extent and scope of responsibility for each decision-point is defined. This responsibility may be limited as one person may be responsible for the labour used in manufacturing a set of equipment in a single department. It may be quite extensive as in the case of a divisional manager who may be responsible for achieving a certain level of profit consistent with the investment under his control.

Essentials

Conceptually it is an ideal system to ensure cost control, but putting it into practice is difficult. The principal preliminaries are:

(1) The effectiveness of responsibility accounting is determined by how successfully costs can be segregated into controllable and non-controllable categories at each level of management. A manager's performance versus budget can best be measured by evaluating those costs (and revenues) over which he or she has some control. This controllable-uncontrollable dichotomy is crucial for the success of responsibility accounting. It is important, therefore, that costs are segregated for each level, through the fact remains that all costs are controllable at some level. Rent expense, for example, may not be control help at the level of a supervisor but it is so at the level of the plant manager.

(2) Control of production an of costs is a matter of timing. The effectiveness of control is often in direct proportion to the speed with which a change is recommended after an unsatisfactory condition is discovered. The performance reports are less effective if they are not available to management immediately after the event in order to improve similar future events. A month and generally even in a week, is to long a period for many off-standard conditions to remain unchecked and uncorrected. The time interval may prevent positive identification of employees who are responsible for the unsatisfactory work. In addition, there may be many hours and days during which there has been waste and inefficiency in the use of materials and labour representing total losses of some magnitude before corrective measures are taken. It is for this reason that in concerns with enlightened management, daily tabulations of operating results are recorded on blackboards and charts by shifts, cost centres and departments so that employees are informed of their production as contrasted with standards.

Daily and weekly accumulation of the results are equal to or better than standards are rewarded through recognition or prizes or bonuses.

(3) Ideally the organisation itself arid its processes must be thoroughly appraised, understood, and altered if necessary, before a system is constructed. That is, the design of a system and the design of an organisational structure are really inseparable and interdependent. The point is that the most streamlined system is not a cure all or a substitute for basic organisational ills or management ineptitude. On a practical level, there may be a powerful temptation to separate the design of the system, from the design of organisational processes by assuming that the organisational structure is given and therefore not subject to change. A manual, of course, is invaluable in getting up such a system.

(4) A fragile balance must be struck between careful delineation of responsibility on the one hand, and a too rigid separation of responsibility, on the other. Buck passing is a pervasive tendency that is supposedly minimised when responsibility is fixed unequivocally. But often the motivation impact boome-rangs; to much falls between the chairs. Managers often wear blinders and concentrate more than ever on their individual worlds. Family cooperation is replaced by intracompany competition.

DIFFICULTIES IN RESPONSIBILITY ACCOUNTING

While implementing the system of responsibility accounting, the following difficulties are likely to be faced by the management:

(1) Separate departmental pursuits may lead to inter-departmental rivalry and it may be prejudicial to the interests of the enterprise as a whole. Managers may act in the best interests of their own, but not in the best interests of the enterprises. A consistency should be tried to be achieved in the departmental goals and enterprise goals so that a conflicting situation does not arise.

(2) For responsibility accounting system to be effective, a proper classification between controllable and non-controllable costs is a prime requisite. But practical difficulties arise while doing so on account of the complex nature and variety of costs. An example would make the point clear. Responsibility for getting the repairs and maintenance job done may be entrusted to one departmental manager. Other departmental managers may not have any say in negotiating and settling the terms and conditions of the service contract to be given to some outside party. However, they shall be charged with the proportionate share of the cost which may distort their budget figures. The negotiating manager is not at fault. But, how under responsibility accounting system, can the other departmental managers be held accountable for costs that they did not incur personally?

(3) Responsibility accounting cannot be relied upon completely as a tool of management control. It is a system just to direct the attention of management to those areas of performance which require further investigation. No doubt it plays a significant role in appraising, co-ordinating and motivating departmental performance, but it cannot be taken as the definitive mechanism for appraising performance and principal means of motivating good behaviour.

(4) Responsibility reports may be got delayed. The duration of reporting also may not be satisfactory Any system cannot effectively function unless and until suitable safeguards are taken beforehand for plugging the loopholes likely to creep into it. If something goes wrong, it must be reported immediately to invite managerial intervention in the matter, without even waiting for the procedural formalities.

(5) Responsibility accounting reports may be overloaded with all available information. This danger is inherent in the system but with clear instructions in management as to the

functioning of the system and preparation of reports etc., only relevant information may flow in.

The problems arising from any form of management control system have been summarised by Horngren as "overemphasis on short-run goals, presence of slack failure to pinpoint responsibility cooperation versus, competition, inaccurate source documents and faulty cost analysis."

Advantages

The benefits of responsibility accounting are many and varied. These are well explained by the statement: "A man will go out of his way to make a plan work if he feels that it is his own creation rather than something that has been forced upon him. He often finds ways and means of effecting savings that the front office would never dream of." The main benefits may be spelt out as below:

(1) Since responsibility accounting hinges on the redesigning of the Corporate organisation, it paves way for the delegation of authority and placement of responsibility. In a business of modern size and complexity, neither planning nor control can be effective unless the management has worked out a satisfactory method of decentralization.

(2) Since the emphasis responsibility accounting is on decentralisation of authority and delineation of objectives, the system of Management by Objectives (MBO) gets established. The heads of divisions/departments understand quite clearly what is expected of them which enables the top to exercise managerial action. Pre-determined objectives hold them accountable for target attainments in their respective cost centres. Deficient and potential areas of managers' performance are identified for necessary action.

(3) When an organisation designs its accumulation and reporting system on the basis of areas of responsibility, its management is able to relate efforts and achievements, responsibility accounting is the process of machining the costs and benefits with the unit (and manager) whose

activities led to their achievement. If the assignment of responsibility for costs and benefits has been strictly defined, it shall be difficult for individual managers to pass the buck when unfavourable results appear.

(4) A business in unlikely to continue to operate at a profit even with the existence of high monetary rewards for employees. The rewards for work must include not only economic incentives but also those which stem from participating, form doing a good job, from belonging. These are the characteristics of morale and necessary ingredients of efficient performance. Considerable frustration will be generated over the results of a decision in which he had no opportunity to participate.

(5) An organisation in which there is clearly defined authority and corresponding placement or responsibility, it identifies the area if the unsatisfactory operating condition. Such a system immediately draws attention towards the off-standard condition which forms the basis for an investigation into the reasons, resulting hopefully, in remedy and correction.

DIFFERENCES BETWEEN MANAGEMENT ACCOUNTING & FINANCIAL ACCOUNTING

Financial accounting and management accounting as a part of the accounting system of business, enterprises, differ from each other in several respects. The notable ones are outlined below.

(A) Statutory. The first difference between financial and management accounting pertains to the *need* of preparing such accounts. Financial accounting, as already observed, caters to the needs of outsiders who on the basis of the financial statements commit their funds in the business. The preparation of such accounts is a statutory obligation. In fact, the corporate laws and the regulations governing the functioning of corporate enterprises not only make it mandatory to prepare such accounts but also lay down the model/format which such accounts are to be prepared. The corporate laws also prescribe independent audit by professional auditors to ensure that the accounts have been properly prepared so as to *reflect a true and fair view* of the affairs of the firms. That apart, tax regulations also require the maintenance of records by business firms. For these reasons a business enterprise must prepare financial accounts. In sharp contrast, management accounting is entirely optional. It is prepared only if it is useful to management. There are no outside requirements for its preparation. The format as also the items to be included are exclusively dependent on management discretion.

(B) Segment Reporting. The financial accounting relates to the business as a whole. While there is no doubt that some firms on their own prepare financial accounts on a segmented basis for the main lines of business, the fact remains that the emphasis is on the entire business. Management accounting focuses on parts of the business. For purposes of management accounting the business is divided into responsibility centres-cost, profit and investment. The term responsibility centre refers to the division of the enterprise into sections, departments, products, individual activities, and so on, In brief, financial accounting relate to the business as a whole but management accounting focuses on parts.

(C) Means an Objectives. Financial accounting and management accounting also differ in respect of their ultimate objectives. Financial accounting is prepared to serve the purpose of external reporting. From the view point of management, therefore the purpose of financial accounting can be said to have been accomplished when it is reflected in the three financial statements, *i.e.*, balance sheet, profit and loss account and statement of changes in financial position. It is, in a sense, an end in itself. But management accounting is only a means to end. In other words, management accounting is designed to serve the purpose of managerial decision-making. With the help of management accounting, management can discharge the planning, directing and controlling activities of the firm. In planning, the manager decides what actions should be taken to help the organisation achieve its goals. In directing, the manager-oversees the conduct of day-to-day operations. And in controlling, steps are taken to ensure that the responsibility centres are operating in the best possible manner.

(D) Historical. As observed earlier, the end-product of financial accounting is three financial statements, namely, balance sheet, profit and loss account and statement of changes in financial position. While the balance sheet and the profit and loss account report the financial position on a particular date and the results of the operations of the firm during the accounting period respectively, the statement of changes in financial position reports the inflows and outflows of financial resources during a period of time. Thus, they essentially record what has happened in the past. They are, therefore, aptly called historical accounts. On the other hand, management accounting does not record the financial history of an enterprise. While there is no doubt that what has happened in the past is included in management accounting, a major part of its contents pertains to future plans. It is, therefore, future-oriented. It aims at providing data for budgeting and planning, and so on. Thus, management accounting has more emphasis on the future.

(E) Information. Yet another difference between financial accounting and management accounting is the type of information contained in them. It has already been pointed out that a basic concept in financial accounting is money measurement. Financial accounting, therefore, contains primarily monetary information. Management accounting, in contrast, includes besides monetary information, non-monetary information also such as quantity and weight of materials, number of employees, units of products sold, and so on. Management accounting can, thus, be said to be more informative than financial accounting.

(F) Structure. One aspect of the differences between financial accounting and management accounting relates to their respective structures of formats of presentation of information. Financial accounting can be said to have a single unified structure in the sense that the information relating to the operations of various enterprises is presented more or less on a uniform basis. It may be recalled that the end products of financial accounting are the three financial statements: *(1)* the balance sheet, *(2)* the profit and loss account/ income statement, and *(3)* the statement of changes in financial position. The balance sheet reports the financial position of a business at a particular point in time the results of operations for a specified period of time, usually a year, are contained in the profit and loss account. The statement of changes in financial position reports the inflow and outflow of financial resources during a period of time. That the various financial statements are prepared according to a model or equation implies that while preparing their financial accounts all firms arrange the information uniformly.

Why is the structure of financial accounting uniform? Financial accounting has the primary objective of providing information to outside parties, namely, shareholders creditors, government, the general public, and so on. These outside users of financial statements are interested in information from many different businesses. In order to enable inter-firm comparison, there is a distinct need to present the financial accounts on a uniform basis within a unified structure. The unified structure of financial accounts, therefore, facilitates communication between a business and outside parties interested in it.

In contrast, management accounting is concerned with accounting information that is useful to management only. Since this type of accounting is prepared for internal use, its structure varies depending upon the requirements and circumstances of a particular case. In other words, management accounting is tailored to meet the needs of the management of a specific business. It, therefore, lacks a single unified structure. It consists of three types of information, namely, full cost accounting, differential accounting and responsibility accounting. A brief account of these is given in the next section of this chapter.

(G) Accepted Accounting Principles. A related aspect is the impact of the generally accepted accounting principles on the preparation of the two types of accounting. Financial accounting, it may be noted, is prepared in accordance with accepted accounting principles (AAP). Accounting is the "language of business", as it provides the principal formal means by which information about a business is communicated to those interested in it. If, therefore, the information is to be effectively communicated and properly understood it should be prepared in accordance with a mutually understood set of rules. These ground rules are referred to as AAP, represents general law or rules to be used as guides in the preparation of financial accounts. In other words, AAP provides a *normative framework* for the preparation of financial accounts. These norms or standards have evolved over the years from experience, reason, usage and necessity. Thus, AAP assures that the financial accounts are prepared in accordance with certain norms and standards so as to enable users to understand their meanings, and be aroused of their reliability. On the other hand, management accounting is for the exclusive use of the management of a firm. Outsiders have neither access to, nor are they in need of, such accounts. Therefore, there is scope for flexibility in their preparation. They can be tailor-made to the needs of the management, accounting to the circumstances in each case. The test of inclusion of any information in management accounting is its usefulness. In brief, while financial accounting, which essentially caters to the needs of outsiders, is prepared according to norms set by AAP, the preparation of management accounting, as an aid to managerial decision-making, is dependent upon, and largely influenced by, the internal requirements of management.

AAP which has evolved over the years comprises the following concepts:

(i) One of the elements of AAP is the assumption of going concern, that is, while preparing the financial accounts it is assumed that the business is a going concern. The term "going concern" means that the business will continue to operate in future and will not cease doing business, sell its assets and make final payment to its creditors and owners. The operational implication of this principle is that while placing value against items/assets of a firm, what is taken into account is not the value which can be realised by the sale of the assets in the market, but the value in terms of the value of the goods/services produced by the use of the assets. Another way of saying the same thing is that for purposes of preparing the financial accounts a business is viewed as a mechanism for adding value to the resources it uses and its success is measured by the difference between the value of its output and the cost the resources used in creating that output. In valuing assets, therefore, current resale value is irrelevant as they will not be sold as such, but rather, they will be used in creation of future output values. The going concern value is, thus, an antithesis of liquidation value.

(ii) One principle which guides the preparation of financial accounts is that information is expressed in monetary terms. There are two aspects of the money measurement concept. In the first place, the operations of a firm involve several dimensions which are expressed in different units. For instance raw materials may be expressed in terms of numbers or weights, labour charges and consumption of electricity are expressed in different units, and so on. In order to enable a comparison it is needed that all the items are shown in common terms. Expression of facts in monetary terms in financial accounts provides such a common denominator. A related aspect is that facts about a business which cannot be expressed in monetary terms would be excluded. For example, the ability of management, the quality of assets, the nature of competition, and so on are not amenable to expression in monetary terms, and, therefore, lie outside the scope of financial accounts. Thus, financial accounting is incapable of giving all information about the operations of a business. The second aspect of the money measurement concept is that transactions are recorded in monetary terms at their value; at the time they take place. In other words, any changes in monetary value as a result of changes in the purchasing power of money have no effect on the financial accounts.

(iii) Another concept is consistency concepts. In the preparation of financial accounts, an item can be treated in several ways. For example, a firm has various alternatives to value its stock, or charge depreciation on its assets, and so on. Which of these alternatives a firm would adopt is a matter of business policy. The consistency concept requires that once a company has decided to adopt one of the alternatives, it will continue to adopt the same basis in future also. The reason underlying this concept is that if a company does not follow a consistent policy, comparison of accounting figures over-a-period of time would be vitiated.

(iii) The realisation concept relates to the basis of recognising revenues. According to the realisation concept, revenue is considered as being earned on the date at which it is realised, that is, on the date when goods and services are furnished to the customers in exchange for cash or some other valuable consideration. It may, however, be noted that earning revenue has nothing to do with the actual receipt of cash.

(v) The accrual concept is another important concept. Financial accounts are prepared after certain time intervals which are usually referred to as the accounting period. The usual accounting period is one year. In preparing the accounts relating to a particular accounting period, a basic principle is the accrual concept. It is often described as the "matching" concept. According to it, the expenses recognised in an accounting period should be matched with the revenues recognised in that period. For example, when certain units of a product are sold in the "current year", and their sales value is recognised as revenue in the "current year", the cost of manufacturing those units should also be recognised as expense in the current year. Two steps are involved in matching the revenue and expenses: First, to determine the revenues to be recognised in a given accounting period and, second, to determine the expenses that are associated with these revenues.

(vi) Yet another AAP is the principle of conservation. It has a reference to the basis on which income/profits and expenses/losses have to be accounted for in financial accounts. The conservative concept implies a prudent policy by which profits are considered only when actually realised but account must be taken of all expenses actual as well as anticipated. The dictum is: *Anticipate no profit, and provide for all possible losses*. In relation to the valuation of assets, the conservative principle implies that the basis would be the cost or the current replacement value whichever is lower.

(vii) Another fundamental accounting concept, closely related to the going concern concept, is the cost concept. According to it, an asset defined as resources owned by a business, is ordinarily shown in financial accounts at cost, that is, the price paid to acquire it. The basis to value assets is cost and not current market value or current worth. The cost basis has two merits. First, it provides a relatively objective basis for accounting as compared to the alternative of attempting to estimate current value. Secondly, the market value/current value concept is difficult to apply. The difficulty arises from the fact that those responsible for preparing accounts would be compelled to keep a track of the changes in the market prices. The cost-based system is much more feasible usually, the term book value is used for amounts (cost) as shown in the financial accounts and the term market value is used for the actual value of the asset as reflected in the market price.

(viii) Financial accounting, based as it is on double entry systems, follows the duality concept. According to it, there are two aspects of each transaction. In other words, each transaction affects two items. For example, X starts a business and deposits a certain amount of money in a Bank. The dual aspects of this transaction is that the business has cash (resources) and the owner has a claim against this. The resources owned by a business are called assets, while the claims against it are of two types: *(1)* the claims of creditors and *(2)* the owner's claims. These are called "equities".

(ix) The business entity concept implies that financial accounts are prepared on the premise that a business has a separate entity from its owners. Therefore, while recording the various items in financial accounts, the approach is to consider the transactions from the viewpoint of the firm and not from the viewpoint of those who own the business. One probable reason for treating the business as separate from its owners is that since the funds from owners and creditors are placed at the dispose of the management who are responsible for the wise and efficient use of funds, the accounts prepared on the assumption of separate entity of business enable us to judge whether or not the management has succeeded in the task assigned to it.

THE MANAGEMENT ACCOUNTANT

Management accounting provides significant economic and financial data to the management and the Management Accountant is the channel through which this information efficiently and effectively flows to the Management.

The Management Accountant has a very significant role to perform in the installation, development and functioning of an efficient and effective management accounting system. He designs the framework of the financial and cost control reports that provide each managerial level with the most useful data at the most appropriate time. He educates executives in the need for control information and ways of using it. This is because his position is unique with respect to information about the organisation. Apart from top management no one in the organisation perhaps knows more about the various functions of the organisation than him. He is, therefore, sometimes described as the Chief Intelligence Officer of the top management. He gathers information, breaks it down, sifts it out and organises it into meaningful categories. He separates relevant and irrelevant information and then ranks relevant information management with information concerning the company as a whole, he supplies detailed information to the line officers regarding alternative plans and their profitability, which help them in decision making. As a matter of fact the management Accountant should not bother himself regarding the decision taken by the line officials after tendering advice unless he has reasonable grounds to believe that such a decision is going to affect the interest of the corporation adversely. In such an event also he should report it to the concerned level of management with tact, patience, firmness combined with politeness.

Position of Management Accountant in the Organisation

The organisational designation and position of the official who is entrusted with the management accounting functions vary from company to company. In large concerns, his designation may be that of 'Controller' or 'Comptroller' or 'Management Accountant'. He is essentially a staff official and acts in co-ordination with the executive heads of all functional and service departments. The Cost Accountant reports to the Chief Accountant when cost accounting is organised as a part of general accounting. The Chief Accountant reports to the Controller or Management Accountant, and the latter reports to the Director (Finance) or Vice-president (Finance). Alternatively, the Cost Accounting Department may be placed directly under the Controller or Management Accountant. In that case, the cost accounting function is organisationally interlinked with controllership function, and the Cost Accountant reports directly to the controller. The organisation chart given hereafter shows the position of the Controller in relation to other departmental heads. He is generally placed directly under the Managing Director with access to the Board of Directors as an invited to the Board meetings or in his capacity as an adviser to functional directors.

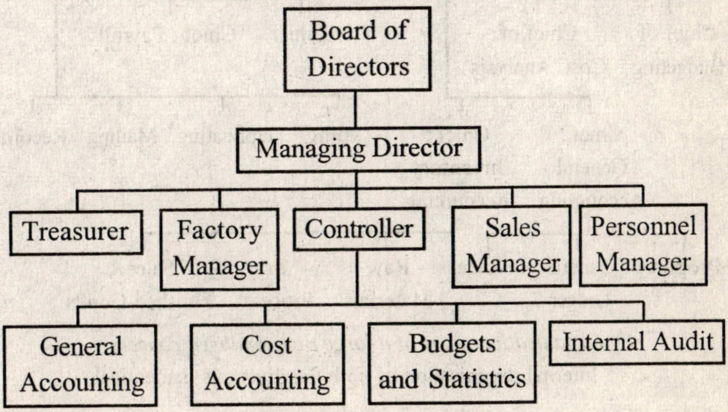

INFORMAL (STAFF) LINK

The position of the management accountant in the organisation has been rightfully explained by Mr. P.L. Tandon in the following words:

"The management accountant is exactily like the spokes in a wheel, connecting the rim of the wheel and the hub receiving the information. He processes the information and then returns the processed information back to where it came from."

The following chart depicts the position of controller in a large divisonalised concern and the responsibilities which accompany the

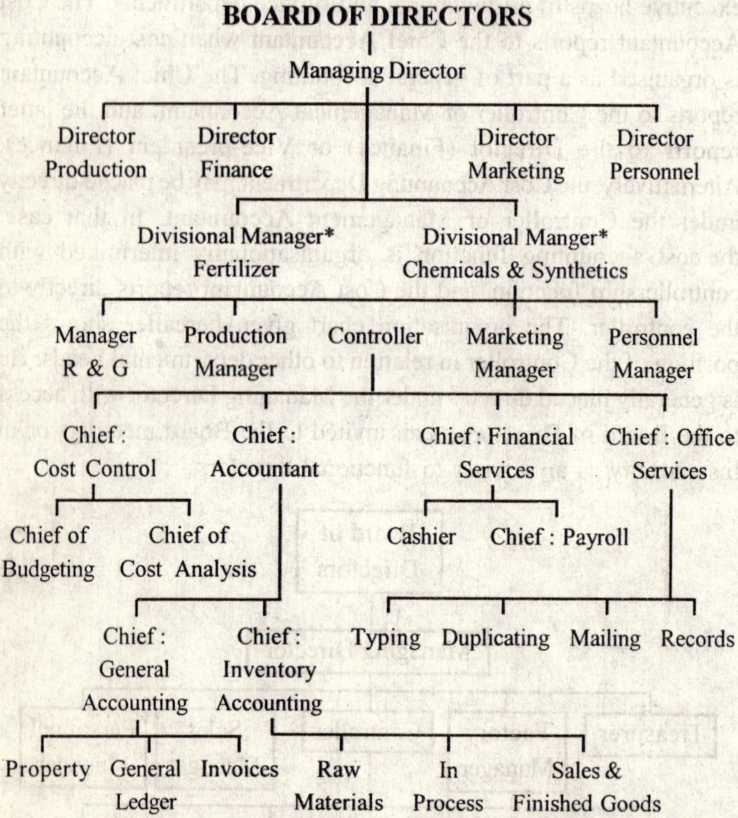

Organisation chart of a large divisionalised concern

* Internal organisation of both the divisions is identical

controllership function with various service departments under the Controller's charge.

In public sector undertakings, the role of the management accountant is in many cases assigned to an official designated as Financial Adviser and Chief Accounts Officer (FA & CAD). The following organisation chart of Bharat Heavy Electricals Limited (BHEL) shows the position of FA & CAO in the organisation.

The relationship between the Management Accountant (Controller) and top management has to be one of mutual confidence. The Management Accountant is not generally concerned with top management decisions. But his rank in the organisational hierarchy enables him to be in direct touch with the top rungs of management. He often attends Board meetings and participates in the deliberations of the Board as an aide. Besides, he has direct access to, is closely associated with, and assists the Managing Director in his day-to-day work. It is not necessary that his suggestions and advice would be always accepted and acted upon. But in all cases, the Managing Director is aware of the implications of each alternative as interpreted by the Management Accountant.

The Management Accountant acts in close liaison with the Cost Accountant, the General Accountant and the Internal Auditor in matters relating to standard costing, budgeting and the financial controls. Moreover, he will have to get the co-operation of the production engineer, sales manager and other heads of functional departments whenever he has to investigate operational matters arising out of the control reports. For performance evaluation, the Management Accountant is often required to make inter-firm comparison of productivity and other indices. For this purpose he must obtain financial data from the accountant, cost break-ups from the cost accountant, and information regarding plant capacity, utilisation of capacity, machine speed and machine load, power transmission and other technical matters from the engineers. On policy matters, the Management Accountant has to evaluate the pros and cons of different alternatives on the basis of business forecasts.

He must obtain necessary information in that connection from the functional managers in the purchases, production and sales departments.

Functions of the Management Accountant. It is the duty of the management accountant to keep all levels of management informed of their real position. He has, therefore, varied functions to perform. His important functions can be summarised as follows:

1. ***Planning.*** He has to establish, coordinate and administer as an integral part of management, an adequate plan for the control of the operations. Such a plan would include profit planning, programmes of capital investment and financing, sales forecasts, expense budgets and cost standards.
2. ***Coordinating.*** He consults all segments of management responsible for policy or action. Such consultation might concern any phase of the operation of the business having to do with attainment of objectives and the effectiveness of the organisation structures and policies.
3. ***Controlling.*** He has to compare actual performance with operating plans and standards and to report and interpret the results of operations to an levels of management and the owners of the business. This is done through the compilation of appropriate accounting and statistical records and reports.
4. ***Other Function.***
   (a) He carries out continuous appraisal of economic and social forces, and the government influences, and interprets their effect on the business.
   (b) He ensures fiscal protection for the assets of the business through adequate internal control and proper insurance coverage.
   (c) He administers tax policies and procedures.

(d) He supervises and coordinates the preparation of reports to government agencies.

It should be noted that the functions of a Management Accountant are more of those of a 'staff official'. He, in addition to processing historical data, supplies a good deal of information concerning the future operations, in line with the management's needs.

QUALITIES OR A MANAGEMENT ACCOUNTANT

A successful accountant has thus to create in himself abilities to perform a variety of functions. He is, therefore, expected to have:

(i) A very good grasp of the economic environment in which the firm is placed.

(ii) An understanding of the methods to forecast economic activities under expected varying conditions. He will find that appreciation of mathematical and statistical tools as also the behavioural aspects of problems will be of great assistance to him in his work.

(iii) Knowledge of the means of recording the company's performance and describing its current condition for the purpose of management review and control and to provide information to interested parties.

(iv) An understanding of the elements that determine the values offered by alternative uses of resources and the means of comparing promised alternative values of one to the other.

(v) A knowledge of the ways to forecast the funds movements associated with alternative activities under consideration.

(vi) An understanding of the ways in which various means of raising funds can be combined to produce greater values for the enterprise.

(vii) An appreciation of the stock of funds already at the company's disposal, and of the ways to use this stock more efficiently.

(viii) An analytical mind which can see through implications of alternative courses.

(ix) Last, but not the least, the ability to get along with people at all levels.

With the above abilities, an accountant can render adequate service expected of him. However, these new dimensions of accounting and a growing number of useful analytical techniques are not expected to supplant the activity of keeping accounts. But the keeping of accounts becomes a relatively minor task in the challenging job of a management accountant by whatever designation called.

❐

3

Budgeting in Managerial Decisions

A budget is a blue print of the projected plan of action expressed in quantitative terms for a specified period of time and the process of preparing a budget is called budgeting. Budgetary control refers to the principles, procedures and practices of achieving given objectives through budgets.

The difference between budget, budgeting, and budgetary control has been stated thus: "Budgets are the individual objectives of a department, etc. whereas budgeting may be said to be the act of building budgets. Budgetary control embraces all this and in addition includes the science of planning the budgets themselves and the utilisation of such budgets to effect an overall management tool for the business planning and control."

A budget is defined as a "comprehensive and coordinated plan, expressed in financial terms, for the operations and resources of an enterprise for some specified period in the future." According to this definition, the following are the essential elements of a budget:

(1) **Plan.** The first ingredient of a budget is its plan. The term "plan" with reference to budgeting has a specific connotation. It includes two aspects which have a bearing on the operations of an enterprise. One set of factors which determine a firm's future operations are wholly external and beyond its control. Included in this category of factors are general business conditions, government policy and size and composition of population. The second

set of factors affecting future activities are within the firm's control and discretion, *i.e.*, they are internal. Promotional programmes, manufacturing processes are illustration of these factors. Budgeting, as a plan, covers both these aspects. In other words, budgeting not only suggests what will happen but should also make things happen. In brief, a budget (plan) is an expression partly of what the management expects to happen and partly of what the management intends to happen.

(2) **Specified Future Period.** A Budget relates to a specified period of time, usually one year. If it is not related to a time horizon, it will be meaningless. Planning merely for a given amount of, say, sales/profit will not constitute a budget unless a time dimension is added, *i.e.*, the budgeted sales/profit is planned to be achieved in a pre-determined time framework.

(3) **Coordination.** Budgets are prepared for the different components/segments/divisions/ facets/activities of an organisation so as to take care of the situations and problems of each component. The budgets for each of the components are prepared in harmony with each another. This is called coordination.

(4) **Comprehensiveness.** A budget is comprehensive. The term "comprehensive" here means that all the activities and operations of an organisation are included in it. It covers the organisation as a whole and not only some segments. The *modus operandi* is that budgets are prepared for each segment/facet/activity/division of an organisation and these are integrated into an overall budget for the entire organisation. The overall budget is referred to as the master budget.

(5) **Operations and Resources.** A budget is a mechanism to plan for the firm's operations and resources. The operations are reflected in revenues and expenses. This means that a

budget should quantify the revenues to be realised from products/services and the expenses to be incurred on goods/services used in generating revenues.

The plan also covers the resources of the firm. The planning of resources means the planning of the various assets and the sources of capital to finance these assets. The assets could be fixed assets as well as current assets.

(6) Financial Terms. Budgets are prepared in financial terms, *i.e.*, in terms of monetary value such as the rupee, dollar, and so on. The reason is that the monetary unit is a common denominator. The various activities and operations are expressed in different units, *e.g.*, material in terms of weight, labour in terms of number/man-hours, sales in terms of territories, advertisement in terms of magazine space, and so on. If they have to be integrated in a plan, they must be expressed in comparable units of measurement. Monetary units provide such a measure.

The essentials of a budget are:

(i) It is prepared in advance and his based on a future plan of actions;

(ii) It relates to a future period and is based on objectives to be attained;

(iii) It is a statement expressed in monetary and/or physical units prepared for the implementation of policy formulated by the management.

Budget is a financial plan, budgeting is the art of planning and budgeting control is the art of adhering to the plan. Whatever programmes and policies are chalked out by the management, budgets put them in a concrete form. The follow-up action to see that the plans are adhered to completes the system of budgetary control. Adherence to plan means that effort is made to contain the actual costs within targeted limits.

Most human endeavour is more fruitful if directed by a well-advised and intelligently conceived programme. The conduct of business is no exception. Sometimes no sustained and continuous effort is made to chart a future course which would seem, all circumstances considered, to point the surest way towards the ultimate part of business success. If management carefully studies and gives proper attention to planning its activities in advance, operations would be more efficiently conducted and profits would be higher. The fundamental purpose of budgeting is to find the most profitable course through which the efforts of the business may be directed in meeting its primary service objective. The purpose of budgetary control system is to assist management in holding the business as early as possible on that charted course. Thus, the emphasis of budgeting is on the necessity for advance decision on future course of action to be followed. However, budgeting control system points out the result which would accrue by following that course of action.

According to the Institute of Cost and Management Accountants, England, budgetary control consists of "the establishment of budgets relating the responsibilities of executives to the requirements of a policy and the continuous comparison of actual with budgetary results either to secure by individual action the objective of that policy or to provide a basis for its revision."

Thus, budgetary control involves:

(a) Revision of budgets in the light of changed circumstances;

(b) Placing the responsibility for failure to achieve the budget figures;

(c) Continuous comparison of actuals with budgets for achievement of targets;

(d) Establishment of budgets.

In the words of J. Batty, budgeting control is "a system which uses budgets as a means of planning and controlling all aspects of producing and/ or selling commodities or services."

Budgetary control system operates through different budgets, prepared for various departments and activities. According to the Institute of Cost and Management Accountants, England, a budget is a "financial and/or quantitative statement; prepared prior to a defined period of time, of the policy to be pursued during that period for the purpose of attaining a given objective."

DIFFERENCE BETWEEN A FORECAST AND BUDGET

Forecasts and budgets both refer to the anticipated actions and events in a specified future period but there is a wide difference between the two. The points of difference have been explained hereunder:

Forecast	*Budget*
(i) Forecasts can be made in those spheres also where budgets cannot interfere.	(i) Budgets can be made of phonemenon non-capable of being expressed quantitatively.
(ii) Forecasting is a preliminary step for budgeting. It ends with the forecast of likely events.	(ii) It begins when forecasting ends. Forecasts are converted into budgets.
(iii) Forecasts, being statements of future events, do not connote any sense of control.	(iii) A budget is a tool of control since it represents actions which can be shaped according to will so that it can be suited to the conditions which may or may not happen.
(iv) Forecast is a mere estimate of what is likely to happen. It is a statement of probable events a which are likely to happen under anticipated conditions during specified period of time.	(iv) Budget shows the policy and programme to be followed in a future period under planned conditions.

CLASSIFY THE BUDGETS

Though budgets can be classified according to various points of view, the following bases of classification are generally in vogue:

(I) Functional classification;

(II) Classification according to flexibility factor;

(III) Classification according to time factor.

I. Functional Classification

According to this basis of classification, budgets correspond, and are co-terminous, with a particular function and are integrated with the master budget of the business. These are called 'functional budgets' whose number depends on the size and nature of the business. The usual functional budgets of a business are:

(a) ***Sales Budget.*** This is a forecast of total sales classified according to groups of products, salesman and geographical locations.

(b) ***Selling and Distribution Cost Budget.*** It is concerned with an estimate of the cost of selling and distribution of goods.

(c) ***Production Budget.*** It is a forecast based on sales, productive capacity and requirements of inventories, etc.

(d) ***Purchase Budget.*** Correlated with sales forecast and production planning, it deals with purchases that are required for planned production. Purchases would include both direct and indirect materials and goods.

(e) ***Production Cost Budget.*** This is related to the cost of production including direct material cost, direct labour cost and expenses-fixed, variable and semi-variable.

(f) ***Cash Budget.*** It is a sum-total of the requirements of cash in respect of various functional budgets as well as anticipated cash receipts.

(g) ***Personnel Budget.*** This has reference to the utilization of men and would include labour employed in productive activity. This would be split up between direct and indirect labour.

(h) ***Plant Utilization Budget.*** This is intended to cover the plant and machinery requirements to meet the budgeted production during the period. Schedules will be produced showing the available load in each department expressed in standard hours or units.

(i) ***Research Budget.*** It relates to improvement in the quality of the products or research for new products.

(j) ***Office and Administration Budget.*** This budget represents cost of all administrative expenses, such as, management director's salary, staff salaries, and expenses of office management like lighting and cleaning.

(k) ***Capital Budget.*** It is a forecast of outlay on fixed assets as also of the sources of capital required. The budget period in the case of capital budget may differ from that of other budgets; as such expenditure is frequently planned number of years in advance.

(l) ***Master Budget.*** The ultimate integration of separate budgets by the accountant provides the Master Budget which includes estimated profit and loss account for the future period and an estimated Balance Sheet as the end thereof.

II. Classification According to Flexibility

(a) ***Fixed Budget.*** It is a budget in which targets are rigidly fixed. Such budgets are usually prepared form one to three months in advance of the fiscal year to which they are applicable. Thus, twelve months or more may elapse before figures forecast for the December budget are used to measure actual performance. Many things may happen during this intervening period and they may make the figures go widely out of line with the actual figures. Though it is true that a fixed, or static budget as it is sometimes called, can be revised whenever the necessity arises, it smacks of rigidity and artificiality so far as control over costs and expenses is concerned. Such budgets are preferred only where sales can be forecast with the greatest of accuracy which means, in turn, that the costs and expenses in relation to sales can be quite accurately ascertained.

(b) ***Flexible Budget.*** The figures used in this form of cost and expense budget are made adaptable to any given set of

operating conditions within any month of the fiscal year. The figures range from the lowest to the highest probable percentages of operating activity in relation to the standard operating performance. From this point of view, a flexible budget prepared for an expense group can be used for the entire fiscal year or as long as there is no need of material changes in the standards. Thus, "the flexible budget possesses a distinct advantage over the static budget, particularly where it is difficult to forecast sales, costs and expenses with any great degree of accuracy.

(III) Classification According to Time Factor

In terms of time factor, budgets are broadly of the following three types:

(a) ***Long-term Budgets.*** They are concerned with planning the operations of a firm over a prospective of five to ten years. They are usually in form of physical quantities.

(b) ***Short-term Budgets.*** They are usually for a period of year or two and are in the form of production plan in monetary terms.

(c) ***Current Budgets.*** They cover a period of a month or so and are the short-term budgets adjusted to current conditions or prevailing circumstances.

Sometimes, within the framework of short-term budget, there are quarterly plans which are prepared by recasting it for a still shorter period on the basis of the performance of immediate past. In a way, these quarterly budgets are meant to be an elaboration of annual budget.

FUNDAMENTALS OF BUDGETING

The fundamentals are concerned directly with effective implementation of budget plans as the management process. The fundamentals tend to represent desirable management orientations, activities, and approaches that are basically necessary conditions for proficient, sophisticated and effective application of the concept of budgeting. These are environmental conditions that need to be established on a sound foundation of managerial commitment. The more important fundamentals, some of which have been referred as essentials may be enumerated thus:

(a) **Responsibility accounting system,** tailored first and foremost to the organisational responsibilities.

(b) **Goal orientation,** entailing the acceptance on the part of management of the concept of management by objectives (MBO).

(c) **Full communication,** ensuring full and clear understanding, by the executive and subordinates alike, of responsibilities and goals as well is full and open reporting in performance reports.

(d) **Realistic expectations,** by avoiding both under conservation and irrational over-optimism.

(e) **Individual and group recognition,** identifying and recognising in the management process individual accomplishment, both outstanding and substandard performance. The system of individual evaluation must be fair, understandable, and accurate.

(f) **Timeliness that is,** a definite time schedule for formal planning performance reports, and certain other related activities.

(g) **Flexible application,** to avoid rigidity and "strait jackets" so that budgets do not act as a severe constraint on the decision-making freedom of managers and supervisors.

(h) **Follow-up,** This fundamental holds that both good and substandard performance should be carefully investigated the purpose being three-fold: *(i)* in the case of substandard performance, to lead in a constructive manner to immediate corrective action; *(ii)* in the case of outstanding performance, to recognise it and perhaps provide for transfer of knowledge to similar operations; and *(iii)* to provide a basis for better planning and control in the future.

(i) **Organisational adaptation,** to ensure sound and clearly defined organisational structure with a clearing designation of lines of authorities and responsibilities.

(i) **Managerial involvement and participation,** including top-management support.

ADVANTAGES OF BUDGETING

1. Correlation of Human Effort with in Business Structure. If in some divisions of business, there is uncertainty of programmes, full steam cannot be applied in other divisions. To secure full power of united action, it is essential to properly time and co-ordinate the effort of all divisions. Budgeting helps in achieving co-ordination of human effort within the organisation.

2. Relation of Business Activities to General Economic Trend. The plans of the business must reflect courage or caution depending upon the expected general trend of business or economic conditions. Budgeting assists the management to co-ordinate the activities of the business to the signals of high and low economic trends. Particularly the danger signals which act as forewarners to the business are reflected in budgeting which cautions the entire organisation well in advance.

3. Optimum Use of Available Facilities. Budgeting entails in itself the most effective use of physical equipment and other facilities. It helps in checking waste related to their uneconomical use.

4. Fixation of Objectives. When the objectives are not the product of hope but rather the logical sequence of carefully laid plans, the executives can command the cooperation and loyalty of their associates. This leads to successful execution of the programmes.

5. Elimination of Uncertainty. The organisation should be schooled in basic policies, which are the real guide to a business. The budget procedure provides a vehicle through which basic policies are periodically re-examined, restated and set forth as guiding principles for the organisation at large.

6. Combined Judgment of Entire Organisation. The budgeting process takes the assistance of the entire organisation in determining the most profitable course, thus the bias or prejudice is eliminated and the final plans are expressive of the combined judgment of entire organisation.

7. Employment Stability. The days have gone when workers could be shunted out at will when not required like flasks or patterns in the foundry. Intelligent budgeting offers the greatest hope for providing stability of employment.

8. Early Study of Problems. Most of us prefer to postpone difficult decisions until necessity compels. In the business also, people are normally opportunists, they wait till a decision is forced. Intensive study, which is to many a distasteful exercise, is not taken up beforehand and when the troubles crop up abruptly, easiest immediate escape is resorted to. Budgeting instills into the organisation the habit of thorough study before decision is put to action.

9. Prevention of Waste. A searching inquiry into every contemplated expenditure and the reason therefore-an analytical approach extending to every function and every department of the business—will constitute an effective prevention of waste.

10. Most Profitable Channelisation of Capital and Effort. Budgeting leads to a balanced and unified programme and through it the capital and efforts are directed into the most profitable channels. Where planning and decision-making is made on a day to day basis, the programme frequently becomes unconsciously warped. Careful advance planning results in balancing of factors and a proportionate emphasis on sales, finance, production, inventories etc. This leads to attainment of goals laid down.

11. Control of Specific Operations. The budget provides a valuable tool of control over certain business operations, *e.g.*, investment in plant, quantity to be produced, quantum of expenditure to be incurred for sales promotion etc. Expenditures are limited and directed into the channels which affered most promise. Certain activities can be controlled if sales and production performance does not meet the expectations.

12. Curtain-raiser Over Weaknesses. Budgeting reveals the weaknesses in the organisation, since the responsibility for the execution of budgets is delegated. The responsibility, however, will be acceptable to executives only when lines of authority are so delineated that they remain unhampered in the execution of their tasks.

Thus, budgeting serves as a communication device which permits a full and free interplay of ideas with the objectives of selecting the best plan. This is the role of budgeting as a management tool for planning. The most feasible plan is put to action and budgeting is used as a control mechanic by the management through assigning responsibilities for execution of the plans. In an effective environment, the necessary co-ordination is achieved in both planning and control aspects of budgeting. To summarise, budgetary control acts as a friend, philosophy and guide to the management.

LIMITATIONS OF BUDGETING

Budgetary control can be a powerful technique in the hands of management to achieve the objectives, but it rests on the quality of management and the attention given to motivating staff to react favourable to the discipline the technique imposes.

In the words of J.R. Batliboi, "The success of budgetary control must depend on the adequacy and reliability of records, the past and the present performances, on the interest of all executives and subordinates in the purposes of such control, proper departmentalisation and subdivision of factory activities, a close classification and proper division and analysis of the expenditure, and the most suitable system of cost and financial accounts."

Budgetary control can be used as a motivator by allowing those responsible for budget achievement to be involved in the budgeting process and by supplying them with monitoring information to facilitate control. In order to be fully effective, the budgetary control should have participative type of budgeting rather than merely serving as authorisation procedures.

1. **Regarded as a Pressure Instrument.** The technique is regarded by staff as a pressure instrument rather than a procedure to assist the executive to do a better job. Thus, there is opposition against the very spirit of budgeting.
2. **Danger of Rigidity.** As budgets are prepared by quantifying all relevant data, there is tendency to attach some sort of finality to budget figures but, as they are meant to deal with business conditions which are constantly changing, they would lose much of their usefulness if they acquire rigidity. Therefore, It is essential that budgetary programme must be continuously adapted to changing conditions in and off a business unit.
3. **Misplacement of Motivation.** Managers may be satisfied with budget performance when better performance is possible and could reasonably be attained if a low level of attainment had not been in the budget.
4. **Thinking too Ahead.** If forecasting is practised too for into the future, the budgetary control technique may not be that fruitful. Appropriate techniques must be developed before the purpose.
5. **Managers Discretion in Submitting Budget Estimates may be Fatal.** If it is left entirely in the hands of managers to submit budget estimates and the same are accepted as such the performance may not improve since the estimates may not be too demanding on their performance.
6. **Prohibited Cost.** It is quite common to find that the structure of the budgetary system becomes top heavy and costly so much so that small concerns cannot afford to adopt it. However, it is essential that there must be some correlation between the cost of the system and the benefits obtained from it. No cast iron rules can be laid down for this as much depends on the size and nature of the activities of individual business.
7. **Weak Organisation Structure.** The entire organisational structure should be very solid and sound. Wherever there

are inherent weaknesses in the organisational structure, no control system would prove to be effective. Delegation of authority and responsibility should be very specific.

8. **Ineffective Accounting System.** If the accounting system, which is the bedrock of successful budgeting is not effective, the control technique would not work.

9. **No Action or Delayed Action.** If even after knowing that particular person or department is responsible for off-budget performance, no action is taken or the action is delayed, the technique of budgetary control could be blamed unnecessarily for unsatisfactory achievements of targets in future also.

10. **Gestation Period not Allowed.** The system, itself, demands Some time to be developed fully within the organisation. The required experience, if not there, can lead to a failure of the system in its initial stages.

11. **Change in Conditions.** If the conditions that are anticipated are changed, the budgetary targets cannot be achieved. The budget may be revised for the future, but still in these days of uncertainty, even the revised estimates may go wrong. The utility of the technique lies in correctly estimating as for as possible the influence of future contingencies.

12. **Budget Plan is Based on Estimates.** Absolute accuracy is not possible in forecasting and budgeting though a high standard is always aimed at. The adequacy or otherwise of a budgetary programme depends to a very large extent on the accuracy with which estimates are made. If the budgeted figures are removed from reality, very little purpose would be served by them. The fact of the budget being based on estimates must be kept in view in interpreting the results thereof.

13. **Impersonal Approach.** Sometimes it is managed that the introduction of the budget system is alone sufficient to ensure its success and to guarantee future profits. After

the preparation of the budget, it is necessary that the energies and efforts of the entire organization are harnessed for the realization of budgetary goals. In this connection, in must always be kept in view that budgeting can never be more than a perfect way of observing results, to indicate more closely and quickly than any other system as to how far more rationalization is necessary; it is not rationalization it itself. Thus, it constitutes only an impersonal approach to the conduct of business activity and has to be supplemented with proper management and administration.

OBJECTIVES OF BUDGETING

1. To ensure that adequate working capital is available for the efficient operation of the business.
2. To show management where action is needed to remedy a situation.
3. To obtain a more economical use of capital.
4. To centralize management control.
5. To aid in controlling cash.
6. To provide more definite assurance of earning the proper return on capital invested.
7. To provide a method of measurement of operating activities and financial position both where standards are and are not used.
8. To aid an obtaining better inventory control and turnover.
9. To prevent waste, to, reduce expenses and to obtain the income desired.
10. To forecast operating activities and financial position.
11. To establish divisional and departmental responsibilities.
12. To operate most efficiently the divisions, departments and cost centres of a plant.
13. To co-ordinate the various divisions of a business, namely production, marketing, financial and administrative

divisions, by consultation among the divisional heads and mutual agreement on company policies.

14. To conform with good business practice by planning for the future.
15. To smooth out seasonal variations in production by developing new 'fill-in' products and thereby accomplishing one phase of economic planning.

Guidelines for a Better Budgeting

The success of the budget programme may well hinge upon proper administration, for the human element is so important. To assist the budget officer of any company in initiating and selling a sound budget system, the Committee on Management Planning and Control of the Controllers Institute of America prepared the following check list of do's and don' ts" [The Controller, Vol. XVIII, No. 12 (Controllers Institute of America), pp. 550-53.]

1. The following points should be considered with respect to budgeting organisation and preparation:

(i) Budgeting Policy

DO	*DON'T*
(a) Use an organisation or operation chart to show the functional responsibility of each executive whose activities justify a separate budget.	(a) Dont's install a budget system if management is unwilling to accept or comply with full cooperation.
(b) Make certain that the final responsibility for execution of the budget rests with top management. If top management does not really desire a budget, and your efforts to promote the principle are unavailing, better abandon the thought altogether.	(b) Don't fail to secure executive approval of budgets before issuing statements.

Contd.

DO	*DON'T*
(c) Adapt the budget procedure to the needs of the organisation, *viz.* cash requirements, inventories, capital assets, sales, expense control, etc.	(c) Don't divide responsibility below. the level of policy determinations.
(d) Remember that it is a basic principle of budgeting procedure that the preparation of and responsibility for a sound budget rest with the respective department heads and not with the budget officer. The budget should, at all times, be considered as a consultant or to advisor to the operating heads of a business.	(d) Don't let the budget be a creation of the budget officer alone. It is essentially an operation function of department heads. The budget officer is the coordiantor and advisor. Variances from budget are then the responsibility of the department supervisor to explain.
(e) Provide for detailed review and approval of programme before expenditure are permitted for-items included in budget. Accept approvals of divisional supervisors up to specified limits to save time of generai executives.	(e) Don't classify all capital expeditures on the same basis. Consider as "Urgent", "Current", or "Desirable" projects.
(f) Require specific approval for projects not budgeted and for expenditures in excess of stated amount or percentage compared with budgeted amount.	
(g) Plan ways and means of keeping everyone interested in the planning and control programme. For example: use "easier" reports to stimulate interest in budgeting.	(g) Don't present a master budget plan without consulting all parties concerned.

Contd.

DO	*DON'T*
(h) Arrange educational meetings to obtain cooperation in the successful operation of a budget.	(h) Don't force budgets on department heads. Make the budget a joint venture. Work out the results together.
(i) Determine management's objectives as to the economy as a whole, competition within industry, internal expansion, and operating efficiency before establishing the forecast.	(i) Don't place budget authority in hands of anyone with partisan influences.

(ii) Preparation

DO	*DON'T*
(a) Make the budget easy to accept. Offer to test or trial run your ideas.	
(b) Classify expenditures carefully and diligently. Avoid arbitrary allocation of expenses between departments.	
(c) Prepare master budgets from summaries of departmental budgets.	(c) Don't depend entirely up a tailor-made budget from a publication. A general outline of a budget may be available for a particular industry but usually this from will require an adaptation to your specific requirements.
(d) Budget accounts must correspond with the established chart of accounts.	(d) Don't fail to praise individuals who are responsible for good planning and performance and don't fail to assist those whose planning is below par.

Contd.

DO	*DON'T*
(e) Express budget objectives and plans in writing. Supplement written material with verbal instructions when necessary.	(e) Don't fail to keep and circulate an up-to-date budget procedure or budget manual. Refer to it frequently.
(f) Select the toughest foreman or division head in the company and sell him on it, then watch the gospel spread.	(f) Don't permit anyone on the budget staff to have an indifferent attitude towards budgeting. An enthusiastic attitude is a requisite of a successful budget staff.

(iii) Organisation of Budget Department

DO	*DON'T*
(a) Be properly staffed for the budgeting job. Judicious expenditures for this department will pay dividends.	(a) Don't fail to have a definite plan for the administration of the budget after it is established.
(b) Vigorously and continually sell the values of practical budgeting. Promote it up the line of authority and down the line of authority. Design it. Dress it. Enthusiastically tout it at every opportunity written and spoken.	(b) Don't try to perfect the budget immediately.
	(c) Don't overlook the unique oportunity afforded to the budget direct to act as a liaison officer between the various operating and staff departments.

(A) Planning

DO	*DON'T*
(a) Do an adequate job of research before starting to forecast.	(a) Don't budget too far in advance. Short term budgets (usually for one

Contd.

DO	*DON'T*
	year of less) permit more realistic comparisons with actual results and they also permit closer adjustment to charging conditions.
(b) Make provisions in the budget for every principal activity.	(b) Don't depend exculsively on past experience. Keep an open and inquiring mind for cost reduction, otherwise inefficiencies are cultivated.
(c) Furnish past performance guides to each Department executive for preparation of future budgets. Explain unusual and non-recurring items.	(c) Don't oppose current and future trends in forecasting without adeqate reasons therefor.
(d) Classify expenses realistically as between variable, semi-variable and fixed categories.	(d) Don't prepare budgets until determination of plant production goals is established.
(e) Budget net results in point of cost per unit when possible. Reach the lowest possible common denominator that will highlight the results of budgeting.	(e) Don't prepare budgets until determination of personnel required for all phases of operations is established.
(f) Have alternate plans available for emergencies. Variable budgets are widely used for this purpose.	(f) Don't release your forecasts with out through study.
(g) Carefully consider discontinuance of low margin lines or the effect of new product lines.	(g) Don't set budgets on variable rates too tight. To be stimulating, rates must be on a basis that will permit a better-than-even chance of attainment.
	(h) Don't criticize too often.
	(i) Don't recommend planning as a panacer for all evils.

(B) Forecasting

DO	*DON'T*
(a) Base the sales budget on a reasonably attainable and expected : volume of sales, neither too optimistic nor nor pessimistic.	(a) Don't establish a budget that is too elablorate at the outset. It is better to start with a basic operation set up and enlarge the scope as conditions warrant.
(b) Use budget period which coincide with sales and production cycles.	(b) Don't fail to consider the favourable effect of capital exenditures on operating budgets. Stress the advisability of capital additions which will increase production improve product or reduce operating costs.
(c) Set production budgets on sales volume after considering existing inventories and the effect of inventory fluctuations and purchasing policies.	(c) Don't overlook external statistic and assistance.
(d) Use these vital factors in forecastting sales: (a) Past experience; (b) Pricing policy; (c) Production capacity and cost; (d) General business conditions; (e) Position in business cycle; (f) Nature of competition; (g) Consumer demand; (h) Consumer purchasing power; (i) Relate probable results from varying advertising appropriations;	(d) Don't fail to recognize that certain departments operate at various stages of căpcity.

Contd.

DO	*DON'T*
(j) Sales promotion plans; (k) Gross profit margins by product, operating profit and net profit.	
(e) Determine and record the reasons. or statistics behind each forecast.	(e) Don't compute all budget expenditures on the same basis. Usually there are three classifications as follows: (a) Variable-(vary with volume); (b) Semi-variable-(increase and decrease not usually in proportion to volume); (c) Fixed-(rent, taxes, etc.)
(f) Make certain that each executive clearly outlines the practical objectives that are expected to be accomplished in the budget period.	(f) Don't forecast to the last detail. Concentrate on items of importance.
(g) Anticipate trade, seasonal and economic changes in the establishment of expense budgets.	(g) Don't resort to bromidic euphemisms. Be realistic and to the point. Slangy sayings sometimes rebound to your own embarrassment.
(h) Point out prior and proposed forecast errors tactfully.	(h) Don't be misled by executive optimism or possimism in forecasting.
	(i) Don't disregard ideas of others affected by the plan.

(C) When Comparing Results, these Ideas should be Considered

DO	*DON'T*
(a) Consider the advisability of using functional charts and graphs for readable interpretations. Compare results of one division or department with another to develop a	(a) Don't hesitate to recommend vigorous corrective action when necessary.

Contd.

DO	*DON'T*
competitive spirit with respect to results.	
(b) Study budget and operating-data carefully for recommendations, suggestions and future action.	(b) Don't set controls too tight at first. Revise controls as experience is gained.
(c) Review results regularly with management, department heads, supervisors and others.	(c) Don't forget that a budget is based on estimates.
(d) Make reports that are clear and concise. They will command greater executive respect and attention.	(d) Don't accept variances without reasonable explanation.
(e) Make certain that budget reports are issued on a timely schedule.	(e) Don't present reports at such a late date they are ineffective.
(f) Issue daily, weekly, monthly or other regular reports showing the conforming actuals with budget as well as explanations of principal variances.	(f) Don't issue budget statements without comparisons to prior periods or without measurements of departmental efficiency.
(g) Present progress reports of capital expenditures with emphasis on cumulative costs, completion dates, and resulting economies or improvement of product.	
(h) Check operating results and budgeting methods with contemporaries for new ideas and techniques.	

(D)

DO	*DON'T*
(a) Remember that budgets and budget reports are essentially tools of management, not merely accounting reports.	(a) Don't stop trying to improve results with new methods, procedures and ideas.

Contd.

DO	*DON'T*
(b) Eliminate transfer of labour between departments except when absolutely necessary.	(b) Don't overlook the objective viewpoint. Sit in the other fellow's chair when making recommendations: department head, banker, stockholder, executive, Board of Directors, etc.
(c) Observe, record and consider those daily incidents that are likely to develop into future variations.	(c) Don't fail to establish definite objectives of performance within the budget.
(d) Provide for possible curtailment because of unforeseen adverse changes in business conditions or prospects.	(d) Don't fail too recognize that manufacturing or other difficulties are variable.
	(e) Don't allow the budget to take the place of management and administration.

(E) Follow-up

DO	*DON'T*
(a) Review corrective action with the department head respecting those daily incidents that are likely to result in budget variations.	(a) Don 'ttakecreditforall the favourable results.
(b) Reflect savings resulting from capital expenditures in the operating expense budget.	(b) Don't forget that good budget performance does not occur as a matter of course but is brought about by constant surveillance.
(c) Regularly analyse transfers of direct to indirect labour and expense and *vice versa*.	(c) Don't fail to stimulate the development of newer and better ways and means of obtaining results from department executives.

Contd.

DO	*DON'T*
(d) Compare results with benefits anticiated before expenditure to see if mechanical or engineering faults may be remanded at little extra cost and thus fully realise the intended objectives.	(d) Don't fail to forecast the effect of management's current decisions on future results.
	(e) Don't be content and conclude that your job is done after publication of the budget.

ESSENTIALS OF AN EFFECTIVE BUDGETING

(1) Support Management. Though a budget programme, in order to be successful, must have the whole-hearted support of every member of management, the impetus and direction must come from the top. This requires commitment of top management to the budget idea as well as to the principles, policies and philosophy underlying it.

(2) Clearly Defined Organization. In order to carry out budgeting in a manner that will provide maximum benefits, organization within the business is essential. There should be a sound plan with responsibilities well defined and adequately maintained. Further, records should be clear, consistently departmentalized and established in such a manner as will indicate definite responsibility on each unit or section of the business.

(3) Recognition of People. For the most effective budgeting, the best human engineering is needed. If any plans are to be made, the departmental heads and minor executives should also participate. Most people want recognition and therefore those who are made responsible for execution of the plans must have a role in making them. Men must be dealt with as human beings.

(4) Co-operation. One of the important pre-requisites in effective budgeting is a willingness on the part of each echelon of management to participate in the preparation of a budget and to be judged against it. The budget must be viewed, not as a pressure tool, but as a challenge, a goal, an objective, that can be attained and surpassed.

(5) Motivation. Budget is a device to control costs through people; hence human relations aspects are of paramount importance in dealing with the subject. No management tool can be used to maximum effectiveness without motivation.

(6) Responsibility Accounting. The transactions or events should be recorded in such a manner as to identify them with the individual in the organisation who controls the activity and is to be held accountable for it. The business plan must be developed by the responsibility centres.

(7) Satisfactory Accounting. The historical facts must be made available in such a manner so as to determine the relationship of costs and results and the efficiency of individual divisional and functional performance.

Moreover, the information system must provide the data in usable form to assist in making sound management decisions.

(8) Continuous Budget Education. An essential condition for the success of budgeting is that it must be able to sustain the interest of those who shoulder the responsibility of putting budget proposals into effect. This needs continu-ous 'budget education' which is concerned with briefing the employees of the undertaking on the objectives, potentials and techniques of budgeting as well as making them understand its uses and limitations.

(9) A Degree of Flexibility. It is always desirable to provide for both possible and unforeseen circumstances. In fact, control is increased and strengthened though the provision of an arrangement whereby differences are automatically catered for, as in flexible budgets, rather than an amendment to the budget plan as would be necessary in the case of fixed budget.

(10) Unambiguous Policy. A Budget programme is always based on certain fundamentals, the collection of which is called the 'policy' of the business. Naturally, therefore, no programme can be prepared without the knowledge of the business policy to be adopted during the period covered by the budgets. In its absence, any attempt to make estimates for the current year would be an exercise in the dark and is bound to affect usefulness for future.

(11) Logical Sequence in the Budget Preparation. It is essential that proper procedures should be evolved for the preparation, submission, examination and review of budget figures in logical sequence. Budget preparation is often exacting and demands much careful though and attention on the part of the entire staff of business unit engaged in the compilation of the various figures.

(12) Constant Vigilance. An effective system of budgetary control requires that provision must be made for the comparison of budgeted and actual results at frequent intervals. As soon as unfavourable trends are detected, immediate action should be taken to remedy them.

(13) Preparation by Responsible Executives. Subject to the natural control of the budget personnel and the chief executive, arrangements should be made to ensure the participation of those entrusted with the performance of the budget in the formulation of budget proposals. Such an approach would guarantee to a certain extent, the proper implementation of the programme contained in the budget.

CASH BUDGET

For any business activity, cash is very important power. Without money nothing moves. So, though the cash budget is discussed after all other budgets, it does not mean that it is not important. It is being discussed at this stage since only when all activities are planned and targeted can one get an idea of the total cash requirement.

A cash 'forecast' is the statement of receipts and payments of cash as it is expected to be in the budget period. For the sake of convenience, the forecast or budget is prepared month by month. The objective of the exercise is to establish whether at the end of each month, there will be a deficit or plus of cash. If the payments are expected to be more than receipts, suitable arrangement should be made in that period so that the shortage is covered. Conversely, if receipts are expected to be more than payments and a large surplus is expected, decision regarding how to utilise that surplus profitably has also be taken. It has often been stated that a cash budget is particularly necessary for an enterprise which operates on a narrow margin of cash. This is certainly so. But a cash budget is also of great importance to all undertakings, even those which have large funds available in excess of requirements. In such a situation it will show the amount and the period during which excess cash is likely to be available. Management then has the responsibility of investing the funds properly, say, in short-term bonds or treasury notes instead of keeping the funds idle and unproductive. When decisions as indicated above are taken and a full picture is presented in respect of receipts and payments based on all other budgets the statement is a 'cash budget'. Cash budget is just a sophisticated and enlarged form of what a housewife does to balance her budget. To have a rather exact picture, instead of monthly cash budgets, weekly budgets may be drawn up. But usually that is not necessary.

The cash budget may have two clear sections-capital and revenue. Capital receipts would be *(a)* any process on issue of shares or debtentures or any loans to be raised; *(b)* sale proceeds of any long-term investments, and *(c)* sale proceeds of any fixed assets.

Revenue receipts would be *(a)* amount receivable on sales or services; *(b)* amount receivable from customers or clients. This depends upon the credit period allowed. Thus, the January cash budget may contain collections of December sales or earlier if the credit period allowed is a month or more than a month; collections shall be including sales tax but net of discounts; and *(c)* usual business receipts like commission, income from investments, etc.

Capital expenditure may be routine replacement expenditure or project expenditure. In both the cases, such of those expenditures as according to plan is to be spent in the 1st month or 2nd month, etc., would suitably be included in the respective months.

Revenue expenditures usually are the following items:

(a) **Payment of Wages.** This depends upon the periodicity of payments, whether fortnightly, the wages are paid.

(b) **Payment for Materials Supplied.** This depends upon the credit period allowed by the suppliers. Thus, if one month credit period is allowed the cash budget for the month of January may include payments for supplies received in the month of December.

(c) **Payments, of Overhead Expenses.** These expenses may be monthly payments or weeldy payments. For instance, rent paid monthly in advance, telephone bills paid every quarter, sales tax paid every quarter, insurance paid annually, etc. Depending upon the periodicity they would be included in the budget of the appropriate month.

(d) **Payments in Respect of Appropriation,** for instance, tax paid or dividends paid, interest on borrowings paid etc. These items will have to be included in the appropriate month in which the payment is expected to be made.

ADVANTAGES OF CASH BUDGET

(1) It enables an organisation to maintain sound liquidity. By planning ahead, the credit position of the enterprise may be strengtgened.

(2) It acts as a standard for evaluating the performance of operation.

(3) Cash budget is an important basis of long term financial planning. It is mainly useful for the study of long term financing with respect to probable amounts, timing, forms of security and methods of repayment.

(4) It assists in maintaining a sound dividend policy consistent with the liquid position of the company. Cash dividend is

always preferred by shareholders. They maintain prestige ensure good relations with shareholders and facilitate any stock financing.

(5) It helps in maintaining an adequate cash balance of expected requirements and provides a reasonable margin for the unexpected.

(6) Cash budget helps in advance to test the influence of proposed programme on cash position. It serves as a device for coordinating the financial aspect of the growth.

(7) It helps as a control device. The expenses of various departments can be best controlled so as not to exceed the available means.

(8) Cash budget helps in cash planning. It shows the cash surplus as well as deficiency of such cash at selected points of time.

PREPARATION OF CASH BUDGET

There are three methods usually used in preparation of a cash budget. These methods are:

(a) Receipts and Payments Method.

(b) Adjusted Profit and Loss Method.

(c) Balance Sheet Method.

Examining different approaches to the preparation of cash budget, the first method is found useful over short period while the other two methods are generally used over long periods. Therefore, we shall discuss here only first method of preparing a cash budget, *i.e.*, Receipt and Payment Method.

Receipts and Payments Method

This is the most simple and popular method of preparing a cash budget. It is similar to Receipts and Payments Account in technique. It shows the yearly cash position with proper breakdowns by quarters and months. It is divided into two parts. One part shows the amount and timing of cash receitlots while the other part shows the amount and timings of cash disbursements. The method involves the following steps:

(i) **Estimation of Cash Receipts.** Estimates of cash receipts prepared on a monthly basis and depend upon estimated cash sales, collection from debtors and anticipated receipts from other sources such as sale of assets, borrowings, etc. Delay in cash receipts should also be taken into account while making estimates.

(ii) **Estimation of Cash Disbursement.** Requirements of cash are based on estimated cash purchases, payment to creditors, employee's remuneration, bonus, advance to suppliers, interest and principal payable in respect of outstanding and budgeted loans, dividend payments, and capital expenditures for expansion, etc. The minimum cash balance desired to be maintained is added with the required disbursements and then provision is made for additional borrowings or capital issues, etc.

(iii) **Form of the Cash Budget.** Budgeted cash receipts and budgeted cash requirements are then brought together to form a total cash budget. From the figures of cash receipts the total cash requirements will be deducted. Then the budget will show the cash position at the end of each control period. If the receipts exceed payments then there will be cash balance at close. If such balance is larger, the management must plan to invest in short term investments for its profitable utilisation. On the other hand, if there is a cash shortage, the management must plan borrowings for short period.

According to this method, the cash budget can be prepared in the following form:

Global Engineering Co. Ltd.

CASH BUDGET

(For six months ended 30th June)

Particulars	*Jan.*	*Feb.*	*Mar.*	*April*	*May*	*June*	*Total*
	Rs.	Rs.	Rs.	Rs.	Rs.	Rs.	Rs.
Opening Balance							
Add-Budgeted cash receipts							
(1) Cash Sales							
(2) Collection from Drs.							
(3) Sale of assets							
(4) Issue of Sec.							
(5) Other receipts							
Total							
Less-Budgeted cash Dis-bursments:							
(i) Purchases							
(ii) Wages							
(iii) Overheads							
(iv) Dividend							
(v) Taxes							
(vi) Purchases. of assets							
Total							
Excess or deficiency of cash							

Illustration.

Z Ltd. closes its books on 31st March each year. On 1st January 2002 it wants to prepare a cash forecast for the first quarter (April to June) of the ensuing year. The following information is available:

	Rs.		*Rs.*
March, 2002	50,00,000	May, 2002	55,00,000
April, 2002	60,00,000	June, 2002	70,00,000

The details of cost of sales for the month of March:

Materials	22,50,000	Variable overheads	5,00,000
Wages	7,50,000	Fixed overheads	7,50,000

Fixed overheads include an amount of Rs. 2,00,000 for depreciation on plant and machinery.

l/5th of the sales are for cash and the rest on credit. Customers are allowed a credit period of one month which happens to be the credit allowed by the suppliers also.

Wages and variable overheads are paid in the month which follows that in which they are incurred. Material and labour costs are strictly variable. Fixed overheads are to be paid in the same month.

During June, 2002 income-tax of Rs. 6,00,000 is to be paid. The staff is to be paid a bonus of Rs. 3,00,000 in May. A uniform gross profit on variable cost is maintained by the company. A loan installment of Rs. 26,00,000 is to be paid in June.

The cash balance in hand on 1st April is expected to be Rs. 2,50,000.

Prepare a cash forecast for the 3 months and also suggest how the shortfall or excess can be filled up or utilised as the case may be. Assume that each month's production is sold out in full.

Solution.

X. Ltd.

CASH FORECAST FOR THE PERIOD 1ST APRIL TO 30TH JUNE, 2002

Particulars	*April*	*May*	*June*
	Rs.	*Rs.*	*Rs.*
Balance b/d	2,50,000	14,00,000	22,50,000

Receipts:			
Cash Sales	12,00,000	11,00,000	14,00,000
Collection from debtors	40,00,000	48,00,000	44,00,000
Total	54,50,000	73,00,000	80,50,000
Payments:			
Material supplied	22,50,000	27,00,000	24,75,000
Wages	7,50,000	9,00,000	8,25,000
Variable overheads	5,00,000	6,00,000	5,50,000
Fixed overheads	5,50,000	5,50,000	5,50,000
Staff bonus		3,00,000	
Income-tax			6,00,000
Loan Instalment			26,00,000
Balance c/d	14,00,000	22,50,000	4,50,000
Total	54,50,000	73,00,000	80,50,000

Date..........

Prepared by............. Checked by.............. Management Accountant...........

CASH BUDGET

(For six months ended 30th June, 2004)

Particulars	*Jan.*	*Feb.*	*Mar.*	*April*	*May*	*June*	*Total*
Opening Balance	....	....	....	....	....	....	....
Add-Budgeted cash receipts							
(1) Cash Sales	....	....	....	....	....	....	....
(2) Collection from Drs	....	....	....	....	....	....	....
(3) Sale of assets	....	....	....	....	....	....	....
(4) Issue of Sec.	....	....	....	....	....	....	....
(5) Other receipts	....	....	....	....	....	....	....
Total	....	....	....	....	....	....	....

Contd.

Particulars	*Jan.*	*Feb.*	*Mar.*	*April*	*May*	*June*	*Total*
Less-Budgeted cash Disbursments :							
(i) Purchases	....	....	....	....	....	....	....
(ii) Wages	....	....	....	....	....	....	....
(iii) Overheads	....	....	....	....	....	....	....
(iv) Dividend	....	....	....	....	....	....	....
(v) Taxes	....	....	....	....	....	....	....
(vi) Purchases of assets	....	....	....	....	....	....	....
Total	....	....	....	....	....	....	....
Excess or deficiency of cash							

PRODUCTION BUDGET

The production budget is a forecast of the production for the budget period. It provides an estimate of the total volume of production product wise with the scheduling of operations by days, week and months. The budget also includes a forecast of the closing finished goods inventory. The preparation of production budget is generally taken up after the sales budget is completed. The factory manager is the person generally made responsible for its preparation, administration and execution. The production budgets can be prepared, department wise, and in such, a case departmental manager will be responsible for the departmental budget and the overall responsibility of the total production budget will be that of the factory manager. The budget is prepared with the following objectives in mind:

(a) To co-ordinate between the sales department and production department.

(b) To serve as a basis for preparation of costs of production budget.

(c) To chalk down and organise the production programme in such a way that will ensure the delivery of finished products according to the requirements of the sales budget.

(d) To know the quantities to be produced product-wise, department wise good period-wise.

Basically, there are two problems connected with the production budget: *(a)* determining the annual production required; and *(b)* pro-rating it throughout the year. The following advantages accrue as a result of the operation of a production budget:

(i) inventory investments within reasonable limits;

(ii) Most effective utilisation of available resources;

(iii) Sticking to delivery promises and hence maintaining goodwill;

(iv) Scheduling labour requirements;

(v) Cost reduction because of uniformity of production.

The following factors must be considered while preparing a production budget:

(i) Production policy should be chalked out in such a manner that the production is, as far as possible, evenly distributed throughout the year. Even in case of seasonal industries, an attempt is made to rationalise the production schedule on an equitable basis. All this leads to reduction of cast stability in employment and better utilisation of production facilities.

(ii) The minimum and the maximum level of finished stocks to be maintained must be pre-determined so as to avoid shortages as well as surpluses. Both result in losses to the business.

(iii) How much is to be produced will largely depend upon the quantity likely to be sold during a given period; hence, sales budget precede the production budget except when production is the limiting factor.

(iv) There is always a setting up time involved in production and the actual production process also consumes a fixed time. The planning of commencement of production must be made after due consideration of the same.

(v) The maximum capacity and the optimum capacity of the plant must be borne in mind before finally drafting the production budget.

(vi) The inputs primarily raw material and labour must be available in right quantity and in right time, otherwise, it will adversely affect the production programme. The budget plan ensures the same.

The following example illustrates the preparation of a production budget:

Illustration.

Prepare a production budget for 3 months ending March 31, 2003, for a factory producing four products, on the basis of the following information:

Type of Product (Units)	*Estimated Stock on Jan. 1, 2003 (Units)*	*Estimated Sales during Jan. March, 2003 (Units)*	*Desired Closing Stock on March 31, 2003)*
I	2,000	10,000	3,000
II	3,000	15,000	5,000
III	4,000	13,000	3,000
IV	3,000	12,000	2,000

Solution.

PRODUCTION BUDGET FOR THREE MONTHS TO MARCH 31, 2003

			Units
Product I	Estimated sales	10,000	
	Add: Desired closing stock	3,000	
		13,000	
	Less: Estmated opening stock	2,000	11,000
Product II	Estimated Sales	15,000	
	Add: Desired closing stck	5,00	
		20,000	

	Less: Estimated opening stock	3,000	17,000
Product III	Estimated sales	13,000	
	Add: Desired closing stock	3,000	
		16,000	
	Less: Estiamted opening stock	4,000	12,000
Product IV	Estiamed sales	12,000	
	Add: Desired closing stock	2,000	
		14,000	
	Less: Estimated opening stock	3,000	11,000
	Total unit to be produced		51,000

Production Cost Budget

When a definite shape has been given regarding the expected and targeted production for the budget period, the production budget (expressed in quantities to be produced) can be converted into a production cost budget. This does not mean that a production budget is framed without taking into account the cost factors. While framing the production budget, if alternative choices of production are there, naturally cost would also be taken into account.

When we talk of production cost, the tripod of *(a)* material, *(b)* labour, and *(c)* overheads has to be considered.

I. Materials Budget. Determination of material cost involves quantities to be used and the rate per unit. Both the quantity to be used and the rate at which such materials are available depend upon the quality of the materials, which in turn depends on the quality of the finished product. It should be noted that usually not one material but many of varying prices and degrees of importance are required. Therefore, a schedule of materials required for a given output is drawn up.

The task of determining the quantities required is that of the production engineering department, which will know the exact processes to be used. The quantity required is also influenced by normal wastage in production expected. As regards the rate, the purchasing department has the responsibility. A statistical treatment of past experience as regards the prices together with an assessment of the effects of changes that are likely to occur will help the purchase department in its task.

The Purchase Budget. It is a natural outcome of the materials cost budget. Since production volume is likely to be different at different times of the year, the requirements of materials will also differ. This will also be the case when production of one product is emphasised more at one time and less at another.

In addition, the question of inventory levels to be maintained in respect of various items of materials will affect the quantity to be purchased. Keeping these factors in view, one can draw up the programme of purchase.

II. Labour Cost Budget. The labour cost budget can be drawn uponly when the time required to do one unit of work and the wages to be paid for it are known. Normally, in modem industrial undertakings, the processes are complex and various types of workers, possessing different skills, are required. The production engineering department, working in close collaboration with the works study department, determines the exact processes to be performed and the sequence of various operations together with the types of machines and men to be used. The production engineering department draws up the production plan and an attempt is made to ascertain the total time required, of various types of workers, for achieving the budgeted output. Thus the total number of hours required for each category of workers is determined. The personnel department will advise regarding the wage rates that are likely to prevail. In this manner, the labour cost budget can be drawn up. This exercise also leads to the determination of the programme of fresh recruitment and training which is essential for efficient work in a modern concern.

III. Overheads Budget. Budgeting for overheads is a little more involved than the other two components of cost. For an approximately realistic forecast of this cost, a classification of the overheads has to be made into: *(a)* Fixed Overheads; and *(b)* Variable

Overheads. "Fixed Overheads are otherwise known as period costs which are to be incurred irrespective of the volume of production. 'Variable Overheads' are overheads which are related to the level of production aimed at. But the difficulty in the above is that a clear line of demarcation cannot be drawn between the 'fixed' and the 'variable' due to the presence of 'semi-variable costs'. These costs contain a hard core of 'fixed costs' too, but will start moving up after production goes up substantially. If the distinction between fixed and variable overheads could be made in an organisation, the overheads budget can be easily drawn.

Another view may be taken of overheads as 'controllable overheads' and 'uncontrollable overheads. Of course, the classification can be on the same lines as 'variable overheads' and 'fixed overheads'. But here the basis of the classification centres round the division of the organisation into various 'responsibility centres'. Each 'responsibility centre' indicates a unit under the charge of a person, for instance, various production shops, stores, repairs, buying departments, etc. The overhead forecasts for ail these responsibility centres are obtained from these departments. When they submit their own forecasts, they provide details of expenses classified as controllable expenses and uncontrollable expenses.

In addition to the two categories of expenses mentioned above, there may be another, *viz.*, policy cost which has been defined by the Institute of Cost and Management Accountants of London as: "Cost which is additional to normal requirement, incurred in accordance with the policy of an undertaking." For example, a firm may decide to build houses for workers and charge rent based on wages rather than the market rent. The cost thus incurred with be policy cost. Strictly speaking, such costs should not form part of overheads, though normally they do. However, for purposes of control, it is better to separate such costs from normal costs.

When the overheads of all the departments are consolidated, the third leg of the tripod is also complete. Thus a full production cost budget can be prepared. The general rules for presentation of any budget are applicable to production cost budget too. Production cost budget is generally presented in the form of a cost shelling a cost sheet presentation, the noticeable points are the drawing up of columns for total and per unit cost, the arrangement of the cost into prime cost, works cost, and so on. As in other budgets, here also the corresponding previous period's budgeted cost and actual cost in total and per unit may be stated.

SALES FORECAST

A sales forecast is a statement showing the quantity and value of projected sales product-wise, area wise or period-wise. It is merely as passive estimate of future sales. It is based on the present amount of sales efforts what the management can except sales to run at about the same level as currently. Some people confuse sales budget with a sales forecast. While it is not so. There is a great difference between these two. The sales budget is more than a sales forecast. A forecast is merely passive, while a budget reflects the positive actions that management plans to take in order to influence future events. To distinguish between a sales budget and a sales forecast this may .be the sales forecast: "With the present amount of sales efforts, we expect sales to run at about the same level as currently." On the other hand, the sales budget may show a substantial planned increase in sales, reflecting management's intention to add salesmen, increase advertising and sales promotion, etc. As a matter of fact, the term 'sales budget' has more wide implications and 'sales forecast' is only first step in the direction of budgeting process.

Sales forecasts can be made both for long term as well as for short term period. The long term sales forecast, normally covers a period of five to ten or more years. It reflects as a matter of fact, the long term sales plans policies of the enterprise. A short term forecast is made normally for one year ahead. The term 'sales forecasting' is more commonly used for the yearly sales forecast.

Factors to be Considered in a Sales Forecast

In the preparation of a sales forecast, the sales people should take into consideration the following factors:

(1) **Availability of Raw Materials and Other Supplies.** Adequate supply of raw materials and other supplies should be ensured before preparing the sales estimates. Sales estimates should be adjusted according to the availability of raw materials if the raw materials are in short supply.

(2) **General Trade Prospects.** The probability of the sales going up or down depends on the general trade prospects. In this connection valuation information may be gathered from financial papers and magazines such as Economic Times, the Financial Times, the Commerce.

(3) **Seasonal Fluctuation.** In the preparation of the sales budget, seasonal fluctuations should be considered because sales are affected by these fluctuations. In order to have an even flow of production, efforts should be made to minimise the effect of seasonal fluctuations on sales by giving special concessions or added inducements during the off-season.

(4) **Orders on Hand.** In boom periods or where production is a very lengthy process, the value of orders on hand may have considerable influence on the amount of sales to be budgeted.

(5) **Adequate Return on Capital Employed.** The sales volume budgeted should produce an adequate return on the capital employed.

(6) **Financial Aspects.** The sales budget should be within the financial capacity of the concern. Sales expansion usually requires are increase in capital outlay. Thus, if any big sales expansion is planned, it must be ensured that facilities are available to finance the operations.

(7) **Competition.** The nature and degree of competition within the industry should be considered in the preparation of the sales budget to have a realistic sales budget capable of being achieved in the face of competition.

(8) **Past Sales Figure and Trends.** The record of previous year's sales is the most reliable basis as to future sales as the past performance is based on actual business conditions. Hence past sales figures must be analysed and to determine the future trends, other factors affecting future sales, *e.g.*, seasonal fluctuations, growth of market, trade cycles, etc., should also be considered.

(9) **Other Factors.** In addition to the above factors the government policies as regards to taxation and business, trends in population, possible changes in the buying habits of the people and their purchasing power, etc., should also be considered. These are actually external and uncontrollable factors so their best possible estimate will help the management in making sales forecast more dependable and reliable.

(10) **Salesmen's Estimate.** The salesmen's estimate should also be given due weightage while preparing sales estimate for the whole concern. It is fruitful to consider the estimates of sales received from salesmen because they can make more accurate estimates being in direct contact with the customers. However, it should be observed that salesmen's estimates should neither be over-optimistic nor too conservative.

(11) **Plant Capacity.** The sales budget should be within the plant capacity available and should ensure proper utilisation of plant facilities. Proposed plant extensions should be allowed for in the preparation of the sales budget.

In almost all companies, the most difficult estimate to make is that of sales. Many practical and technical difficulties have to overcome before a reliable forecast can be developed. There are two ways of proceeding to prepare a sales forecast first, to make an internal forecast on the basis of opinions of executives and salesmen, and second, is based on external factors—a statistical forecast on the basis of an analysis of general business conditions, market conditions, extent of competition, etc. A sales forecast can be made in the following ways:

(1) **Market Research and Statistical Techniques.** The first method of forecasting the sales is the market research conducted by a' specialised department known as Economic Statistics department. Only very big enterprises adopt this method. They have experienced economists and trained statisticians in their market research department. The analyse the market for their products with the field surveys and other techniques. They specifically analyse the external factors such as nature of demand, customer's tastes, substitutes and their markets, price situation and extent of competition, etc. In analysing the demand of the product they use trend analysis, cycle projection analysis, correlation and regression techniques, moving average and other statistical techniques. Though this method is quite scientific but costly one. All enterprises cannot afford it.

(2) **Group Executive Judgement Method.** Under this method, the basic targets of sales forecast are developed by the head office people (senior executives). When the market situation is intricate and beyond the mental capacity of salesmen, products are few, the sales are limited, the forecasts can be prepared by head office people also. Under this method, group executive intelligence is utilised and they consider internal factors as well as external factors fully. The method of sales forecasting is simple and immediate also. In such forecast considered judgement the management is after taken to be the basis of development of sales forecasts. But, such projections, however, must be viewed as a mere guesswork.

(3) **Sales Staff Method.** In this method, the forecast of sales is initiated by the salesman, who can rightly be called as 'on the job man'. First of all, he prepares a sales forecast for his area. He is duty provided by the historical data

regarding past sales, market competition and other factors, etc. The necessary format is also provided by the department. He is only to fill up the blank.

SALES BUDGET

In most cases, sales budget is not only the most important but also the most difficult to prepare. It forecasts what the business can reasonably expect to sell to its customers during the budget period. Including within its fold both the sales quantities as well as sales revenue, sales budget represents the income side of the planning budget.

Rationale

The company earns profits only when it is able to sell its products and not when it produces them. It is no use producing goods that are no likely to be sold and for which there is a limited demand. In some businesses, it is necessary to establish that the product will sell even before it is produced *e.g.*, a large luxury liner will not be built without a prospective customer agreeing beforehand to buy on completion. It is only during boom times, when a company has full order book, that sales budget loses its prime importance. In normal times of keen competition, the sales forecast must be realistic.

Preparation of Sales Budget

The usual steps in the preparation of a sales budget are as follows:

(a) Sales Forecasts. A sales budget is the direct outcome of sales forecast. A sales forecast is a statement depicting the quantity, value of projected sales, product-wise, area-wise and period-wise. Assuming that the organisation of the sales department is on the useful pattern, *i.e.*, sales manager, divisional sales manager, area sales manager, sales inspectors and salemen; first of all, each salesman will estimate the sales he can make in his area in the budget period. He will forward his forecast to his area manager who will collate all such forecasts from his area. Then, area sales manager will prepare his area budget and forward it to divisional sales manager. He will forward these papers to the sales manager. He will prepare the sales budget for the whole organisation on the basis of the sales estimates. Thus, sales budget is built from the bottom and not from the top.

(b) **Consideration of Various Factors.** In developing a sales budget, sales manager should take into consideration the following factors-past sales figures and trends salesmen's estimates, plant production capacity, availability of raw materials and other supplies, general trade prospects, orders on hand, seasonal fluctuations, financial aspect, competition expected etc.

The sales manager, after taking into consideration the above factors, should prepare the sales budget in terms of quantities and amounts and the sales estimates must be analysed for products, period and territories. The sales budget should include an estimate of selling and distribution costs in addition to an estimate of the total sale proceeds.

(c) **Organisation for Sales Budget.** Preparation of Sales budget is the direct responsibility of sales manager. In this work, he is helped by all people working in the sales department. Sales representatives area and divisional sales manager all provide necessary help and initial forecast of sales and they are ultimately responsible for carrying out their share of the plan.

The following factors may be taken into consideration while preparing the sales budget.

1. **Salesmen's Estimates.** Salesmen should be asked to submit their estimates, since they are in touch with the field. Their estimates would be the most realistic, if they submit it objectively and they are skilled enough to do the job. However, the estimates submitted by then should be scrutinised thoroughly by the sales manager and due pruning should be made.

2. **Orders in Hand.** The present is always taken into account while estimating for the future. Particularly, in certain business, orders are received in advance and production takes place afterwards. Available orders are, therefore, accounted for first, while preparing a sales budget.

3. **General Trade Prospects.** The business in particular is greatly influenced by the overall conditions of the trade and the forthcoming changes in them. The economic indicators, available in the published and unpublished form, assist management a lot in this regard.

4. **Proposed Management Policies.** If the management has a policy to expand, diversify or contract the business, the budget would automatically take it into consideration.

5. **Past Behaviour.** The sales pattern of the past is always a grade for the future. Mathematical and statistical techniques may be employed for prediction of sales for the budget period on the basis of analysis of past sales data-long-term trend, seasonal and/or cyclical fluctuations can be estimated; extrapolation may be done; regression technique may be employed; graphic methods may adopted, etc.

6. **Availability of Finance.** Finance is a very big constraint in a many undertakings and it is the life-blood of entire organisation. Moreover, additional sales can take place only when finance is available for additional production. Hence, finance is an important factor to be considered while preparing a sales budget.

7. **Potential Market.** Market surveys and research are to be conducted to know the market potentials. The expected population growth, purchasing power of consumers, buying habits of the people, changes in tastes, fashions etc., all these factors affect the market.

8. **Other Factors.** The following other factors should also be taken into consideration:

(i) National and international political and economical scene.

(ii) Government policies;

(iii) Selling and distribution overheads;

(iv) Extent of competition.

9. Seasonal Fluctuations. Umbrellas sell in rainy season, fans in hot, woollens in winter—the demand is higher in a particular season—the budget will be prepared accordingly. The policy of off-season discounts and special rebates can be framed to boost up sales in off-seasons.

10. Plant Capacity. Sales can't exceed production and the production capacity maybe limited. The quantity which can be produced with available physical facilities should be considered while preparing the sales budget.

10. Availability of Materials. Raw material and other types of materials needed for production should be available required quantity at the proper time. The position in regard thereto will affect the preparation of sales budget, particularly when material is scarce.

The following illustration would throw light on the aspect of sales budgeting.

Illustration.

Mr. Atulya manufactures two types of toys, Raja and Rani and sell them in Agra and Bombay markets. The following information is made available for the current year:

	Market	*Budgeted Sales*	*Actual Sales*
Agra:	Raja	400 at Rs. 9 each	500 at Rs. 9 each
	Rani	300 at Rs. 21 each	200 at Rs. 21 each
Bombay:	Raja	600 at Rs. 9 each	700 at Rs. 9 each
	Rani	500 at Rs. 21 each	400 at Rs. 21 each

Market studies reveal that toy Raja is popular as it is under-priced. It is observed that if its price is reduced by Rs. 1 it will find a ready market. On the other hand, Rani is over-priced and market could absorb more sales if its selling price is reduced to Rs. 20. The management has agreed to give effect to the above price changes.

On the above basis, the following estimates have been prepared by Sales Manager:

Product	*% increase in sales over current budget*	
	Agra	*Bombay*
Raja	+10%	+ 5%
Rani	+20%	+ 10%

With the help of an intensive advertisement campaign, the following additional sales above the estimated sales of Sales Manager are possible:

	Agra	*Bombay*
Raja	60 units	70 units
Rani	40 units	50 units

You are required to prepare a budget for sales incorporating the above estimates.

Solution.

SALES BUDGET

Period................

		Budget for the current year			*Actual Sales*			*Budget for the future period*		
		'Units	*Price Rs.*	*Value Rs.*	*Units*	*Price Rs.*	*Value Rs.*	*Units*	*Price Rs.*	*Value Rs.*
Agra	Raja	400	9	3,600	500	9	4,500	500	10	5,000
	Rani	300	21	6,300	200	21	4,200	400	20	8,000
	Total	700	–	9,900	700	–	8,700	900	–	13,000
Bombay	Raja	600	9	5,400	700	9	6,300	700	10	7,000
	Rani	500	21	10,500	400	21	8,400	600	20	12,000
	Total	1,100	–	15,900	1,100	–	14,700	1,300	–	19,000
Total	Raja	1,000	9	9,000	1,200	9	10,800	1,200	10	12,000
	Rani	800	21	16,800	600	21	12,600	1,000	20	20,000
	Total	1,800	-	25,800	1,800	-	73,400	2,200	-	32,000

Notes: Budget estimates:

		Agra	Bombay
Raja:	Budgeted	400	600
	Increase	40 (10%)	30 (5%)
		440	630
	Advertisement effect	60	70
		500	700
Rani:	Budgeted	300	500
	Increase	60 (20%)	50 (10%)
		360	550
	Advertisement effect	40	50
		400	600

SELLING AND DISTRIBUTION COST BUDGET

This budget is the forecastable costs incurred in selling and distributing the company's products during the budget period. It is closely connected with the sales budget inasmuch as it is mainly based on the volume of sales projected for the period. However, the fact must be kept in view that expenditure may be contemplated during the budget period which will have no effect on sales until a future budget period. For example, an advertising campaign may be launched this year which will have no immediate effect but should influence sales in future.

The sales manager is normally responsible for the preparation of the selling and distribution cost budget. Nevertheless, he will co-operate with the sales office manager, distribution manager and the advertising manager or the advertising agents. Advertising is gradually becoming an increasingly important and costly item in selling-cost budgets so much so that some companies now prepare an advertising budget.

The work regarding the preparation of selling and distribution cost budget is simplified, if it is broken down in the following four parts:

(a) Cost of Sales Office

The expenditure on salaries of staff, rent, rates, right and heat of the sales office, stationery, postage, etc., will be budgeted. Such expenditure will not vary with sales to the same extent as direct selling and distribution expenses. A change in the value of sales does not always represent an increase or decrease in the number of transactions as each transaction may have a higher value.

However, major changes in the number of transactions will effect the number of staff needed with all its concomitants.

(b) Direct Selling Expenses

When preparing the budget, following points must be considered under this head:

(i) The impact of seasonal changes *e.g.*, where the majority of annual sales are made in certain months of the year, the expenditure on commission to travellers may be heavier in those months.

(ii) The effect of anticipated in changes the volume and/or value of sales, *e.g.*, where travellers' commission is based on units sold, an increase in budgeted sales in units will result in an increase in travellers' commission.

(iii) The appointment of agents and their remuneration under their agreements.

(iv) The changes in the basis of remuneration to provide an incentive to sell particular products.

(v) The basis of remuneration of travellers *e.g.*, whether travellers are remunerated by a commission on sales only or receive a fixed salary and commission.

(vi) The scope of the representation, *e.g.*, a planned expansion or contraction of the geographical area served may involve variations in the number of travellers and in travelling expenses.

(c) Publicity Expenditure

Normally, the total expenditure on publicity is fixed by management as matter of policy. Frequently, the type of advertising and expenditure thereon is laid down. *e.g.*, press, window displays, posters, exhibition, televisions, etc.

(d) Distribution Expenses

These expenses are incurred either in the storage of finished products to enable orders to be swiftly fulfilled or after a sale to a customer has been made. When preparing the budget the following considerations must be kept in view:

(i) Type of transport used, *e.g.*, own motor vehicles or those of outside contractors.

(ii) Transport costs having regard to the geographical pattern of sales;

(iii) External influences on transport costs, *e.g.*, increase in rail freight charges.

(iv) Handling costs which may be affected by changes in the products sold, where these will require a variation in the method of hand ling;

(v) Expenditure on rent, rates, wages, insurance, etc. in connection with necessary warehouses.

MASTER BUDGET

Most business organisations are too large to permit the detailed planning of the entire business in one budget. It, therefore, become necessary to use various functional or subsidiary budgets and then to co-ordinate them in a Master Budget.

A master budget is a summary budget for the entire enterprise which embodies the summarised figures or various activities. In simple words, it is the co-ordinated and summarised budget of the entire budgetary programme. According to I.C.W.A. England: "The Master Budget is the summary budget incorporating its component functional budget."

A master budget represents the overall plan of the enterprise. It is, therefore, principal planning budget. The various items depicted in the master budget include: "sales cost, production, profits, gross capital and profit appropriations, etc. There is no unanimity of opinions regarding the content and the form of master budget. Management Accountants have often regarded the budgeted Profit and Loss A/c and Balance Sheet as the master budget. Actually, the layout of the master budget is not yet standardised.

Functional or Subsidiary Budget

A master budget is compiled from various functional budgets. A budget relating to a department is known as a functional budget. According to I.C.W.A. England: Functional budget is a budget of a particular junction." The following chart gives a shape-short view of various budgets:

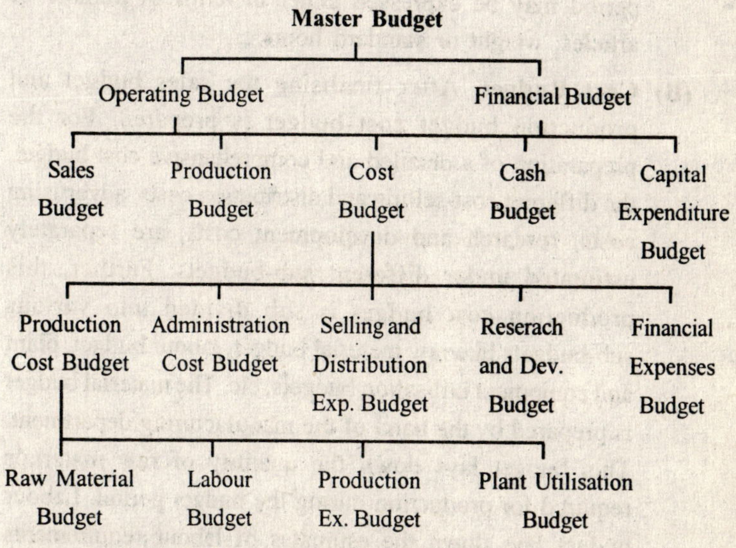

I. Operating Budget

Operating budgets are also known as revenue budgets or income and expenses budget. They assume the form of budgeted income statement covering the entire operations of the firm. The operating budget is prepared in two parts: programme budget and responsibility budget. The main components of the operating budget are: sales budget, production budget and cost budgets. The production is a quantity budget while others are value budgets. A brief description of these budgets are as follows:

(A) Production Budget. A production budget is a quantity budget which lays down the quantity of units to be produced during the budget period. The main purpose of this budget is to maintain no optimum balance between sales, production and inventory position of the firm. It is also known as output budget because it depicts the quantitative estimates of output for the budget period as well as also the estimates at different control period within the budget period. The quantity of output to be manufactured during a budget period may be expressed either in terms of number of articles, weight or standard hours.

(B) Cost Budget. After finalising the sales budget and production budget cost budget is prepared. For the preparation of a detailed and comprehensive cost budget, the different cost-selling and distribution costs, advertising costs, research and development costs, are separately estimated under different sub-budgets. Further, this production cost budget is sub divided into various sub-budgets like raw material budget, labour budget, plant and equipment utilisation budgets, etc. The material budget is prepared by the hand of the manufacturing department. This budget lays down the quantity of raw materials required for production during the budget period. Labour budget lays down the estimates of labour requirements necessary to carry out the estimated production. It may be sub-divided into two parts-direct labour cost and indirect labour cost. An expense budget is prepared for estimation of future costs. These costs relate to the various segments of operating activity, *i.e.*, manufacturing office and administration, etc. As such manufacturing costs budgets, administration costs budget and selling and distribution costs budgets.

(C) Sales Budget. The entire operations of the enterprise are planned around the volume of activity expected during a definite period. A sales bugget, therefore, is a nerve centre of the operating budget. It lays down the sales potential in terms of quantity, value, period, area and product, etc. It lays down a comprehensive sales programme, plan and organisation for developing sales. The preparation of a sales budget starts with the sales forecast. This forecast is prepared for each product separately. In projecting sales for a particular year various factors are taken into consideration for example past historical data of sales, present conditions of the firm and general economic conditions, etc.

II. Cash Budget

The financial budget presents a summarization of anticipated receipts and disbursements for the budget period. Its purpose is to plan for the allocation of working capital as represented by the current assets of the enterprise. It indicates the need of capital at various points of time and helps the management in planning and providing the proper quantity of cash to meet the needs of the business.

III. Capital Budgets

Capital budgets are those budgets which lay down the estimates in respect of the capital resources of the firm. They specify the capital intentions of the management and as such reflect. The management policy in respect of investments, expansion, growth, contraction, production and profits. In setting out these budgets the management usually considers a set of alternative forecasts.

A typical form of Master Budget may be as follows:

MASTER BUDGET

(For the year ending as on)

Normal Capacity... ... ...

Capacity Budgeted.................

(A) Budgeted Profit and Loss Account for the year ending ....

Items	*Budget Period Amount (Rs.)*	*Previous Period Amount (Rs.)*
(1)	*(2)*	*(3)*
A. Net Sales		
Manufacturing Costs:		
Direct Labour		
Direct Material		
Factory Overhead		
Add Opening Stock		
Less Closing Stock		
B. Cost of goods sold		
C. Gross Profit (l minus 2)		
Opening expenses:		
Selling		
Distribution		
Advertising		
Research and Development		
Financial		
D. Operating Costs		
E. Operating Profit (3 minus 4)		
F. Net profit before tax		
G (5 plus 6)		

Contd.

(1)	*(2)*	*(3)*
H. Provision for taxation		
I. Net Profit (7 minus 8)		
J. Profit Appropriations:		
Dividends		
Transfer to General Reserve		
Total Appropriations		
K. Surplus (9 minus 10)		

(B) Budgeted Balance Sheet as at.....

Items	*Budget Period Amount (Rs.)*	*Previous Period Amount (Rs.)*
1. Fixed Assets		
2. Current Assets		
3. Capital Employed (1 plus.2)		
4. Current Liabities		
5. Total fixed Assets and working Capital (3 less 4)		
6. Financed by Capital and Reserves:		
Issued hare Capital		
General Reserve		
Profit and Loss		

BASIC STEPS IN PREPARING MASTER BUDGET

Without going into the minute details of designing, operating and other budgets for their consolidation into a master budget, we propose to identify and discuss, a brief, the basic steps involved in the preparation of the master budget. A simple and clear discussion on these steps, in chronological order, appears in Accounting for Management Control by Charles T. Horngren. The following discussion is adapted from there.

Step 1. The sales forecast is the starting point for budgeting, because inventory levels, purchase production, and operating expenses are generally geared to the rate of sales activity. The sales forecast (as reflected in the sales budget) is, thus, the foundation of the entire operating budgets and the master budget.

The sales forecast is usually prepared under the direction of the top sales executive. A number of factors are taken into consideration for forecasting sales for the sales budget of a given period. These may be: *(a)* past patterns of sales (historical data); *(b)* estimates made by the sales force; *(c)* general economic and competitive condition; *(d)* specific interrelationship of sales and economic indicators, *e.g.* GNP or industrial production indices; *(e)* changes in prices and price-elasticity of demand; *(f)* market research studies; *(g)* existing contracts and orders; and *(h)* advertising and sales promotion plans.

On the basis of the forecast for the period, sales are usually budgeted as a Marketing Plan, both in quantities and value as well as by district or territory, product, and time period.

Step 2. After sales are budgeted, the Purchase Budget may be prepared.

The total merchandise needed will be the sum of the desired closing inventory plus the amount needed to fulfil the budgeted sales demand. The total need will be partially met by the opening inventory. The balance must come from planned purchases.

In the case of a manufacturing concern, the raw materials have to be converted into finished products, requiring the preparation of Direct Labour and Manufacturing Overhead Budgets. All of these will be combined into Production Budget (both in term of volume and value) keeping in view the budgeted sales and the changes in the inventory levels of finished goods.

Step 3. The budgeting of operating expenses (administrative and selling) is dependent upon a number of factors. Many operating/ expenses are directly influenced by month-to-month fluctuations in sales volume (*e.g.*, sales commission and delivery expenses) Other expenses are not directly influenced (*e.g.* rent, insurance, depreciation, salaries, etc.) Here, the 'concept of cost variability' as discussed earlier may be helpful in budgeting operating expenses.

Step 4. Steps 1 to 3 will provide enough information for a budgeted income statement.

Step 5. Cash Budget. Month-to-month effects of the cash position of the levels of operations can be estimated on the basis of the above steps in budgeting. The cash budget (budgeted statement of cash receipts and disburse-ments) has the following major sections:

A. Cash Receipt

(i) The beginning cash balance plus cash receipts will amount to the total cash available for needs (before financing, if any).

(ii) Cash receipts would depend on *(a)* cash sales (scheduled properly), *(b)* collection from customer's accounts receivables, and *(c)* other operating sources, *e.g.* miscellaneous rental income, interest on investments, etc. It may be noted that studies of the forecasting of accounts receivable are a prerequisite to accurate forecasting of cash receipts. Key factors here include bad debt experience and average time lag (number of days) between sales and collection.

B. Cash Disbursements

(i) Purchase, depending upon the credit terms extended and the bill paying habits and procedures. (Schedule).

(ii) Payrolls, depending on wage, salary, or commission terms, and on payroll dates. (Schedule)

(iii) Other costs of expenses, depending on timing and credit terms. (Note depreciation does not entail a cash outlay.)

(iv) Other disbursements, include purchases of assets, long-term investments, installment, etc.

C. Financing Requirements

The cash budget also shows the pattern of short-term, self liquidating financing. Seasonal peaks often result in heave drain on cash, for merchandise purchases and operating expenses, before the sales are made and cash collected from customers. The working capital cycle moves from cash to inventory to receivables and back to cash.

Financing requirements depend on how the total cash available. A above, compares with the total cash needed. Needs include the disbursements, B above, plus the ending cash balance desired. The financing plus will depend on the relationship of cash available to cash sought. If there is an excess, loans may be repaid or temporary investments made. Should there be deficit, borrowings would become necessary. The pertinent outlays for interest expenses usually contained in this section of the cash budget.

The ending cash balance will be equal to (A+C—B) Financing (c) may have a positive (borrowings) or a negative (repayment/ investment) effect on cash balance.

Step 6. Budget Balance Sheet. Each item in the budgeted balance sheet is projected in the light of the details of the business plan for the period expressed in the budget schedules as detailed in the above steps. Effect of capital budgets on fixed and long term assets and their depreciation, etc., will also be taken into consideration for the purpose.

FLEXIBLE BUDGETING

Activity-Capacity-Efficiency Link. Before we proceed to discuss the topic proper, it is necessary to have a clear understanding of the following three terms and their inter-relationship; *(i)* Level of activity, *(ii)* Capacity, and *(iii)* Efficiency.

(i) Level of Activity. Level of activity or production volume refers to the volume of output of a manufacturing concern. The volume of output need not be uniform each year. The management always tries to adjust its volume of output to the maximum extent of production facility available subject to sales and inventory constraints. Sometimes, the actual volume does not turn out to be the budgeted volume. A measurement and expression of actual volume as compared to budgeted volume is known as "the level of activity ratio" or "production volume ratio". If a factory produces different products, the volume can be expressed in terms of standard hours and compared with budgeted volume, also expressed in terms of standard hours. Thus, the level of activity ratio is defined by the terminology as "The number of standard hours equivalent to the production achieved whether completed or not divided by or expressed as a percentage of the budgeted number of standard hours."

$$\text{Actual capacity utiliation ratio} = \frac{50,000 \text{ hours}}{50,000 \text{ hours}} \times 100 = 100\%$$

(ii) Capacity. "Capacity constitutes that fixed quantum of plant and machinery and of human resources to whom management has committed itself and with whom it expects to conduct the business." This activity refers to the total facility available in a factory. Generally, capacity of a manufacturing unit is expressed in terms of quantity. However, production facilities are generally not installed for a single purpose. With minor adjustments, the plant would be capable of being used for other purposes too. Hence, it is appropriate to express the production capacity in terms of the hours the plant is planned to work rather than the units it is planned to produce. Hence, the terminology defines capacity ratio as : "The actual number of direct working hours divided by or expressed as a percentage of the budgeted number of standard hours." But this refers to the actual utilisation of budgeted capacity. The budgeted capacity itself may be different from the installed capacity. It is possible to express the budgeted capacity as a fraction or percentage of installed capacity. This would show the utilisation planned as against capacity available. Actual hours worked can also be compared against the installed capacity.

(iii) Efficiency Ratio. The activity ratio and capacity utilisation ratio need not go together always. Sometimes, the capacity utilisation ratio may be 100% but the activity ratio may be less than 100%. The reverse is also possible. This is because there is another factor intervening, namely, the efficiency of utilisation of production facility.

The Concept of Fixable Budgeting. Budgets are generally prepared by keeping a certain level of activity as the target. All the functional budgets are based on that planned level of activity. If the actual level is different from the budgeted level, a comparison of actual figures with budgeted figures becomes meaningless, as they refer to two different levels. In this case, the budget itself will have to be revised in accordance with the actual level of activity achieved.

Revision of the original budget in accordance with the actual level of activity is not a simple adjustment of scales. Certain figures can be easily adjusted for scales and certain others cannot be. Certain figures do not lend themselves to such adjustments. For example, if the original budget was a production of 500 units and the actual output is 400 units, all costs of production cannot be scaled down to 80% of the original budget. There are certain elements of cost which do not change proportionately to the change in the level of activity. We can identify those elements and determine their degree of variability, then we would be able to revise the figures for any actual level of activity. Thus, sorting out of the figures and determining their variability for different levels of activity is the crux of the problem in flexible budgeting.

A flexible budget is defined by the Terminology as: "A budget which by recognising the difference in behaviour between fixed and variable costs in relation to fluctuations in output or turnover is designed to change appropriately with such fluctuations." This is to be distinguished from a Fixed Budget, *i.e.*, "A budget which is designed to remain unchanged irrespective of the volume of output or turnover obtained."

A fixed budget will practically be of no use, because the actual level of activity does not generally conform to the budgeted level of activity. If the budget is designed in such a way that the figures can be scaled up or down in accordance with the actual level of activity, the utility of the budget is greatly improved. This is exactly what is aimed at in flexible budgeting. Flexible budgeting has immense practical applications. It is particularly applicable to the following industries: *(a)* Industries dependent upon weather conditions, *e.g.*, agro-based industries, *(b)* Industries whose levels of activity fluctuate due to frequent introduction of new products, *(c)* Industries which carry out production on the basis of customers' orders, *(d)* Industries the demand for whose product is based on tastes and fashions, *(e)* Industries which mostly depend upon export markets.

How to Classify Costs. What is evident from the above discussion is that flexible budget is essentially a production cost budget. Though this technique of budgeting also relates to sales, cash, etc., for different levels of activity, we concentrate on production cost alone, because it is the major problem area. All the elements of cost do not lend themselves to easy adjustment for different levels of activity. The revision of the budget cost-for the actual level of activity is to be done by classifying the costs into variable, fixed and semi-variable or semi-fixed. These terms have been used in the following senses: *(a)* Variable cost—a cost which tends to vary directly with the volume of output, *i.e.*, level of activity, *(b)* Fixed cost—a cost which tends to be unaffected by variations in the volume of output, *i.e.*, variations in level of activity, *(c)* Semi-fixed or Semi-variable cost—which is partly fixed and partly variable.

The major problem in the preparation of a flexible budget (in respect of costs) is the neat compartmentalisation of costs into fixed, variable and semi-fixed costs. This problem has been dealt with in the Chapter on Essentials of Cost Accounting. Then are three important methods of classifying costs into fixed and variable categories. They are:

(I) Method of Least Squares. The first method of bifurcating the fixed and various elements is by using the method of least squares. This is only an extension of the method of scatter diagram. In this method, any cost variation for units, *i.e.*, variable of worked out with the help of the following steps.

(a) Determining the variation in total cost from average at each level of output.

(b) Determining the variation in actual output from average output.

(c) Multiplying the variation in cost by the variation in output.

(d) Dividing the total of items in *(c)* above by the total of the square of items in *(b)* above. This gives the variable cost per unit.

The above working is on the basis of the equation y = a + bx, *i.e.*, the sum-total of cost represented by a straight line consists of.

(i) a = fixed element in the total cost; and

(ii) bx = the number of units multiplied by the variable element in each unit cost.

(II) High and Low Points Method. Under this method, the total cost (without distinguishing fixed and variable) of two volumes of output one higher and the other power, are taken. The difference in the two total cost figures (*i.e.*, incremental cost) divided by the difference in the volume of output between the two levels (*i.e.*, incremental output) gives the variable cost per unit. Once the variable cost per unit is determined, the total variable cost for any volume of output can easily be determine. Then the total cost of the volume of output less the total variable cost gives the fixed cost which is theoretically supposed to remain fixed for all levels of output.

(III) Scatter Diagram Method. This method involves plotting the total cost for different volumes of output on a graph in which the total cost is measured along the Y-axis and the volume of output along the X-axis. Then a straight line is drawn by visual inspection in such a manner that the line is nearer to all the plotted points in the graph and coverages on the Y-axis. From that point at which it merges with the Y-axis draw a parallel line to the X-axis. This line will demarcate the 'fixed costs' for all the levels of output.

Preparation of Flexible Budget. It has been stated that a flexible budget is generally a production cost budget. It does not mean that we cannot have a complete master budget on flexible basis. There again cost is the major item which would require adjustments at various levels. Thus one could prepare a master budget showing sales, costs and profits for different volumes of activity. The main problem is that costs have to be classified as 'fixed' and 'variable' for the purpose of evolving budgets for different volumes.

As a matter off act budget for each department can be prepared on the lines of flexible budget by classifying the cost into 'fixed' and 'variable'. In order to appropriately fix up the costs for different volumes, the degree of variability for each item of cost at various levels of output could be evolved on the basis of past experience. This requires a close study of individual items of expenditure, their nature and variability.

Illustration.

From the following particulars prepare a flexible budget for the three months ending 30th Steptember showing the estimated sales costs and profit for 60%, 80% and 100% activity. Assume that all items produced are sold.

Management salaries	Rs. 4,20,000
Rent and Rates	2,80,000
Depreciation of machinery	3,50,000
Sundry office cost	4,45,000
	14,95,000

Semi-variable expenses at 50% activity: Variable expenses at 50% activity.

	Rs.		Rs.
Plant maintenance	1,25,000	Materials	12,00,000
Indirect labour	4,59,000	Labour	12,80,000
Salesmen's salaries & expenses	1,45,000	Salesmen's commission	1,90,000
Sundry expenses	1,30,000		
	8,95,000		26,70,000

Semi-variable expenses remain constant between 40% and 70% activity, increase by 10% of the above figures between 70% and 80% activity and increase by 15% of the above figures between 80% and 100% activity; fixed expenses remain constant whatever be the level of activity. Sales at 60% activity are Rs. 51,00,000; at 80% activity are Rs. 68,00,000; at 100% activity are Rs. 85,00,000.

Solution.

FLEXIBLE BUDGET FOR THE THREE MONTHS END IN 30TH SEPTEMBER 19.........

Particulars	*Level of activity*					
		60%		*80%*		*100%*
		Rs.		Rs.		Rs.
Sales		51,00,000		68,00,000		85,00,000
Variable cost:						
Materials	14,40,000		19,20,000		24,00,000	
Labour	15,36,000		20,48,000		25,60,000	
Salesmen's com.	2,28,000	32.04,000	3,04,000	42,72,000	3,80,000	53,40,000
Semi-variable costs:						
Plan maintenance	1,25.000		1,37,500		1,43,750	
Indirect labour	4,95,000		5,44,000		5,69,250	
Salesman's salary	1,45,000		1,59,500		1,66,750	
Sundry expenses	1,30,000	8,95,000	1,43,000	1,43,000	9,84,500	1,49,500
Fixed costs:						
Managements salaries	4,20,000		4,20,000		4,20,000	
Rent and rates	2,80,000		2,80,000		2.80,000	
Dep. of mach inery	3,50.000		3,50,000		3,50,000	
Sundry office cost	4.45.000	14,95,000	4,45,000	14,95,000	4,45,000	14,95,000
Prolit (loss)		4,94,000		48,500		6,35,750

Date.............

Prenared by........................ Checked by.................. Management Accountant...........

It would be evident from the above discussion that the degree of variability of costs is determined by a study of the behaviour of costs over a period of time. This study leads to the delineation of the variable costs from the total costs, thus leaving the fixed core which remains unchanged for different level of activity. The study of different levels of activity would also lead to identifying the normal level of activity". This level is free form of any short-term influences and irons out violent fluctuations in the short run. But the normal level of activity need not mean full utilisation of capacity because level of activity is also very much dependent upon the sales volume. But, over a long period of time, if the sales volume is not sufficient enough, then naturally the capacity would be left out as idle capacity. Hence, 'normal level of activity' is defined as: "A satisfactory and logical balance between plant capacity and sales volume". The total costs have to be linked to the normal level of activity and their variability has to be expressed with reference to the normal level of activity.

ZERO BASE BUDGET (ZBB)

ZBB is a cost-benefit approach whereby it is assumed that the cost allowance for an item is zero, and will remain so until the manager responsible justifies the existence of the cost item and the benefits the expenditure brings. In this way a questioning attitude is developed whereby each cost item and its level has to be justified in relation to the way it helps to meet objectives and hew the expenditure benefits the organisation. This is a forward looking approach as opposed to the all too common method of extrapolating past activities and costs, which is a feature of the incremental budgeting approach.

ZBB is formally defined by the CIMA thus; A method of budgeting whereby all activities are re-evaluated each time a budget is formulated. Each functional budget starts with the assumption that the function does not exist and is at zero cost. Increments of cost are compared with increments of benefit, culminating in the planning maximum benefit fer a given budgeted cost.

ZBB can be applied in both profit seeking and non-profit seeking organisations. The technique gained wide publicity when the then President Carter directed that all US government departments adopt zero base budget.

In a manufacturing firm. It is best applied to service and support expenditure including, administration, marketing, personnel, information and computer services, research and development, finance and accounting, production planning and so on. These activities are less easily quantifiable by conventional methods and are more discretionary in nature. Manufacturing costs such as direct materials and labour and production overheads can be more easily controlled by well established methods which compare production outputs with resource inputs rather than using ZBB. Budgeting and controlling manufacturing expenditure uses techniques such as work study and standard costing which are described later in the manual

Zero base budget can successfully be applied to service industries and to a wide range of non-profit seeking orgnisations. For example local and central government departments, educational establishments, hospitals and so on. It could be applied in any organisation where alternative levels of provision for each activity are possible and the costs and benefits can be separately identified. It is concerned with alternatives and means that established activities have to be compared with alternative uses of the samè resources. It takes away the implied right of existing activities to continue to receive resources, unless it can be shown that this is the best use of those resources.

There are several formal stages involved in implementing this type of budget but of greater importance is the development of an appropriate questioning attitude by all concerned. There must be a 'value for money' approach which challenges existing practices and expenditures and searching questions must be asked at each stage; typical of which are the following:

(a) Is the activity essential or one of the frills?

(b) How much should the activity cost? Is this expenditure worth the benefits achieved?

(c) What is the best way to provide the function? Have all alternative possibilities been considered?

(d) What is the correct level of provision? Has too much or too little been provided in the past?

(e) How does the activity-existing or proposed-contribute to the organisations objectives?

(f) Does the activity need to be carried out at all? What would be the effects, if any, if it ceased? and so on.

The overall process of implementing this type of budget can be. sub-divided into three stages thus:

I. Definition of Decision Packages

A decision package is a comprehensive description of a facet of the organisation's activities or functions which can be individually evaluated. The decision package is specified by the managers concerned and must show details of the anticipated costs and results expected expressed in terms of tasks accomplished and benefits achieved.

Two types of decision package are possible:

(a) **Mutually-exclusive Decision Packages.** These are alternative forms of activity, tasks and expenditure to carry out the same job. The best option among the mutually exclusive packages is selected by comparing costs and benefits, and the other packages are then discarded. Naturally, mutually-exclusive packages would only be prepared when there are quite clearly different approaches for dealing with the same function. As an example, an organisation with a distribution problem might consider two alternative decision packages: Package 2 might be an in-house fleet of lorries, whereas Package 2 could involve contracts with independent hauliers.

(b) **Incremental Decision Packages.** These packages reflect different levels of effort in dealing with a particular activity. There will be what is known as the base package, which represents the minimum feasible lever of activity, and other packages which describe higher activity levels at given costs and resulting benefits. As an example, a base package for a Personnel Department might provide for staff engagement and termination procedures and payroll administration. Incremental packages might include; education and training, welfare and social activities, pension administration, trade union liaison and negotiations etc. Each package would have its costs and benefits clearly tabulated.

II. Packages are Evaluated and Ranked

When the decision packages have been prepared, management will then rank all the package on the basis of their benefits to the organisation, This is a process of allocating scarce resources between different activities, some of which already exist and other that are new.

Minimum requirements which are essential to get the job done and activities necessary to meet legal or safety obligation will naturally receive high priority. It will be found that the ranking process focuses management's attention on discretionary or optional activities.

Because of the large number of packages prepared through out the organisation the ranking process can become onerous and time consuming for senior management. One way of reducing this problem is for lower level managers to rank the packages for their own budget centre and for these rankings to be consolidated, with others, at the next level up the hierarchy. Alternatively, there could be a cut-off-limits for expenditure so that packages for a lower amount say less than £2,000, could be ranked within the department and need not be referred higher.

III. Resources are Allocated

When the overall budgeted expenditure level is decided upon the packages would be accepted in the ranked priority Sequence up to the agreed expenditure level.

Where the ranking of lower cost pakages has been delegated to departments the proportion of the expenditure budget remaining after the more expensive packages have been ranked would be allocated to individual departments. The departments would then rank their own small packages up to their allocated expenditure level.

Advantages of Zero Base Budget

(a) It is a systematic way of challenging the *status quo* and obliges the organisation to examine alternative activities and existing cost behaviour patterns and expenditure levels.

(b) This leads to greater staff and management knowledge of the operations and activities of the organisations and can increase motivation.

(c) It focuses attention on value for money and makes explicit the relationship between the input of resources and the output of benefits.

(d) It develops a questioning attitude and makes it easier to identify inefficient, obsolete or less cost-effective operations.

(e) Properly carried out, it should result in cl more efficient allocation of resources to activities and departments.

Disadvantages of Zero Base Budget

(a) It may emphasise short term benefits to the detriment of longer term ones which in the end may be more important.

(b) There are considerable problems in ranking packages and there are inevitable many subjective judgements. Political pressures within organisations also contribute to the problem of ranking different types of activity, especially where there are qualitative rather than quantitative benefits.

(c) ZBB is not always acceptable to staff or management or trade unions who may prefer the cosy *status quo* and who see the detailed examination of alternatives, costs and benefits as a threat not a challenge.

(d) It may encourage the wrong impression that all decisions have to be made in the budget. Circumstances change and new opportunities and threats can arise at any time and organisations must be flexible enough to deal rapidly with these circumstances when they occur.

(e) There is considerable management skill required in both drawing up decision packages and for the ranking process. These skills may not exist in the organisation.

(f) It is a time consuming process which can generate volumes of paper work especially for the decision packages.

PERFORMANCE BUDGET

The system of budgeting and budgetary control explained above ensures that the concerned organisation can prepare the next year's Profit and Loss Account and Balance Sheet. This is because the budgets are meant to be implemented in terms of physical activities-production and sales. In other words, the performance has to match the targets and the expenditure that is budgeted must result in the achievement of physical targets. In a way, therefore, the system of budgetary control stated above is system of performance budgeting.

In government, however, so far the emphasis on physical activities was totally submerged in monetary expenditure so much so that government budgets never correlated expenditure with performance. The budgets themselves were drawn up by natural heads such as salaries and establishments, rent, stationery, telephones and postage, travelling, etc. and not by functional heads. The result was that if the budgeted amount was spent, even if it resulted in no benefit or physical achievement, it was considered enough. The disadvantage is manifest the system often led to wastage.

Government has realised that budgeting should be on the basis of what is meant to be achieved and that expenditure has to be judged in the light of achievement of targets. The name given to such a system is "Performance Budgeting" .

The very first requirement is determination of the various activities to be under taken and the targets to be achieved. For example, the Education Ministry must decide how many institutions for the training of the handicapped shall be opened and where and how many handicapped persons shall be trained and in what skill. Then the expenditure involved should be listed under various heads for each institution and for the activities as a whole. The performance of the people and departments concerned shall be judged not only by the amount of money spent but also by the number of handicapped persons trained in different skills. Thus expenditure will be linked with performance and the amount spent shall be fruitful.

In performance budgeting, Government must give up the cash system of accounting and adopt the accrual system. Otherwise, it is possible that in one year, when payments are not made, it may appear to be dismal. It goes without saying that performance budgeting will succeed only if budgets are drawn up realistically on a careful assessment of the available resources and of what is feasible and possible. Also, there must be prompt reports, at short intervals, showing the amount spent (under different heads) and the results achieved. Government has taken the correct step of decentralising accounting work, otherwise such a system of reporting would not be possible. In over words, performance budgeting has to be akin to the system of budgeting and budgetary control in a good industrial concern.

PROGRAMME PLANNING AND BUDGETING SYSTEMS

Non-profit seeking organisations such as local and central government hospitals, charities and so on, often prepare detailed conventional budgets showing the different categories of expenditure, classification by classification. A particular problem of such organisations is that the measurement of outputs is difficult and sometimes impossible. As a consequence the budgeting process frequently just compares current expenditure to budgeted expenditure with little or no attempt to compare expenditure against performance achieved. By contrast, in profit seeking organisations the comparison of expenditure on resource inputs to outputs in terms of revenue and profits is much more straightforward.

In addition to the problems of relating inputs to benefits achieved, non-profit seeking organisations also have difficulties with long term strategic planning and realistic resource allocation. The short-term financial process of annual expenditure budgets is, on occasions also being used for long term policy planning with obvious disadvantages.

In an attempt to overcome these problems the Programme Planning & Budgeting System (PPBS) system was evolved.

PPBS is a sophisticated concept developed in North America and is usually considered in relation to State and Federal government activities although there is no reason why the system principles could not be more widely applied. PPBS is based on systems theory and is output and objective oriented with a substantial emphasis on resource allocation based on economic analysis. The system is based, not on traditional organisational structures and divisions, but on 'programmes' grouping of activities with common objectives. As with corporate planning, conventional short-term budgeting—year by year—takes place within the PPBS long term framework.

PPBS requires that the organisation prepares a long term plan relating to the objectives of the organisation sub-divided into programmes. These programmes are expressed in terms of objectives to be achieved over the medium to long term, say 3 to 5 years. The key point is that the programmes are objective related and spread across several conventional departments. The total estimated costsare for the programme as a whole and are not initially expressed in relation to departments. When the various programmes for the organisation have been agreed they form the long term plan for the organisation. PPBS covers activities spanning several years and conventional annual expenditure budgeting would take place within this framework. Each year the departments contributing to a given programme would prepare, and be monitored by, normal expenditure budgets for their share of the programme's activities for the year in question.

PPBS requires as ophisticated information system able to monitor progress towards meeting systems objectives. The PPBS reporting system should be able to report upon results in, terms of the programmes of activities unlike conventional reporting which is geared to existing organisational sub-divisions and usually deals only with expenditures.

BUDGET ORGANISATION

The installation and operation of a budgetary control system requires the co-operation of managers at all levels. The budgeting function is usually vested in the office of the Controller or the Chief Accounts Officer. The Budgeting Function is normally the responsibility of the Budget Officer or the Budget Director. The Budget Officer' or the Budget Director would report to the Controller of the Chief Account Officer if the Budgeting Function is vested within the domain of the Controller's Office. On the other hand, if the Budgeting Function is an independent set-up outside the Controller's office then the Budget Officer or the Director would head the department and report to the Chief Executive. A slightly deterrent practice is to have a Budget Committee. The Committee would comprise a number of top management executives. It would be responsible to develop general and basic concepts as to the economic conditions likely to prevail. The company practices in respect of budget administration were as follows:

(1) In this company the budget was administered by weekly managers meeting rather than any specific budget meeting or committee. The preparation of the budget and monthly reporting of variances were the responsibility of the Cost Accountant who was at the Manager's level.

(2) The company had a budget centre headed by a budget director. Broad targets were laid down in the form of general budgets. However, accounting department controlled the budget. The Chief Accountants co-ordinated budget activity. The budgets were reviewed by a budget review committee composed of representatives from finance, technical, marketing and personnel departments.

(3) The company did not have a budget officer as such but management planning and control system was installed and cost control and budget control were practised by fixed lines of executive responsibility.

(4) In this company there was a finance planning department which looked after the budget activity. There was an

assistant treasurer who co-ordinated and consolidated the budgetary operations of the company.

(5) In this company every department carried out is own responsibilities and had to report on its achievements every quarter.

(6) In this company line management was responsible for budgetary control. The Branch Sales Managers prepared the budget. The Deputy General Managers In consultation with the All India Sales Manager finalised the budget and placed it before the board of directors.

EXHIBIT

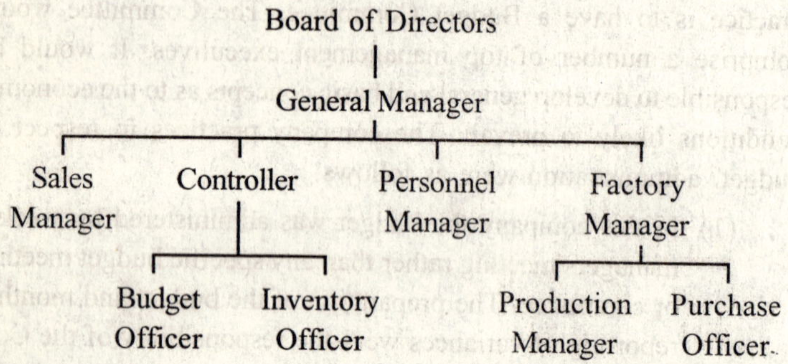

Organisational Chart Showing the Budget Function

Note.

(a) In the chart shown the Budget Officer reports to the Controller and the Budgeting Function is within the domain of the Controller's Office.

(b) In very large organisations the Budgeting Function may be vested under a Budget Director/Planning Manager in a separate department styled as Planning Department outside the Controller's Office. In this situation the Budget Director/ Planning Manager would report to the President of the Company.

(c) In the chart shown the Inventory Function is vested in the office of the Inventory Officer who reports to the Controller.

The Inventory Officer will have to get the necessary information from the sales department, production department and the purchase department to arrive at finished goods, work in process and raw material inventory. His function is co-ordination.

RESEARCH AND DEVELOPMENT BUDGET

Research has now become a continuous activity in many industries. Research has now become a continuous activity in many industries. Research and development programmes should be identified and their corresponding cost should be budgeted. The Financial Accounting Standards Hoard defines the two terms, "research and "development", in the following manner:

A. Research is planned search or critical investigation aimed at discovery of new knowledge with the hope that such knowledge will be useful in developing a new product or service (hereinafter "product"), or a new process or technique (hereinafter "process"), or in bringing about a significant improve-ment in an existing product or process.

B. Development is the translation of research findings or other knowledge into a plan or design for a new product or processor for a significant improvement to an existing product or process whether intended for sale or use. It includes the conceptual formulation, design, and testing of product alternatives, construction of protypes, and operation of pilot product alternatives plants. It does not include routine or periodic alterations to existing products, production lines, manufacturing processes, and other on-going operations even though those alterations may represent improvements and it does not include market research or market testing activities.

The research and development budget is the most important tool for planning and controlling research and development costs. It compels management to think in advance about the fairness of these expenses both in total amounts and in each field of a research programme. It helps in coordination with the company's other plans and projects. Since the research and development programmes compete with other desirable activities in allocation of funds, coordination is needed to balance financially immediate and long-term company plans. Also, this budget guides the research and development department to plan correctly the staff and equipment requirements and special facilities needed for the work. The preparation of research and development budgets should be based on reasonably accurate estimates and should be flexible. Research projects should be planned and evaluated and then grouped into long-term and short-term projects. A short-term research programme is needed to earn a satisfactory rate on return of the funds invested. A long-term research programme is developed to ensure that the research programmes are in line with future market trends, and demand and research costs are in conformity with budgeted financial position. Research and development is discretionary costs and therefore in case of decline in operating income and financial.

Programmes Budget

A budget set for a plan or programme of action of the concern is known as a programme budget. Such budgets can be prepared for each plan or programme separately. It helps management in assessing the economies of various programmes. The estimated revenues and costs of the programmes are given in the budget. The budgets are not suitable to exercise control over individuals since so many persons may be assigned with the task of completing the programme and no one individual may be responsible for the entire operation.

Responsibility Budget

The budget set for operation by a department or by an executive responsible for it is termed as a responsibility budget. Thus, it is a budget identifying the revenues and costs, with an individual responsible for their incurrence. The main advantage flowing from such budgets is that management can exercise better control over the entire business. The achievement of the individual is tested by comparing it with the budgeted target and the individual can be taken to task for non-performance. The budget may be prepared for each responsibility centre separately.

Budgeted Balance Sheet

A projected balance sheet represents the expected financial position at a particular date. The .projected balance sheet is prepared from the budgeted balance sheet at the beginning of the budget period and the expected changes in the account balances reflected in the operating budgets, capital expenditure budgets, and cash budget. If any of the accounts or relationships among the accounts appearing on the projected balance sheet are not according to management's requirements and objectives, the operating plan might have to be changed. For example, if a bank or financial institution requires a business firm to maintain a certain minimum current ratio and debtequity ratio, the operating plan would have to be changed if these ratio are indeed too low. Furthermore, unfavourable ratios may decrease the value of company shares in the stock exchange and lows the creditability of the firm in the investment market. The projected balance sheet also automatically determines the arithmetical accuracy of other budgets since they are used in preparing the forecasted balance sheet.

❐

4

Standard Costing

Standard costs are the scientifically pre-determined costs of manufacturing a single unit or a number of units of product or of rendering a service during a specified future period. According to the Terminology, it is "a pre-determined cost calculated in relation to a prescribed set of working conditions, correlating technical specifications and scientific measurements of materials and labour to the prices and wage rates expected to apply during the period to which the standard cost is intended to relate with an addition of an appropriate share of budgeted overhead. Its main purposes are to provide bases for control through variance accounting for the valuation of stocks and work-in-progress and in exceptional cases for fixing selling prices."

What is evident from the above definition is that standard costs are planned costs of a product under current, or anticipated operating conditions. The dictionary meaning of the word 'standard' is that it is a "thing serving as a basis for comparison", "thing recognised as model for imitation". But it should be noted that 'standard' is a relative term. Admittedly, what is standard for one may be sub-standard for another and vice versa. However, what is significant is that within an organisation, it serves as a desirable target.

The term 'standard cost' consists of two parts, *viz.*, 'standard' and 'cost'. Standards can be established in respect of qualities and quantities like materials and labour. Cost involves the expression of the standards so established in values:

Standard costs are highly detailed scientifically pre-determined costs of material, labour and overhead chargeable to a product or service. Standard costs represent excellent target costs that should be obtained. This Institute of Cost and Management Accountants defines standard cost as "a predetermined cost which is calculated from management's standards of efficient operation and the relevant necessary expenditure. It may be used as a basis for price fixing and for cost control through variance analysis". The Institute in its terminology defines standard costing as "the preparation and use of standard costs, their comparison with actual costs, and the analysis of variances of their causes and points of incidence, "Standard cost expresses what costs should be under attainable good performance, They are projections of what actual cost should be under an assumed set of conditions', The term "standard", has been called by different names in accounting *e.g.*" "a norm", "a model or example or comparison", "a measure of comparison", "a criterion, of excellence", "a yardstick", "a benchmark", "an index of waste or potential savings", "a sea-level from which to measure cost attitudes", "a gauge", A standard may be a norm or a measure of comparison in terms of specific items such as pounds or kilograms of materials, labour hours required, hours of plant capacity used.

The definition given by W.W. Bigs makes the concept of standard costing more clear. According to him, "Standard Costing discloses the costs of deviations from standard and classifies these as to their causes, so that management is immediately informed of the sphere of operations in which remedial action is necessary.

Thus, standard costing statistics are prepared to show:

(i) the standard cost.

(ii) the actual cost.

(iii) the difference between these costs which is termed as variance.

Standard costs are determined for each element of cost-direct materials, direct labour, overhead (fixed and variable)—separately and then variations from actual costs are in respect of each element distinctly so as to detect which part of the costs needs control and which department, process or operation, the responsibility may be placed. The standard costs are organised to uncover and report off-standard conditions. The management should strive for the attainment of standard costs because they are attainable ideal costs and are practical from the point of view of business.

OBJECTIVES OF STANDARD COSTING

The companies using standard costing reported to management at various levels the significant variances with written explanation. In some companies standard costing was a part of regular costing system, while in others it was used on an *ad hoc* basis. The following represented the broad objectives of the standard costing system:

(1) Exert effective control and an adequate check at various levels and in different areas of management.

(2) Determine future managerial policy in respect of marketing and production and.

(3) Ensure accuracy in costing.

The few companies having effective standard costing system used such system to attain the following specific objectives.

(A) Cost Control. Cost control was exercised by comparison of actual costs against the standard. Such comparison took place in respect of each element of expense, departmental or cost centre, costs and product costs. In many cases costs were broken down into controllable and non-controllable components with a view to focussing the management attention only on such costs which were control lable.

In respect of purchase activity standard costing system enabled the management to control purchase prices. With regard to production activity by use of standard costing, the management was able to control material usages and reduce waste. Some companies considered benefit of economy of usage by bulk issues to cost centres. These companies were also able to use labour with greater efficiency and derive optimum usage of power and coal by efficient running of the equipment.

(B) Pricing. Standard costs were used to set prices where companies offered products of jobs under terms of contracts. Prices were also determined on the basis of standard costs by companies which operated in a competitive industry, but where they had certain measure of control in fixing prices.

(C) Evaluating Performance. Standard costing system was used to evaluate the performance of executives operating at various levels of management. Far example, a foreman may be held responsible if he is not able to achieve certain output which is laid down as a standard. In one company standard costing system was effectively used to grant bonus to executives where performance was better than standard.

(D) Cost Reduction. Cost reduction was possible by implementation of industrial engineering specifications. Variance analysis could locate inefficiencies and could bring a level of innovation which could increase productivity and reduce costs. A few companies had well-established cost reduction programmes where special efforts were made to reduce costs in certain directions pointed out by variance analysis.

ADVANTAGES OF STANDARD COSTING

Standard costing is a system of cost accounting which facilitates the performance of the entire managerial process-planning, organisation, coordination and control. Among the many advantages generally attributed to standard costing, the most important may be listed as follows:

(1) Cost Control. Cost control and cost reduction are probably the most important aims of any costing system; and standard costing gives due recognition to this fact. Cost control has the objective of production of the required quality at the lowest cost attainable under existing conditions. Effective control requires detailed standards, to show how much of each material should be used, how much labour should be required for each operation, and what facilities and services will be needed. Standards enable management to make periodic comparison of actual costs with standard costs in order to measure performance and to take action to maintain control over costs. Standard costs help management in cost control through the principle of exception, *i.e.*, highlighting only those activities which fail to come up to standard or which exceed standard. The off-standard conditions can be investigated and proper action can be taken before they continue for a long time. Standards help develop cost conscious attitudes, because it makes cost variances clearly observable by management. Cost consciousness tends to reduce costs and encourage economies in all phases of the business and guides management towards improvement.

(2) Economical Means of Costing and Record-keeping: The use of standard costs can reduce clerical labour and expense by avoiding the detailed record keeping which is necessary when actual costs alone are used. The following benefits are derived which reduce the cost of record-keeping:

(a) By carrying inventory at standard cost, store ledgers can be kept in terms of quantities only. This eleminates much clerical time in pricing and balancing items on the stores ledger. Total standard cost of inventory can readily be obtained at any time by multiplying the quantity in stock by the standard unit cost.

(b) When standard costs are used, requisition or bills for materials to be put into production can be written and priced more rapidly than when the goods must be priced at actual cost. In fact, materials, requisitions, labour time tickets, and production cost cards can be prepared in advance of production.

(c) The time required to assemble cost data for budget preparation or special cost studies such as pricing is reduced because it is not necessary to devote so much time to the analysis and collection of past actual costs.

(d) The time which must be devoted by management to the study and analysis of cost reports is much reduced when standard costs are used. Standard costs tend to eliminate unnecessary details and focus on those aspects which require management attention and thus bring economies and effectiveness in management reporting.

(e) The time required to prepare reports which are used by management can be reduced. Since most reports are useful in proportion to their timelines, standard costing helps management to take remedial action promptly by providing useful and timely reports of variances.

(f) The standard cost of goods finished can be obtained immediately upon completion since it is necessary to multiply the quantity by the unit standard cost. Simple and economical costing methods can be used in place of elaborate costing methods.

(3) Managerial Planning. Planning is a process of using all resources in such a manner that maximises business profits. Management must plan for efficient and economic operations for standard costs to be effective. The standard costs, carefully determined, will disclose inefficiencies in operations, which can be thoroughly investigated and remedial action taken. Standard costs are more convenient than actual cost for budget preparation because the standard costs at different production levels and for different product mixes are readily built up into total costs as called for by the budget. On the other hand, using actual costs requires a great deal of analysis and adjustment when extensive changes in product volume or product-mixes take place. Furthermore, actual costs are influenced by many temporary or random influences which make it difficult to predict the future behaviour of unstandardised costs.

(4) Coordination. The establishment of standards coordinates all functions-manufacturing, marketing, engineering, research, and accounting towards the achievement of a common goal. Setting standards involves defining and communicating targets so that they can work towards the attainment of the goal.

(5) Standards as Incentives to Employees. If standards are reasonable and attainable they act as incentives to employees to improve their performances and to maintain the quality of the product. Each worker performs his job with advance knowledge of the standard set for the particular job; he knows that if his work is less than the standard, he is responsible for the variance.

Standards motivate workers, supervisors and foremen to work more efficiently in the accomplishment of their respective standards. Many incentives like cash bonus, individual and group bonus, prizes, vacation time, and promotions can be given for equalling or surpassing standards. Similarly, management can decide upon action to be taken for below standard performance.

(6) Formulating, Price and Production Policies. Standard costs as compared to actual costs can be used for estimating selling prices. When standard unit costs are available, expected costs and sales prices can be computed on the basis of standard costs. Standards already established can easily be modified to reflect current conditions and changes in material prices or labour rates and the price of the product can lie determined on a realistic basis. Also, the problem of absorption of fixed overhead is better tackled and simplified by using standard costs. Standard costs are predetermined costs which help management in the decision process by providing standard unit costs for various levels of activity. Standard costs are thus useful to management in determining price policies, preparing bids for prospective orders, planning production of new products and new methods, and furnishing cost estimates in all managerial decisions.

Actual costs, on the other hand, may reflect excessive usage of material, abnormal labour times or an inequitable charge for overhead. Actual overhead cost per unit at any given time may be so influenced by temporary fluctuations in production levels as to make actual cost entirely unusable for pricing. Standard costs on the contrary, are based upon carefully determined and planned usages of material, labour and overhead facilities and thus are free from accidental and temporary distortions caused by.

Necessary adjustments in standards to incorporate changing conditions can be done without any difficulty whenever required. Standard overhead rates are determined upon a normal production or activity level and therefore, provide an acceptable base for determining product prices which will recover full overhead costs in the long run.

LIMITATIONS OF STANDARD COSTING

There are certain disadvantages in the Standard Costing System which are noted below:

(1) **Sometimes Standards Create Adverse Psychological Effects.** If the standard is set at a high level, its non-achievement will lead to frustration and resistance. This acts as a discouragement rather than an incentive for better efficiency.

(2) **For Fixing Responsibility for an Adverse Variance.** The controllable and the non-controllable portions of the variances should be segregated. This may be quite a difficult task.

(3) Even if the initial standards are fixed up with a certain amount of accuracy the management should be alert to factors which would necessitate an alteration to these standards. Unless standards are current, they are useless as incorrect standards. Such out of date standards will do more harm than any benefit.

(4) **Establishment** of standards may be costly and may require high degree of technical skill. This may make a standard costing system beyond the reach of small business concerns.

(5) **It is Difficult to Fix up Reliable and Workable Standards.** Unless the standards are correctly fixed, the control and study of variances on which the whole system is built up will not be effective. The standards are merely approximate and may adversely affect the values of standards as tools of control.

STANDARD COSTING *Vs.* HISTORICAL COSTING *Vs.* ESTIMATED COSTING

Standard costing can be distinguished from historical costing and estimated costing. Under historical costing, the costs are the actual costs and, therefore, the question of exercising control does not arise at all. It is simply an analysis of costs after they have been incurred and, therefore, pertain to past data. Estimated costing, on the other hand, refers to that system of costing under which costs are estimated in advance-meaning thereby that the costs which are likely to be incurred during given period of time are conceived of well before their being incurred. This is done with reference to historical costs and the prevailing condition of business. It is, thus, an estimation of the actual costs or historical costs of a business in anticipation. As apart from it, standard costing refers to that system of costing whereunder the costs which ought to be there and should be attained are determined in advance. Standard costs strive to make the actual costs equal or approximate to the predicted costs, whereas in estimated costs, the estimated must come into line with the actual costs. Thus, the term standard costs under standard costing does not referred what the costs are or what the costs shall be but refers to what the costs should be or ought to be. Standard costs are, therefore, above the efficiency level of normal or expected costs so that management can make efforts to achieve the goal and bring down the costs to that level.

Estimated costs represent merely figures based on average of past experience or personal opinion; while standard costs are based on carefully and scientifically established figures in respect of a product. The estimated costing simply plans the affairs while standard costing besides planning acts as a dynamic instrument of measurement of performance, comparison and control.

There is a point of similarity between the estimated costs and standard cost that both are determined before the process of production commences, but they differ in regard to their purpose. The main points of difference are as under:

Historical cost systems are principally associated with recording of historical, or as they are commonly called, actual costs. Historical costing is the ascertainment of costs after they have been incurred. It indicates to management the results actual transactions that have taken place in an organisation during some previous period. The recording of historical costs is useful as it determines the cost of resources used towards achieving organisational, objectives. Historical costs, however, have the following limitations:

1. Historical costs are collected after they have been incurred and therefore are ineffective in cost control. The costs have been incurred, they can not be undone and no steps can be taken to correct inefficiencies.
2. Historical costs are not helpful in cost reduction since they contain no standards or goals towards which employees can work.
3. Historical costs do not provide reliable guides to management in the tasks of budgeting, planning, and decision-making. Historical costs reflect a situation in a previous period. But the company, in facts, may be working under conditions different from those prevailing during that previous period. Therefore, historical costs are not useful in budget making, performance evaluation, detecting above or below-standard performance.

The need of standard costing arises because the historical costing system which is usually adopted in every business concern has certain deficiencies. In case of historical costing costs are known only after the production takes place while the policies are to be determined before the production begins, and hence it may not be much useful. Thus operating efficiency cannot be measured with the help of historical costing. Moreover, the historical costs may be too expensive to compile.

STANDARD COSTS AND ESTIMATED COSTS

The term "standard costs" should not be confused with "estimated costs" Standards costs and estimated casts differ in the following respects:

A. Estimated costs are frequently less accurately determined. Estimated costs are developed from projections using averages of past data regarding performance. Standard costs are predetermined realistically and much more scientifically through the use of time and motion studies, engineering estimates and specifications, selected measures of plant capacity, cost behaviour patterns. Thus the fund mental difference between an estimated cost and a standard cost is depth of analysis, prediction techniques and amount of effort used to develop cost information.

B. Estimated costs are not helpful to management in accomplishing managerial functions as they are not scientifically predetermined costs. But standard costs involve more sophistication, operation analysis and evaluation and comprehensive review of internal and external factors. They become reliable measures for product costing, product pricing, planning, coordination and cost control purposes.

C. Estimated cost emphasises on actual cost with which it is compared at the end of the accounting period. If the estimated costs are found higher or lower than actual costs they are revised for use in the next accounting period. Revisions in estimated costs are made in accordance with changes in actual cost conditions which are expected to continue during the next accounting period. In standard costing, the emphasis is on standard costs, *i.e.*, what costs of material, labour and overhead should be incurred if the factory is to be operated as a highly efficient unit with each manager, foreman, worker, plant and machine functioning as an efficient part of the production process. Under standard costing, actual costs are ascertained on by to facilitate their comparison with standard costs.

STANDARD COSTING AND BUDGETARY CONTROL

Both standard costing and budgeting are control systems. But each has got its own special features.

The principle points of difference between standard costing and budgetary control lie in *(a)* their scope of coverage, and *(b)* the approach to planning.

The scope of budget is wide. It is an integrated plan of action a coordinated plan in respect of all functions of an enterprise.

(i) It is possible to introduce standard costing into the accounting routine itself (as well as comparing actuals from books with standards outside the books). In such a case, the variances are given out by the accounting system itself. In a budgetary control system, the targets are not introduced into the accounting system; the comparison is made outside the books of account and forms the subject of reports outside the accounting system.

(ii) Budgets require functional coordination, whereas standard costing does not require such coordination since it is possible to think even of one aspect of cost. Mostly it is costs alone which form the subject-matter of standard costing—while considering one function, other functions can be ignored and hence functional coordination is not essential.

(iii) In India, at present, the approach to budgeting is generally through forecasts an expression of how things are expected to be rather than how things should be. Standards, in order to serve any useful purpose, must necessarily be exact and determined scientifically. Of course, budgets, too should be similarly drawn upon the basis of most careful study of what can be achieved given the realities of the situation. Thus budgets relating to costs can be drawn up using the information provided by standard costing. As far as possible that should be ensured.

(iv) The scope of standard costing, however, is limited to the operating level. Here too it is further linked to the costs. As the name suggests, its average is limited to costs whereas budgets embrace revenues as well as costs and all functions and activities—sales, finance, capital expenditure, personnel, purchase, etc., in addition to production. Budgets are mast useful when they are well coordinated.

In both the systems actuals have to be compared against standards; actual information has to be obtained. For the standard costing system, actual information can be obtained only from a well-maintained costing system, whereas for a budgetary control system, information may be obtained from the financial accounting system, supplemented by costing data.

One must remember, however, that the two control systems are never treated as exclusive. Standard costing is a specified system in respect of costs, budgets are also concerned with costs among other things; therefore, it would add strength to a budgetary control system if it adopts standard costs in respect of cost data. The two are complementary to each other. The distinction between the two systems is mainly on account of the field or scope and technique of operation.

Budgeting	*Standard Costing*
1. Budget can be operated without standards.	1. Standard costing cannot exist without budgets.
2. Budgetary control can be adopted in part also.	2. It is not possible to operate this system in parts.
3. Budget is a projection of financial accounts.	3. Standard cost is the projection of cost accounts.
4. It does not necessarily involve. standardization of products.	4. It requires standardization of products.
5. Budgetary control is concerned with the operation of the business as a whole and hence it is more extensive.	5. Standard costing is related with the control of expenes hence, it is more intensive.

In spite of the above differences, there are some similarities between standard costing and budgeting. Both have in common the establishment of predetermined measures of performance and the comparison of actual and planned performance so as to disclose deviations which are used for the purpose of cost control. Both have the same objective of managerial control and are therefore interrelated and cannot function independently. Both help in the preparation of reports which compare actual costs and predetermined costs for management planning and control. Matz and Usry have observed that standards are almost indispensable to the work of establishing and operating a budget. A study made by the National Association of Accountants (U.S.A) concludes that standard costs are especially valuable in developing the cost side of the budget because they provide a reliable and convenient source of data for converting the budgeted production schedule into requirements for raw materials, labour and services.

Manufacturing Cost Standards *vs* Non-manufacturing Cost Standards. Standards can be laid down for the manufacturing sector and the non-manufacturing sector. The manufacturing sector, however, more readily subjects itself to the process of planning and controlling *via* standards and standard costing. This is because the activities in the manufacturing sector lend themselves to statistical measurement, industrial engineering studies and time and motion studies. For example, input-output ratios can be prescribed for the usage of materials, efficiency of labour or Overhead incidence in the manufacturing sector. Standards and Standard Costs can be prescribed for the elements of manufacturing cost *i.e.*, Direct Material, Direct Labour and Manufacturing overhead. However, in the non-manufacturing sector; the activities are associated mainly with the external economic environment. A salesman would not now whether he would attract customers before visiting them or making telephone calls. Input-output ratios cannot be easily prescribed for these activities. At least not as rigidly and as accurately as in the manufacturing segment. Further, the non-manufacturing activity has always been neglected mainly because cost accounting techniques gained currency initially in the manufacturing sector. While it is rightly believed that the non-manufacturing costs do not lend themselves to the standards continued complacency may endanger the prosperity of strong companies and the viability of weak ones. Therefore, attempts should be made to subject the non-manufacturing costs also to as close a control as possible. In fact, there should be no discrimination between manufacturing costs and non-manufacturing costs in this regard.

FACTORS FOR FRXING STANDARDS

Certain factors are to be borne in mind while fixing the standards:

Period of Use

The first important criterion for establishment of standard costs is the length of the operation, period for which standards are to be used. Long-term as well as short-term standards may be fixed ranging for different periods. For long-term planning and growth standards for a longer duration, say 3 to 5 years, may be justified while for planning and budgeting for the accounting period short term standards for a year or so are beneficial. For measuring the performance and exercising control over costs, short-term standards are most suited. The standards according to length of time may be categorised as:

(a) Basic Standards. These are not altered over a long period of time; revisions are not frequent and there is a stability and stagnancy in standards fixed. These 'basic' or 'bogey' standards remain constant for a very long time and, therefore are applied in industries where only a small range of products are manufactured and long-term planning is required. But since the conditions do not remain static in this dynamic world, the standards become obsolete and require overhauling and, therefore, the long-term basic standards are not realistic.

(b) Current Standards. Short-term standards are known as current standards. These are more suitable for business since they take into account the current conditions and are related to the budget period.

In business, it will be useful to set both—long term as well short term standards. This will help in finding out variations in respect of both these standard in advance of actual production.

Reasonable or Desirable Level of Attainment

This we have discussed at length already in the foregoing pages and it can be said that standards are to be set assuming efficient working conditions and reasonably good performance.

Activity Level

The level of activity or performance required must be decided upon before establishing any standards. The level or output of production which shall be attained over the forthcoming period for which the standards are to be computed, is to be assumed or judged with regard to the capacity of the plant and the marketability of the products. The sales potential and production capacity decide the quantum of output to be manufactured within a particular period. The idle capacity, unutilised capacity and other limiting factors should be taken into consideration before determining the attainable level of output.

After bearing the above factors in mind, we can proceed to set up the standards for the different elements of cost separately.

How to Determine Standard Costs

Cost in its totality can be compared to a triangle. The three elements which constitute the triangle are material cost, labour cost and overhead cost. As already stated, standard cost involves fixing standards in quantitative terms and converting them into values. It is a coordinated exercise, though at the operational level, unlike the coordination required at a higher level for budgeting. It is important to think for all the three elements or cost at the same times while setting up standards. There is obvious connection between labour and overheads since the question whether to use manual labour or machines will have to be decided. Further, the time required to accomplish a task will also depend on the conditions in which materials are bought. If some cutting or further treatment is required, not only will there be some wastage of materials but also more time will be needed. Buying materials absolutely ready for use may mean some extra cost of materials but may mean less wastage and lower labour cost. Thus standard for all three elements of cost must be considered together. Setting up of standard cost involves two processes, *viz....*

(i) Determination of quantitative standards consistent with quality, and

(ii) Converting such quantitative standards into monetary values.

To start with, the production engineering department considers, approves and circulates the drawings for a proposed job (if it is an engineering concern) to the various concerned sections/departments. The engineering department itself has experts specialising in studies of materials, labour and machine requirements, etc. The approved designs provoke the concerned department/sections to study the implications and set standards in respect of their area of specialisation. Material specialists, fix standards for materials consumption, time and motion study experts determine the exact process and sequence of operations and standard time; and the buying department fixes the material prices, and so on. Then all the above data go to the 'standard cost committee' (comprising representatives of all the departments/ sections concerned) where the standard cost is finalised.

The main departments involved (co-operating in building up the standards) are following:

Material cost	:	Production Engineering Department (Material specialists) and Buying Department.
Labour Cost	:	Production Engineering Department (Time and motion study experts) and Personnel Department.
Overhead Cost	:	Production Engineering Department and Production and Service Departments.

The cost accounting department acts as the coordinator.

Determination of standard material cost involves first the laying down of quality standards for the finished products; the quantity of materials required depends upon the desired quality of the output. The standard quantity of materials is often dependent if the material is of better quality and vice versa. The quantity required is converted into money values on the basis of prices expected to prevail (in current standards). An ideal price can be used if ideal standards are expected, but this is only hypothetical. Price standards should take into account freight costs, discounts, etc. Ideal purchase efficiency should be assumed.

Determination of standard labour cost involves determining the standard time to be taken for each operation or each job as a whole on the basis of motion study and time study. It is the production engineering department which has to prescribe the categories of labour required and the time to be taken by each category. The time to be taken for each unit of output can be known from 'standard hour'. The standard time is converted into money values with the assistance of the personnel department which would know the wage rates likely to prevail. Thus, a current standard for labour can be determined. Determination of overheads cost standard is a little involved. "Overheads" is the aggregate of indirect materials, indirect labour and indirect expenses. The term 'indirect' is used here with reference to the costing unit these items of cost, however, may be 'direct' as far as the cost centre (*i.e.*, "the department") is concerned. Hence, a simple way is to fix standards for materials cost, labour cost and expenses in respect of each department both production and service. To the departments these costs are direct and hence it is easier to fix the standards. Before fixing the standards, the level of activity of each department is to be determined. This process can be simplified by classifying the costs as "variable" and "fixed". Variable would very according to the level of activity budgeted and fixed would remain constant for the period.

As ultimately the standard overhead cost per unit has to be determined, it is necessary to link the standard overheads of the departments to the products. For this purpose, the standard overheads of service departments have to be redistributed to the production departments. This should be done on a standard basis. For instance, the power house standard cost for a period is Rs. 7,20,000 and the standard output is 24,00,000 Kwh, the standard rate per kwh amounts to 30 paise. Depending upon the standard consumption for actual output, the standard cost charged for actual production will differ. Assuming that the standard consumption of power for one unit of output is 200 Kwh and actual production is 10,000 units, the standard cost applied to actual production would be Rs.6,00,000 (*i.e.*, 30 Paise × 200 kwh × 10,000 units). If the actual expenditure on power amount to Rs.7,30,000 the variances in power cost would amount to Rs.10,000 adverse. The above is a simplified example of power cost which can be easily linked to the final product.

For the cost of other overheads which cannot be linked with the final product so conveniently, again the same principle applies. The service departments' standard costs should be predetermined. It should be assigned to the production departments on standard recovery basis. For instance, the standard cost (budget) of "time office" is Rs.80,000. The standard working time of the three production departments is 20,000, 20,000, 10,000 hours respectively. Accordingly the time office's 'standard cost to .be distributed is Rs.32,000, Rs.32,000 and Rs.16,000 respectively among the three production departments. The production department's overheads collected like this would be converted into standard recovery rates.

Recovery rate for each production department is fixed on the basis of standard house. The rate is arrived at by dividing the standard overheads by the standard hours budgeted to be worked. The standard hours budgeted means the budgeted production muliplied by the standard time per unit. Thus the recovery rate for a production department is standard (budgeted) overheads divided by standard hours. This rate is determined in advance. This rate will adopted to coarge overhead for each unit, The recovery will be at the standard rate for standard hours of actual production, That is, if one unit takes 6 hours whereas the standard time is 5 hours, the unit will be charged with 5 hours multiplied by recovery rate per hour. The actual cost of a unit would be actual direct cost applied plus the overhead charged on predetennined recovery rate for the standard hours of actual output. The overheads charged to the production will differ from the overheads actually spent due to more less spending as well as due to volume of production being more or less than what is budgeted, These would be reflected in variances.

Illustration.

Standard recovery rate	Rs. 5 per standard hour
Units produced	100 units
Standard time per unit	2 hours
Total actual time taken	250 hours

Actual overhead charged from Service Department to Production Department Rs.500

Actual overhead incurred in the production department Rs.600.

Calculate the overheads charged and incurred.

Solution.

Actual overhead charged to production department	Rs. 500
Actual overhead incurred in the production department	Rs. 600
Total	Rs. 1,100

Total overhead charged to the costing units at Rs. 5 per standard hour (Rs. 5 × 2 hours × 100 units) Rs. 1,000

The above illustration shows that there is an under-recovery of overheads to the extent of Rs. 100 (Rs. 1,100-Rs.1,000). The overhead of production department is Rs. 1,100 which consists of Rs. 500 charged from service, department and Rs.600 incurred in the production department. The former sum itself is on the basis of predetermined rates of recovery from the service department. The actual overhead in the service department may itself be different. The amount charged from the the service department to various production departments (like the Rs. 600 charged) may differ from the actual cost of the service department. Thus there can be overhead variance for the service department as well. Hence overhead variance can arise in the production department as well as at the service department stage. The discussion about overhead variances in this book is mainly based on production department.

How a Standard is Fixed?

The preparation of standards calls for liaison between many departments. It is not a responsibility of the costing department only. The Productions Engineer and the Cost Accountant will have to collaborate in setting standards. The Cost Accountant must have a detailed study of the functions necessary for the manufacture of the product. It is the task of the costing department to reflect in units of thing and money values the budgets standards and standard costs that result from the decisions of the operating management. After being done so standards are generally fixed for:

Production

(i) Direct Material:	(a)	quantity per unit of output;
	(b)	price per unit of quantity;
	(c)	wastage per unit of input; and
(ii) Direct Labour:	(a)	number of men per machine;
	(b)	grade of men employed
	(c)	wage rate for each grade; and
	(d)	machine/man hours required per unit of output.
(iii) Indirect Materials:		Cost per machine, production hour.
(iv) Indirect Labour:		Cost per machine/production hour, or percentage of direct labour.
(v) Fixed Expenses:		Total amount for the period of budgeted production hours.
(vi) Variable Expenses:		Cost per unit of output, or cost per product hour.

The setting of Standard Costs requires consideration of the following:

(1) Quantities	for each element of cost entering into a
(2) Prices or rates	product *i.e.* Material, Labour, Overhead.
(3) Quantities or grades	

The Cost Accountant will have to collaborate with the Production Engineer for the purpose of fixing the standards.

HOW TIGHT SHOULD STANDARD BE?

The establishment of standards or standard cost is decided by the use to be made of them. It can be rightly said that a single standard may not be suitable for all purposes. For the purposes of cost control, tight standards need to be established. The attainable performance standards are useful for purposes of inventory valuation, product costing and income determination. Realistic standards are needed for pricing decisions and capital expenditure decisions.

High Standards

A high standard helps in cost reduction and motivating employees to try to reach the targets established. High standards represent the best possible performance and, if achieved, raise the levels of performance and efficiency as compared to poor or loose standards. High standards being unattainable in practice may not be good for the employees. Employees may not seriously accept them because they know that they are unattainable and impossible excuse the failure to reach them. High standards are also not realistic and therefore cannot be used in product costing, inventory valuation, financial statement, planning, and capital investment decision.

Low (Loose) Standards

A standard which is low or loose can be attained by poor performance. However, it defeats the purpose of standard costing and fails to disclose in efficiencies. Similarly, standards set in terms of average past performance expect too little. Since jobs on which performance is poor are likely to be more numerous than are jobs on which performance is exceptionally good, average past performance standards are usually considerably looser. Such standards do not help management in cost control as they are not accurate measures to compare actual results.

In conclusion, it can be said that accountants generally seem to favour currently attainable standards which are most appropriate for performance appraisal, accounting purposes, cost control and decision making. Such standards produce good performance, promote employee motivation and include unavoidable elements, such as spoilage, lost time, capacity not utilised in setting standards. The National Association of Accountants argues:

Revision of Standards

Standard Costs may be fixed for a period of three, six or eleven months or for an indefinite period. There are no definite rules for the selection of a particular period and each case is to be decided after considering the conditions prevailing in that business and the type of standard required to be established. Normally a period of one year is more realistic, as it coincides with the normal accounting period. Frequent revision of standards is very expensive and besides this it will defeat the purpose for which they are fixed. Periods longer than a year have the advantage of savings in clerical costs and continuity and uniformity in standard costs which would show trends over a longer period. A high degree of flexibility in the procedure is, however, necessary so that the long-term standards may be adjusted to suit current conditions. Where the prices of materials and wage rates are not likely to fluctuate appreciably, standard costs may be established for indefinite periods.

The main purpose of establishing Standard Costing System is to control actual performance by comparing with the standards. After standards are set, conditions may change because of change in methods of production, change in price level (revision of materials prices, labour rates, charges of gas, water, electricity, rates and taxes etc.) changes in specifications or designs of products (requiring more or less matereal or labour or change in the product mix and grades of labour required), and technological advances. Under such circumstances the management will have to change the entire standard cost structure. Some of the changes might have been anticipated and adjustments for the same might have been made while fixing the standards, but some of them might not have been anticipated. If the changes are of a temporary or a minor nature, then it is not advisable to revise the standards. It has already been stated that frequent revision caused by each change in working conditions is neither practicable nor desirable because if it is done, it loses its importance as a "measuring tool".

Any variance of costs due to deviations of actual conditions for the standards may be shown separately in variance. Analysis Reports as Revision Variance, so that management can be informed of the extent of change in cost.

TYPES OF STANDARDS

(A) Performance Level Standards

Performance Level Standards mean the quality or productivity expected from the inputs employed in production and other activities, and can be classified into two *viz.*, Theoretical/Ideal/Perfection Standards and Currently Attainable Standards. Theoretical or Ideal or Perfection Standards represent and expectation of the best performance given certain resources and equipment. These standards usually include allowance for rest periods of personnel but do not make any allowance for wastage, spoilage or lost time. These standards are the ultimate objective which the enterprise expects to strive for. The chances of attainment of the theoretical standards in actual day-to-day operations is rather remote. It may not be incorrect to say that the accomplishment of the theoretical performance level is not really possible.

Currently Attainable Standards could be in terms of performance levels which are 'Attainable Performance':

Attainable Performance is defined as Theoretical Performance minus unavoidable losses due to material spoilage, labour rest periods and fatigue and machine set-up time. Unlike theoretical standards, attainable standards are attainable. However, a hıgh efficiency in input management is required to achieve the attainable standards. Also the concept of attainable standards could be nebulous inasmuch as capturing all potential unavoidable losses in the input management process is difficult. Avarage Past Performance Standards are based on the historical data, which is taken as the reference level for building up standards for the future. However, if past performance has been bad then the standards tend to be loose and good performance in the earlier years would render the standard rather tight. The past periods chosen as a representative year has to be a normal year neither super-normal nor abnormal. But if the corporate policy is to employ tight standards then the representative year will be slanted in favour of yearls with extra-ordinary performance. And of the policy is to have loose standards, the years with poor performance will be the representative periods.

Normal Performance standards is a performance level likely to prevail over future period of years-over the product market life or over the phase of the business cycle. In terms of performance level it will lie in between the levels prescribed by Attainable Performance Level and Average Past Performance. Also, the normal standards are expectations which will characterize the average over a future set of years.

(B) Volume of Output

Volume of output standards can be expressed in terms of Theoretical capacity, Practical capacity, Normal activity, Expected activity. These terms have already been defined in the previous Chapter.

(C) Price Level Standards

Price level standards can be thought of in terms of Ideal Standards, Basic Standards, Current Standards and Normal Standards.

Ideal standards are set on the presumption of the most favourable prices likely to prevail for the inputs required. In at inflationary era, the idea of ideal standards will tend to be obsolete even while the standards are being set. Also favourable prices assumed can build-in frustration at the end of the budget period because of the unavoidable unfavourable variances. Also favourable prices imply less provision of cash for meeting obligations on cash account which can allow situations of deficit to emerge and cause difficulties and embarrassment. Ideal standards are strict standards and the performance level tends to be tight. Basic standards refer to the price level prevailing in a particular year. The said years is usually understood to be the first year following the establishment of standards. The basic standards do not undergo change following changes in the price level norms. Thus the basic standards present the index number of prices of the inputs *viz.*, materials, labour and factory overhead. It is analogous to the index number of prices. Current Standards mean the prices likely to prevail in the ensuing fiscal period. Based on the experience of the current year and the conditions likely to prevail in the coming future period the standards undergo revision. Normal Standards are price levels expected to prevail over a future period of time, say the product market life for the business cycle. These standards have a pre-determined tenure and undergo change only after the lapse of the tenure period.

(D) Physical Standards versus Financial Standards

Physical Standards are norms or input-output ratios expressed in physical terms such as the number of kilograms required or labour hours demanded for a given unit of output. It could also refer to broad norms such as number of personnel required for a given repair and maintenance operation or promotion activity. Physical Standards express the yardstick of performance in physical terms.

Financial Standards are norms or input-output ratios expressed in monetary terms, such as the rupee value of the input (material, labour overheads) required for a given unit of output. In fact, financial standards are always the product of the physical standards and the concerned price factor. Thus if the physical standard of materials for unit of output is 5 kgs. and the standard price of one kilogram is Rs. 4, the material price factor for a unit of output is Rs. 20 or the price factor for a kilogram of raw material input is Rs. 4. Again, financial standards can also be expressed in terms of broad norms such as monetary inputs required for any manufacturing or marketing operation. One more point needs to be reiterated. Physical planning precedes finance planning or financial standards stem from some physical standard with the price factor as the conversion link.

(E) Manufacturing and Non-Manfacturing Standards

Manufacturing Standards and standard and standard costs refer to the scientifically predetermined input-output ratios prescribed for production activity. The manufacturing segment lends itself to statistical measurement and hence input-output ratios can be, relatively speaking, easily prescribed. The input-output ratios are laid down after a lot a rigorous exercise with respect to choice of materials (material standards), motion and time studies (labour standards) and technical and engineering studies of production and service department facilities (factory overhead standards). Once again the norms are expressed as standards to begin with and eventually converted into monetary terms *i.e.* standard costs.

Non-Manufacturing Standards refer to input-output ratios for the non-manufacturing activities *viz.*, marketing administration. However, in the non-manufacturing segment input-output ratios cannot be prescribed with the same precision as the manufacturing segment. The activities of the marketing department depend to a great extent on the external economic and social environment. Thus, it is difficult of not impossible to quantify the number of can is to be made by a salesman before he attracts a favourable response from, the customers. Also, customers response in numbers and value is not easy to gauge to provide a yardstick in terms of input-output or 'call-response' ratio. In the marketing segment except for deliveries and commission all other inputs are fixed expenses and hence defy precise measurement through input-output, ratios.

The reason for this differential in behaviour between the manufacturing and non-manufacturing segments is not far to seek. Cost accounting techniques gained initial currency in the manufacturing segment. However, with the advancement in management science it may be possible to improve the situation in the non-manufacturing segment. And in time to come to the discriminating features of the two segments may disappear.

APPLLCATION OF THE TECHNIQUE OF STANDARD COSTING

Standard costing is not a method of costing just as process or job or unit costing. It is a system or technique of cost accounting which can be used in conjunction with process, job or operating costing without any difficulty, whatsoever, Industries where standard costing is more suitable can be categorised as under:

1. Engineering and textile industries where large range of products are manufactured.
2. Process industries where the method of production and nature of output are the same. The examples of such industries are chemical industries, distillaries, paper-making and metal processing etc.

3. Industries where the methods of manufacturing are repetitive and products are more or less homogeneous, *e.g.*, agricultural and food products.
4. Service industries where operation costing is also applicable like transport, gas and water, electricity etc.
5. Extraction industries such as coal, oil and timber.

Where the work is not repetitive, *e.g.*. construction work, contract work, ship-building and erection work etc., it is difficult to set standard and, therefore, standard costing would not be suitable. But in certain cases, it can be applied partially though not fully, at least to some advantage of the concerns.

DETERMINATION OF STANDARD COSTS

Installation of standard costing system for accomplishing the desired objectives require existence of certain pre-requisites. These pre-requisites can be put as follows:

(1) Existence of Budgetary Control System. Existence of budgetary control system is a pre-requisite for the standard costing system. Budgets fix the targets which the executives have to achieve. They create a sense of discipline, financial or otherwise, among employees at different levels. Budgets are the projections for the future and therefore they are of great use to the effective functioning of the standard costing system.

(2) Competent Staff. The successful operation of standard costing system requires existence of well qualified and trained staff for fixing of the standards, measuring performance and reporting variances to different levels of managements. The reports submitted to the management help the management in applying the principles of "management by exception" meaning thereby that the management pays attention only to those cases where performance is below or above the standard.

(3) Acceptance of the System. The standard costing system can have the desired effects only when the system is acceptable both to the management as well as to the workers. The management should take sufficient interest in the system to make it effective,

Similarly the workers should also believe that in the long run, the system would be beneficial to all of them. This is possible by fixing the standards in a way that they are capable of being achieved by an average worker.

(4) Reasonable Size. The system of standard costing can be introduced with advantage in concerns which are of a reasonable size. The system may not be suitable for small concerns since in their case careful scheduling of production may not be possible. For example, in a small concern a worker may be handling different machines and at times he may be called to handle different jobs and therefore, it may not be possible to correctly fix the standard time for different jobs or different operations handled by him. Moreover the system of standard costing requires specialisation of jobs and processes which may not be possible in a small concern.

(5) Efficient Accounting System. An efficient accounting system is also an essential requisite for successful operation of the standard costing system. The accounting information supplied should not only be accuarate but also be complete and up-to-date. The system of coding may be used for speedy recording and analysing the accounting information. Appropriate cost centre should also be set up in the organisation.

It has already been stated that the technique of standard costing requires pre-determination of standard cost. It became therefore, essential for us to understand how the standards are set. But before that it will be proper to consider the true meaning of the term "standard cost". Does it mean "ideal cost" or simply "cost based on past performance, or normal cost?" We are discussing below the different meanings which may be attached to the term "standard cost". There are, therefore, different bases on which standard costs may possibly be determined.

THE CONCEPT OF STANDARD HOUR

A standard hour is the expression of the actual output in terms of standard time instead of units. This would facilitate expression of dissimilar output in terms of a common factor. According to the Institute of Cost and Management Accountants, London, standard hour means: "A hypothetical unit pre-established to represent the amount of work which should be performed in one hour under standard performance." When the term standard hour is used it is assumed that it represents the amount of work to be done in sixty minutes. For example, if a welder welds one piece in 20 minutes according to the standard, the standard output in one clock hour will be 3 units. If the number of units actually produced in one day (of 8 hours) is 30, then the output can be expressed as 10 standard hours, though he has actually worked for 8 hours only. The concept of standard hour enables measurement of activity of a factory for producing dissimilar units and expressing them as a single measure. Accordingly, comparison of levels of activity between two periods can be done by converting the different output into standard hours.

Illustration.

A firm can produce 3 products, A, B and C the standard hours being fixed as 20, 25 and 35 respectively, The firm's output in 1975 were as follows:

	1975	*/976*
	Unils	*Unils*
A	10,00	12,000
B	8,00	5,900
C	5,000	7,000

Express the change in the level of activity in 1976 as a percentage of 1975 activity.

Solution.

Standard hours of output of 1975 and 1976:

		1975		*1976*
A	10,000 × 20	2,00,000	12,000 × 20	2,40,000
B	8,000 × 25	2,00,000	5,900 × 25	1,47,500
C	5,000 × 35	1,75,000	7,000 × 35	2,45,000
		5,75,000		6,32,500

Precautions in Use of Standard Costing

Ordinarily, the various variances that are worked out in standard costing may be relied upon to indicate the state of affairs and remedial action may be taken. For example, materials usage variance, if adverse, will indicate inefficiency in the use of materials; therefore, steps may be taken to remedy the situation and to pull up the foreman concerned. However, a degree of caution is necessary in coming to a conclusion on the basis of variances. Sometimes, they do not reveal the real situation without further inquiry. The following precautions may, therefore, be necessary:

(A) The emphasis should be on removing causes that lead to wastage or loss; for this, it is necessary that worker and staff members should frankly state what has happened. If the emphasis is one punishment, frankness will be missing; if punishment is not the idea, the real causes will come to light arid then proper remedial action should be possible.

(B) Price variance should not always be dismissed as beyond one's control. Could not the purchase be made at different point of time? Could not a substitute material be purchased? Stocks kept for a long time involve extra expense in the form of interest. How is this to be treated? Such questions should not be ignored.

(C) The real cause of the situation should be ascertained; for example, it is quite possible that extra time is being because repairs and maintenance work is not up to the mark.

(D) If the factors that existed when standards were framed have changed, it would be better to revise the standards realistically and them only compare them with actual performance. Suppose materials of a better quality are now available, this will call for revision of the materials standard. If a process has undergone change, the labour standard will need revision.

Standard Costing in India—A Glimpse of the Practices in Leading Companies

A company stated that they used standards only for manufacturing operations. They called these standards as target costs. They had established physical as well as monetary targets. They relied on historical costs, although transition to standards based on engineering specifications were in progress.

Another leading company mentioned that they did not have standards as referred to in accounting text-books. They made use of physical as well as monetary standards for controlling different activities. For example, in respect of service departments a great degree of control is exercised by applying physical standards. Such control is aided by arranging constant visits to the factories by members of the company's management audit team. In respect of production departments, they also applied value standards. In other words, standards were specified for each item of expenditure. However, even in these instances, control exercised was broad and general in nature rather than specific and individualistic. Standards were established to compare and measure the actual input and output and the resulting costs. Usage variance was a regular feature. Consumption standards were based on marginal usage and allowable wastage. This company did not lay down price standards, as it thought such standards would not serve any useful purpose. There was no sense in making price variance analysis. Company faced emergency situations more as a rule than as an exception whereby they were compelled to procure adequate quantities of raw material at an uneconomic price rather than stick to rigid economies of purchase price and face the shortage. It was stated that the economy achieved was more a result of technical development rather than buying policy. For example, company imported raw material, company developed a substitute made form castoroil which was never used before as a useful raw material input. The choice was mainly influenced by the low price of castor oil prevailing in India, as compared to other oils. So essentially the standards kept on changing as did the inputs.

Rationale of Standard Costs

Standard costs aid in the managerial process of planning control, evaluation and motivation. The process of planning starts with the establishment of standards and standard costs which have to be adhered to, if certain performance levels are to be attained.

Then the process of monitoring the extent of conformance or otherwise of the actual events (historic costs) with the intended events (established norms) starts *i.e.* Control. 'Given the variation of the actual events from the intended events attempts are made to evaluate the performance (favourable variance/unfavourable variance) so as to enable initiation of response action. And the favourable/unfavourable variances are also the basis for operating a reward/penalty system—bonuses/incentives for favourable variance and penalties of whatever sort for unfavourable variances. Thus, Standard Costs motivate personnel to achieve them and with a hope of reward or the fear of penalty.

In fact the entire process of initiating, evolving and implementing of a standard cost system is a motivational tool to the top middle and junior management to actively participate in the *modus operandi* of the control system and contribute to the success of the enterprise. By its very nature, the standard cost system involves the management and the managed in a common venture which seeks to steer the enterprise towards the direction of the best possible result-resource ratio. Standards motivate individuals and groups at all levels of responsibility towards organisational objectives, that is to say, it encourages goal directed behaviour. Again since standards and standard costs imply the laying down of norms for individual/group tasks, the structure must be so designed as to facilitate providing authority and pinpointing responsibility centres are evolved. And last but not the least standards/standard cost provide an opportunity and identify the need for all functional areas production, marketing, purchase, personnel and finance to come together and focus their attention towards the common goals that lie at the heart of the enterprise "Economic Performance". In this togetherness of the human resources, the financial controller and staff provide an important link and media of communication

So, we see that the entire process of management gets initiated on account of the installation and operation of a standard cost system—planning, control evaluation, motivation, organisation and co-ordination. Standards and standard costs provide a fillip to the practice of scientific management. In addition to contributing to scientific management within an enterprise, standards/standard costs also aid in specific functions like:

(i) Book-keeping Economy:	The anxiety of quick collection of historical data of current operations and the installation of an elaborate paraphernalia for the efficient data collection can be dispensed with. Informative financial statements can be prepared in advance and as and when actual data are ready comparisons can be made with the norms laid down. Data reporting is more efficient, in terms of time and money.
(ii) Product Costing: (Income determination and inventory valuation)	Pre-determined cost help in building product information in advance and facilitate the timely preparation of financial statements.
(iii) Formulation of Budgets:	Budgets, which represent a quantified expression of the intentions of management, are invariable guided by standards and standard costs. Thus, the budget process gets based on scientifically pre-determined input-output ratios.
(iv) Pricing Decision:	Pre-determined costs provide timely inputs to aid pricing decisions particularly for filling in tenders.
(v) Cost Reduction and Cost Consciousness:	Standards and standard costs discolse the gaps in actual performance *vis-a-vis* intended performance. Further investigation into the

causes of the gap reveal the weak spots of the enterprise and pave the way for corrective action. And the very presence of standards and standard costs inculcate sense of commitment towards cost norms and zeal to attain the cost targets. Thus, standard cost initiates and promotes cost consicousness.

Thus Standard Costs have a dual role in the organisation. As a generic contribution they facilitate the managerial process of planning, controlling, evaluation, motivation, organisation and co-ordination. In terms of specific functions they aid in the product costing, pricing decisions, budget formulation, book-keeping economy, and cost reduction and cost consciousness.

Flexible Budgeting under Standard Costing

In the foregoing pages of this chapter, framing of a budget for different levels of activity was discussed. In a system of standard costing, the levels of activity may be measured in terms of standard hours (Refer to Chapter 12 regarding the concept of standard hour). A flexible budget distinguishes variable costs from the fixed ones. The latter are also known as "capacity costs". This is to indicate that these costs are more relative to capacity rather than to the level of activity. If capacity is under utilised, naturally, level of activity would also be adversely affected, provided the efficiency factor does not intervene. The full impact of capacity utilisation is not reflected in the "Level of activity" due to the presence of the efficiency factor. Hence, in standard costing, while calculating the revised figure for fixed costs calculation is done in such a way that the comparison between fixed cost incurred and the revised budgeted fixed cost would clearly bring out the capacity imbalance.

The "flexible budget allowance" for fixed costs in a system of standard cost will not be constant for all levels of activity as in the case of a flexible budget without standard costing. The "flexible budget allowance" is defined as: "The expense which should be allowed for the level achieved." For example, if the fixed cost budget for 10,000 unit level of activity (100%) is Rs. 40,000, then the revised fixed cost budget for 8,000 unit level of activity (80%) will not be Rs. 32,000 (as it is not a variable cost) nor will it be Rs. 40,000. For, in that case, such a revised budget will not bring out the capacity imbalance prominently. The appropriate revised fixed cost budget is dependent upon capacity utilisation and efficiency. Supposing, in this case, the budgeted working\hours were 40,000 (at the rate of 4 hours per unit) and the actual working hours amount to 36,000 hours, then the level of activity has been affected by both capacity utilisation (less utilisation) and efficiency (adverse in this case). As the actual level of activity is only 8,000 units the capacity of fixed costs of the basis of Rs. 4 per unit $\left(\frac{\text{Rs. } 40,000}{10,000 \text{ units}}\right)$ would amount to only Rs. 32,000. Hence the under-recovery would amount to Rs. 8,000 *i.e.*, Rs. 40,000-32,000. The causes for the under-recovery are two fold, namely, capacity utilistion and efficiency. Under flexible budgeting with standard costing, we aim at reflecting the capacity imbalance prominently, while comparing the actual recovery with the revised budget. Hence, the original budget is revised on account of the influence of the efficiency factor, so that in comparison, the capacity imbalance is prominently brought out.

Thus, in this case, revised fixed cost budget for 80% level of activity, taking the present efficiency level, would be Rs. 36,000. This is arrived at by adjusting the original budget allowance for the efficiency factor. The efficiency is a adverse as 4,000 hours have been wasted. The recovery, therefore, for this 4,000 hours namely, Rs, 4,000, is adjusted against the original budget of Rs. 40,000. Hence, the revised budget is Rs. 36,000. A comparison of the actual recovery with the revised budget would show an adverse variance of Rs. 4,000, *i.e.*. Revised budget is Rs. 36,000-Actua recovery is 32,000. This shows the under-recovery due to capacity utilisation.

The reader could simply keep in mind the following formula in this connection:

Revised fixed cost budget = Original fixed cost budget ± Efficiency variance,

It should also be kept in mind that this sort of adjustment is necessary only under a system of standard costing, that too only in respect of fixed costs. Variable costs would always be proportionate to the volume.

Illustration.

The under mentioned information is available in respect of a factory for a period:

Budgeted working hours	= 50,000
Budgeted production	= 1,00,000 units
Budgeted fixed costs'	= Rs. 1,50,000
Actual working hours	= 48,000
Actual production	= 90,000 units
Actual fixed costs	= Rs. 1,45,000
Standard recovery rate for fixed cost	= Rs. 1.50 per unit

Work out the fixed cost allowance for the flexible budget. Also work out the variances.

Solution.

Revised fixed cost allowance = Original budgeted fixed cost ±
Efficiency Variance

Evidence variance = (Standard hours of Actual production –
Actual time taken × Standard recovery rate per hour)

(The standard recovery rate per hour in this case is Rs. 3, because budgeted fixed costs + budgeted working hours, *i.e.*, Rs. 1,50,000 + 50,000 hours=Rs. 3 per hours).

= (90,000 units ×½ hour per unit 48,000 hours) × Rs.3 per hour.

= Rs. 9,000 (Adverse).

Revised flexible budget allowance = Rs. 1.50,000 Rs. 9,000 = Rs. 1,41,000

∴ Capacity variance = Revised flexible budget-Actual recovery of fixed costs

= Rs. 1,41,000 Rs. 1,35,000

= Rs. 6,000 (Adverse).

Rs. 1,35,000 refers to recovery on 90,000 units at Rs. 1.50 per unit

Budget expenditure variance = Original budgetallowance—Actual expenditure.

= Rs. 1,50,000 - Rs. 1,45,000

= Rs. 5,000 (F).

An Alternative Approach. Yet another method of calculating the fixed cost allowance for flexible budget is by using the level of activity and capacity ratios instead of by calculating the variances. Here, again, in substance, the original budget is adjusted for the efficiency factor so that a comparison of the actual recovery with the revised budget would reflect the capacity imbalance. The original budget is increased/decreased by such percentage of that budget, the percentage being the difference between the level of activity ratio and capacity utilisation ratio. If the level of activity ratio is more than the capacity ratio, the difference percentage on original budget will be added to the original budget and if less, it will be deducted. For example,

Original budget	= Rs. 2,00,000
Level of activity ratio	= 90%
Capacity utilisation ratio	= 80%

Therefore, the difference between level of activity and capacity ratio is 10% (the former being higher).

Revised budget allowance

= Original budget ± (Level of activity ratio – Capacity utilisation ratio) × Original budget)

= Rs. 2,00:000 + [(90%—80%) × Rs. 2,00,000]

= Rs. 2,20,000.

6. (i) Ideal Costs

These are costs which should be there under ideal working conditions, ideal management and ideal plant capacity. Such an ideal is a myth, far from reality. Such a flight to imagination does not have any material significance in the eyes of a practical manager who is aware of certain limitations which exist in spite of every possible check, control, care and caution. Perfection can never be achieved when one has to deal with men, materials and machines and not simply figure. The feasibility of perfection is not possible, even in biological and mathematical sciences, what to talk of management science with involved handling of man in particular whose behaviour is totally unpredictable at any given time. Sometimes miraculous results are achieved due to certain abnormalities but with whatever is feasible if strived for. When the plant is working at maximum capacity or even at more than its capacity level perfection is a far cry and hence deal costs cannot be regarded as standard costs for managerial control.

(ii) Normal Costs

Such costs can be determined on the basis of the prevailing conditions of the business of industry. Thus, here it is assumed that plant is working at normal level of capacity and efficiency, workers are engaged in production activities performing their normal functions and the normal efficiency operations are being carried out. The cost shall thus be an average standard cost which is normally there in the business. Then, where would the management need control? How would the business progress and brighten its prospects, broaden and widen its field of activities and achieve prominence and success in the competitive market? Besides that, the meaning of 'normal' differs from one business to another. This suggests that normal levels of workmanship, efficiency, capacity and managerial operations are not significant and of worth for practical planning and control of costs.

(iii) Reasonably Attainable Costs

Costs which can be attained reasonably if the management tries for them, *i.e.* it makes a sincere and integrated effort to achieve the targets set in, can be regarded as a satisfactory yardstick or benchmark for standards. Her , we assume a level of operation which is certainly above the normal level of efficiency. It neither means perfection (an idea) nor the current conditions nor even the normal conditions. The management by fixing costs at such a level can make whole hearted efforts to bring down the actual cost to the level of standards and can achieve better efficiency in the field of business operations. Some authors feel that reasonable attainable standards cannot be regarded as standards for our purpose because it is difficult to set in the level between actual costs and ideal costs. But as a matter of fact, it is not at all difficult to set in such standards because we assume a better efficiency level than what is prevailing at present or even what shall prevail for which standards are being fixed.

Such standards are not a myth, a miracle or a moon for a baby but are practical, realistic, capable of being attained if conditions are improved, strict control is exercised wastes and in economies are checked and the utilisation of the present capacity is at the maximum or fullest possible level of efficiency. Such costs can serve the purpose of management as standards and hence can be adopted for comparison with actual costs. These standards will, of course, be elastic and dynamic. Elasticity and adaptability according to needs, is one of the foremost requisites of any good system and so is the case with the system of standard costs too. The standard fixed in the manner mentioned above is capable of being modified in accordance with the requirements of time and suitability of enterprise. Nevertheless they are not to be frequently changed; a suitability is tried to be maintained so that they can serve as useful guide for long-term planning and budgeting. It provides an incentive both to the workers and the executives and creates cost consciousness among them. An integrated effort shall be made round every corner to reduce the costs to the level of standards, and effective implementation of the system may prove to be a boon to the management. Thus standard cost of a product may be defined as "pre-determined cost based upon engineering specifications and representing highly efficient production for quantity standards and forecasts of future market trends for price standards, with a fixed amount expressed in rupees for material, labour and overhead for an estimated quantity of production."

(iv) Anticipated Costs or Expected

The costs which are expected to be incurred during a particular following period are cost which closely follow the pattern of present costs, though adjusted according to past behavioral pattern as well as future tendencies. But such cost would be on estimate of what the actual costs will be after the completion of the period for which the estimates have been prepared. As pointed out while distinguishing estimated costing from standard costing, such estimated costs do to provide any basis for comparison and control. Estimated cost is just a prediction of the actual costs, it is, in away, better than what the cost is or what the cost shall be under normal conditions. A standard should be fixed assuming a somewhat higher level of efficiency than what is reflected under the simple estimation of actual costs.

(v) Current Costs

The costs which are currently or presently being incurred are also not a useful guide for standard costs since they are neither in rhythm with past trends nor are inclusive of factors and conditions following ahead. Present is always to be adjusted for past as well as future. Current costs have even weaker ground for being regarded as a suitable basis for treatment as standards.

Current actual costs are, in one way, the costs which are most accurate to be assumed as standards if the conditions remain static and circumstances do not change. But this is seldom true in business and moreover we need cost control, the scope of which is absent if we adopt the current costs as standards.

Standards for Distribution and Administrative Activities

Most of the companies did not establish standards for distribution and administrative activities. Few companies did make use of distribution standards in formulation of budgets. For example, a budget to sell 1,000 tons of a product was the basis for forecasting requirements of salesmen on the business of number of calls a salesman could make to sell this product. Having once prepared the budgets, actual control of distribution expenses was effected by comparing actual with budgeted expenditure.

Even a company engaged mainly in selling and distribution activities and not establish and use standards to control these activities. The company thought that it was unrealistic to do so. They had two hundred product lines the cost of which varied from Rs.1 million for engineering equipment to 10 paise for a brand of a tablet for headache. The range of marketing operations included machinery, general engineering services, pharmaceuticals, baby food, etc. It is, therefore, necessary to modify such standards in light of experience and expected operations. Standards can be of two types—perfection and attainable. The perfection standards are strictly scientifically & determined and the attainment of which is a long-term objective. Whereas attainable standards are modified to suit the actual operating conditions.

❐

5

Capital Budgeting

Capital budgeting decisions, as already pointed out, pertain to fixed assets or long-term assets, which, by definition, refer to assets which are in operation, and yield a return, over a period of time, usually exceeding one year. The capital budgeting decision, therefore, involves a current outlay of outlays of cash resources in return for an anticipated flow of future benefits. In other words, the system of budgeting is employed to evaluate expenditure decisions which involve current outlays but are likely to produce benefits over a period of time longer than one year. These benefits may be either in the form of increased revenues or reductions in costs. Capital budgeting, therefore, includes addition, disposition, modification and replacement of fixed assets.

Capital budgeting deals with investment expenditure, implementation of projects and control over expenditure and resources. The disinvestment decisions having long-term implications should also be covered under capital budgeting decisions. Moreover, since running of a capital project does not require investment in fixed assets along it entails current asset investment also; therefore, the proposal should be examined in totality *i.e.* investment in the entire project involving expenditure on fixed assets as well as on current assets should be considered as a capital investment.

Capital budgeting is concerned with initiating a project or in expansion suggesting the desirability or otherwise of a given project considering the cash flows throughout the effective life of the project. If the availability of funds is ensured, an entrepreneur is interested in knowing the most appropriate choice among several proposals which met the basic objectives of business.

Capital budgeting refers to the long-range planning process that involves investing the firms' resources for a period longer than a year.

To make a capital budgeting decision, the financial consequences of each of the alternatives should be determined and the time period or time relationship of such consequences should be known. Thus "how much cash is received or paid out", together with, "when the cash is received or paid out" are important to determine before a comparison of different projects can be proceeded with. The non-financial considerations also play an important role sometimes, and they should also be taken care of.

The future success of a business depends on the investment decisions made today. The business is continually faced with the problem of deciding whether the commitments of resources-time or money are worthwhile in terms of the expected benefits. The solution of the problem is relatively easy if the benefits are to accrue reasonably some after the expenditure is made. However, the solution is more complex if the expected benefits are likely to accrue over several years.

Capital budgeting is a many-sided activity that includes searching new and more profitable investment proposals, investigating engineering and marketing considerations to predict the consequences of accepting the investment, and making economic analyses to determine the profit potential of each investment proposal.

The distinguishing features of capital budgeting decisions are:

1. The future benefits will occur to the firm over a series of years;
2. Current funds are exchanged for future benefits; and
3. There is an investment of funds in long-term activities.

Thus, time element lies at the core of capital budgeting.

The process of capital budgeting involves:

(i) Identification of potentially desirable investments;

(ii) Evaluation of the alternative proposals;

(iii) Selection of investments that meet the criteria laid down.

Before the process of capital budgeting is started, the criterion for evaluation must be determined. This will however depend on managerial objectives.

The capital budgeting analysis involves:

(i) A forecast of the costs and benefits of the project;

(ii) Discounting the funds invested in the project at an appropriate rate since money has a time value;

(iii) Assessment of the risk associated with the project; and

(iv) Follow-up to determine whether the project is performing according to expectations.

Nature

By its very nature, the capital budgeting decision is multi-disciplinary. As pointed out earlier it requires:

1. **Identification of Opportunities,** which in turn needs a close watch on the technological innovations, trends in markets and the economic environment.

2. **Appraisal of Alternative Proposals,** which requires the knowledge of costs and likely revenues in the future. It can be had by translating the technical parameters like machine speeds capacity, throughout rates, maintenance schedule etc., into appropriate costs and revenues besides making pricing decisions and the like.

3. **Examination of Organisational Ability to Undertake Complex Project,** the level of technology to be harnessed and managerial capabilities and other organisational support systems like information system etc. This is essential since investment decisions involve commitment of not only financial resources, but also the human and organisational resources. The skill of top managements is required to achieve this involvement and coordination, besides mobilising the needed resources.

4. **Anticipation of Likely Risks,** it includes balancing of these risks against likely returns from the investment. It

would also need the skill of the top management. Its attitude to wards risk is also very relevant for the purpose. The nature of the problem requires the involvement of heads of responsibility centres also, besides the top management.

CAPITAL BUDGETING IMPORTANCE

Capital budgeting decisions are of paramount importance in financial decision-making.

(a) **Such Decisions Affect the Profitability of a Firm.** They have also a bearing on the competitive position of the enterprise. This is mainly because of the fact that they relate to fixed assets. The fixed assets represent, in a sense, the true earning assets of the firm. They enable the firm to generate finished goods that can ultimately be sold for profit. However, current assets are not generally earning assets. Rather, they provide a buffer that allows the firm to make sales and extend credit. True, current assets are important to operations, but without fixed assets to generate finished products that can be converted into current assets the firm would not be able to operate. Further, capital budgeting decisions are "strategic" investment decisions as against "tactical"—which involve a relatively small amount of funds. Therefore, such capital investment decisions may result in a major departure from what the company has been doing in the past. Acceptance of a strategic investment will involve a significant change in the company's expected profits and in the risks to which these profits will be subject. These changes are likely 10 lead stockholders and creditors to revise their evaluation of the company. Thus, capital budgeting decisions determine the future destiny of the company. An opportune investment section can yield spectacular returns. On the other hand, an ill advised and incorrect investment decision can endanger the very survival even of large-sized firms. A few wrong decisions and the firm may be forced into bankruptcy.

(b) **A Capital Expenditure Decision has its Effect Over a Long Time.** Span and inevitably affects the company's future cost structure. To illustrate, if a particular plant has been purchase by a company to start a new product, the company commits itself to a sizeable amount of fixed costs in terms of labour, supervisor's salary, insurance, rent of the building, and so on. If the investment, in the future, turns out to be a successful or yields less profit than anticipated, the firm will have to bear the burden of fixed costs, break-even points, sales and profits will all be determined by the firm's selection of assets.

(c) **Capital Investment Decisions.** Once made, are not easily reversible without considerable financial loss to the firm. This is because there may be no market for second-hand plant and equipment and their conversion to other uses may not be financially feasible.

(d) **Capital Investment Involves Costs and the Majority of Firms have Scarce Capital Resources.** The underlines the need for wise and correct investment decisions, as an incorrect decision would not only result in losses but also prevent the firm from earning profits from other investments which could not be undertaken for want of funds.

Limitations

Capital expenditure decisions are of considerable significance to the firm as the future success and growth of the firm depends heavily on them. Unfortunately, they are not easy to take. There are a following limitations:

(i) The benefits from investments are received in some future period. The future is uncertain. Therefore, an element of risk is involved. For instance, a decision to acquire an assert that is going to last for 15 years requires a 15-years forecast. A failure to forecast correctly will lead to serious errors which can be corrected only at considerable expense. Revenue involves estimating the size of the market for a product and the expected share of the firm in that. These estimates depend on a variety of factors, including price, advertising and promotion, and sales effort. Adding to the uncertainties are the possibilities of shits in consumer preferences, new moves by competitors, technological developments and changes in the economic or political environment.

(ii) It is not often possible to calculate in strictly quantitative terms all the benefits or the costs relating to a particular investment decision.

(iii) Problems also arise because costs incurred and benefits received from the capital budgeting decisions occur in difference time periods. They are not logically comparable because of the time value of money.

RATIONALE OF CAPITAL BUDGETING

Where outlays of funds are made and results continue over an extended period of time, several implications of far-reaching importance follow in their wake and it is these implications which constitute the rationale of capital budgeting.

(1) Proper capital budgeting would also lead to better timing of assets acquisition and improvement in quality of assets purchased. This is due to the nature of demand for and supply of capital goods. The former does not arise until sales impinge on productive capacity and such situations occur only intermittently; on the other hand, production of capital goods involves a relatively long period of time so that the business would have ordinarily to wait for about a year or so before new capital goods become available. The matching of the need for capital goods with their availability is one of the functions of capital budgeting.

(2) A asset expansion is related to future sales, the economic life of the asset purchased represents an indirect forecast of sale for the duration of its economic life. Any failure to accurately make such a forecast would result in over-

investment or under-investment in fixed assets. An erroneous forecast of asset needs can result in serious consequences for the firm. If a firm has too much investment in fixed assets, it will be burdened with avoidable heavy expenditure and if it has not spent enough on such assets, its productive operations would be affected by inadequate capacity.

(3) By making a capital investment, the decision maker makes a commitment into future lossing some of his financial flexibility in the process. Thus the purchase of an asset based on an economic life often years requires a long period of waiting before the result of this action works itself out and, to that extent, he is at the mercies of future events.

(4) Asset expansion requires substantial funds which might not be immediately and automatically available. Therefore, a determined effort would have to be made to procure them. It is natural that capital expenditure programme of a sizeable amount would entail arrangements for finance well in advance to ensure their availability at the right time.

Thus, the size of funds involved in asset expansion and the fact that expenditures are designed to be recovered in future, which is distant and seemingly imperceptible, makes capital budgeting one of the most critical and crucial, delicate and difficult areas of managerial decisions. This is also due to the fact that so many variables-changes in the quality of the product, changes in the quantity of output, changes in the quality and quantity of direct labour, changes in the amount and cost of scrap, changes in maintenance expenses, down-time, flexibility etc. are involved in capital budgeting decisions that neat generalisations are impossible. This is not a routine clerical work to be performed on a mechanical basis though the electronic equipment has facilitated the same to some extent. It requires a continuous monitoring.

APPROACHES TO CAPITAL BUDGETING DECISIONS

There are three types of approaches to capital budget decisions, depending upon the quality of management. These are:

1. **Disaster Approach.** In many cases, the capital expenditure decisions are taken by management only when a disaster as, for example, a plant break-down. Similarly, when repair or overhaul of plant and machinery is not possible or when it has reached beyond its economic life, capital expenditure becomes inevitable. The disaster approach to capital budgeting is, thus, a situation of management by crisis and a glaring example of bad management.

2. **Passive Approach.** Under this approach, the emphasis is placed only on current needs. It is a situation of "manage as we go," living day-to-day basis. It is certainly an improvement over the first approach to capital budgeting, but this approach also lacks the wider perspective and long-term realities of changing horizons. In this situation, management is not a plan but an ongoing basis of making current decisions for total expenditure. Most of the large companies in India fall under this category.

3. **Dynamic Approach.** This is the most modem and effective approach to capital budgeting decisions. In this approach, the emphasis is on long-range planning where by symptoms are identified in advance and capital expenditures are the results of advance planning. Here, the capital budgeting decisions are based on market research, R and D, and technological changes. In India, there is now a growing awareness in most large companies especially in the public sector, to shift from the Passive to Dynamic approach to capital budgeting, wherein they study or scan the changing environments and opportunities of the industry both in India and abroad and plan their capital expenditure decisions accordingly.

STEPS INVOLVED IN PREPARING CAPITAL BUDGET

Capital budgeting decisions of a firm have a pervasive influence on the entire spectrum of entrepreneurial activities. They require a complex combination and know ledge of various disciplines for their effective administration. For example, Economics, Financial Mathematics, Economic Forecasting, flow projection and timing techniques and techniques of control. In order to tie all these elements, a financial manager must keep in mind the three dimensions of capital budgeting programme: Policy, Plan and Programme. These three P's constitute a sound capital budgeting programme. Dean proposes 10 specific elements in an investment programme, which are as follows:

(1) The first stage in the capital expenditure programme should be the conception of a profit making idea. It may be rightly called the organisation of investment proposals. The proposals may come from a rank and file worker of any department or from any line executive. To facilitate the organisation of such ideas a periodic review and comparison of earning, costs, procedures and product line should be made by the management.

(2) When a specific proposal is made to management, its consistency with the long-range plans of the company must be verified. It requires the determination of over-all capital budgeting policies before hand based upon the projections of short and long-run developments.

(3) Once the timeliness and priority of a proposal have been established, it should be listed on the one-year capital budget, as an indication of its approval.

(4) This stage involves the tentative acceptance of the proposal with other competitive projects, within the selection criteria of the company. Small projects under a certain rupee amount could be approved by the departmental head. Larger projects should be ranked according to their rate of return. Any one or more tests of profitability maybe used for it.

(5) This stage involves the comparison of a proposal with other projects within the selection criteria of the firm. This is done either by financial manager or by a capital expenditure planning committee. Such criteria should encompass the supply and cost of capital and the expected returns from alternative investment opportunities. Once the proposal passes this stage, it is authorised for outlays.

(6) Then comes the stage of establishing the priorities. When the accepted projects are put in priority, it facilitates their acquisition or construction, avoids costly delays and serious cost overruns.

(7) Once the financial manager has reviewed the projects, he will recommend a detailed programme, both of capital expenditures and of sources of capital to meet them, to the top management. Possibly, the financial manager will present several alternative capital expenditure budgets to the top management, it will finally approve the capital budget for the firm.

(8) This is a continuous phase that involves the preparation of reports for every other phase of the capital expenditure programme of the company.

(9) This phase makes the end of the cycle in tile life of a project. It involves more than the recovery of the original cost plus an adjustment for replacement programmes.

(10) An important and last step of the capital budgeting process is an evaluation of the programme after it has been fully implemented. Was the net investment greater than anticipated? Were the expected net cash benefits actually realised? Management can improve its capital budgeting techniques for the future as a result of an evaluation of past performance. Such an evaluation also has the advantage of forcing department heads to be more realistic and careful.

COMPONENTS OF CAPITAL BUDGETING PROGRAMME

The capital expenditure decisions are not the decisions of the Finance Department or top management alone. Involvement of line managers and staff men at different levels of management is essential for successful formulation and implementation of the programme. Capital budgeting is, therefore, regarded as an exercise in inter-dependency.

The basic components of capital expenditure programme of the following:

1. Setting up of corporate and divisional goals as well as plans and policies-both short-term and long-term.
2. Strong organisation base to ensure proper delegation of authority, team work, effective communication and coordinated efforts.
3. Developing basic criteria to be used in the choice of a project. These will have to be objective, relevant, reliable and sound and not based on whims and likes and dislikes of individuals. The different criteria used in capital budgeting may be enumerated in brief as follow:

   (a) ***Feasibility of the Project.*** Technical, economic, financial, organisational and social and political.

   (b) ***Return on Capital.*** Pay back of capital to determine the ability of the project *(i)* to yield a minimum desired rate of return, or *(ii)* to pay back the amount of capital investment as quickly as possible.

   (c) ***Risk Evaluation.*** The risk involved in a project to be carefully analysed, evaluated and, wherever possible, quantified. The quantification of risk is important as we expect higher returns from risky investment.

   (d) ***Essentiality.*** In many cases, urgency and essentiality would require abandonment of economic feasibility.

4. Developing effective framework for the formulation of capital expenditure programme. This will depend upon a number of factors *viz.*

   (i) Creative and systematic search for profitable opportunities through research and development.

   (ii) Formulation of management (ROI) and risk, etc.

   (iii) Administrative procedures; covering all the components of the programme, to be simple, uniform and inexpensive.

   (iv) Initiation, screening and preliminary scrutiny of the proposals.

   (v) Evaluation and final scrutiny. Regarding the justification of the project, its feasibility, and risk evaluation of assumptions and promises etc., consideration of available alternatives and then choice.

   (vi) Budgeting and approval. All the three parts of the budgets, current, short-term and long-term, to be prepared, taking into considerations financial and other constrains.

5. **Management of Capital Project.** This will involve, *(a)* assignment of responsibility for incurring expenditure; *(b)* control during the progress of the project of cost, time, value, and quality of work done; and *(c)* coordination and motivation for the effective implementation of the programme:

6. **Post-completion Audit.** A project completion report is prepared wherein the entire operations are reviewed by top management and policies, procedures and organisation adopted in the light of the past experience. Mistakes are identified, evaluated and corrected for future projects. This basis objective of post-completion audit is not finding faults but learning from the past mistakes to do better in the future.

A capital budgeting programme thus involves the entire organisation and is a continuous process. It may, however be noted that the first four components—(1) to (4)—of the capital budgeting the programme relate to the formulation or pre-completion phase of the programme while the last two—(5) and (6)—relate to the implementation or post-completion phase. The success of the programme depend on both.

DATA FOR CAPITAL EXPENDITURE DECISIONS

The type of costs required in capital investment decisions differs from those reflected in the accounting records because only future costs are relevant for such decisions. Recorded costs may be useful but only to extent that they furnish a starting-point for future costs projections.

All estimated cash costs pertinent to the project under consideration should be included; and expected savings in material costs, particularly those arising from an expected reduction in scrap, should be reflected; prospective changes in direct labour, materials, handling, inspection etc., should be reckoned; anticipated increases or decreases in specific overhead costs, such as taxes, insurance power; maintenance, repairs, supplies, etc., must be considered.

The use of plant overhead rate should be avoided. Very often the new equipment is more automatic than the old and a different cost pattern will emerge. Thus, there is a reduction in supervision, overtime premiums and other overhead costs which have a tendency to vary with direct labour while there is an increase in repairs, maintenance, power and other costs varying with machinery usage.

Opportunity Costs

These costs play an important role in capital budgeting decisions. Opportunity costs represent the loss of alternative income as a consequence to actions adopted. To illustrate, in an expansion project, the economic rather than the book value of the space required for expansion should be taken into account against a proposed investment; in a replacement decision, the realizable value of the existing asset should be treated as a reduction of the cost of replacement.

Estimating the Revenue from Proposed Capital Investments

In capital investment studies, differential revenue, where measurable, cannot be ignored. There are to facets to this problem the potentiality or capacity for the asset under consideration and the marketability of increased output.

The estimation of the potential output of an asset is an engineering exercise and generally can be determined without much difficulty. Estimating the marketability of the product is considerably more difficult. In some situations, where the demand for a company's products is expected to remain unsatisfied, the estimated capacity of the prospective asset would be more or less equivalent to units sold. Generally, however, the determination of future revenue possibilities is more hazardous and involves a multitude of factors, such as consumer reactions, economic conditions and activities of competitors, etc. Under such conditions, and particularly where the proposed capital expenditure is substantial, a formal market survey may be warranted.

Depreciation

Depreciation is another cost whose treatment in capital investment analysis differs from other cost accounting reports and analysis. In calculations designed to reveal the desirability of replacing existing machinery and equipment, depreciation of the unabsorbed book value of an existing asset is a sunk cost and is not relevant except for its tax effects it is only the economic value of the asset that has relevance in replacement decisions. The common error, except for tax savings, of including a loss on the undepreciated book balance of the existing asset in the replacement analysis imposes an unjustifiable penalty on the prospective asset and injects an unwarranted element of conservatism into the replacement decisions.

Interest Cost

Accounting reports and statements typically give recognition to contractual interest but ignore imputed interest on capital. While the inclusion of interest is indispensable studies, the determination of an appropriate rate presents difficulties. Interest sometimes is misunderstood as being the same as: return on investment which consists of two elements of interest and profit. The former represents the cost of money while the latter is the reward or risk and uncertainty. Interest cost constitutes the minimum acceptance criterion for capital investment projects undertaking for profit. A firm must at least recover its money costs before it can realise a profit on its own investment. On the other hand, the minimum acceptance criterion that can be considered as a reward for risk and uncertainty varies with the nature of the risk assumed.

Income-taxes and Capital Investments

Payment of income-tax results in cash expenditure. Income-tax is an important element in capital-investment decisions as capital investments are based on cash flows. Though the undepreciated book balance of a displaced asset is a sunk cost; it does constitute a tax-deductible cost and, to that extent, is pertinent in replacement decisions. The sale of an old asset also effects income-taxes so that losses sustained on the disposition of an old asset are first applied against any capital gains available, any excess being deductible in full form ordinary taxable income.

Income-taxes have other effects on capital-investment decisions. The privilege of being able to carry forward operating losses encourages capital expansion by reducing the risk involved. The complexities of tax laws and applicable legal decisions emphasize the need for skill in this area. Therefore, it is desirable for a company to have its own tax cell, or outside tax consultant, to participate in all major capital-investment decisions.

METHODS OF RANKING INVESTMENT PROPOSALS

In most business firms there are more proposals for projects than the firm is able and willing to finance. Some proposals are good, others are different and yet anothers poor. A screening process has to be devised for finding out the real content of such proposals; methods of differentiating between them have to be developed and for this purpose, a ranking procedure has to be evolved. Essentially, the ranking procedure envisages relating of a stream of future earnings to the cost of obtaining those earnings. Among the many methods of ranking investment proposals the following four, are very widely used, though there are many variations in the technique and there are strong as well as conflicting opinions on the fundamentals of different basic approaches:

(1) Urgency or Essentiality.

(2) Pay Back Method.

(3) Average Rate of Return Method or Accounting method.

(4) Discounted Cash Flow Method:

  (a) Time adjusted rate of return or internal rate of return method.

  (b) Excess Net Present Value Method.

  (c) Terminal Value Method.

  (d) Profitability Index or Benefit Cost Ratio.

(1) Urgency or Essentiality

Many phases of business operations are managed in an ad-hoc manner instead of as part of a well-conceived plan. Thus, if there is a breakdown of an old machine, it must be hastily, though uneconomically, replaced in order to avoid disruption in production. However, all repairs, maintenance and replacements should be within the framework of an overall equipment policy which considers future cost comparisons and timings because outlays on all these should be compounded together and matched against future benefits and alternatives. In case this fundamental principle is ignored, though the pressure of the moment may lead to quick remedial action which might be correct on logical grounds, such action is correct in most cases by coincidence rather than methodical analysis. It is, therefore, natural that, when a projected outlay is large and far-reaching in its effect, urgency should not be a convincing influence. Further, the considerations of urgency import extraneous factors into capital budgeting decisions thereby relegating economic considerations into the background as individual manager's power of persuasion influences the spending decision of policy makers.

(2) Pay Back Method

The pay back method is the other traditional method of capital budgeting. It is the simplest and, perhaps, the most widely-employed, quantitative method for appraising capital expenditure decisions. This method answers the question. How many years will it take for the cash benefits to pay the original cost of an investment, normally disregarding salvage value? Cash benefits here represent CFAT. Thus PB measures the number of years required for the CFAT to pay back the original outlay required in an investment proposal.

There are two ways of calculating the Pay back (PB) period. The first method can be applied when the cash flow stream is in the nature of annuity for each year of the project's life. *i.e.* CFAT is uniform. In such a situation, the initial cost of the investment is divided by the constant annual cash flow:

$$PB = \frac{\text{Investment}}{\text{Constant annual cash flow}}$$

For example, an investment of Rs. 40,000 in a machine is expected to produce CFAT of Rs. 8,000 for ten years. Then,

$$PB = \frac{\text{Rs. } 40,000}{\text{Rs. } 8,000} = 5 \text{ years}$$

The pay back period of 5 years signifies that the investment in the purchase of the machine will be recovered in five years. In other words, 20% of the capital invested in the zero time period is recovered every year.

The second method is used when a project's cash flows are not equal, but vary from year to year. In such a situation, PB is calculated by the process of cumulating cash flows till the time when cumulative cash flows become equal to the original investment outlay. Following Table evaluates an investment proposal which costs Rs. 50,000 and yields CFAT of Rs. 8,000, Rs. 12,000, Rs. 15,000, Rs. 20,000, Rs. 21,000 and Rs. 24,000 in years I to 6 respectively.

Table

Year (1)	*Annual CFAT* (*Rs.*) (2)	*Cumulative CFAT* (*Rs.*) (3)
1	8,000	8,000
2	12,000	20,000
3	15,000	35,000
4	20,000	55,000
5	21,000	76,000
6	24,000	1,00,000

From above Table, it is apparent that the PB period would lie between the third and the fourth year. The cumulative cash flow at the beginning of the fourth year is Rs. 55,000 which exceeds the initial cost of the investment of Rs. 50,000. Therefore, the recovery of the investment lies some where between the third and the fourth year, the pay back period being three years plus a fraction of a year. To calculate the fraction, we are required to simply divide the amount of funds needed to recover the investment in the fourth year by the amount of cash flow in that year. The amount recovered up to the end of the third year is Rs. 35,000, the balance amount required is Rs. 15,000 to recover the total investment of Rs. 50,000. The cash inflow of the fourth year is Rs. 20,000. The pay back fractions is 0.75 *i.e.* $\frac{\text{Rs. } 15,000}{\text{Rs. } 20,000}$ Thus, the PB period for the project is 3.75 years.

The pay back period can be used as a decision criterion to accept or reject investment proposals. One application of this technique is to compare the actual pay back with a pre-determined pay back, *i.e.*, the pay back set up by the management in terms of the maximum period during which the initial investment must be recovered. If the actual pay back period is less than the pre-determined pay back, the project would be accepted, if not, it would be rejected. Alternatively, the pay back can be used as a ranking method. When mutually exclusive projects are under consideration, they may be ranked according to the length of the pay back period. Thus, he project having the shortest pay back may be assigned rank one, followed in that order so that the project with the longest pay back would be the lowest. The term "mutually exclusive" refers to proposals from which only one can be accepted to the exclusion of others. Obviously, projects with shorter pay back period will be selected.

Advantages

(a) It is easy to understand and simple to operate.

(b) A firm, which is short of cash, must necessarily place a premium on quick return of its funds and, therefore, lays much stress by the payback method. It is, thus, clear that such a situation puts an undertaking under conditions of a nature which leaves no other alternative for it than to adopt the payback method not so much because it leads to the best decisions but because best decisions are not alternatives available to the firm due to pressing needs of cash flows.

(c) The short-term approach typified by the payback method reduces the possibility of loss through obsolescence.

(d) The use of payback method is preferred on the ground that returns beyond three or four years are so uncertain as to disregard them altogether in a planning decision.

(e) It is an improvement over the criterion of urgency.

Thus, it is a handy device for evaluation investment proposals where precision in estimates of profitability is not important, preliminary screening of a number of proposals is necessary, a weak cash and credit position has an all-important bearings on the selection of investment possibilities and the contemplated project is extremely risky.

Limitations

(a) The first major shortcoming of the pay back method is that it completely ignores all cash inflows after the pay back period. This could be very misleading in capital budgeting evaluations. Under the pay back method, however, both the projects would be given equal ranking which is apparently incorrect. Therefore, it cannot be regarded as a measure of profitability. Its failure lies in the fact that it does not consider the total benefits accruing from the project.

(b) Another deficiency of the pay back method is that it does not measure correctly even the cash flows expected to be received within the pay back period in that it does not differentiate between projects in terms of the timing or magnitude of cash flows. It considers only the recovery period as a whole. This happens because it does not discount the future cash inflows but rather treats a rupee received in the second or third year to be as valuable as a rupee received in the first year. In other words, to the extent that the pay back method fails to consider the pattern of cash inflows, it ignores the time value of money.

(c) Another flaw of the pay back method is that it does not take into consideration the entire life of the project during which cash flows are generated. As a result, projects with large cash inflows in the latter part of their lives may be rejected in favour of less profitable projects which happen to generate a larger proportion of their cash inflows in the earlier part of their lives.

The above weakness notwithstanding, the pay back method can be gainfully employed under certain circumstances. In the first place, where the long-term out look, say in excess of three years, is extremely hazy the pay back method may be useful. In a politically unstable country, for instance, a quick return of the investment is the primary goal, and subsequent profits are almost unexpected surprises. Likewise, this method may be very appropriate for firms suffering from a liquidity crisis. A firm with limited liquid assets and no ability to raise additional funds, which nevertheless wishes to undertake capital projects in the hope of easing the crisis, might use pay back as a selection criterion because it emphasis so quick recovery of the firm's original outlay and little impairment of the already critical liquidity situation. Thirdly, the pay back method may also be beneficial in taking capital budgeting decisions for such firms which lay more emphasis on short-run earning performance rather than long-term growth. In brief, the pay back period is a measure of liquidity of investments rather than their profitability. Thus, the pay back period should more appropriately be treated as a constraint to be satisfied than as a profitability measure to be maximised. Finally, the pay back period is useful, apart from measuring liquidity, in making calculations in certain situations. For instance, the internal rate of return can be computed easily from the pay back period. The pay back method is a good approximation of the internal rate of return which otherwise requires atrial and error approach. A detailed account of this is given while discussing the Internal Rate of Return Method (IRR) as a time-adjusted technique to evaluate capital expenditure decisions.

To conclude, there are two major drawbacks of the traditional techniques of appraising capital investment decisions as discussed above. They do not consider the total benefits associated with an investment proposal. In addition, they ignore the pattern of benefits in terms of the magnitude and timing of cash inflows. For these reasons the traditional methods are unsatisfactory as capital budgeting decision criteria. The two essential ingredients of a theoretically sound appraisal method, therefore, are that *(i)* it should be based on a consideration of the total cash stream, *(ii)* it should consider the time value of money as reflected in both the magnitude and the timing of expected cash flows in each period of a project's life. The time-adjusted or discounted cash flow techniques satisfy these requirements and, to that extent, provide a more objective basis for selecting and evaluating investment projects.

The remaining two methods such as: Average rate of return method, and

Discounted Cash Flow methods are discussed in detail in next questions.

AVERAGE RATE OF RETURN METHOD

The average rate of return (ARR) method of evaluating proposed capital expenditure is also known as "the accounting rate of return method". It is based upon accounting information rather than cash flow. There is no unanimity regarding the defmition of the rate of return. There are many alternative methods of calculating the ARR. The most common usage of the average rate of return expresses it as follows:

$$ARR = \frac{\text{Average annual profits after taxes}}{\text{Average investment over the life of the project}} \times 100$$

Average annual profits after taxes Average investment over the life of the project The average as profits after taxes are determined by adding up the after tax profits expected for each year of the project's life and dividing the result by the number of years. In the case of annuity, the average after-tax profits are equal to any year's profit.

The average investment is determined by dividing the net investment by 2. This averaging process assumes that the firm is using straight-line depreciation, in which case the book-value of the assets declines at a constant rate from its purchase price to zero at the end of its depreciable life. This means, that on the average, firm will have one-half of their initial purchase price in the books. Consequently, if a machine has salvage value, then only the depreciable cost (cost minus salvage value) of the machine should be divided by 2 in order to ascertain the average net investment, as the salvage money will be recovered only at the end of the life of the project. Therefore, an amount equivalent to the salvage value remains tied up in the project throughout its life time. Hence, no adjustment is required to the sum of the salvage value to determine the average investment. Likewise, if any additional net working capital is required in the initial year of the project life which is likely to be released only at the end of the project's life, the full amount of working capital should be taken in determining the relevant investment for the purpose of calculating ARR. Thus, the average investment consists of the following:

Net working capital + Salvage value + 1/2 (Initial cost of machine-Salvage value)

Example.

	(Rs.)
Initial investment	
(Purchase of machine)	11,000
Salvage value	1,000
Working capital	12,000
Service life	5 years

The straight-line method of depreciation is adopted. The average investments is:

Rs. 2,000 + Rs. 1,000 + 1/2 (Rs. 11,900 – Rs. 1,000)

= Rs. 8,000

Example.

Determine the average rate of return from the following data of two machine A and B:

	Machine A	*Machine B*
Cost	Rs.56,125	Rs.56,125
Annual estimated income after depreciation and income tax:		
I Year	3,375	11,375
II Year	5,375	9,375
III Year	7,375	7,375
IV Year	9,375	5,375
V Year	11,375	3,375
	36,875	36,875
Estimated life in year	5	5
Estimated salvage value	3,000	3,000
Average income tax rate	55%	55%

Depreciation has been charged on a straight-line basis.

Solution.

$$ARR = \frac{\text{Average income}}{\text{Average investment}} \times 100$$

$$\text{Average income} = \frac{\text{Total income}}{\text{Number of years}}$$

$$\text{Average income of machine A} = \frac{\text{Rs. } 36,875}{5} = \text{Rs. } 7,375$$

$$\text{Average income of machine B} = \frac{\text{Rs. } 36,875}{5} = \text{Rs. } 7,375$$

Average investment

= Salvage value + ½ (Cost of machine – Salvage value)

= Rs. 3,000 + 1/2 (Rs. 56,125 – 3,000)

= Rs. 3,000 + 1/2 (Rs. 53,125)

= Rs. 3,000 + Rs. 26,562.50 = 29,562.50

Average investment for machines A and B would be 29,562.50

$$\text{ARR machine A and B} = \frac{\text{Rs. } 7,375}{\text{Rs. } 29,562.50} \times 100$$

= 24.95% Approximately

The average rate of return for machine A and B is 24.95%

In addition to the above, there are other approaches to calculate the ARR. One approach, which is a variation of the above involves using original rather than the average cost of the project. In the case of this alternative approach the ARR for both the machines would be 13.14% (Rs. 7,375 ÷ Rs.56,125).

Another approach towards calculating the ARR involve using annual cash flows instead of the average annual accounting profits as the numerator. It requires calculation of the relevant cash inflows. To find out cash flows after taxes (CFAT), we have simply to add back the amount of depreciation (D) to each year's earnings after taxes (EAT). Depreciation charges per year for both the machines of

Example 2 would be Rs. 10,625 [Rs.56, 125 – Rs. 3,000) 5]. Thus, Rs. 10,625 will be added to EAT every year to find the CFAT.

With the help of the ARR, the financial decision-maker can decide whether to accept or reject an investment proposal. According to the ARR as an accept-reject criterion, the actual ARR would be compared with a predetermined or a minimum required rate of return or cut-off rate. A project would qualify as acceptable if the actual ARR is higher than the minimum desired ARR, otherwise it is liable to be rejected. Alternatively, the ranking method can be used to select or reject proposal. Thus, the alternative proposals under consideration may be arranged in descending order of magnitude, starting with the proposal with the highest ARR and ending with the proposal having the lowest ARR. Obviously, projects having higher ARR would be preferred to projects which have lower ARR.

Advantages

The average return method of ranking investment proposals in considered to be superior to the payback method and, in the position of some, it is probably the most satisfactory method. It takes into account savings over the entire economic life of the project even though estimates of distant future may be subject to wide margins of errors. Hence, correct comparisons of the value of projects can be made. In case this method is used, the fact that projects may differ widely in character does not impede comparisons. Further, new product investments can be compared with cost reducing projects or a proposal this year can be compared with one which will not be ready until next year. Another strong point in favour of the method has been held out to be that it embodies the concept of net earning after allowing for depreciation as it is of vital importance in the appraisal of a proposal.

Limitations

However, this method of evaluating investment proposals also suffers from some serious deficiencies.

(a) The main shortcoming of the ARR approach arises from the use of accounting income instead of cash flows.

Earnings calculations ignore the reinvestment potential of a project, while the cash flows take into account this potential and, hence, the total benefits of the project. This drawback can be overcome by using the modified ARR approach which involves average cash flows instead of the average profits.

(b) Secondly, the ARR criterion of measuring the worth of an investment does not differentiate between the size of the investment required for each project. Competing investment proposals may have the same ARR, but may' require different average investments. The ARR method, in such a situation, will place the firm in an indeterminate position.

(c) Thirdly, this method does not take into consideration any benefit which can accrue to the firm from the sale or abandonment of equipment which is replaced by the new investment. The "new" investment, from red in terms of incremental cash outflows due to new investment the ARR method does not make any adjustment in this regard to determine the level of average investments. Investments in fixed assets are determined at their acquisition cost.

(d) Final, shortcoming of ARR is that it does not take into account the time value of money. That the timing of cash inflows and outflows is a major variable in financial decision-making is a well established fact. Accordingly, benefits in the earlier years and later year cannot be valued at par. To the extent that the ARR method treats these benefits at par and falls to take account of the differences in the time value of money, it suffers from a serious deficiency. Thus, the ARR in case of both machines A and B is the same, although machine B should be preferred since its return in the early years of its life is greater compared to that of machine A. Clearly, the ARR method of evaluating investment proposals fails to consider this.

DISCOUNTED CASH FLOW METHOD

Importance of Time and Cash Flows

An investments are essentially outlays of funds in anticipation of future returns, the presence of time as factor in investment fundamental, rather than incidental, to the purpose of emanating investments. Time is always crucial for the investor so that a sum received today is worth more than the same sum to be received tomorrow. Thus, in evaluating investment projects, it is important to consider the timing of returns on investments. In a way, time is the dimension through which the monetary variables involved in investments—the capital outlays and subsequent receipls—must be related.

Discounted cash flow technique considers the net cash flow as representing the recovery of original investment, plus a return on capital invested.

Time-Adjusted Rate of Return or Internal Rate of Return Method

Time-adjusted rate is used when the cost of investment and the annual cash inflows are known while the unknown rate of earning is to be calculated. Thus; net cash investment on a capital expenditure proposal, its economic life and the annual net cash earnings therefrom having been determined, these relationships can be combined to compute a rate of return on investment and concurrently, the return on investment. In a language of compound interest, the rate of return will be that rate—the internal rate of return or time-adjusted rate of return—at which the present values of cash inflows and out-flows set off each other. Discounted cash flow method, therefore, treats as separate variables in an equation each year's cash receipts from an investment project and applies discount factors, which go on increasing as earnings become more remote in time, with the object of computing a rate of return so that a project's cash flow discounted at this rate will equal the initial investment. As a matter of fact, determination of this rate of return is one of the difficult problems connected with this method.

The method's mathematical formulation is based on algebraic treatment which is common to all calculations involving compound interest. To illustrate, where Rs. 200 are invested at 5 per cent compounded annually for two years, at the end of the first year the amount would become Rs. 210 *i.e.* Rs. 200 plus Rs. 10 interest, which may be algebraically stated as 200 (1 + r); for the second year it would be 200 $(1 + r)^2$ and so on. In case it is known that initial investment of Rs. 200 would accumulate to Rs. 220,50 at the end of the second year, the rate of return can be computed by solving the value of r in the equation 200 $(1 + r)^2$ = 220,50 or 200 = 220.50 $(1 + r)^2$. If for this simple example, symbols are substituted for numbers making C stand for initial investment and E return, the essential symbolic formulation of discounted cash flow method would be:

$$C = \frac{E}{(1+r)}$$

Of course, earnings may accrue not only during one year but during many years. Accordingly, as many earning symbols are required as there are years during which earnings have been generated so that the formula used by the discounted cash flow method would be:

$$C = \frac{E_1}{(1+r)} + \frac{E_2}{(1+r)} + \frac{E_3}{(1+r)} + \frac{E_n}{(1+r)}$$

Where E_1, E_2, E_3 are the cash earnings of years, 1,2,3 et., C is required investment and r is the rate of return.

Thus, it is clear that, when using the discounted cash flow method, the analyst must determine the amount of required investment and estimate the net cash flow over the investment's life in order to solve for the remaining unknown, the rate of return. It is possible that the algebraic formulation of the method may be felt to be a little involved and its application difficult, so that time-adjusted rate of return can also be calculated, where cash flow is the same during the life of an investment, with the held of Annuity Table (No. II) showing present value of Re. 1 received annually over no years by using the following two steps:

The factor to be located in the relevant annuity table (No. II) is to be calculated. This factor reflects the same relationship of investment and cash inflows as do the payback calculations. Thus

$$F = \frac{1}{C}$$

Where,

F = Factor to be located.

I = Original Investment.

C = Cash inflow per year.

The factor thus calculated is located in Table II on the line representing the number of years corresponding to the estimated useful life of the asset and the relative discount percentage, representing the rate of return, would be estimated.

To illustrate, when the initial cost of an equipment is Rs. 6,000 and the cash flow for five years estimated to be Rs. 2,000 per year, the factor to be located in Table II would be 3 $\left(\frac{\text{Rs. } 6,000}{\text{Rs. } 2,000} = 3\right)$ and, when placed on the line of five years, the discount percentage would be somewhere between 18 percent (Rs. 3.127 present value of Re. 1) and 20% (Rs. 2.99 present value of Re.1), thereby indicating that the time-adjusted rate of return for the equipment proposal is more than 18 per cent but less than 20 per cent Though it is possible to interpolate a more specific rate between 8 per cent and 20 per cent the resulting accuracy must be regarded as spurious in view of the future cash inflows and the life span of the asset being only estimate; it would ordinarily be enough for the management to know that this proposal promises a return of slightly under 20 per cent.

In economic term or the rate of return, is the rate of interest at which the investor could borrow the needed investment funds and just repay his loan with interest by means of return therefrom, leaving nothing for himself. In other words, it is the maximum rate of interest he could afford to pay without having to subsidize a project. The profitability of prospective interest by means of return therefrom, leaving nothing for himself. In other words, it is the maximum rate of interest he could afford to pay without having to subsidize a project. The profitability of prospective investment is then judged by comparing this rate with the rate at which money can actually be obtained. Higher the rate of return relative to the market cost of capital, the more profitable is the investment.

The discounted cash flow method is useful in selecting among two or more competing capital proposals with different cash flows and estimated lives under certain conditions. This is illustrated by the following example.

Comparison of Competing Proposals—Discounted Cash Flow Method

	Machine A	*Machine B*
Estimate Life	15 years	10 years
Initial Cost	Rs. 8,000	Rs. 10,000
Estimated average annual cash revenue	Rs. 2,200	Rs. 2,700
Less: Estimated average annuai cash costs	Rs. 900	Rs. 1,000
	Rs. 1,300	Rs. 1,700
Rate of Return (As per Table II)	14% app	11% app.

Thus, machine A yields a higher rate of return though its annual cash income is Rs. 400 less than that of machine B. Such a situation has arisen due to the longer life of machine A.

The discounted cash flow method is particularly useful in situations where the estimated net cash receipts do not follow an even flow pattern.

EXCESS OR PRESENT VALUE

This method generally establishes 'a target'—a minimum rate below which a proposal would be rejected by management as undesirable in the light of the prpfit goals and above which it would be considered favourable and seeks to determine whether present value of estimated future cash inflows at management's desired rate of return will be greater or less than the cost of the proposal. Thus, cash inflow, initial investment and desired rate of return are given in this method while the present value of cash inflows and its deviation from initial investment are to be determined.

The profitability of a project ascertained by comparing the amount which meets the stated condition, *i.e.*, pre-determined minimum rate, with the actual amount of investment required by the contemplated project. If a project's earnings could return with interest at the market rate an amount of capital greater than that actually required for investment in the project, the project is adjudged profitable. The basis for such a conclusion is that, in case a business could borrow more than is actually required for investment in a project and repay this greater amount with interest from the projects earnings, it follows that it would borrow exactly the smaller amount needed and, after paying this with interest, retain some of the earnings for itself.

In terms of the formula of the discounted cash flow method given above, r is the known cost of capital under the present value method while the first part of the equation is the value of all future earnings discounted to the present by the market cost of capital. Thus, the algebraic formulation for the method is

$$V = \frac{E_1}{(1+i)^1} + \frac{E_2}{(1+i)^2} + \frac{E_3}{(1+i)^3} + \frac{E_n}{(1+i)^n}$$

where E_1, E_2, E_3, are the net cash earning of the years 1, 2 and 3 etc., it is the market cost of capital, and V is the present value of market cost of capital.

The profitability of investment project is determined by comparing V with C, *i.e.*, required investment in the project; the greater the ratio V/C, the more profitable is the project. Only those projects are profitable for which V/C is greater than unity because, where this condition is not fulfilled, the funds required for investment cannot be fully repaid with interest from out of the earnings.

In simple language, the steps involved in the method on the-basis of Annuity Table (No.II), showing the present value of Re. 1 received annually for no years, are as follows:

(i) The present value of the stream of cash savings from the equipment at management's desired rate of return is computed. This is done by multiplying the annual cash, inflow with the factor located from the Annuity Table at the point of intersection of the given interest rate column with the line number of years corresponding to the life of the asset.

(ii) The investment is subtracted from the present value of cash savings, thus determined, to arrive at the excess present value.

To illustrate, where the initial cost of an equipment is Rs. 6,000, cash inflows for five year are estimated to be Rs. 2,000 per year and the management's desired minimum rate of return is 15% after taxes, the present value of the stream of cash savings, would be Rs. 6,704 (Rs. 2000 × 3.352) and the excess present value would be Rs. 704 (6,704 – 6,000). The equipment proposal is 'attractive according to this method inasmuch as, though the management would be willing to pay Rs. 6,704 for a stream of cash payments of Rs. 2,000 each for the five years, it can buy the equipment for Rs. 6,000 only there by enabling the management to net the difference of Rs. 704 which is the excess present value of the asset.

A further step in the refinement of the excess present value approach, known as the excess present value index (sometimes called the profitability index), reflects the percentage relationship between the present value of the stream of future payments at the desired rate of return and the initial investment so that, in the above example, the excess present value index would be:

$$\text{Excess Present Value} = \frac{\text{Present Value of Cash Savings}}{\text{Original Investment}} \times 100$$

$$= \frac{\text{Rs. } 6,704}{\text{Rs. } 6,000} \times 100 = 1.117 \times 100 = 111.7$$

The main advantage of the use of excess present value index is the ready comparability it affords between investment proposals of different magnitudes. For example, at a certain desired rate of return, an investment costing Rs. 1,00,000 may show excess present value of Rs. 13,000 while another costing Rs. 10,000 may show an excess present value of Rs. 2,000 only; in this case the second investment would be viewed as more favourable owing to its excess present value index being 120 as compared with 113 for the first.

Advantages

(a) Erratic flow of revenues and expenses over the project's life are directly considered under this method while they are averaged under other methods.

(b) Conceptually, discounted cash flow techniques are superior to those of the other methods. It is more objective because its conclusion is not directly influenced by decisions regarding depreciation methods, capitalisation versus expense decisions and conservatism.

(c) It is strictly comparable to cost of capital ratios so that decisions can be made quickly and safely by comparing rate of returns and the value of money to the firm.

(d) The method enables a ready comparison to be made between projects having different lives and different timings of cash inflows because: the discounting process allows comparison to be made at the same point in time.

(e) Discounted cash flow method automatically gives more distant while, under other methods, distant units of money are unealistically treated with the same weight as present units.

Disadvantages

(a) Though the method represents an advance over the other methods of analysing investment proposals, it is not a dependable ranking method in as much as it does not reflect the firm's cost of capital.

Table 1-Present Value Re. 1

No. of Years	4%	5%	6%	7%	8%	9%	10%	12%	15%	20%	25%	30%	35%	40%
1.	.9615	.9524	.9434	.9346	.9259	.9175	.9091	.8929	.8696	.8333	.8000	.7692	.7407	.7134
2.	.9246	.9070	.8900	.8734	.8573	.8417	.8264	.7972	.7561	.6944	.6400	5917	.5487	.5102
3.	.8890	.8638	.8396.	.8163	.7938	.7722	.7513	.7118	.6575	.5787	.5120	.4552	.4064	.3644
4.	.8548	.8227	.7921	.7639	.7350	.7084	.6830	.6335	.5718	.4823	.4096	.3501	.3011	.2613
5.	.8219	.7835	.7473	.7130	.6806	.6499	.6209	.5614	.4972	.4019	.3277	.2693	.2230	.1859
6.	.7003	.7462	.7050	.6663	.6302	.5963	.5645	.5066	.4323	.3349	.2621	.2072	.1652	.1328
7.	.7599	.7107	.6651	.6227	.5835	.5470	.5132	.4523	.3759	.2791	.2097	.1594	.1224	.0949
8.	.7307	.6768	.6274	.5420	.5403	.5019	.4665	.4039	.3269	.2326	.1678	.1226	.0926	.0678
9.	.7026	.6446	.5919	.5339	.5002	.4604	.4241	.3606	.2843	.1938	.1342	.0943	.0671	.0484
10.	.6756	.6139	.5584	.5083	.4632	.4224	.3855	.3220	.2472	.1615	.1074	.0725	.0497	.0346
15.	.5553	.4810	.4173	.3624	.3152	.2745	.2394	.1827	.1229	.0649	.0352	.0195	.0111	.0064
20.	.4564	.3769	.3119	.2584	.2145	.1784	.1486	.1037	.0611	.0261	.0115	.0053	.0025	.0012
25.	.3751	.2953	.2330	.1842	.1460	.1160	.0933	.0588	0.334	.0100	.0038	.0014	.0005	.0002
30.	3083	.2314	.1741	.1314	.0994	.0754	.0537	.0334	.0151	.0942	.0012	.0004	.0001	0
40.	.2083	.1420	.0972	.0668	.0460	.0318	.0221	.0107	.0037	.0007	.0001	0	0	0
50.	.1470	.0872	.0543	.0339	.0213	.0134	.0085	.0035	.0009	.0001	0	0	0	0
100.	.1098	.0076	.0030	.0012	.0005	.0002	.0000	0	0	0	0	0	0	0
	0	0	0	0	0	0	0	0	0	0	0	0	0	0

Table II—Present Value of Aeauly of Re. 1

No. of Years	4%	5%	6%	7%	8%	9%	10%
1	.9615	.9524	.9434	.9346	.9259	.9574	.9091
2	1.8861	1.8594	1.8334	1.8080	1.7833	1.7591	1.7355
3	2.7151	2.7232	2.6730	2.6943	2.5771	2.5313	2.4869
4	3.6299	3.5461	3.4651	3.3872	3.3121	3.2397	3.1699
5	4.4518	4.3295	4.2124	4.1002	4.9927	3.8897	3.7908
6	5.2421	5.0757	4.9173	4.7665	4.6229	4.4859	4.3553
7	6.0021	5.7864	5.5824	5.3893	5.2064	5.0330	4.8684
8	6.7327	6.4632	9.2098	5.9713	5.7466	5.5348	5.3349
9	7.4353	7.1078	6.8017	6.5152	6.2469	4.9952	5.7590
10	8.1109	7.7217	7.3601	7.0236	6.7101	5.4177	6.1446
15	11.1184	10.3797	9.7122	9.1079	8.5595	8.0607	7.6061
20	13.5903	12.4622	11.4699	10.5940	9.8181	9.1289	8.5136
25	15.6221	14.0939	12,7834	11.6536	10.6748	9.8226	9.0770
30	17.2920	15.3725	13.7648	12.4090	11.2578	10.2737	9.4267
40	19.7928	17.1591	15.0463	13.3317	11.9246	10.7574	9.7191
50	21.4822	18.2559	1.5.7619	13.8007	12.233	10.9617	9.9148
100	24.505	19.848	16.618	14.269	12.494	11.109	9.9993
	25.000	20.000	6.662	14.289	12.500	11.111	10.000

TABLE II (Continued)

12%	*18%*	*20%*	*25%*	*30%*	*35%*	*40%*
.8229	.8696	.8333	.8000	.7692	.7407	.7143
1.6901	1.6257	1.5270	1.4400	1.3609	1.2894	1.2245
2.4018	2.2832	2.1065	1.9520	1.8161	1.6959	1.5889
3.0373	2.8550	2.5817	2.3616	2.1662	1.9959	1.8492
3.6048	3.3522	2.9906	2.6893	2.4356	2.2260	2.0352
4.1114	3.7845	3.3255	2.9514	2.6427	2.3852	2.1680
4.5618	4.1604	3.6046	3.1611	2.8021	2.5075	2.2628
4.9676	4.4873	3.8372	3.3289	2.9247	2.5082	2.3360
5.3282	4 7716	4.0310	3.4631	3.0190	2.6653	2.3790
5.6502	5.0188	4.1925	3.5705	3.0915	2.6150	2.4136
6.8106	5.8474	4.6735	3.8553	3.2682	2.8255	2.4839
7.4694	6.2593	4.8696	3.9539	3.3158	2.8501	2.4970
7.8431	6.4611	4.9476	3.9849	3.3286	2.8556	2.4994
8.0552	6.5660	4.9799	3.9950	3.3321	2.8568	2.4999
8.2438	6.6418	4.9966	3.9995	3.3332	2.8571	2.5000
8.3045	6.6605	4.9995	3.9999	3.3333	2.8571	2.5000
8.3332	6.6666	4.9999	3.9999	3.3333	2.8571	2.5000
8.3333	6.6667	5.0000	4.0000	3.3333	2.8511	2.5000

(b) It is pointed out that other methods of ranking investment proposals are easier to understand and apply than the discounted cash flow methods. The supporters of discounted cash flow methods rebut this argument by asserting that the difficulty of the method is over-estimated and the reluctance to use it is based more on unfamiliarity than on its complexity. Tables and other short cuts are available to facilitate the use of the method.

However, the fact remains that discounted cash flow method is admittedly less familiar.

(c) Another deterrent to the use of the method is the fact that it does not correspond to accounting concepts for recording costs and revenues with the consequence that special analysis is necessary for the study of a capital investment.

TERMINAL VALUE METHOD

The terminal value approach (TV) even more distinctly separates the timing of cash inflows and out flows. Behind the TV approach is the assumption that each cash inflow is re-invested in another asset at a certain rate of return from the moment it is received until the termination of the project.

Example.

Original outlays	= Rs. 10,000
Life of the project	= 5 years
Cash inflows	= Rs. 4,000 each for 5 years
Cost of capital, K	= 10%

Expected interest rates at which cash inflows will be re-invested:

Year-end	
1	6%
2	6%
3	8%
4	8%
5	8%

Solution.

We would re-invest Rs. 4,000 received at the end of year 1 for 4 years at the rate of 6%. The cash inflows in year 2 will be reinvested for 3 years at 6%, the cash inflows of year 3 for 2 years, and so on. There will be no reinvestment of cash inflows received at the end of the fifth year. The total sum of these compounded cash inflows is then discounted back to the present at K and compared to the present value of the cash outflows, *i.e.* Rs. 10,000 in this case.

If K is 10%, the PV of the terminal sum is given in following

Table

Year	*Cash inflows (–Rs.10,000) (Rs.)*	*Rate of*	*Years for investment*	*Compounding factor**	*Total compounded sum (Rs.)*
(1)	*(2)*	*(3)*	*(4)*	*(5)*	*(6)*
1	4,000	6%	4	1,262	5,048
2	4,000	6%	3	1,191	4,764
3	4,000	8%	2	1,166	4,664
4	4,000	8%	1	1,080	4,320
5	4,000	8%	0	1,000	4,000
	Total compounded sum				22,796

*Table has been used to fmd the compounded sum.

Now, we have to fmd the present value of Rs. 22,796. The discount rate would be the cost of capital, K (10%). The sum of Rs. 22,796 would be received at the end of year 5. Its present value will be

$$\text{PV} = \frac{\text{Rs. } 22{,}790}{(1+\text{K})^5} = \frac{\text{Rs. } 22{,}796}{(1.10)^5}$$

Present value of Re.1, received 5 years hence, as per table at a 10% discount rate is 0.621. The sum of the present values would be Rs. 14,156.31 (Rs. 22,796 × 0.621).

The decision rule is that if the present value of the sum total of the compounded re-invested cash inflows (PVTS) is greater than the present value of the outflows (PVO), the proposed project is accepted, otherwise not.

Symbolically,

If PVTS > PVO, accept,

If PVTS < PVO, reject,

The firm would be indifferent if both the values are equal.

Thus, since the PVTS of Rs. 14,156.31 exceeds the original outlay of Rs. 10,000, we would accept the assumed project under the TV criterion. A variation of the terminal value method (TV) is the net terminal value (NTV). Symbolically, it can be represented as NTV = (PVTS – PVO). If the NTV is positive, accept the project, if the NTV = NTV is negative, reject the project. In the above examine, the NTV is positive. Its value is Rs. 4,156.31. Therefore, the project is acceptable.

The NTV method is similar to the NPV method, with the difference that while in the former values are compounded, in the latter they are discounted. Both the methods will give the same results, provided of course, the same figures have been discounted as have been compounded and the same interest rate (rates) are used for both discounting and compounding.

Advantages

The NTV/TV methods have a number of advantages. *(a)* Firstly, these method explicitly incorporate the assumption that the cash inflows are rein-vested once they are received and avoid any influence ofthe cost of capital on the cash inflow stream itself, *(b)* Secondly, they are mathematically simpler processes of evaluating the investment worth of alternative capital projects, *(c)* Thirdly, these methods are easier to understand for business executives who are not trained in accountancy or economics than NPV or IRR as the "compounding technique" appeals more than "discounting", *(d)* Fourthly, they are better suited to cash budgeted requirements. The NPV presentation in spite of being a cash flow approach does not explicitly show all the cash inflows. It does not take into account cash inflows in respect of interest earnings.

Profitability Index or Benefit Cost Ratio

Yet another time-adjusted capital budgeting technique is the Profitability Index (P) or Benefit Cost Ratio (B/C). It is similar to the NPV approach. The PI approach measures the present value of returns per rupee invested, while the NPV is based on the difference between the present value of future cash inflows and the present value of cash outlays. It was observed in a preceding section that a major shortcoming of the NPV method is that being an absolute measure, it is not a reliable method to evaluate projects requiring different initial investments. The PI method provides a solution to this kind of problem. It is, in other words, a relative measure. It may be defined as the ratio which is obtained by dividing he present value of future cash inflows by the present value of cash outlays.

Mathematically,

$$PI = \frac{\text{Present value of cash inflows}}{\text{Present value of cash outflows}}$$

This method is also known as the B/C ratio because the numerator measures benefits and the denominator costs.

Using the B/C ratio or the PI, a project will qualify for acceptance if its PI exceeds one. When PI equals I, the firm is indifferent to the project.

When PI greater than, equal to, or less than I, the net present value is grater than, equal to, or less than O, respectively. In other words, the NPV will be positive when the PI is greater than 1; it will be negative when the PI is less than one. Thus, the NPV and PI approaches give the same results regarding investment proposals.

The selection of projects with the PI method can also be done on the basis of ranking. The highest rank will be given to the project with the highest PI, followed by others in the same order.

Though it is common to define PI as the ratio of the PV of the cash in flows divided by the PV of cash out flows, the PI may also be measured on the basis of the net benefits of a project against its current cash outlay rather than measure its gross benefits against its total cost over the life of the project. This aspect becomes very important in situations of capital rationing. In such a situation the decision rule would be to accept the project if the PI is positive and reject the project if it is negative.

Advantages

Like the other discounted cash flow techniques, the PI satisfies almost all the requirements of a sound investment criterion. It considers all the element of capital budgeting, such as the time value of money, totality of benefits, and so on. Conceptually, it is a sound method of capital budgeting. Although based on the NPV, it is a better evaluation technique than NPV in a situation of capital rationing. The PI method is superior to the NPV method as the former evaluates the worth of projects in terms of their relative rather than absolute magnitudes. However, in some problems of a mutually exclusive nature, the NPV method would be superior to the PI method. The comparison of PI and NPV is further explored subsequently.

This method is, however, more difficult to understand. Also, it involves more computation than the traditional methods but less than IAA.

DISTINGUISH BETWEEN TIME ADJUSTED RATE OF RETURN AND EXCESS PRESENT VALUE METHODS

Though both these method of evaluating capital investment proposals are the species of the same genus, *viz.*, discounted cash flow technique, and, therefore, there is a widespread impression that they represent one and the same thing, they look at the problem from two different viewpoints and answer different questions thereby indicating certain fundamental differences between them.

Both the method are based on the unexceptionable principle of business finance that money has a time value but similarity between them ends there are important distinctions to be emphasized. First, while the time-adjusted rate of return method seeks to find the maximum rate of interest at which the funds invested in any given project could be repaid with earnings generated by the project itself, the present value method arrives at the amount to be invested in a given project so that its anticipated earnings will exactly suffice to repay the amount with interest at the market rate. Second, in the algebraic formulation, the farmer method treats the required rate of return as an unknown factor but the latter method takes it as the business's known cost of capital.

However, the present value method is considered more superior because it explicitly recognizes availability of a market for funds and assumes that individuals, as well businesses, will use the market rationally to enhance their earnings. The time-adjusted rate of return method, on the other hand, does not recognize the existence of such a capital market and, had it been doing this, it would be equivalent to the present value method.

The distinction between the time-adjusted rate of return and the excess present value approaches to the discounted cash flow method of evaluating investment proposals, when applied in practice, is highlighted by the presence of two mutually exclusive alternatives and can very well be brought out by illustrate or example.

To illustrate, the position in connection with the calculation of the time adjusted rate of return for the purchase of a grinding machine, costing Rs.5 lakhs with an annual cash savings of Rs. 1,00,000 per year spread over ten years and discounted at rates of interest of 15 percent and 20 percent, is as follows:

Years	*Cash Inflow Outflow + –* *Rs.*	*Present 15% Discount Factor* *Rs.*	*Value 20% Discount Factor* *Rs.*
(1)	*(2)*	*(3)*	*(4)*
At the time of Purchase	-50,00,000	-5,00,000	-5,00,000
1	+ 1,00,000	+92,860	+90,630
2	+1,00,000	+79,930	+74,210

Contd.

(1)	*(2)*	*(3)*	*(4)*
3	+ 1,00,000	+68,790	+60,750
4	+1,00,000	+59,210	+49,740
5	+ 1,00,000	+50,960	+40,720
6	+ 1,00,000	+43,860	+33,340
7	-1,00,000	+37,750	+27,300
8	+1,00,000	+32,500	+22,350
9	+ 1,00,000	+27,970	+ 18,300
10	+ 1,00,000	+24,070	+14,980
Total	Rs.+5,00,000	Rs.+17,900	Rs.-7,680

According to the Table, the present value of cash inflows, when discounted at 15 per cent exceeds the immediate cash outlay of Rs.5 lakhs on the purchase of a grinding machine by Rs.17,900 thereby indicating that the proposal earns at a rate more than what might be required to pay interest at 15 per cent on the sum to be invested. However, the discounting of cash inflows at 20 per cent yield as present value a negative amount of Rs.67,680 which means that the proposal is not likely to earn enough during the life time of the machine to enable interest to be paid off at 20 per cent on the cost of the asset. The exact discount factor involved would, of course, have to be interpolated between these two rated and it may settle at about 16 per cent leading to the obvious conclusion the proposal can afford to pay from its annual cash flows that initial cash investment of Rs.50,000 plus interest 16 per cent and can yet be well off. Thus, the proposed investment in grinding machine seems to satisfy the criterion of acceptability with any minimum cutoff rate of 15 per cent or belows.

It is quite clear that only two alternatives—to but the machine or not to buy-were alone available in the above example. Another complication can, however, be introduced at this stage of the analysis in the form of the availability of a third alternative to purchased a different type of plant at a cost Rs. 7.5 lakhs with estimated cash savings of Rs. 1,30,000 per year over it serviceable life often years.

The time-adjusted rate of return on the latter proposed investment works out to approximately 12.24 per cent which just exceeds the acceptability limit if the same happens to be 12 per cent. Nevertheless, that cannot be the end of the story because the return on the entire original investment of Rs. 7.5 lakhs investment, which would have to be procured in the event of the purchase of more expensive plant, while the incremental cash inflow to justify this increased outlay is Rs. 30,000 every year. This estimated quantitative information would give a discounted rate of return of a little less than 4 per cent on the additional investment. In this context, the third alternative proposed investment should not be preferred over the less expensive grinding machine despite the fact that the proposal requiring additional investment given an overall rate of return of 12.24 per cent which represent a satisfactory profitability rate if the minimum acceptable limit is 12 per cent.

The excess present value method tries to solve this problem a little differently though directly. According to this approach, the acceptable criterion, technically known as cost of capital of say 12 per cent and the alternative investment to be taken up would be the one which gives the maximum estimated net present value of this rate. This can be presented as follows:

	Proposal X	*Proposal Y*	*Proposal Y – X*
Initial Investment	– Rs. 5,00,000	– Rs. 7,50,000	+ Rs. 2,50,000
Annual Cash Earnings	+ Rs. 1,00,000	+ Rs. 1,30,000	+ Rs. 30,000
Present Value for			
10 Years at 12%	+ Rs. 5,82,380	+ Rs. 7,57,094	+ Rs. 1,74,714
Net Present Value	+ Rs. 82,380	+ Rs.7094	– Rs. 75,286

The choice of investment to be taken in hand is beyond doubt for Proposal X inasmuch as it is likely to add more to the present value of the firm than Proposal Y. Thus, neither the differential calculations are required nor is it necessary to adopt trial and error method to arrive at the time-adjusted rate of return for each proposal.

Though any of the two methods can lead to the solution desirable from the point of view of the larger interests of a business undertaking, there are circumstances in which it is difficult to decide the priority to be given to a particular alternative from out of a number of them in order to obtain information on incremental rate of return. Dealing with such cases is considerably facilitated by the use of excess present value approach instead of the computation of differential rate of return. This is due to the reason that the present value method does not need a decision regarding the sequence in which different alternatives have to be compared.

Similarities

The two methods--IRR and NPV—would give consistent results in terms of acceptance or rejection of investment proposals in certain situations. That is, if a project is sound, it will be indicated by both the methods. If, however, it does not qualify for acceptance, both the methods will indicate that it should be rejected.

The situations in which the two methods will give a concurrent accept-reject decision will be in respect of conventional and independent projects. Thus, in the case of such investments, cash outflows are confined to the initial period, that is, to the beginning. The independent proposals refer to investments, the acceptance of which does not preclude the acceptance of others, so that all profitable proposals can be accepted and there are no constrains in accepting all profitable projects. The reason why both the methods are equivalent and support or reject a proposal is simple. The decision criterion with these methods may be recalled here. According to the NPV method, the decision rule is that a project will be accepted if it has positive NPV, *i.e.* NPV exceeds zero. The IRR method would support projects in whose case the IRR is more than the requirement rate of return (when IRR exceeds K). When the NPV equals zero or the IRR equals K, the project may be accepted or rejected. Projects which have positive net present values will have an IRR higher than the required rate of return.

❑

6

Marginal Costing

Marginal Costing is a system of ascertaining cost and not a method of costing like Single or Output Costing Contract Costing or Process Costing. It is a technique of determining cost and helping the management to know the effect on profits of changes in the volume or type of output. It has been defined by the Institute of Cost and Works Accountants, London, as, "the amount at any given volume of output by which aggregate costs are changed if the volume of output is increased or decreased by one unit". Marginal Costing necessitates the classification of costs into fixed and variable. These two types of costs behave differently with changes in the volume of output. Fixed costs tend to change with time rather than the level of output. They tend to remain constant for all volumes of production within the installed capacity of plant. For example, rent of office or factory manager's salary, insurance charges, telephone rent etc. shall remain the same even if the production goes up or comes down. They are related to period or time and not to volume of output hence are known as period costs. Variable costs, on the other hand, are known as product cost as these are related to the volume of output, *i.e.* it increases or decreases directly with the change in the volume of output.

Marginal costing is basically concerned with the ascertainment of product or variable cost of the product *i.e.,* direct materials, direct wages, direct expenses and variable overheads. Thus marginal cost is the aggregate of variable cost of a product. Marginal costing is also known as Variable Costing.

By analysing this definition, we find that with the increase in one unit of output, the total cost is increased and this increase in total cost from the existing level to the new level is known as marginal cost. For example, a company produces 1,000 exhaust fans per annum. Total Fixed cost is Rs. 50,000 per annum. Variable cost per exhaust fan is Rs. 400. Total cost of 1,000 exhaust fans will he as follows:

	Rs.
Variable (Marginal) cost (1,000 × 400)	4,00,000
Fixed Costs	50,000
Total cost	4,50,000

If output is increased by one exhaust fan, the cost will appear as follows:

Variable cost (1,001 × 400)	4,00,400
Fixed Cost	50,000
Total cost	4,50,400

Marginal cost per unit is, therefore Rs. 400

From the above, it will be clear that in marginal costing, costs are separated into fixed and variable. Only variable costs are regarded as the costs of the products being manufactured. The fixed costs are treated as period costs which will be incurred during the period regardless of the volume of output and are charged directly to the Profit and Loss Account.

The advocates of Marginal Costing plead that the cost of production should constitute the variable expenses incurred in production, as they are direct expenses incurred in production. The fixed costs are time costs and are incurred irrespective of the fact whether the production is carried on or not, hence they should not form part of the cost of production. There is no justification for apportioning such costs to the volume of work-in-progress or finished goods at end of the period. Such costs should be recovered from the margin (contribution) derived after deducting the variable costs from the value of sales. By doing so, the time cost of performing a particular a activity can be ascertained and used as a basis for sound managerial decision and cost control.

Difficulty in Classification of Variable Overhead Costs

Overhead cost may be broadly sub-divided into fixed and variable. Examples of fixed costs are, rent, insurance premimum, manager's salary, office salary etc. and that of variable are electricity costs, factory supplies, power etc. Overheads are taken into account for the determination of costs. It may not be easy to find out the amount of variable overhead costs. Many costs may be semi-variable, *i.e.* part of it may be fixed and part variable. For example, telephone charges will include telephone rent (fixed) and call charges (variable) and it may be difficult to find out variable portion out of the semi-variable overhead costs: Similarly, electric power, depreciation, repairs etc. are examples of semi-variable expenses. We shall discuss briefly how the problem can be solved.

A semi-variable cost is a cost which varies in total amount with changes in the volume of output, but the change is not proportionate to the change in output.

There are several methods for the separation of variable cost out of semi-variable cost, but one of them which is simple is explained below.

Two levels of production are chosen and on the basis of past experience, respective total semi-variable costs are found out. The difference in the volume of output and that in the cost shall suggest the answer. It is found that when the total production in a month was 100 units, the invariable cost amounted to Rs.400 and in another month, when the total output increased to 120 units, the semi-variable cost amounted to Rs.440.

Units produced	*Semi-variable costs*
	Rs.
100	400
120	440

An analysis of the above position shows that with an increase in production by 20 units, the semi-variable cost increased by Rs.40 *i.e.,* average increase is Rs. 2 per unit. Now we can ascertain that when 100 units were produced, total variable overhead cost would have amounted to Rs. 200 (Rs. 400 - Rs. 200) was fixed overhead cost out of the semi-variable cost of Rs. 400. The variable cost of Rs. 200 is the marginal cost to be used in marginal costing.

Features

From what has been discussed above we come to the conclusion that the following are the special features of marginal costing.

(i) Profit is calculated in a special manner. Marginal costs are deducted from the value of sales arid the difference is termed as "contribution", which is meant to cover the fixed casts and profits, if any. If the contribution exceed the fixed casts, there will be net profit and if it is less than the fixed costs, there is loss.

(ii) The unit cost of a product means the average variable cast of manufacturing the product which varies directly with production. Fixed casts are not allocated to the products and are charged against the revenue of the period. Generally variable selling and dispibutive costs are not considered here.

(iii) The valuation of work-in-progress and finished goods is done at the marginal casts. The reason being that fixed costs are period casts, that is, they relate to a particular period of time, hence if any portion of such costs is apportioned, to the work-in-progress or finished goods, that portion of fixed cast will be carried over to the next year and will remain recouped during the period in which these expenses have been incurred.

The contribution can be Gross or Net. If only the manufacturing variable expenses have been deducted from the sales revenue, the difference is termed as Gross Contribution. If variable administration costs are deducted from the Gross Margin, the balance will be the Net Margin.

There are two terms which confuse the students generally. These are marginal cost and marginal costing. Marginal cost, is the change in the aggregate costs with the increase or decrease of one unit of production. If 1,000 units are produced and the marginal cost is Rs.3 per unit then the total cost will be Rs. 3,000. If the production is increased to 1001 units of production then the total cost will be Rs.3,003. The change in the aggregate cost is Rs. 3 and is marginal cost. In this context a unit may be a single, a batch of articles, an order, a stage of production capacity or a department. It relates to the change in output in the particular circumstances under consideration.

Marginal costing is the ascertainment of marginal costs by differentiating between fixed costs and variable costs and to see the effect of profit of changes in volume or type of output. Thus marginal costing includes two things *i.e., (i)* the ascertainment of marginal cost and *(ii)* the cost volume-profit relationship.

ASCERTAINMENT OF MARGINAL COST

We have already seen how total cost is presented in the cost sheet with various divisions of costs. The presentation is made under the method of absorption or total cost method. Under this method the total cost as absorbed in the units of production. But presentation under marginal cost is different from the absorption costing. Under marginal costing the cost is ascertained as under:

	Rs.	
Sales.	XXXXXXX	
Less: Marginal cost:		
Direct Material	XXXXX	
Direct Wages	XXXXXX	
Direct Expenses	XXXXXX	
Variable Overhead	XXXXXX	XXXXXXX
	------------	------------
Contribution	XXXXXX	
Less: Fixed Costs	XXXXXXX	

Profit (or Loss)	XXXXXXX	

Thus, we find that out of sales, marginal cost is deducted in order to calculate the gross margin or contribution.

Economists' and Accountants' views on Marginal Cost

Economists define. Marginal Cost as "the amount at any given volume of output by which aggregate costs are changed if the volume of output is increased or decreased by one unit". Suppose the aggregate cost of production of 1,000 units of a product is Rs. 10,000 and that of 1,001 units is Rs. 10,008, then the marginal cost of producing one additional unit is Rs. 8 (Rs. 10,008-10,000). Thus the additional cost of producing one additional unit is the Marginal cost according to the economists. According to economists variable costs are supposed to increase or decrease at a charging rate. At low level of activity, the variable cost per unit is supposed to decline with every additional unit of production as a result of increased efficiency of workers or better utilisation of production facilities. The law of increasing return or diminishing cost operates at a low level of activity, on the other hand, at a very high level of activity, variable cost per unit is supposed to rise with every additional unit of production on account of bottlenecks, over-crowding or excessive use of facilities. The law of diminishing returns, or increasing cost comes into operation. Against this, according to accountants it is assumed that with changing volume of activity variable cost per unit remain constant with changing volume of production or sales. Hence Marginal Cost in accounting refers to the difference in the total variable cost which results from the addition or reduction of a certain number of units, not of a single unit. It is the aggregate of variable costs, that is, Prime Cost plus variable overhead. For example, if Rs. 20,000 of Direct Materials, Rs. 10,000 of Direct Wages and Rs. 10,000 of variable overheads are incurred in producing 10,000 units of a product, the marginal cost will be:

Rs. 20,000 + 10,000 + 10,000/1000 = Rs. 4 per unit

MARGINAL COSTING AND DIFFERNTLAL COSTING

Marginal Costing is sometimes confused with Differential Costing. The term 'Differential Costing' means a technique used in the preparation of *ad hoc* information in which only cost and income differences between alternative courses of action are taken into consideration. Thus, in case of differential costing a comparison is made between the cost differential and income differential between two or more situations and decision regarding adopting a particular course of action is taken if it is on the whole profitable. This is illustrated with the following example.

Example.

Pioneer manufacturing Company, makers of a specialized line of toys, receives an order for 2,000 units of toy battle tanks, from a large mail order house at a price of Rs.3 per unit.

The company sells this type of toy to its other customers at Rs. 5 each but it has surplus capacity and can take the special order without adversely affecting its regular operations for the coming month.

The income statement of the company for the preceding month is as follows:

Net Sales - 10,000 units @ Rs. 5	50,000
Costs:	*Rs.*
Direct Material: Rs. 1.50 per unit	15,000
Direct Labour: Rs. 1 per unit	10,000
Factory Overhead	10,000
Selling and Administration Expenses	10,000
Total Costs	Rs. 45,000
Net Profit	Rs. 5,000

Direct material and direct labour costs to be incurred on the special order are estimated to be of the same amount per unit as for the regular business. Special tools costing Rs. 500 would be required to meet the specifications of the mail-order house.

You are required to prepare a differential cost analysis for deciding about the acceptance of the order.

You are required to prepare a differential cost analysis for deciding about the acceptance of the order.

Solution.

DIFFERENTIAL COST STATEMENT

Existing situation	*Proposed situation*	*Net Increase*	*Decrease*
	10,000 units	12,000 units	2,000 units
Sales (i) Rs.	50,000	56,000	6,000
Cost:			
Direct Materials	15,000	8,000	3,000
Direct Labour	10,000	12,000	2,000
Factory Overhead	10,000	10,000	
Selling & Adm. Expenses	10,000	10,000	
Special tools	—	500	500
Total Cost	45,000	50,500	5,500
Profit (i)-(ii) = (iii)	5,000	5,000	500

In the above case differential costs are Rs. 5,500 while differential sales are Rs. 6,000. Thus, acceptance of order from a large mail order house gives an extra profit of Rs. 500. The order may be accepted provided it does not adversely affect the present sales at Rs. 5 per unit.

Thus, in case of Differential Costing, the change in total costs (both fixed and variable) is taken into account. The term 'Differential Cost' means the net increase or decrease in total cost resulting from a variation in production. The differential cost is termed as 'Incremental Cost' when the cost increases and 'Decremental Cost' when the cost decreases. Thus, Differential Costing, Incremental Costing and Decremental Costing are alternative terms and they are different from Marginal Costing and Direct Costing.

The difference between Marginal Costing and Differential Costing can be summarised as follows:

1. In case of Marginal Costing, the entire fixed cost are excluded while in the case of Differential Costing such

fixed costs which are relevant for decision-making are considered.

2. Differential Costs are worked out separately as analysis statements while marginal costs may be embodied in the accounting system itself.

3. In Marginal Costing, the contribution and the profit-volume ratio are the main yardsticks for the purposes of performance evaluation and decision-making. While in case of Differential Costing; the differential costs are compared with incremental or decremental revenue as the case may be.

4. Differential Costing can be used both in case of Absorption Costing and Marginal Costing.

The manner of application of Differential Costing is somewhat different from that of Marginal Costing. Under Differential Costing, differential costs of various alternatives are compared with the differential revenues and the decisions are taken on the basis of maximum net gain. While evaluating the viability of different projects, making a choice out of several alternative proposals. Differential Costing helps in a better way than Marginal Costing. If under Marginal Costing, while deciding about the profitability of products or making cost-benefit analysis, fixed costs are also considered at some stage, it takes the shape of Differential Costing. Hence, practically the purpose of applying the two techniques is the same and here also we have not made any difference in the application of these techniques to the problems which management has to face in its routine or otherwise decision-making process.

ABSORPTION COSTING OR FULL COSTING

Absorption Costing technique is also termed as Traditional or Full Cost Method. According to this method, the cost of a product is determined after considering both fixed and variable costs. The variable costs, such as those of direct materials, direct labour, etc. are directly charged to the products while the fixed costs are apportioned on a suitable basis over different products manufactured during a period. Thus, in case of Absorption Costing all costs are identified with the manufacture products. This will be clear with the help of the following example.

Example.

A company is manufacturing 3 products A, Band C. The costs of their manufacture are as follows:

	A	*B*	*C*
Direct Material per unit	Rs. 3	Rs. 4	Rs. 5
Direct Labour	2	3	4
Selling Price	10	15	20
Output	1,000 units	1,000 units	1,000 units

The total overheads are Rs. 6,000 out of which Rs. 3,000, are fixed and rest are variable. It is decided to apportion these costs over different products in the ratio of output. You are required to prepare a statement showing cost of each product and profit according to Absorption Costing.

Solution.

The cost of each product would be ascertained according to Absorption. Costing as follows:

STATEMENT SHOWING COST AND PROFIT
(According to Absorption Costing Technique)

	A		*B*		*C*	
	Per Unit *Rs.*	*Total* *Rs.*	*Per Unit* *Rs.*	*Total* *Rs.*	*Per Unit* *Rs.*	*Total* *Rs.*
Direct Materials	3	3,000	4	4,000	5	5,000
Direct Labour	2	2,000	3	3,000	4	4,000
Overheads:						
Fixed	1	1,000	1	1,000	1	1,000
Variable	1	1,000	1	1,000	1	1,000
Total Cost	7	7,000	9	9,000	11	11,000
Profit	3	3,000	6	6,000	9	9,000
Selling Price	10	10,000	15	15,000	20	20,000
Total Profit	Rs, 3,000 + Rs. 6,000 + Rs. 9,000 = Rs. 18,000					

Under Absorption Costing each unit of product has to bear its total share of cost. It may be true that some products may not be able to bear their full share of cost but may be able to contribute to the overall profitability of the firm. For example, a product can be sold at a price which is sufficient to recover more than its variable cost required to produce it, but may not be sufficient to recover its full share of fixed cost. On the other hand, there may be products which contribute much more than their share of variable and fixed costs. Under absorption costing, the management is interested in knowing whether or not a product can produce an adequate return on investment after absorbing its share of the overall cost whether fixed or variable or direct or indirect. This is because in the long run, all costs must be more than recovered to assure a satisfactory return to the investors on their investment.

However, charging of fixed costs creates problems. These costs are apportioned to different products on some suitable basis, *e.g.*, as a percentage of direct material, a percentage of direct labour or a rate per article, etc. But, there is always some doubt about the suitability of the method adopted for apportionment of these fixed costs. It cannot be said with definiteness that the fixed costs so charged are really the costs which should have been charged to each of the different products. It, therefore, brings more inexactness in costing. Moreover, fixed costs have to be incurred whether there is production or no production. It means cost of a product not only depends upon the costs which are directly incurred but also on the volume of output. For example, if the cost of direct material and direct labour for a unit is Rs. 3 and 4 respectively and the fixed costs are Rs. 2,000 and the volume of output is 1,000 units, the total cost of production will be as follows:

Costs of Direct Materials	Rs. 3,000
Cost of Direct Labour	4,000
Fixed Overheads	2,000
Total Costs	9,000

The cost per unit comes to Rs. 9. In case, the output is 800 units only, the cost of production will be as follows:

Direct Material	Rs. 2,400
Direct Labour	3,200
Fixed Overheads	2,000
Total Cost	7,600

The cost per unit comes to Rs, 9,50 per unit.

From the above example, it is clear that the cost of the product has gone up by 50 paise per unit not because of any increase in price of direct materials or increase in the rates for direct labour, but because of lower volume of production. This seems to be a bit illogical. Some people, therefore argue that the fixed costs should not be considered while computing the cost of the product. But this should be charged against the total fund arising out of excess of selling price over variable cost. Marginal Costing, as explained below, is a technique of costing which deals with this concept.

Absorption and Marginal Costing

Both the types of cost accounting determine the cost of product, job or service either individually or collectively for the enterprise. Both the systems lend themselves to adoption of historical or estimated basis of absorption of costs.

The most differentiating features are as follows:

(a) In Marginal Costing the variable expenses are absorbed in the product cost or cost of goods sold whereas Fixed costs in their entirety are charged against the revenues of that period. Against this, in Absorption Costing not only variable but also fixed costs are charged to the cost of production to the cost of goods sold. Hence fixed cost is not entirely charged against the revenue of the period. Thus, under Absorption Costing, a portion of fixed cost will remain submerged in the value of closing inventories. The carry-over in opening inventories will bias computation.

(b) The main cause of difference between the profits in the two systems is the variation between the fixed costs absorbed in the opening and closing inventories. The net operating income under Marginal Costing is to be reconciled with that in Absorption Costing by adjusting of the difference in fixed overheads merged in the valuation of opening and closing inventories.

(c) In Absorption Costing the concept of period cost assumes a lesser significance as a portion of it is absorbed in the inventory cost and not viewed as an expense till sales are affected. Thus the profitability for a period may not be true till the quantum of fixed charges merged in the opening and closing balance of inventories is allowed to play its part in full in the computation of profitability.

(d) The profitability as realised in both the systems will differ. In Marginal Costing, the entire fixed costs are treated as period cost and thus are charged off against the revenues of that period without any relation to sales and production quantities. If the sales turnover in quantities is more than the production output in quantities, the profits will stand inflated and *vice-versa*.

(e) The Marginal Costing, either on a historical basis or estimated, rates of recovery of overheads are developed only for variables while in Absorption Costing two rates are developed, one for the fixed cost and the other for variables or alternatively a comprehensive rate to recover the entire cost. Both these systems permit computation of overheads for any volume of activity.

(f) The main elements of cost like Direct Material, Direct Labour and Direct Expenses, if any, will be accounted for in both the systems alike. The difference is only in overheads.

(g) In Marginal Costing the entire fixed expenses actually incurred are charged off, overhead variance due to variation in volume does not affect the computation while in Absorption Costing it does as over-absorption or under absorption.

However, Marginal Costing is easy to operate and facilitates a better and quicker understanding of the position of profitability with reference to anticipation and enables management to frame a future course of action.

The following example will show how presentation of accounts differs from each other.

Example.

ALLIED Co. LTD.

The following data relate to selling price and cost of a product:

Fixed Costs.

Manufacturing	Rs. 40,000
Selling & Administrative	Rs. 10,000

Variable Cost per unit.

Manufacturing	Rs. 4 per unit
Selling and administrative	Rs. 2 per unit
Selling price per unit	Rs. 15 per unit

The company produced 10,000 units of the product during the year and there was no opening inventory.

Solution.

	Absorption Costing	*Marginal Costing*
Units sold	10,000	10,000
	Rs.	*Rs.*
Sales Revenue (10,000 units @ Rs. 15 per unit)	1,50,000	1,50,000
Cost of goods sold:		
Variable manufacturing cost	40,000	40,000
Fixed Manufacturing cost	40,000	
Total manufacturing cost	80,000	40,000
Gross Profit	70,000	—
Contribution margin (Gross)	—	1,10,000
Less: Selling and administrative expenses:		

Variable selling & administrative expenses (10,000 × Rs. 2)	20,000	20,000
Fixed selling & administrative expenses	10,000	—
Tortal Selling & Administrative expenses	30,000	20,000
Net Profit	40,000	—
Contribution Margin (net)	—	90,000
Less Fixed costs:		
Manufacturing		40,000
Selling & admipistrative		10,000
Total period costs		50,000
Net Profit		40,000

The above data shows that there was neither any stock of finished goods at the beginning of the year nor at the end because the firm manufactured 10,000 units and sold all of them. As no portion of fixed costs was transferred to this year (because there was no opening stock) and no fixed costs have been transferred from this year to the next year, the amount of profits under the two do not differ. The difference arise under the two because of the price at which the opening and closing stocks have been charged.

It should be noted that while, under absorption costing, the cost of manufacturing the product has been calculated by taking both variable and fixed manufacturing costs which amount to Rs. 8 per unit (variable cost Rs. 4 per unit plus fixed cost Rs. 4 per unit), whereas in Marginal Costing, the same amounted to Rs. 4 per unit *i.e.*, the variable manufacturing cost.

MARGINAL COSTING AND STANDARD COSTING

Standard costs are the scientifically poredetermined costs of manufacturing a single unit or a number of units or product or of rendering a service during a specified future period. According to the terminology standard cost is a pre-determined cost calculated in relation to a prescribed set of working conditions correlating technical specifications and scientific measurements of materials and labour to the prices and wage rates expected to apply during the period to which the standard cost is intended to relate with an addition of an appropriate share of budgeted overhead. Its main purposes are to provide bases for control through variance accounting for the valuation of stocks and work-in-progress and in exceptional cases for fixing selling prices. The standard costs are planned costs of a product under current or anticipated conditions. The term standard cost consists of two parts, *viz.* standard and cost. Standards involve the expression of standards so established in values. Standard costing is the system of costing which seeks to control the cost of each unit or batch through determination beforehand of what should be the cost and then its comparison with actual cost. Thus the system of standard costing is based on standard cost.

The essential nature of standard costs is that in represents costs that should have been incurred rather than cost that were incurred. On the other hand marginal costs are direct costs or variable costs which vary according to the volume of production. Though an estimate of future marginal costs can be made but if the cost figures have been obtained for the expired period they will be historic costs. As a matter of fact, standard costing and marginal costing both are variable tools of cost control and marginal planning.

If a firm practises standard costing on proper lines *i.e.*, standards are themselves determined in a way which will not impose too great a burden on the workers or other employees of the firm, it may infuse in the minds of the staff a desire to achieve the standards and thus show greater efficiency. The objective of standard costing is avoidance of all losses and wastages as far possible.

Marginal costing also known as direct costing or variable costing is a comparatively new area in the field of accounting. It is very useful in decision making. It refers to the method of costing which is concerned with changes of any product. It deals primarily with changes in future cost. Projected cost provide very helpful guidelines for managerial decisions on pricing, sales, budgeting, production planning and marketing. According to the Institute sales. Cost and Works Accounts, London, "marginal costing is an ascertainment by differentiating between fixed costs and variable costs, of marginal cost and the effect on profit of changes in volume or type of output". Marginal Costing is a process of determining and analysing the marginal costs. Marginal cost it the amount of any given volume of output by which aggregate costs an changed if the volume of output is increased or decreased by one unit.

The concept of marginal costing is based on the important distinction between product costs and period costs, the former being related to the volume of output and the latter to the period of time rather than the volume production. Marginal costing regards as product costs only those manufacturing costs which have a tendency to vary directly with the volume of output. This is the complete contrast to the conventional system of costing under which all manufacturing costs—fixed as well as variable are treated as product costs variability with volume is the criterion for the classification of cost into product and period categories.

Thus marginal costing necessitates analysis of costs into fixed and variable. Even the semi-variable costs have to be closely and critically analysed in order to resolve themselves into their fixed and variable components depending upon whether they tend to remain fixed or vary with the compute.

Differential Costs and Incremental Costs

The terms have been defined by John G. Blocker and W. Keith Weltmore as:

> "The increase or decrease in total costs that result from producing and distributing additional or fewer units of a productor from a change in method of production of distribution such as the use of improved machinery, addition of a product or territory, or selection of a additional channel".

Incremental cost measures the addition to unit cost which results from an addition to output. The incremental cost is generally expressed as a cost perunit while differential cost is expressed in aggregate.

USEFULNESS OF MARGINAL COSTING OR VARIABLE COSTING OR DIRECT COSTING

(1) Profit Planning. With the rising cost and shrinkage in profit margin attention is now directed more and more by management towards a better and fuller understanding of the relationship between profit and the major factors affecting it like sales volume, production, selling price, sales mix, production and selling costs etc. This is simply because all these factors are variable in nature. Unless these relationships are known, there can be no assurance that the plans and subsequent actions to control activity will lead to the anticipated profits. Marginal or variable costing as method of evaluating the result of operation is designed to specify the need for a simple presentation of operating results which clearly show the cost volume-profit relationship. It attempts to improve the procedure for collecting and presenting information regarding these relationships. This type of information is not necessary for the determination of net income or for the measurement of production cost, but it is important to have such information for purposes of budgeting and profit planning, in selecting product lines and in deciding upon the relative importance to be given to each line of activity, in appraising the performance of sales personnel, in establishing price policy, and as a basis for decisions involving choice amongst alternatives.

(2) Decision-making. The technique of marginal costing is a valuable aid to management for decision-making under changing conditions. Business policies which form the basis of budgeting and which must be followed to secure desired results are formulated with the help of marginal cost analysis. Thus, one of the important duties of the cost accountant is to advise management on business policies arising out of marginal costing. Some of the important areas of decision-making where marginal cost analysis becomes unseful are mentioned below:

(i) ***Determination of Selling Price and Volume of Output.*** If the total revenue can be projected on the basis of anticipated prices and volumes of production, the increase in revenue at different levels of Production and at different prices can be compared with the marginal costs at those

levels of activity. Then the selling price which will maximise profits can be determined fasily by comparing the marginal costs and incremental revenue. Production should be increased as long as the increment in revenue is more than the marginal cost of producing the additional output. It will not be profitable any more to increase production when marginal revenue is equal to the marginal cost.

(ii) ***Make or Buy Decision.*** Manufacturers have sometimes to decide whether components or parts should be bought from the market or produced in the factory. The marginal cost of producing the parts compared with the market price gives an accurate basis for taking the decision to make or buy.

(iii) ***Determining Optimum Product or Sales-mix.*** Business firms producing and selling two or more products often face the problems of determining the ratio in which the different items should be produced and sold so as to maximise profits or minimise costs. As the fixed overheads are constant whatever be the mix, the most profitable mix is that which would give the highest amount of gross margin (excess of selling price over the variable costs). Application of the marginal costing technique is very appropriate in this connection. The decision will naturally depend on the effect of alternative combinations on the use of labour, materials, machine time, selling techniques, storage space, etc.

(iv) ***Replacement of Machinery.*** Whether it would be more profitable to replace existing machinery by new and improved ones is question which management in every concern has to face from time to time. The differential cost of keeping the old machine in use and using new machinery is the proper basis for making decisions of this nature.

(v) ***Acceptance of Special Order.*** If a special order is proposed and the price offered is less than the average total cost, a

comparison of the additional revenue and marginal cost is necessary to decide whether the order is worthwhile to accept. Assuming that the order executed at the offered price will not affect the selling price in the market, it will be profitable to accept the offer so long as the additional revenue exceeds the marginal cost of supplying the order.

(vi) ***Submitting Tenders and Quotations.*** When a tender is submitted, the additional production involved will mean an increase in total cost. To make a competitive bid, the minimum price has to be quoted. The marginal cost indicates the floor below which the quotation will be unprofitable. This implies that any price above the marginal cost may be quoted so as to increase the total profit, provided the quoted price does not lower the normal price for the rest of the market.

(vii) ***Alternative Use of Plant Facility.*** If the manufacture of a particular product or component is possible by different methods techniques it needs to be decided whether one machine should be used instead of another, or how many operators should be used with a machine, or whether the processing should be carried out by manual or machine work. Marginal costing may be used in comparing the effect of alternative techniques on profit. The variable cost affected by alternative technique will lead to varying gross margins and this can be on the basis of deciding upon the best alternative.

(3) Cost Control. The importance of cost controller accomplishing the objective of profit maximisation is widely recognised in business houses. But neither all costs are controllable by any individual nor are all costs controllable by management at all times. Therefore, it is appropriate and logical that a clear distinction should be made between controllable costs. However, it is also necessary for effective cost control that the responsibility of control must lie with those who make the cost incurring decisions. This is possible to ensure through the marginal cost technique where variable and fixed costs are normally separated.

As Marginal Costing recognises the behaviour of costs in relation to volume and/or time, only variable costs are charged to product processes or functions per unit basis while the fixed expenses incurred to keep capacity and sell in readiness for use, are not charged to products and can be controlled by functional responsibility centres. Hence, the foreman is no longer accountable for depreciation and rent over which he has no control. Fixed costs are referred to the controlling authority involved. Thus, marginal costing ensures reporting only such costs to individual managers which are relevant and appropriate.

Further, under Marginal Costing it is possible to accumulate costs by cost centres, the smallest area of responsibility like, for instance, a department. Thus reports to foremen include only those costs which are subject to his control. Reports to higher managers include costs items in either detailed or summary form, because more costs are controllable as the scope of management responsibility enlarges. For instance, the production superintendent is responsible for all costs of the production department and own office costs. The production manager is responsible for costs of the production and service departments. The reports sent to management thus summarise the controllable costs at each stage.

Fixed costs are collected and reported in the income statement as separate deductions from marginal income *i.e.*, contribution margin instead of being merged with the cost of goods sold and inventory. This helps management to clearly understand the expense behaviour and not to loose sight of individual items of fixed expenses.

In short, the most important requirement of cost control, that costs within the functional area of responsibility be identified and controlled by people who make the cost incurring decisions; is fulfilled in marginal costing it follows a logical principle that costs which are not controlled by the responsibility individual should be omitted or separated from the costs which the individual is expected to control. This is technically referred to as "Responsibility Accounting".

Marginal Costing facilitates management by exception by focussing attention of the management towards results which are moving out of line and prompt them to initiate timely action for correction. Moreover, it helps higher level management personnel in evaluating the performance of men responsible to them. The impact of fixed expenses over specific functions and in the firm as a whole is conveyed to management in a more meaningful form under marginal costing. This helps management to ensure better utilisation of existing facilities and personnel.

To sum up, as a tool of management, the marginal costing technique highlights relationships between profits and the major factors affecting profits. The significance of marginal costing is particularly established, in multi-product companies and situations in which there is under-utilised capacity, and in connection with cost reporting to managers at different levels in the organisation. Variable costs and fixed costs require different approaches for purposes of control. From this point of view, marginal costing followes a logical principle that costs which are not controllable by operating managers should be separated from costs which are expected to be controlled by them.

Limitations of Direct Costing/Marginal Costing Variable Costing

Under certain conditions, some of the advantages listed in the previous section can be considered disadvantages of for example, the management of a company were prone to make all decisions both short and long-term, on the is of contribution, it might be a disadvantage to have the monthly accounting statements reflect contribution. In addition to these disadvantages that may apply in particular cases there are five disadvantages to direct costing.

(1) Inventories are Undervalued. The first disadvantage of direct costing is that inventories are undervalued. There is no question that inventories will have a lower value under a direct costing system than under a full absorption system and, in this respect, could be considered undervalued. Whether this disadvantage applies to any situation will depend on what effect this lower inventory value has. (The same disadvantage applies to the LIFO method of inventory valuation.) To the extent that in, direct costing inventories are smaller than in full absorption costing, internal statements will show a lower profit (in the year of the change over).

(2) Internal Financial Statements Differ from Published Reports. The Second disadvantage is that the internal financial statements will differ from the published reports. This results because most direct costing methods are not considered acceptable by the public accounting profession for external financial statements. Consequently, when a company uses direct costing, it is necessary to increase the value of the inventory to reflect full accounted costs. This adjustment may cause confusion because the internal profit figure will be different from that included in the annual report.

The seriousness of this disadvantage depends on the ability of management to understand the situation. If management understands and agrees that a direct costing system is more useful there should be little problem. If, however, management is not able (or willing) to understand why internal and external statemen' are different, this factor could be an important consideration in deciding whether to adopt a direct costing system.

The calculation to adjust the inventories to full cost is usually not an involved problem with respect to either the public accountant or the Internal Revenue Service. Acceptable methods are available that can be applied to the entire inventory value so that it is not necessary to recalculate the cost of each item. The clerical cost of making this calculation is relatively small.

(3) Monthly Profits Tend to Fluctuate more Widely. The third disadvantage of direct costing is that monthly profits will tend to fluctuate widely where the demand is seasonal. Under a full absorption system, if production is relatively constant, the effects of seasonal than changes in sales will be considerably mitigated. With direct costing, however the same amount of fixed costs will be reflected in the income statement each month regardless of the sales volume; therefore, profits will be higher in above-average months and lower in below-average months.

The seriousness of this disadvantage will depend upon several things, first, upon whether seasonal demand exists; if it does exist, upon whether production is more constant than sales (if it is not, the monthly profit fluctuations will not be mitigated), third, upon whether management, understands the limitations of the monthly profit estimates. As in the other situations, this is considering the adoption of a direct costing system.

(4) Direct Costing Requires a Change in the Present System. The fourth disadvantage of direct costing is that for most companies it entails a departure from accounting methods that have been in effect for some period of time. Any change causes a certain amount of trouble and confusion. A change to a direct costing system, therefore should not be made unless there are positive advantages for doing so. A company should not change its internal accounting system simply because "it appears to be the thing to do". Direct costing (or any other costing) is not a panacea for management ills. A direct costing system may aid management to make better decisions but it will not compensate for inadequate management.

(5) It is Difficult to Calculate Variable Costs. The fifth disadvantage, offered by proponents of full costing, is the inability of some companies to calculate variable costs, or even to agree on a definition. Management must make decisions based on differential costs and, consequently, these costs must be estimated. No matter how inexact the estimate, it is generally better than no estimate at all. The objection refers to having these variable costs reflected on the books of account. Since the variability of costs will differ under different circumstance, the usefulness of a single calculation of the variability of overhead costs is questioned. The answer to this question must also be decided in the context of a specific situation. If management must take many decision where variable cost may be very widely, a separate study will be required for each decision. Under these circumstances, little would be gained in having a single, arbitrarily deemed variable cost reflected on the books of account. If however, the variability of overhead costs does not differ much for different types of decisions, the fourth objection to direct costing is not valid.

❒

7

Emerging Trends in Management Accounting

A. Inflation Accounting

One of the important objectives of maintaining financial accounts is to measure true profit and prepare Balance Sheet which represent true and fair economic portion of an enterprise. This objective can be achieved only if the account books are rightly maintained and any external factor affecting them is duly recognized and its effect is shown in the final accounts. Historical accounting system is based on certain well accepted accounting concepts and principles which guide in the maintenance, preposition and presentation of accounts. Anything which is not consistent with conventional accounting principles is ignored despite the fact that it considerably effects the nature of financial reports and statements which are prepared for internal and external purposes. One such important thing is the 'Inflation' which effect the Final Accounts but its effect is not appreciated by conventional accountants who are attached dearly with the 'cost principle' of historical accounting system. It is only recently that the accountants have started realising the impact of inflation on financial accounts and report the same, in one form or the other, to their users.

Effects of Inflation

Under condition of inflation the price of raw materials, wages, and every other input of production goes an increasing. Similarly, the replacement cost of fixed assets is much higher than their cost values when inflation shows rapid increase in price level. In other words, the inflation pushes down the value of money which can, now buy lesser amount of similar goods with the same amount of money.

Traditional Accounting is based on the assumption of stable value of money which is quite unrealistic under inflationary conditions. The values attached to unsold stock, fixed assets, etc. change with changes in price level; hence the Balance Sheet will fail to show current economic portion if historical values are shown in the Balance Sheet. The profit measurement based on historical valuation of inventory and depreciation charges will also not be fair under conditions of rising prices. Historical accounts may mislead outside uses and the management itself may not rightly interpret the accounts in the absence of inflation accounting as the historical accounts present nothing but a distorted picture of business affairs. The comparison of the one period's performance and economic position with any other period is not proper and fruitful due to distortion in accounts.

Financial analysts should properly understand the manner in which distortions arise in conventional accounts based on traditional concepts and conventions of accounts. Following distortions are notable.

1. Under-valuation of Inventory. Under conventional accounting, the inventories are valued at lower of cost or market value. The closing inventory of the current year becomes opening inventory of the next year. The real value of raw materials purchased for the current year's production is also more than the cost but they are shown at cost values. Thus the cost of goods sold is much less than its real cost. In this manner, the calculated gross profit and hence, net profit is inflated or over-stated. The distortion is caused due to the fact that the cost of sales (at cost value) is matched against the current value of sales.

2. Under Provision for Depreciation. According to traditional costing depreciation is charged on the cost values of assets which are purchased at different periods of time at different price levels. The depreciation change is matched with sales at current prices having low purchasing power. The amount of depreciation is much less than when considered on the real values of assets. It leads to over-statement of profit due to inadequate provision for profits.

3. Current Position not Reflected. Fixed assets are shown at cost less depreciation and inventory which form a sizable proportion of working capital is also shown at cost price, or market price, whichever is less. This type of treatment is, not fair when their actual values are much higher. The Balance Sheet based in traditional accounting practices fails to reflect the current economic picture of an enterprise.

4. Capital Erosion. There is always a danger that the capital may be eaten away by the distribution of dividend out of capital when the profits have been over-stated. Non-recovery of cost of exhaustion of fixed assets, endangers, the long-term financial stability of the firm.

5. Different Replacement of Assets. The management may find it difficult to replace the retiring assets by the new ones due to the fact that the amount represented by Depreciation Fund Account is much less than the amount required to buy new assets which obviously cost more due to increasing price level. It becomes almost impossible to maintain capital without recognising inflation Accounting.

6. Loss Gains on Monetary Assets Liabilities. Holding of monetary assets such as cash balances, bills receivables and debtors cause loss to a firm as their real value declines due to inflation. Against it, a firm gains on the delayed payment to its creditors. Such losses and gains need to be brought into financial statements if real position is to be conveyed to their users.

Thus, the historical financial accounting suffers from the serious limitations and posses a there at of the very existence of an enterprice in the long-term. Therefore, we need a system of accounting which could contribute in the meansurement of true profit and show the true and fair economic values of assets and liabilities in the Balance Sheet. Inflation Accounting is a newly developed technique which is helpful in achieving the desired objectives. It may be defined as an accounting technique which appreciate objectives. It may be defined as an accounting technique which appreciate the impact of inflation on accounts of an undertaking and provides for the same by allowing the assets and liabilities to be shown at current values through adjustments in the Income Statement of that year.

There is a lot of controversy as to the measurement of impact of inflation on an enterprise and method of showing the impact in the Final Accounts. Radical thinking on the subject is that the traditional method of presentation of Final Accounts should be entirely replaced by the current accounting techniques. A large number of academicians and practitioners believe that this type of change will complicate the matter and a greater degree of subjectivity will enter into the accounts. Hence, the benefits of Inflation Accounting may be reaped if the a Final Accounts are allowed to be prepared and reported in the usual manner and the impact of inflation is shown as a supplementary information attend to the historical accounts.

Techniques of Inflation Accounting

Accounting for inflation has been one of the most controversial subjects. There is no dearth of persons in the accounting profession; who are opposed to the introduction of inflation accounting by the modification of historical accounting system. But nobody can deny the fact that the inflation causes distortions in accounts which need to be rectified by some kind of method which may be of general acceptability.

Partial Price Level Accounting

Since price level accounting is not statutory in case of Indian companies and other organizations, a partial price level accounting may be resorted to neutralise the effect of inflation and produce some degree of improvement in profit measurement. The price level accounting is said to be partial if the accounts are modified along the following lines:

1. Use of UFO method for valuation of inventory so that the cost of goods sold is valued at the most current cost so as to measure realistic gross profit.

2. Use of replacement cost in place of historical costs of assets for the purposes of depreciation charges and Balance Sheet figure.
3. Creation of Depreciation Reserve Account out of current year's profits to enable the enterprise to accumulate reserve to facilitate replacement of the retiring assets.

An enterprise can serve its purpose to a great extent by doing the above but the problem of reporting the current economic position of the enterprise still remains unresolved. The partial method does not specify any method method for the estimation of anticipated replacement cost of assets. It fails to recognize the effect of inflation on monetary assets as a result of change in the value of money as a measuring rod. Thus it does not provide a comprehensive method to deal with Inflation Accounting problem.

Full Price Level Accounting

According to full price level accounting, all the items- monetary and non-monetary is appearing in historical final accounts are recast according to a particular method so as to bring in them the full effect of purchasing power variations. Broadly speaking, two methods to deal with accounting for price level changes have been developed, as explained below:

CURRENT PURCHASING POWER ACCOUNTING (CPPA)

According to CPPA method the historical costs are adjusted by indices in terms of general purchasing power of money at the end of the year. For this reason, this method is also known as General Purchasing Power Accounting (GPPA) or General Price Level Accounting (GPLA) method. Under conditions of rising prices (Inflation), the price Index at the end is higher than at the beginning of the year. The current purchasing power of any item is converted as per the following formula:

Current Purchasing Power (CPP)

$$= \frac{\text{Current Price Index}}{\text{Index at Beginning}} \times \text{Conversion Amount}$$

It may be noted that the historical costs for an item, say, inventory are incurred at different points of time at varying price index. The CPPA method converts the mixed historical costs into an equivalent rupee of current purchasing power and thus makes all the accounting numbers comparable in terms of general purchasing power. General Price Index is fairly a good measure to convent the historical costs into an equivalent purchasing power. It is assumed that the movements in prices of materials, labour and fixed capital equipments, etc., are in the same direction and at the same rates as in case of general price index. The wholesale price index or consumers price Index can also be applied for cost conversion with almost same degree of accuracy. Historical cost multiplied by conversion factor gives the current cost which, if spent, can buy the same amount of goods as could be bought by incurring the cost at the beginning.

The conversion factor is determined as under:

$$\text{Conversion Factor} = \frac{\text{Price Index at end}}{\text{Pirce Index at beginning}}$$

Illustration.

On 1st January 2003, a Company purchased a machine for Rs. 50,000 when the General Price Index was 100. The inflation has pushed up the Index to 120 to 31st December 2003. The Company wishes to show the asset at current cost based on General Price Index. You are required to convert the historical cost into current cost and show how the asset would appear in the Balance Sheet if depreciation @ 20%cost to be changed on current cost.

Solution.

Current cost = Historical × Conversion factor

$$= 50{,}000 \times \frac{120}{100}$$

$$= 50{,}000 \times \frac{6}{5}$$

$$= 50{,}000 \times 1.2 = 60{,}000$$

Balance Sheet

	Historical costing	*Current purchasing power*
Machine less depreciation	4,000	48,000

Monetary Items

Monetary items are those items of a Balance Sheet which are fixed or otherwise remain unchanged despite the change in the general price Index. For example, Sundry debtors is an item of current asset which is fixed in the sense that a firm will realize neither more nor less than the amount stated in the historical accounts. Other examples of monetary items are the cash balances, Bills Receivables, Sundry Creditors, Accrrued Incomes, outstanding expenses, etc. Since monetary items are fixed by contract or otherwise, they are shown in the inflation Adjusted Balance Sheet as their historical values. However net gains or loss on holding monetary items is calculated and taken into account in determining net income /loss.

There is always loss in holding monetary assets as they loose purchasing power during inflation. On the other hand, there is a gain in holding monetary liabilities which can be discharged by paying the same fixed amount which has lost purchasing power, during inflation. The net gain or loss in monetary items is to be calculated and included in current income or treated as capital item.

Illustration.

Suppose a firm has a cash balance of Rs.5,000 in the beginning of the current year-1st Jan. 2003 and it holds the same Rs 5,000 on 31st Dec. 2003 as there was no transaction during the year. Calculate the loss due to holding this monetary asset if the General Price Index has gone up from 100 at the beginning of the year to 120 at the end of the year.

Solution.

The firm must hold cash balance which is more than 5,000 in order to neutralise the effect of inflation. It must hold

$$5,000 \times \frac{120}{100} = \text{Rs. } 6,000$$

whereas it holds the same fixed Rs. 5,000. Then there is a loss of Rs. 1,000 (6,000-5,000) in holding cash.

Non-Monetary Items

Non-monetary items include all those assets and liabilities which do not represent a fixed amount to be received or paid. Examples of non-monetary items are equity capital, reserves and surplus, land, building Machinery, etc. There is no gain or loss on non-monetary assets the way it accrues on monetary assets which carry fixed amount. The values of non-monetary items may change over time. This is the reason that the non-monetary assets and liabilities are shown at adjusted values in the CPPA adjusted Balance Sheet. The conversion factor for non-monetary items is determined as under:

(a) Conversion factor for non-monetary asset

$$= \frac{\text{Price Index on date of Balance Sheet}}{\text{Price Index on acquisition of Sheet}}$$

(b) Conversion factor for capital

$$= \frac{\text{Current year's Index}}{\text{Index on date of capital acquistion}}$$

(c) Reserve & Surplus (retained earnings) will be the residual figure after restatement of all items in terms of general purchasing power in the year when Inflation Accounting is introduced for the first time.

Adjusted Income Statement

For the preparation of adjusted Income Statement according to CPPA method, the adjustment are required to be made in respect of each item of revenue and expenses which must be converted in terms of the purchasing power equivalent to year-end rupee. The procedure for conversion is almost the same as in case of monetary and non-monetary items as explained earlier. Consider the following in this connection:

Items	*Methods of Conversion*
Open Inventory	$\frac{\text{Index at the end}}{\text{Index at Beginning}} \times \text{Opening Inventory}$
Purchases	$\frac{\text{Index at end}}{\text{Average Index}} \times \text{Amount of Purchase}$
Wages & Salaries and other expenses	$\frac{\text{Index at end}}{\text{Average Index}} \times \text{Conversion cost}$
Closing Inventory	Depends upon the method used for issue of inventory for consumption *i.e.* : LIFO or FIFO method
Depreciation written off	$\frac{\text{Index at end}}{\text{Index when asset acquired}} \times \text{Amount of depreciation}$ Alternatively, the assets may be first restated in terms of current Purchasing power and then the depreciation on such a cost at a particular rate calculated.
Interest and dividend	Interest and dividend paid or received at the end of the year need no adjustment as they represent current purchasing power.

Illustration.

Balance Sheet of a Public limited company for the year end on 31st Dec. 2002 stood as under:

Liabilities	*2002 (Rs)*	*2003 (Rs)*	*Assets*	*2002 (Rs)*	*2003 (Rs)*
Capital	2,00,000	2,00,000	Land & Buildings	75,000	7,50,000
Retained Earnings	—	65,000	Plant & Machinery	1,00,000	1,00,000

Accumulated Depreciation	—	20,000	Monetary assets	65,000	45,000
Liabilities	1,00,000	1,00,000	Investories —2002 = 4000 units —2003 = 3000 units	60,000	45,000
	3,00,000	3,25,000		3,00,000	3,25,000

The income statement for the year 2003 was as under:

Sales (6000 units @ 50	3,00,000	
Less:		
opening Inventory		
4000 units @ 15	60,000	
Purchases-	1,00,000	
5000 units @ 20	1,60,000	
Less: closing Inventory		
3000 units @15	45,000	
		1,15,000
		1,85,000
Less Expenses:		
Interest changes		15,000
Administration exp.	85,000	
Depreciation	20,000	1,20,000
Net Income		65,000

Calculation of Purchasing Power Gains/Loss

	Unadjusted	*Conversion*	*Adjusted*
Net monetary assets on 1-1-2003	(35,000)	180/100	(63,000)
Add monetary receipts during 2003	3,00,000	180/120	4,50,000
Net monetary Items	2,65,000		3,87,000
Less monetary Payments			
Purchases	1,00,000	180/150	1,20,000

Interest	15,000	180/120	22,500
Administration Expenses	25,000	180/120	1,27,000
	2,00,000		2,70,000
Net monetary assets on 31-12-95	65,000		1,17,000
Less Actual net monetary assets on 31-12-1995			65,000
Purchasing power loss			52,000

Adjusted Income Statement for the Year Ending 2003

	Unadjusted	*Conversion factor*	*Adjusted*
Sales: 6000 units @ 50/-	3,00,000	180/120	4,50,000
Loss: Cost of goods sold:			
opening stock: 4000 units	60,000	180/100	1,08,000
Purchases: 5000 X 20	1,00,000	180/150	1,20,000
	1,60,000		2,28,000
Loss: Closing Inventory 3000 × 15	45,000	180/100	21,000
Cost of goods sold	1,15,000		1,47,000
Gross margm	1,85,000		3,03,000
Other Expenses:			
Interest	15000	180/120	22,500
Admn. Expenses	25,000	180/120	1,27,500
Depreciation	20,000	180/100	36,000
	1,20,000		1,86,000
Net Operating Income	65,000		1,17,000

Reconciliation of Adjusted Earnings

Retaining Earnings 1-1-2003	nil
Adjusted net operating income	1,17,000
Less purchasing power loss	52,000
Net Income transferred to B/S	65,000

Price Level Adjusted Balance Sheet As on 31-12-2003

Liabilities	*Unadjusted (Rs.)*	*Conversion*	*Adjusted (Rs.)*	*Assets*	*Unadjusted (Rs.)*	*Conversion*	*Adjusted (Rs.)*
Liabilities	1,00,000	180/180	1,00,000	Monetary Assets	1,65,000		1,65,000
Capital	2,00,000	180/100	3,60,000	Inventories	45,000	180/100	81,000
Retained Earnings	65,000		65,000	Land & Buildings	75,999	180/100	1,35,000
Accumulated Depreciation	20,000	180/100	36,000	Plant & Machinery	1,00,000	180/100	1,80,000
	3,85,000		5,61,000		3,85,000		5,61,000

Merits of CPPA Method

The chief merits of CPPA method of inflation accounting may be noted as under:

1. This method is conceptually a sound method as it is rightly concerned with the change in the general level of prices *i.e.* inflation.
2. The method provides an objective basis for converting the historical costs into current costs as it uses the current price index which is published by a reliable agency.
3. The inter-firm comparison of annual accounts is objective and dependable as the same criterion to represent the current values is used by different firms.
4. The capital of the enterprice is maintainable as the method attempts to provide depreciation on current cost and recognize the loss on holding the monetary assets.
5. Replacement, cost of assets is nearer to the current purchasing power of which adjustments in accounts are made. The management is in a position to replace any asset conveniently when CPPA method is used to incorporate the effect of inflation in account books and accordingly manage the finances.

6. Income measurement is scientific as the matching of revenues and expenses is based on the same value.
7. The CPPA method provides useful information to management to understand the impact of inflation on different firms working with different capital-mix and asset structure and adjust its own policies for optimising income of shareholders.

Limitations of CPPA Method

The method has been criticised due to the following limitations:

1. General price level may not necessarily reflect the current cost of an asset for which we need specific price index. Therefore, the method should be applied with due care.
2. Selection of an appropriate Index Number is itself a difficult task. The result based on cost of living Index Number may be different from that of indices of producers goods. Sometimes, the correctness of available Index Numbers is also doubtful.
3. Calculation of purchasing power loss/gain on monetary items does not serve any tangible gain except that it leads to more confusion in the minds of users of inflation adjusted statements. A highly levered company is likely to show high gains on borrowed funds and over-statement of its profits in a period of inflation.
4. Tax authorities do not agree to the method of profit measurement for tax purposes under Inflation Accounting method. This limits the use of the technique for reporting profits on current purchasing power basis.
5. The CPPA is not suitable for small scale undertakings due to its being a costly affair as it requires technical knowledge and other resources for its proper implementation on regular basis
6. Maintenance of operating capability of an enterprise remains unsolved in a period of inflation due to gradual depletion of working capital.

The CPPA method is considered a true Inflation Accounting method despite its limitations for the simple reasons that it offers a simple and objective solution to the problem, specially in a period when an economy is passing through a phase of high degree of inflation when the prices of all goods move in the same direction.

Current Cost Or Replacement Cost Accounting

The basic problem concerning assets management is the replacement of existing capital equipments by new ones at the time of expiry of their life without economic difficulties. This is possible when adequate funds in the form of accumulated depreciation have been created during the life time of assets. Another related problem is the presentation of current cost ,or replacement cost in the Balance Sheet for rational decision-making by users of Balance Sheet. The Current Cost (replacement cost) Accounting (CCA) for truly reflecting the impact of inflation takes into account the current cost of individual assets by using specific Index Numbers instead of general price indices which are used in case of CPPA method. In order to ascertain current cost of assets, the services of expert valuers may also be utilized. The financial analyst should clearly understood the concept of current cost which is defined as the amount of cash or other consideration which is needed to buy a new asset of more or less similar nature.

Sandiland committee headed by Mr. Francis C.P. Sandiland appointed by the British Government in 1975 to examine various issues relating to Inflation Accounting had recommended the Current Cost Accounting (CCA) to deal with the changes that arise in the economic position of an undertaking as a result of inflation. According to CCA method, the accounts have to be readjusted as under:

1. Preparation of Income Statement for current year to determine current operating income by the application of matching principle.
2. Calculation of holding gains /loss for showing the same in Balance Sheet.
3. Presentation of Balance Sheet on current cost basis.

Following illustration clarifies the redrafting the annual accounts based on current cost Accounting technique.

Illustration.

Arti Products Ltd. reported the following annual accounts:

Liabilities	*2002*	*2003*	*Assets*	*2002*	*2003*
Capital	80,000	80,000	Land & Building	70,000	70,000
Loans	70,000	70,000	Plant & Machinery	80,000	80,000
Reserve &			Inventives	44,000	33,000
Surplus	70,000	87,000	2002-4000 units		
			2003-3000 units		
Accumulated					
Depreciation	16,000	32,000	Debtors	26,000	46,000
			Cash	16,000	40,000
	2,36,000	2,69,000		2,36,000	2,69,000

Income Statement For 2003

Sales: 7000 units @ 50 per unit	35,000	
Less: cost of goods sold:		
opening inventory 4000 × 11	44,000	
Purchases 6000 × 20	1,20,000	
	1,64,000	
Less: Closing stock: 3000 × 11	33,000	1,31,000
		2,19,000
Gross Margin		
Operating Expenses		
Usual Expenses	1,75,000	
Depreciation	16,000	
Interest	10,500	2,02,000
Net Profit		17,000

You are required to redraft the Income Statement and the Balance Sheet for 2003 providing for the following as for the current Cost Accounting method of Inflation Accounting.

1. Replacement cost of land during 2003 was Rs. 130000 and the current cost of Plant & Machinery was estimated at Rs. 1,75000
2. The sales were made at the end of 2003 when the replacement cost of inventory was Rs.25 per unit.
3. The company has used FIFO method of inventory valuation.
4. Plant & Machinery has a life of 5 years.

Solution.

Income Statement for the Year 2003
(Current Cost Method)

Sales- 7000 units @ 50 per unit		3,50,000
Less cost of sales:		
Opening Inventory 4000 × 25		1,00,000
Purchase 6000 × 25	1,50,000	
	2,50,000	
Less closing Inventory 3000 × 25	75,000	1,75,000
Gross Margin	1,75,000	
Less : Usual Expenses	1,75,000	
Interest	10,500	
Depreciation 20% of $\frac{(175000 + 80000)}{2}$	25,500	211,500
		(36,500)
Net operating profit (Before holding gains & losses)		

Reasised Holding Gains

On Inventory:	
(a) Purchases 6000 (25 – 20)	30,000
(b) Opening Inventory 1000 (25 – 11)	14,000
On Depreciation:	9,500
(25,500 – 16,000)	53,500

BALANCE SHEET
As on 31st December 2003

Equity capital		80000	Land & Buildings		1,30,000
Loans		70,000	Plant & Machinery		
Reserve & Surplus				175,000	
Beginning Balance			*Less* Accumulated		
	70,000		Depreciation	70000	1,05,000
Operating Profit	(36,500)		Inventories 3000 × 25		75,000
Realised holding			Debtors		46,000
gains	53,500		Cash		40,000
Unrealised		87,000			
holding gains		1,59,000			
(Balancing figure)		3,96,000			3,96,000

Merits of CCA Method

1. Profit is realistically ascertained as the current revenue income is matched against the current cost of earning that revenue.
2. The method suggests the maximum amount which an undertaking can distribute by way of dividend without disturbing productions capability.
3. Segregation of operating income from that of holding gains is important from management point of view. Management can formulate realistic dividend policy when realized and untealized holding gains are also considered in such policy-making.
4. The method is simple as it can be applied easily in re-drafting the annual accounts.

Demerits of CCA Method

1. The concept of current cost is not rigidly defined. The current cost of an existing asset will be different from the current cost of similar asset with some kind of technical improvements.

2. Ascertainment of current or replacement cost is a difficult problem. Expert valuation, introduces a lot of subjectivity in calculations.
3. The method ignores the gains or losses on holding monetary assets and liabilities.
4. It cannot be used with equal advantage in fixed assets and inventory intensive industries and in industries with few fixed assets and a high turnover of inventory.

Inflation Accounting Standards and Practices

During the last two decades or so, the Inflation Accounting has attracted the attention of professional accounting institutes, and other bodies of accountants and academicians both in developed as well as under-developed countries in the world. In 1969, the Accounting Principles Board (APB) in U.S.A. issued APB statement No.3 which recommended for the disclosure of supplementary price-level changes informations. Since them, the regulatory bodies *i.e.* the Financial Accounting standards Board and the Securities and Exchange Commission have issued Exposure Draft (1974) and Accounting series Release No. 190 (1976) respectively, which required the firms to furnish supplementary information regarding impact of inflation on their performance and economic position. The Financial Accounting Standard No.33 (FAS 33) issued by FASB in 1979 requires mandatory supplementary informations regarding inflationary impact with a view to meeting the users objective of better informations on firms working. In the United Kingdom, Inflation Accounting was favoured by a statement of Accounting active No.7 (1974) which required the supplementary informations balled on general Purchasing power accounting. Sandilands Committee in 1975 had recommended the Current Cost Accounting method for readjustment of final accounts prepared on historical cost accounting principles. The statement of Standard Accounting Practice-16 (SAP-16) in U.K. presently guides the preparation of accounts which should incorporate the impact of inflation.

The developments in U.A. and U.K., have encouraged other countries to think of inflation Accounting as a means of proper education to management and other users of final accounts for rational decision-making. So far as India is concerned, the inflation accounting is still optional in the absence of any prescribed standard and majority of the Indian Companies publish the accounts based on historical costing. The Institute of Chartered Accountants of India had issued a Guidance Note on Accounting for price level changes in 1982. Few enlightened and progressive companies is private and public sector such as Hindustan Organic Chemicals Ltd., Bharat Heavy Electricals Ltd., Hindustan Machine Tools Ltd., Tata Iron & Steel Co., etc., have started publishing price-level adjusted final accounts for the information of the interested parties. Inflation accounting in India can be made compulsory by an amendment in the Indian Companies Act to the best advantage of companies and other users. The companies will be willing to reconstruct accounts as per the rules provided the tax authorities allow enhanced depreciation on replacement cost.

SOCIAL RESPONSIBILITY ACCOUNTING

Investors and those dealing in companies shares and debentures are directly interested in the operations of such undertakings. The government agencies such as Securities and Exchange Board of India and Board of Industrial and Financial Reconstructive (BIFR) are also keenly interested in the published accounts and other accounting defects of public limited companies. In the modern time, the consumers and general public has also started taking interest in the economic affairs of large scale business enterprises which effect public life in a number of ways. The people of a particular region in which a large scale factory is set up, cannot ignore its effects on their life. Large scale industrialization brings economic prosperity to the people and effects substantial change in their life style. Simultaneously, it also brings some changes in physical and social environment in which their health and happiness deminish. The disadvantages of unplanned industrialization at a bigger scale are widely known. The welfare governments try to eliminate or minimise the harmful effects of setting up of large scale factories through various legislative measures. Efforts are also made to bring out improvements in the prevailing condition by encouraging public awareness and developing a sense of social responsibility among the industrialists.

The manufacturers and sellers earn a part of profit at the cost of the public. They are not required to pay any extra cost, *e.g.*, for the environmental pollution which the factories create by virtue of the very nature of production. The pollution is injurious to public health and the public has to bear the cost in the form of additional expenditure on medical care and reduced incomes. Therefore, public would expect some kind of compensation against the cost it bears and it would also like to know the policies and programmes of the factories to safeguard the interests of the public. With public awareness and interest taken by the government, the social accounting or social responsibility accounting is a new area in accounting which is emerging fastly with the rapid industrial development in the developing countries in the world.

Social responsibility accounting is not a separate branch of accounting but it is simply on accounting technique which seeks to highlight the social responsibility of business in addition to its economic obligations. Social responsibility of business firms is increasingly being recognised by the government and by all those who feel concerned for public welfare. The enlightened business enterprises realise their responsibility towards the society at whose cost they earn super-normal profits. The public through its elected representatives have started questioning the performance of large scale enterprises in terms of social benefits and the progressive public limited companies provide informations relating to their activities for social good Social responsibility accounting is concerned with identification of the areas of social concern, measurement of social costs and social benefits and reporting the same informations alongwith the published accounts to satisfy public interest and also with a view to show true and fair view of the operations and economic position of business enterprises. The terms such as Social Accounting and Societal Accounting have also been used in place of social responsibility accounting without disturbing the nature and scope of the subject. Therefore, the usage of one term in place of another does not make any difference. However, the term social accounting gives an impression of national accounts and may be avoided in the interest of the clarity of message.

The main objectives of social responsibility accounting are: *(a)* Creation of public awareness regarding social costs and social benefits of a factory in their locality or regions, *(b)* Government involvement in safeguarding the health and well-being of the public which is exposed to handful effects of the industry, *(c)* Developing consciousness among other social welfare organisations regarding industrial locations and their impact on society, *(d)* Construction and publication of annual accounts which incorporate social responsibility of business.

The achievement of the above objectives is vital in the interest of the society and enterprisers. With increasing public awareness, the entrepreneurs will be forced to create facilities to neutralise the harmful effects on society of their enterprises and they will also be able to understand realistic economic position of their enterprises and accordingly inform the outside interested parties for their investment decisions. It may be pointed out that in the developed countries, a public limited company which is engaged in large scale business activity is not regarded an economic business entity exclusively for profit-making but it is also required to perform its social responsibility by undertaking social activities for public welfare. In developing countries the social responsibility is also gaining grounds.

AREAS OF SOCIAL RESPONSIBILITY

Social responsibility of business is not only confined to prevent and minimise the hannful effects of pollution but it is extended to other equally important areas such as community involvement, human resource development, product improvements and fair business practices, energy conservation, etc. Each area of social responsibility covers wide range of activities such as mentioned below:

1. **Community Involvement.** Social performance in (his area relates to corporate support to educational institutions, cultural activities, recreational performances, health and welfare activities. Aid in personal problems concerning

physically handicapped and child care is considered as a great social responsibility of business in modern times. Encouraging and providing time for employees and to be active as volunteers in community activities is also an important part of corporate social responsibility.

2. **Environmental Contribution.** A clear and clear environment is highly important for the health of the society. The establishment of factories in a particular region pollute the environment through the emission of different gases and its waste materials and thus cause harm to the social health. The study of the benefits being enjoyed by the industry and the cost being borne by the society in terms of injury to its health is a subject-matter which form part of the social accounting.
3. **Conservation of Physical Resources.** Physical resources conservation is considered as one of the important social responsibility of today's manufacturing firms. Energy and scarce raw materials need to be used economically, and new resources developed to meet the industry requirements. Society in general and the investors in particular want that the information on these issues is disclosed in the annual accounts of companies.
4. **Product Contribution.** It is the social responsibility of business that it does not ignore the interests of the consumers and provide right type of goods at reasonable rates with assured supply and attend to all consumer complaints promptly. Consumers education is regarded as one of the important components of social responsibility of modern entrepreneurs, through the supply of relevant literature and media programmes to keep the consumers informed of the characteristics of product or services.
5. **Human Resources.** Creation of job opportunities, enhancement of workers skill through education and training, continuity of employment, recruitment in depressed areas, adequate wages, provision of congenial working

condition recognition of workers ability and providing equal opportunity for promotion etc., are the vital areas of social responsibility of business enterprises. Provision of education and counselling for employees to prevent or alleviate problems arising out of use of drugs and alcohol by employees is an area of social responsibility which is emerging fastly.

Method of Presentation

The social responsibility of business has been widely recognised and as such the society has the right to be informed of the activities which have been undertaken to compensate it for the cost it bears for the economic benefits of the industry. It is on the basis of such an information alone the society can decide to support or oppose the business programmes of an interprise. The evil effects of an industrial enter rise in a locality are so indirect and slow that the members of the locality pay no attention to it. With an increase in education and knowledge, a lots of awakening is witnessed these days among the ordinary members of the society that they are always prepared to come out openly against the government and industry which may cause harm to their life through the industrial activities in the long-run. Thus the industry cannot ignore the interests of the society while planning their business activities.

So far as the publication of information on social activities by Indian Companies is concerned, the picture is quite grim as majority of enterprises do not care for social good and the publication of such information is not statutory. However, there are some enlightened companies which publish information relating to their social activities for the information of the society. Most of the information provided is in a descriptive form as there is no standard format on which such information could be furnished. Generally, the information relating to social responsibility areas is provided in the Directors Report. Tata Iron and Steel Company one of the premier private sector giant gives sufficient details of expenditure on its social activities for the benefits of employees and the community of the surrounding areas. Some of the public sector companies not only provide social accounts in descriptive form but also in an account from which give a better and accurate idea about their social responsibilities. Public Sector Companies such as SAIL, BHEL, MMTC, IPCL, etc. have been publishing detailed accounts of their social cost-benefits. At present the public sector companies are required to disclose an account of benefits and social overhead costs alongwith the annual accounts.

The Steel Authority of India Limited (SAIL) prepares Social Income Statement and also a Social Balance Sheet. The Social Income statement in divided into: *(i)* Social benefits and cost to employees, *(ii)* Social benefits and costs to community, and *(iii)* Social benefits and costs to General public. The statements also show net social income/cost to employees, community and the general public. The Social Balance Sheet depicts the social funds and the social capital investments on the date of Balance Sheet. The company generates funds through own-equity and social equity contributed by employees. The funds are utilised for purchase of land, residential and other buildings, roads and budget, electrification, water supply and severage, furniture and fittings, human resources investment, etc.

The social responsibility accounting relating to general public includes various items of social benefits to general public and social cost to general public as shown below:

Social Benefits and Cost to General Public

A. Social Benefits to General Public

(a) Taxes, duties and levies paid to :	
(i) Central Government	—
(ii) State Governments	—
(b) Business generation	—
(c) Foreign Exchange	—
(i) Earned	—
(ii) Saved	—
(d) Research and development efforts	—
Total Benefits to General Public	____

B. Social Cost to General Public

(a) Social services and facilities consumed	—
(b) State services and facilities consumed	—
(c) Foreign exchange spent	—
Total Social Cost to General Public	___
Net Social Income/Cost to General Public	___

The statements in terms of monetary units give a better and accurate idea of the social responsibility of business. But the preparation of accurate quantitative statements is in itself a challenge. It is felt that the quantification of the cost in money value is a very difficult task. It is not possible to exactly calculate the social services and facilities consumed by the enterprise. Similarly it is a complex problem to calculate the damage done to the wealth of the society (social cost) due to environmental pollution caused by a factory in a particular area. The expenditure which is required to treat the ailments of the community, due to environmental pollution is the social cost which should ultimately be borne by the enterprises. An estimation of such a cost is possible and the entrepreneur should either pay the cost to government who provides the medical facilities or make necessary provision for preventive or curative methods of treatment. The social costs payments to government will be in addition to the corporate tax imposed on companies but this showed be a tax deductible item.

HUMAN RESOURCE ACCOUNTING

Human Resource is an important element in any production endeavour though the machines are rapidly replacing labour in the modern scientific age of production. Material resources-machines and materials cannot be put to economic use without human resources which means energies, skill and knowledge of people which are available to a firm for productive purposes. In fact human resources are as good as any other asset as the former actively contribute in the profitability of an organisation whereas the role of the latter in achieving the objectives is quite passive. The importance of human assets in an undertaking may be realized from the fact that all the material resources will be rendered useless or unproductive if they are not attended by trained, experienced and sincere work forces. It is a matter of satisfaction that the importance of human resource as a potent force of production is being realised in almost all the productive ventures in the modern time and this resource is being accorded a high status than that of the consumable physical assets.

The industry practice in the past has been to pay special attention for management of physical resources *i.e.*, inventory management, depreciation policy, amortization of wasting assets, treatment of capitalized revenue expenditure, etc. Very little attend on has been devoted to upgrade human resources through investment in the form of additional expenditure on hiring, education, training, health and satisfaction of people who are the real assets in any organisation. The industrial enterprises have shown more interest to evaluate the performance in terms of total funds deployed for product on without any regard to the nature of labour intensity and the role of human resource in total product on. Capital-light industries are likely to show a higher Rate of Returns (RoI) simply because the constitution of man-power is much more than the investment in the form of physical assets. Productivity per worker should, in fact, be a certain to judge the performance in such enterprises.

Most of the organisations have no objection in recognising Human Resource as an asset but they do not fully appreciate the significance of this vital asset as it does not find its due place in their final accounts. The only information available with financial accounts is a certain category of labour drawing salary exceeding cent in limits. The concept of cost of investment in Human Resources or the value of the assets to the organisation is missing in the conventional accounting system which considers the amount spent an hiring, training and development as usual expenditure of business despite the fact that the implications of such an expenditure are long-term and it is for an asset which is full of life and sensibilities. Disregard to human asset consisting of human energies skills and knowledge results in high labour-turnover and frustration amongst the workers which limits the industrial growth. In the absence of adequate data regarding investments in human resources, the management is not in a position to effectively plan and control human resources. Therefore, the Human Resource Accounting should form an integral part of the conventional accounting for generating and reporting information relating to human resources for managerial purposes.

Human Resource Accounting (HRA) may be treated as a process of identifying, measuring and reporting human resources of an organisation. The American Accounting Association has defined HRA as "the process of identifying and measuring data about human resources and communicating this inflammation to interested parties." Thus HRA takes into account: *(a)* human resource as an asset, *(b)* measuring the cost of investment in human resources or estimating of the value of human resource to the organisation, *(c)* periodic evaluation of human asset, *(d)* reporting of HR investment in Balance Sheet or providing additional inflammation with annual accounts. HRA serve useful purpose. It provides necessary data for decision-making by the management and other interested parties, help evaluation of the contribution of human resource in the performance of an undertaking and assist in reporting the worth of human resource to the organisation.

The first important step in Human Resource Accounting is the valuation of human resources. There one two methods of accounting for human resources as explained below:

1. Cost Method

According to this method, the costs incurred by an organisation on the acquisition of human assets and its further development through education and training is taken into account. This is the historical concept of cost, which may be substituted by another concept *i.e.* replacement cost. Thus, the human resource valuation may be done either according to historical costs or replacement costs.

Historical Cost Accounting

Historical Cost Accounting (HCA) takes into account the actual costs incurred on human resources. It consists of the acquisition cost which is aggregation of cost incurred on recruitment, selection and hiring of people to meet the requirement of the organisation and the development costs which is need to develop the quality of human asset through education and training. After having determined the historical costs, the next step would be to capitalise it and deal it the way the cost on acquisition of plant and machinery or any other fixed asset is treated. Since the human resource is employed for fairly long-period, the capitalized cost is to be written off during the period of employment of much resource. For example, if an amount Rs. 80,000 has been spent on the specialised training of an employee aged 50 years, then this amount may be written off during the 8 year's remaining service period before the retirement of the employee, by charging every year Rs. 10,000 to income statement. In case the employee leaves the employing firm for any reason, then the unwritten off amount may be written off in the year in which be leaves the firm. Similarly, if the investment in certain category of human resource becomes unproductive due to obsolescence, then also the remaining amount may be written off. Thus, the Balance Sheet on any given date will show the amount which remains invested in human resources.

From the above, it would appear that the Human Resource Accounting based on historical cost is quite simple. The success of this method depends upon the fair and realistic procedure of organisation to write off the human asset which has been consumed during a financial year. However, this is the most difficult task as it is very difficult to predict the human behaviour and the contingencies involved due to typical nature of assets. It is not possible for management to know the stage at which a particular employee or a group of employees will leave the firm as the labour mobility cannot be restricted through artificial means. There is no specified time for death or abrupt changes in the health conditions of employees. Thus, a firm cannot adopt a particular procedure to write off the investments in human resources. The experience of the management would be quite helpful in developing a satisfactory procedure for amortisation of human assets. The procedure, once adopted may be reviewed from time to time in the light of the changes in the health condition of employees and the development of new production techniques which requires further training of industrial workers.

Advantages of HCA

Historical cost-based accounting for Human Resources offers advantages such as, *(1)* It is simple to understand and apply as it uses the conventional techniques of cost accumulation and cost expiration. *(2)* It provides useful informations which may be used by personnel managers in planning and control of man-power in the best interestories organisation. *(3)* Inter-departmental data with regard to investments in human resource provides useful information which keeps on changing by inter-departmental transfers of workers.

Limitations of HCA

Following limitations reduce the utility of HRA based on historical costs:

(1) The measurement of costs which must be capitalised creates some problem, Cost-expiration procedure causes the main problem for which there is no standard solution. There is always scope for subjective valuation which reduces the reliability of human resources.

(2) It is argued that the investment in human resources as shown in the Balance Sheet represents nothing more than the unamortised costs which was incurred in past years. It is not related in any way to the contribution of human resources to the total production or profitability of the organisation. The energy, skill and capabilities cannot be represented by the cost spent an human resource and development.

(3) Historical cost cannot be used as a basis for decision-making for future under changing business environment. Investment in human resources is undervalued under condition of inflation.

(4) This method is least useful to investors who cannot understand the current costs of human resources.

Replacement Costs

Replacement cost is the cost of replacing the existing human resources by the new resources of the same productive capabilities.

In other words, it is the current valuation of the historical cost of human resources. Replacement cost can be positional or personal. Positional replacement cost may be defined as the sacrifice which must be incurred to replace a person with another person of the same capability. It consists of three elements *i.e.*, acquisition cost, development cost and separation cost. The concepts of acquisition and development costs are quite clear. Separation cost refers to the cost which an organisation has to bear as a result of leaving the position or job by an employee. On the termination of an employee, three types of cost arise. They are separation compensation cost, differential pre-separation performance cost and vacant position cost. Separation compensation cost is the payments made to the employees leaving the firm. Differential pre-separation performance cost is the cost of lost productivity prior to separation of employees whose tendency is to go slow before leaving a firm, and the vacant position cost is incurred during the period the search for replacement is continued. Under Replacement Cost Accounting method, the Balance Sheet will show the replacement cost of investment in human resources instead of historical costs. Replacement Costing method of Human Resource Accounting suggests process of finding out the replacement cost on continuous basis.

Replacement costing method of human resources valuation attempts to measure the current economic values of investment in human assets which make the Balance Sheet a true statement of current economic position of an enterprise. The replacement cost informations are not only useful to management for internal decision-making but they are equally important to outside investors in understanding the real strength of any organisation. The utility of replacement costs is enhanced if it does not vary widely from the economic value of human resources to the or of ulisation to which it belongs. The replacement cost should, however, be used with care keeping in view the difficulties in its measurement. The replacement cost may not be assessed objectively to give colour to Balance Sheet and it will be a fruitless exercise if the organisation is indifferent or unable to replace an outgoing member of the team by a new incumbent of the similar capability.

2. Human Resource Value Accounting (HRVA)

HRVA seeks to measure the value of human resources in terms of its contribution in the benefits which a firm desires from its operations. The calculation of value of human resources on the basis of benefits accruing to a firm is a technical job for which models have been developed by different authors.

Lev and Schwartz have suggested a model which attempts to estimate the human capital value of a person for a firm. According to their Model, the future expected average earnings of different grades of labour upto the age of retirement are estimated and discounted at the rate which is equal to cost of capital. The calculated aggregate of present values for all categories of employees will represent the value of human capital to the firm. This method is useful in so far as it gives value which can be compared with other non-human capital in order to understand the labour intensity in any firm. It can also be used with the help of the rate of growth in human capital, the structure of labour force *i.e.,* whether the firm has an ageing labour force or a younger labour force. An increasing rate of growth will obviously imply that younger persons are being inducted into the firm. Lew and Schwartz Model has been criticised on the ground that the estimation of a reliable figure of future earnings is not an easy task as the grades of labour keeps on changing and the concept of cost of capital is not always rigidly defined. The utility of the human resources data is reduced due to these limitations.

Another model known as Flamholtz's model seeks to measure the human capital investments on the basis of the contribution of human assets in the total economic value of a firm. The economic value of a firm is to be determined by calculating the present value of future expected earnings. Flarnholtz is of the view that an individual is not valuable in the abstract but he is valuable due to personal attributes and in relation to his role and the characteristics of the organisation. He has identified the variables which determine the value of an individual to a firm. The view that the human resource valuation is closely linked with its contribution in the total economic value of a firm seems sound but the problems associated with such valuations make the economic valuation method merely a theoritical proposition.

There is another model Harmanson's model which has developed the idea of super normal profit (profit in excess of normal profit) as a measure of human resource valuation. The method of valuation of Human Resource as developed by Harmonson is known as Unpurchased Goodwill Method as the super-normal profits give rise to goodwill. According to his model, the human asset valuation may be explained in this manner. Suppose, the average normal return an owned assets (tangible assets) during the last five years has been 10% whereas a firm enjoyed a return of 15% on its owned assets of Rs. 60,000. Total earnings in this case amounted to Rs. 9,000 (15% of 60,000). To earn Rs. 9,000 at 10% normal return, the total assets required are 90,000. Thus unowned assets or Human Resource should be valued at 30,000 (Rs. 90,000 - 60,000). This model fails to explain the existence of human capital in case there is no profit in excess of normal profit.

Advantages of HRA

The advantages of Human Resource Accounting may be listed as under:

1. Information relating to Human Resources is useful in developing man-power budgets.
2. Management is in a position to allocate reasonable funds for the development of human resources in the light of the contribution of human capital in the over-all value of any firm.
3. Incorporation of HRA information and its reporting with annual accounts provide objective assessment of a company's performance for rational decisions. Fair rate of return can be calculated only if the human asset is also taken into account and the Balance Sheet can be made to provide realistic state of economic affairs of the enterprise.

4. HRA is not only useful for human resource planning and control but it is also advantageous to the investors who can properly value a firm only after having studied its human resources.

Limitations of HRA

1. The problems associated with the measurement of human resources are complex. There is no specific objective method of measurement of human resource due to which subjectivity enters into calculations and the data loose much of their reliability.
2. Some persons do not agree even with the idea of treating human resources as an asset owned by the proprietors.
3. HRA involve costs. Small Scale enterprises do not find it suitable for cost considerations.
4. There is no standard practice for measurement and reporting human resource asset. It is also not compulsory except that the companies are required to show few informations about their employees.

Owing to the above, the HRA has not gained favour with the industry. Only few enlightened companies in India both in the public and private sectors have made attempts to provide detailed informations with respect to their labour force and such an informations has been fund quite useful by the investing community.

RESPONSIBILITY ACCOUNTING

The nature of work in a large scale business enterprise is so complex that it is divided into 'divisions' or 'segments' on some basis so as to effectively carry out the work: in each division or department for achieving the over-all objective of the enterprise. Each division enjoys necessary authority to control the business operations under its command to achieve standard performance which forms the basis to evaluate his accountability towards the organisation. The idea underlying such an organisational structure is to achieve over-all efficiency by delegating authority to divisional managers or departmental heads who are held responsible for the results expected of them by the top management. Responsibility accounting is a system of accounting under which responsibility of each divisional executive is established and a system of reporting developed to ensure timely action in cases the responsibility is not being discharged according to the expectations of top management.

Different authors on the subject have defined Responsibility accounting in different manners. According to Anthony and Reece "Responsibility Accounting is that type of management accounting that collects and reports both planned and actual accounting information in terms of responsibility centre." This definition recognises responsibility accounting as a system of management reporting about responsibility centres. More or less similar view has been expressed by J.A. Higgind who says, "It is a system of accounting which is tailored to an organisation so that costs are accumulated and reported by levels of responsibility within the organisation. Each supervisory area in the organisation is charged only with the cost for which it is responsible and over which it has control." Charles T. Homgren defines responsibility accounting as "a system of accounting that recognizes various responsibility centres throughout the organization and reflects the plans and actions of each of these centres by assigning particular revenues and costs to the one having the pertinent responsibility. It is also called profitability accounting and activity accounting." According to this definition, the Responsibility Accounting is concerned with:

(a) Identification and establishment of responsibility centres. A responsibility centre is a sub-unit under the control of an executive officer who may be called a divisional manager.

(b) Charging each responsibility centre with specific functions or activities to perform and

(c) Evaluating the performance of divisional manager in terms of costs and revenues. Costs represent the values of physical and financial resources in monetary terms and revenues measure the output in money values.

Implementation of Responsibility Accounting

Following steps are required to be taken to implement the responsibility accounting in an organisation:

1. Classification of organisation in suitable responsibility entries is the first important step towards the implementation of R.A. A responsibility centre is a sub-unit under the charge of a manager who is wholly responsible for the operation of that responsibility centre. A responsibility centre may be created in such a manner that it is distinguishable as a separate sub-unit of the organisation for operation and control purposes.
2. Defining the authority and responsibility of heads of each unit division in the organisation is necessary for the success of R.A. system, which, infect, is based on authority and responsibility relationship.
3. Designing an effective reporting system so that the manager of a responsibility centre receives necessary information in time and there is continuous appraisal system to keep the managers conscious of costs and revenues.
4. Taking necessary corrective action in cases of less than standard performance (adverse variances) and also reporting the same to the responsibility centres for improving efficiency in future.

Objectives

Responsibility Accounting in an organisation may be implemented with the following objectives:

1. To simplify management problems of a large business undertaking.
2. To achieve over-all efficiency through the performance of responsibility centres.
3. To ascertain the contribution of individual responsibility centres with a view to understand their relative importance to the organisation.

4. To measure the performance of divisional-managers in charge of responsibility centres. It is possible that a responsibility centre might not show satisfactory contribution towards organisational goals despite best efforts by a responsibility centre manager.
5. To motivate divisional managers to perfoım well in the interest of the organisation through a system of responsibility accounting which appreciates and provides incentives for efficient discharge of duties.
6. To provide basis for Management By Exception which means focus sing the attention of management on deviations which exceed tolerable limits.

Responsibility Centres

A responsibility centre in an organisation is a sub-unit for doing specified activities by a responsible officer who is empowered to control over those activities but is held responsible for the performance of the sub-unit under his charge. The size of a sub-unit (Responsibility Centre) which may also be called a department, division or segment, varies according to the nature of work done therein. It can be as large as the production department or as small as an advertising call in an organisation. On the basis of type of data used to measure performance, an organisation may be classified into three centres *viz.* *(a)* Cost Centre, *(b)* Profit Centre and *(c)* Investment Centre.

Cost Centre

A cost centre is a responsibility centre which consumes resources or incur costs which is measured in monetary terms. It may be noted that the cost centre is concerned with costs (inputs) only; the revenue (output) is not considered in the measurement of performance, as the costs do not give rise to revenue directly. The cost which is directly traceable to the cost centre should only be brought in the calculation of Cost Centre Indirect Cost which are incurred for the organisation as a whole are not within the direct control of the manager of a Cost Centre; therefore, such costs are excluded in the measurement of their efficiency. These is some controversy over the exclusion of output (revenue) from the measurement of efficiency of cost centre but majority of experts believe that cost is a satisfactory measure of efficiency as output is not measurable in many cases. It would be quite logical to measure efficiency of Cost Centres such as legal department, labour welfare department, advertising division, etc. in terms of costs as the measurement of output (revenue) is full of complexities. The difference between the actual costs and the standard costs specified for the responsibility centre would reflect the efficiency of Cost Centre.

Profit Centre

Profit Centre is a responsibility centre which takes into account both the cost (input) and revenue (output) in the measurement of its efficiency. The difference between revenue and cost is profit which is compared with some profit figures in the past or standard profit, if any, to measure efficiency of the divisional manager in charge of profit centre. For the purpose of measurement of profit, the concept of cost remains the same as in case of cost centre but the concept of revenue (output measurement) is different from its traditional meaning based an accrual principle. Revenue of profit centre will be arrived at simply by valuing the total output at a rate at which output can be disposed off. The surplus of Profit centre is the profit before the recovery of fixed expenses which are incurred for the organisation as a whole and also before income tax which is also payable for the organisation as a whole.

The Profit Centre in an organisation is a better and more effective measure of efficiency as it considers both input (expenses) and output revenue) as against Cost Centre which traces and measures costs only. It generates consciousness to show satisfactory profit and the management is always in a position to safely de-centralize power and authority to the divisional manager in charge of profit centre. However, the Profit Centre encounters the following problems which should be resolved carefully for the proper operation of the centre.

1. Establishment of a responsibility centre as a profit centre is itself a problem. The successful operation of profit

centre is also governed by the degree of freedom enjoyed by the divisional manager in deciding about the nature of output. If the authority is limited, the profit centre cannot work as an effective control technique.

2. Measurement of cost is another problem which gives rise to controversy about profit centre. Those costs which are traceable directly to a profit centre should be taken into account in the measurement of efficiency and no other cost should be brought into calculations.
3. Inter-centres transfers of goods and services cause problem insofar as the pricing of such transfers is concerned. Cost and revenues of centres are affected by the method of pricing of goods and services exchanged between the departments. The problem of transfer pricing should be carefully solved so that the measurement of performance is not unduly affected by pricing methods.

There are various methods of pricing the goods which are supplied and received between the responsibility centres. Anyone of the following pricing methods may be adopted but no one is without drawback.

Cost Price. It is the unit cost of production to the supplying division. The use of cost price for pricing of goods from one department to another is quite simple and convenient but it is not considered suitable for profit centre analysis due to distortions in profits. The profit of the supplying division will not contains any element of profit on the goods supplied whereas the profit of receiving division will be increased to the extent profit is not included in the goods so received.

Cost Plus Pricing. It is the price which includes some amount of profit in the cost price: In other words, the cost plus price is the cost price plus profit at a specified rate which is either the rate which can be realised if goods are disposed off in the open market or a rate which management considers reasonable for transfer purposes. Fixation of profit rate introduces subjectivity in the performance analysis.

Market Price. It is the price at which goods are actually exchanged in the market. Market Price is determined by market forces and as such it cannot be influenced by individual actions of divisional managers, who should normally agree to pricing the goods at the prevailing market rates. In case the market quotations are not readily available, the cost plus pricing which conform to market pricing, should be taken for the valuation of goods exchanged between the responsibility centres to measure their effectiveness.

Negotiated Price. It is the price which is settled between the parties through mutual negotiations. The pricing of goods transferred from one division to another at negotiated price serves the interests of the supplier as well as the receiver of goods. However proper negotiations are possible if the supplier has a choice to sell outside and the buying segment has also a choice to buy from outside where buyers and sellers for similar goods exist.

Investment Centre

Investment centre is that segment of an organisation which is held responsible not only for costs and revenues but also effective utilization of investments in the form of assets. Assets are said to have been effectively utilised if their utilization yields a fair rate of return. Thus, an investment centre is concerned with controlling inputs (cost) output (revenue) and investment (assets utilization) with a view to perform so well that it earns a reasonable rate of return on investment. Return on Investment (ROI) is the proportion of net income to total assets as shown below:

$$\text{ROI} = \frac{\text{Net Income}}{\text{Total Assets}}$$

Actually, the ROI is a function of profit margin and asset-turnover and as such their combined action determines ROI. Therefore, ROI may be interpreted in terms of profit margin a Sales and the proportion of Sales to total assets.

$$\text{ROI} = \frac{\text{Net Income}}{\text{Sales}} \times \frac{\text{Sales}}{\text{Total Assets}}$$

The performance of an Investment Centre is reported in terms of Return an Investment and is compared with cost of investment or rate specified by management for measurement of performance of the Profit Centre. ROI is fairly a good measure of performance reporting but it involves some practical problems in its calculations due to the problems associated with the assignment of values to different assets and their traceability to investment centre. The determination of net income is also subject to difference of opinion as to the exclusion of interest and taxes from the total income for a year. In view of these difficulties, the concept of residual income may be applied in the measurement of performance of profit centre. Residual income is the excess of income over standard expected Income of the profit centre. If the excess of income so arrived at is positive, then the performance is considered goods; otherwise the performance is bad for which responsibility of the divisional manager is fixed. It may be noted that the application of residual income in the measurement of performance is also not perfect as it is not free from the problem of estimation.

Performance Reporting

A CASE OF A COST, CENTRE

Items	*Budgeted cost*	*Actual cost*	*Variance*	*% Variance*
Raw Materials	2,75,000	3,00,000	25,000 (A)	–9.1
Labour Cost	3,25,000	3,75,000	50,000 (A)	–15.4
Overheads-Directly traceable	50,000	40,000	10,000 (F)	+20.0
Total	6,50,000	7,15,00	65,000 (A)	–10%

The performance report of the cost centre has revealed that the costs of materials and labour have gone up beyond the budgeted costs whereas the responsibility manager has been able to save overhead cost. The manager would explain the increase in costs and the future costs will be set up accordingly.

A CASE OF PROFIT CENTRE

Particulars	*Budgeted figures*	*Actual figures*	*Variance*	*% Variance*
Revenue:				
Outside supplies	2,00,000	1,55,000	– 45,000	– 22.5%
Inter-departmental supplies	6,00,000	6,20,000	+ 20,000	+ 3.3%
Total	8,00,000	7,77,000	25,000 (A)	– 3.1% (A)
Costs:				
Raw Materials	3,25,000	3,07,540	+ 17,550	+ 5.4
Labour	2,60,000	3,21,750	– 23.75	
Overheads	65,000	85,800	– 20,800	– 32.00
Total	6,50,000	7,15,000	65,000 (A)	– 10% (A)
Profit	1,50,000	60,000	90,000 (A)	– 60% (A)

The performance of the profit centre as indicated by a decline of profit by 60% is, obviously, below expectations. According to responsibility accounting, the cause for such a poor state of affairs have to be investigated, responsibility fixed and future plans adjusted. The possible causes for deciine in profit may be the increase in costs, decrease in volume of output, decline in selling and supplies rates, wastages in production, etc. A look into the budget would suggest whether the budgeted figures were realistically fixed. The success of responsibility accounting will depend the consideration of all aspects which affect the costs and revenue and the steps which may be taken to improve the position in the future periods.

A Case of an Investment Centre. As we know that a Investment Centre is not only concerned with the costs, revenue and absolute figure of profit but also the rate of return on assets (investment) employed by the centre. Therefore, the profit and the assets employed to earn those profits have to be correlated to determine rate of return. A comparison ofbudgeted or expected rate of return with actual rate will show the performance of the profit centre. Relevant figures as shown to below show the performance of an hypothetical Investment Centre.

PERFORMANCE REPORT—2002-03

Items	*Budgeted figures*	*Actual figures*	*Variance (±)*	*% Variance*
Revenue	1,50,00,000	1,70,00,000	+ 13.3	
Costs	1,08,00,000	1,10,00,000	– 2,00,000	– 1.8
Profit	42,00,000	60,00,000	+ 18,00,000	+ 42.8
Total Assets	2,30,00,000	2,50,00,000	+ 20,00,000	+ 8.7
Rate of Return (ROI)	18.26%	24%	+ 5.74%	

Plus performance of the Investment centre is indicative of its satisfactory performance which is appreciable by the management. However, there is always scope for further improvement in working and the management may explore the possibilities of enhancing profitability by reducing costs which has shown adverse variance.

❐

8

Application of Marginal Costing

The concept of variable costs (separation of fixed costs from variable costs) is not only useful income measurement but also is very significant in management decision-making. Variable costing is an important tool of profit planning and cost control. The preceding section has established that the contribution margin/marginal contribution is the core of variable costing. It is out of the marginal contribution that the fixed costs are to be met; and the excess of the marginal contribution over fixed costs represents profit. From the above it follows that maximising the marginal contribution would lead to the maximisation of profit. The marginal contribution approach can be applied in making decisions with regard to:

(a) Price fixing on special orders

(b) optimal sales mix

(c) adding a new product line

(d) dropping a product line

(e) developing a production plan if certain input (material or labour) is in short supply

(f) making or buying component parts

(g) selling of a product in a limited market.

Throughout the discussion, it will be assumed that fixed costs will remain unchanged within the relevant range. Thus, as output is changed, within the relevant range, changes will be only in variable costs and revenue; fixed costs, on the other hand, will not change and, therefore, are irrelevant costs for decision-making. Thus, sales revenue and variable costs are the only relevant variables for decisions.

(I) Accepting a Special Order

A company may have a production capacity which is not fully utilised. In that case, the total profit of the company can be increased by using the unutilised capacity to produce and sell goods which yield a positive marginal income. The following example is illustrative of this situation.

Example.

The management of a company is to decide whether to accept an export order for 500 units per month at Rs. 7 per unit. Its present position is as follows:

Present Sales	1,500 units per month
Production Capacity	2,000 units per month
Selling Price	Rs. 10 per unit1
Total Cost	Rs. 8 per unitg
Fixed Cost	Rs.5,500

The result of accepting the export order may be tabulated as follows:

	Present Sale	*Proposed Export Sale*	*Tothi*
Sales (units)	1,500	5000	22,000
Sales Revenue (Rs.)	15,000	3,500	18,500
Variable Costs @ Rs. 5 per unit	7,500	2,500	10,000
	7,500	1,000	8,500
Additional cost for export order	—	500	500
Contribution Margin	7,500	500	8,000
Fixed Costs (Rs.)	4,500	—	4,500
Profit (Rs.)	3,000	500	3,500

Note. Calculation of variable cost per unit:

Fixed cost per unit = Rs. 4,500/1,500 = Rs. 3

Total cost= Rs. 8 per unit

Variable cost = Rs. 8 – Rs. 3 = Rs. 5 per unit

In above example, the use of marginal costing technique reveals that the company will be better off by accepting the offer of export sales and the total profit will improve by Rs. 500. If the total cost were only considered, the contribution to profit of this additional sale would not be known except by recalculating all costs and breaking up the fixed expenses which cannot be promptly done. Otherwise, the decision may be to reject the offer as the selling price is Re. 1 per unit less than the total cost.

Similarly during a period of economic depression when sales are low and tend to decline, it may be wrong to consider total cost while deciding whether production should be continued or not. If production is stopped and no sale is made, there will be no recovery of fixed cost and the firm will suffer a loss. However, if orders are accepted at a price below the total cost but above the variable cost, it will lead to some contribution towards the fixed cost and the loss will be reduced to that extent.

Marginal costing is also helpful in developing data to show which sales-territory or customers, or other segment are contributing most towards fixed cost and in what proportions.

Let us consider the following example:

	Total	*Sales Districts ('000)*			
		I	*II*	*III*	*IV*
Sales Revenue (Rs.)	3,700	1,200	1,000	800	700
Variable costs:					
Production	1,650	550	450	350	300
Selling	795	190	205	200	200
	2,445	740	655	550	500

Contribution Margin	1,255	460	345	250	200
Fixed costs (Districts)	955	560	242	250	240
Profit (Loss) by Districts	260	200	100	0	(40)
Fixed Cost (Total)	160				
Total Profit	100				

From the above figures, it is obvious that the elimination of sales district IV would increase the overall profit of the company by Rs. 40,000 a year.

(II) Replacement Decision

Whether it would be more profitable to replace existing machinery by a new and improved one is a question which management in every concern has to face from time to time. The differential cost of keeping the old machine in use and using new machinery is the proper basis of making decisions of this kind.

(III) Pricing Decisions (Selling at Below Normal Price)

The marginal contribution approach can help management in arriving at correct pricing decisions under special circumstances like the followings.

Situations: When it may be Necessary to Sell at or Below Unit Cost

Usually it is supposed that price charged from customers cover costs fully. This is quite true in normal circumstances and normal cases as otherwise a profit cannot be earned. But in certain circumstances price may be fixed below the total cost *i.e.*, at marginal cost. Circumstances can be cited when selling price of the products may be below the marginal cost.

(a) If the firm has already purchased large quantities of raw materials and if the attempt to sell the raw materials will result in heavy loss or if continued storage will result in deterioration in quantity or quality thus giving rise to an extraordinary loss, it may be better to turn the raw materials into finished stock and sell it at a price below the marginal cost.

(b) If the closure of the business though temporary will mean discharge of old trusted employees and experienced workers the management must continue the production and sell at below marginal cost. If business is closed and restarted later, the services of these experienced hands may not be available. It will create the need of new recruitment and fresh selection of inexperienced persons which may entail expenditure on training etc.

(c) If there is a threat of even a temporary closure of the business which may result into breaking the connection's with the customers, the sale may be made at a lower price.

(d) In the case of a new product it may be sold at a low price to make it popular and acceptable. This is done with the hope that sales will increase with the passage of time and cost of production will come down as a result of increase in sales. Ultimately cost of production will be in line with the selling price and the concern will start earning profit from the new line of production.

(e) When the goods are of perishable nature, they may be sold at a lower price also. It is better to sell the perishable goods at a lower price whichever they can realise otherwise these goods will perish and nothing will be realised if they remain unsold.

(f) When a foreign market has to be explored to foreign exchange, the price may be quoted at a lower value. The same thing also applies to sale to special customers like the government who can be offered price concessions. The concessional price below the total cost but above the marginal cost will bring additional profits if additional sales are made. Several monthly magazines and journals work on the same principle when they offer specially low subscription rate to new customers.

(g) Sometimes prices below cost are charged in the event of keen competition also. When competitors are to be eliminated from the market, losses may be deliberately incurred to defeat and eliminate rivals. It is done in hope that after sometime the quantity of sales will considerably go up and shall be able to earn profit and cover the loss earlier.

(h) There are certain expenses of closing and reopening the business. At the time of closing the works machinery has to be dismantled and greased up. At the time of reopening machinery will have to be reassembled again overhauled thoroughly. These expenses can be avoided if production is continued.

(i) When the sale of one product at a price below the marginal cost will push up the sales of other profitable products, one product may be sold at below prices too. The loss in one product will be made up by profits in other products.

(IV) Make or Buy Decisions

Most firms have to decide sometimes or the other whether they should buy a part from the market and stop making it themselves or whether they should stop buying it and start making it. There are various considerations affecting such a decision, chief of which is cost. As in any other case, the decision will mostly turn, in case the part is already being made and the decision is whether or not to buy it from outside, on the comparison of the price that has to be paid and the saving that can be effected in cost. This, as can be realised, is only the marginal cost or the variable cost normally no saving is possible in fixed expenses.

However, if the decision is whether or not to produce a part being bought at present from outside suppliers, the comparison will have to be between the price being paid to outsiders and all the additional cost that will have to be incurred. Such additional cost will comprise not only materials and wages on the production of the part but also salaries of additional supervisors to be engaged, if any, interest on the capital that will have to be used for buying the necessary equipment as well as the depreciation on it, rent of premises, if present premises are not sufficient to house the new activity.

Besides the comparison of price demanded by the outsiders and the marginal cost, other considerations as below are also important:

1. Opportunity Cost. It may be that the price quoted by the outsider may be higher than the marginal cost and thus the indicated decision may be for 'own' production. But before the decision is taken, the alternative use to which the machines and facilities can be put should also be considered. To take a simple example, suppose a machine produces 10,000 units at a total cost of Rs. 5 of which Rs. 4 is variable. The article can be purchased from outside at Rs. 4.25. Suppose, if the machine is released from this article, it can be hired out at an annual rent of Rs. 3,600. It would be cheaper to hire out the machine and buy the article from outside.

2. The Fixed Expenses Burden. In case a part is produced by the firm itself, it will mean an outlay on machines and other facilities and also employment of staff some of which may be permanent and fixed in nature. Thus, the fixed expenses burden increases. Some firms deliberately buy from outside to keep this burden as low as possible even if the price to be paid is a little more than the cost of 'own' manufacture. A compromise is also often adopted own production is kept at the estimated minimum requirement, keeping in view possible fluctuations in demand, and the excess quantity required is purchased from outside. The effect of such a policy is that should demand fall, orders on outsiders can be cut down; the costs to be incurred will then be in proportion to the effective demand. In other words, the bulk of the cost then becomes controllable.

3. Non-Cost Consideration. It is usually a mistake to arrive at "make a decision only on the basis of costs. Factors which do not affect costs directly are important. Of these the under mentioned are noteworthy:

(a) *Quality.* Given the quality of the final product, there is a certain quality for the various parts and components about which there should be no compromise. If quality cannot be ensured in own production, the article concerned should be purchased from outside; if outside suppliers cannot be relied upon in this respect, the article should be produced by the firm itself, whatever the cost.

(b) *Regularity of Supply.* Interruption of production process is very costly and therefore, before reliance is placed on

outside sources of supplies, one must be sure that supplies will be regular and timely.

(c) Expected Fluctuations in Demand. Case there are large fluctuations in demand up and down, it is better to purchase from outside; but if demand is likely to increase substantially, own production may lead to lower costs later.

(d) Reliability of Supplier. Appart points *(l)* and *(2)* made above, the supplier may land the firm in serious trouble if later on he runs into difficulties himself or adopts an attitude of non-co-operation or tries to extract a high price, knowing that production facilities that previously existed have been dismantled. For checking the dependability of the supplier, the under mentioned points may be kept in mind:

(a) The general reputation enjoyed by the supplier for reliability.

(b) His financial position and reputation in this regard;

(c) The technical know-how and production facilities at his disposal; and

(d) His relation with his workmen, etc.

Example.

A firm purchases 20,000 units of a spare part from an outside source @ 3.00 per unit. There is a proposal that the spare be produced in the factory itself. For the purpose a machine costing Rs. 50,000 with a capacity 30,000 units and a life of 5 years, will be required. A foreman with a monthly salary of Rs. 1,000 p.m. will have to be engaged. Materials required will be 60 paise per unit and wages 45 paise per unit. Variable overheads are 150% of labour and fixed expenses are recovered @ 200% of wages. The firm can raise funds @ 16% p.a.

Advise the firm whether the proposal should be accepted.

Solution.

The decision should be based on the comparison of the price being paid at present and the additional costs to be incurred if manufacture is undertaken. This comparison is made below:

(i) Price being paid at present (20,000 × Rs.3,000) Rs. 60,000

(ii) Cost to be incurred if manufacture is undertaken:

	Rs.
Materials @ 60 p.	12,000
Labour @ 45 p.	9.000
Variable overheads	13,500
Additional foreman's salary	12,000
Depreciation (50,000 ÷ 5)	10,000
Interest (16% on Rs. 50,000)	8,000
	64,500

The cost of making 10,000 units will be higher than the price being paid at present. Hence the proposal is not acceptable.

(V) Operate or Shutt-down Decisions

If the demand of the products are not adequate enough to cover fixed costs, it is better to shut-down the business temporarily. There may be some fixed costs, which can be substantially reduce due to this temporary closing down of operations. Hence, management will have to make a comparison between two situations whether to continue or suspend the production. Marginal costing helps the management in the decisions of such type also.

Example.

Rainbow Paint and Varnish Works, manufactures 2,00,000 medium-size tins of 'spray lac paints' when working at normal capacity. It incurs the following costs of manufacturing per unit.

	Rs.
Direct Material	7.80
Direct Labour	2.10

Variable Overheads	2.50
Fixed Overheads	4.00
Product cost per unit	16.40

Each unit of product is sold for Rs. 21 with variable selling and administrative expenses of 60 paise per unit of product.

During the next three months, only 10,000 units can be produced and sold. Management plans to shut down the plant estimating that the fixed manufacturing costs can be reduced to Rs. 74,000 for the quarter.

When the plant is operating, the fixed overhead costs are incurred at a uniform rate throughout the year. Additional cost of plant shut down for the three months are estimated at Rs. 14,000.

You are required:

(i) To express your opinion, along with calculations, whether the plan should be shut down for three months, and

(ii) To calculate the shut-down point for three months in units of products.

Solution.

(i) Variable Cost of the Product = Rs. 7.80 + Rs. 2.10 + Rs. 2.50 + Rs. 0.60 + Rs. 13 per unit

Contribution = Rs. 21 - Rs. 13 = Rs. 8 per unit

Calculation of Loss, if the Plant is Operated

	Rs.
Total contribution on 10,000 units	80,000
Total Fixed Costs for three months	
(2,00,000 × 4 × 3/12)	2,00,000
Expected Loss on Operation	1,20,000

Calculation of Loss, if the Plant is Shut Down

Unavoidable Fixed Cost	74,000
Additional Cost of Shut Down	14,000
Total Loss on Shut down	88,000

As is clear from the above calculations, the plant should be shut down for three months. If this decision is carried down, the management can reduce its loss from Rs. 1,20,000 (loss on operation) to Rs. 88,000 (loss on shut down).

(ii) Calculation of Shut Down Point

Avoidable Fixed for the period

= Total Fixed Costs for the period – (Unavoidable Fixed Costs + Additional Cost of Shut Down)

= Rs. 2,00,000 – (Rs. 74,000 + Rs. 14,000) = Rs. 1,12,000.

Shut Down Point = Avoidable Fixed Cost/Contribution per unit

= Rs. 1,12,000/ Rs. 8 = 14,000 units

(VI) Key Factor

The limiting factor which prevents an enterprise from earning unlimited profit is known as the Key Factor. In a multi-product company or seasonal business, the question may arise as to which product should be pushed more in the peak season (where production, capacity is limited) so that the company can maximise profits. The concept of contribution margin helps and guides management to determine which products are most profitable to sell and highlights the Key Factor.

The key factor may be the market for sales (as is usually the case) or scarce raw material, skilled labour, machine-capacity, etc. If there is a key factor or constraint, the best position is reached when the gross margin (*i.e.* contribution) is maximised per unit of the key factor. For example, if the available labour supply is inadequate to permit manufacture of all the products, the most profitable course of action would be to use the available manpower to make the products which contribute the largest marginal income per hour of labour. Similarly, if materials are in short supply, management have to generate maximum marginal income per unit of material used. Thus, the contribution per unit of the key factor of production may be ascertained and the products ranked according to the descending order of contribution for selective attention. Consideration of total cost cannot be expected to reveal the significance of this aspect of business policy, nor help in decision-making which is appropriate.

(VII) Fixation of Selling Prices

The fixation selling prices is one of the important functions of management. The technique of marginal costing can be applied to the pricing of products. The theory is that only those products should be produced or sold which make the largest contribution towards the recovery of fixed costs. The selling price fixation is also done under different circumstances. Some important circumstances are as follows:

(i) Under Normal Circumstances. Under normal situation the product giving more contribution should be produced and sold. The selling price of the product should be fixed covering the total cost as otherwise profits cannot be earned. For example,

Product A selling price Rs. 10- p.u. V.C. Rs. 6/-p.u.

Product B selling price Rs. 12- p.u. V.C. Rs. 10/-p.u.

If the maximum number of units of Product A and/or Product B which can be produced and sold by the firm is 100 unit B. the comparison should be made in this manner:

Contribution p.u.	Product A = Rs. 4/- p.u.
	Product B = Rs. 2/- p.u.
Profit + F.C.	Product A = Rs. 4000 total (1000 × 4)
	Product B = Rs. 2000 total (1000 × 2)

If the number of fixed costs is Rs 1500 p.a. it is clear that the product of production A is profitable as maximise the profit Rs.2500 as against Rs.5000nly in case of product B.

(ii) Pricing in Depression. Price fall during depression and the product may be sold below the total cost. In case there is a serious but temporary fall in the demand on account of depression leading to the need for a drastic reduction in prices temporarily, the minimum selling price should be equal to the marginal cost. If the selling price at which the goods can be sold is equal to marginal cost or more than marginal cost, the product should be continued. Fixed expenses will be incurred even if the products discontinued during depression for a short period. If the product can be sold at a price which is a little more than marginal cost, loss on account of fixed expenses will reduce because price will recover fixed expenses to some extent. This will be clear from the following example:

Suppose, marginal cost per unit is Rs. 10 and fixed expenses amount to Rs. 150,000. Selling price per unit is Rs. 11 and 40,000 units can be sold at this price.

	Rs.
Marginal Cost: 40,000 units @ Rs. 10	= 4,00,000
Fixed Expenses	= 1,50,000
Total Cost	5,50,000
Cost p.u. Rs. 13.75	

Here, selling price of Rs. 11 is below the total cost, yet it is advantageous to sell the product at the selling price of Rs. 11 which is more than the marginal cost of Rs. 10. This will reduce the loss on account of fixed expenses (if the product is discontinued) by Rs. 40,000 as below:

	Rs.
Selling Price of 40,000 units @ Rs. 11	= 4,40,000
Less: Total cost (calculated earlier)	= 5,50,000
Loss	= 1,10,000
Loss if the product is discontinued (Fixed expenses)	= 1,50,000
Loss reduced if the product is continued	40,000

(VIII) Production Mix With and Without Constraints

If there are no production contraints, that is, raw material and labour are in abundant supply, the product with the highest contribution margin per unit should be produced until demand is satisfied. Next, relate the next product with the next highest contribution margin per unit and so on. This criterion will maximise profit.

Let us suppose that the management of a hypothetical company has the following data relating to its two products per unit basis:

TABLE

	Product X	*Product Y*
Selling price	Rs. 330	Rs. 500
Direct material	Rs. 40	Rs. 240
Direct labour (skilled)	Rs. 150	Rs. 100
Variable overheads (20% of labour)	Rs. 30	Rs. 20
Fixed overheads	Rs. 2,80,000 per annum	

Problem 1. How much of each product should be produced if there are no production and sales constraints?

Decision. The management should concentrate on producing product Y only because it gives a higher (Rs. 140) marginal contribution per unit than product X (Rs. 110).

Problem 2. How much of each product should be produced if there are no production but sales constraints in terms of volume of rupees?

Decision. Management should produce X units exclusively because its profit volume ratio (marginal contribution to sales ratio) is higher ($33\frac{1}{3}$%, *i.e.* Rs. 110 + Rs. 330) than that of product Y (28%, *i.e.*, Rs. 140+ 500).

Let us further suppose that the sales level is Rs. 3,00,000. Then, product X will generate a marginal contribution of Rs.1,00,000, while the corresponding amount will be Rs. 84,000 in the case of product Y.

Let us incorporate some more in formation to explain the problem of production mix with a scarce supply of inputs.

Further information	*Product X*	*Product Y*
Materials used (per unit)	2 kg	12 kg
Labour hours (per unit)	30 hours	20 hours
Power consumed (per unit)	20 kwh	28 kwh
Demand for products	5,000 units.	4,000 units

Problem 3. How much of each product should be produced if capacity is limited to 1,40,000 labour hours?

Decision. The production mix will depend on which product has a higher contribution per hour (See following Table)

	Product X	*Product Y*
Selling price	Rs. 330	Rs. 500
Less: Variable costs:		
Direct material	40	240
Direct labour	150	100
variable overheads	30	20
Total variable costs:	–Rs. 220	–Rs. 360
Marginal contribution per unit	Rs.110	Rs. 140
Labour hours	30	20
Marginal contribution per hour	Rs.3.67	Rs.7.0

The basis of our decision should be the marginal contribution per direct labour hour. The firm should produce as many units of product Y as it can sell. If any labour hours are still available, they should be used in manufacturing the product which gives the next higher marginal contribution per direct labour hour. Accordingly, the following solution emerges:

(Time taken in producing a unit × Expected sales in units)

= Total Hours left hours (Capacity used-Hours used)

Product Y	20 hours × 4,000	= 80,000	60,000
Product X	30 hours × 2,000	= 60,000	Nil

Accordingly, a production mix of 4,000 units of product Y and 2,000 units of X is the most suitable under the circumstances. Such a combination will yield income greater than any other combination, given labour hours as a key factor. The amount of income generated by such a combination will be Rs. 5,00,000 as shown in Table.

TABLE 1

	Product X	*Product Y*	*Total*
Marginal contribution per unit	Rs. 110	Rs. 140	
Total units sold	2,000	4,000	
Total marginal contribution	Rs. 2,20,000	Rs. 5,60,000	Rs. 7,80,000
Less: Fixed cost			– 2,80,000
Net income			Rs. 5,00,000

Problem 4. How much of each product should be produced if only 22,000 kg of material is available?

Decsion. Maximising, marginal contribution per kilogram of material will be the guiding criterion for the decision.

(i) Maintaining Desired Level of Profits. Management may be interested in maintaining a desired level of profit. The volume of sales needed to have a desired level of profits can be ascertained by the marginal costing technique. As per formulae,

Desired Sales = Fixed cost + Desired profit / P/Y Ratio

(ii) Evaluation of Profitability of Departments. The decision whether a department should continue or be closed depends to a costing technique helps the management in taking such decisions.

Product Decisions

The concept of marginal contribution guides management to determine which products are most profitable to sell and highlights the key factor of production. Such a key factor may be some scarce raw material, skilled labour, machine capacity, etc. If the available labour supply is inadequate to permit manufacture of all products the most profitable course of action is to use the available manpower to make the products which contribute the largest material income per hour of labour. If materials are in short supply, management should produce according to the largest marginal contribution per input of material. Thus, the contribution per unit of the key factor of production should be determined and the products ranked according to descending order of contribution for selection. Absorption costing just cannot explain such an important aspect of a production decision affecting the total profits of the enterprise. This is illustrated in the following examples.

(i) Dropping a Product Line

Example.

A hypothetical company makes a profit of Rs. 40,000 from the manufacture and sale of three products in following Table.

TABLE

	Products			*Total*
	X (Rs.)	*Y (Rs.)*	*Z (Rs.)*	*(Rs.)*
Sales	50,000	60,000	80,000	1,90,000
Less Costs:				
Variable costs	– 16,000	– 40,000	26,000	82,000
Fixed costs (allocated)	– 2,000	– 36,000	– 20,000	– 68,000
Profit (loss)	22,000	(16,000)	34,000	40,000

Problem. On the basis of the income statement prepared under absorption costing and supplied to management, management is considering dropping product Y because it is incurring a loss of Rs. 16,000. Should the management carry out the proposal?

Decision. The decision would depend on the fact whether the facilities represented by Rs. 36,000 fixed costs allocated to product Y can be better used elsewhere in the company, that is, new sales line may be added or it may be possible to produce and sell existing more profitable products X and Z. If neither of the things is possible, management will be advised not to eliminate product Y, otherwise profits will be reduced by Rs. 20,000 as shown in this Table.

TABLE

	Products		*Total*
	X (Rs.)	*Z (Rs.)*	*(Rs.)*
Sales	50,000	80,000	1,30,000
Less: Variable costs	– 16,000	– 26,000	– 42,000
Marginal contribution	34,000	54,000	88,000
Less: Fixed costs Net profit			– 68,000
Net Profit			20,000

Although product Y is an unprofitable line, its elimination has converted Rs. 40,000 profit to a much lower figure of Rs. 20,000. The reason is that this product was making a marginal contribution of Rs. 20,000 (Rs. 60,000 sales Rs. 40,000 variable costs) to fixed costs which are to be incurred, irrespective of the fact whether product Y is continued or eliminated.

(ii) Adding A New Product Line

Let us modify Example 16.6 on the assumption that management has found a substitute product W in place of product Y. The marketing and production departments of the company have furnished to management the following information regarding the new product. W:

Sales revenue: Rs. 1,00,000

Variable costs: Rs. 60,000

No additional fixed costs will be required.

Problem. Advise the management whether product W should be introduced.

Decision. Yes, product W should be introduced because it will increase the existing profit by Rs. 20,000 as shown in this Table.

TABLE

	Products			*Total*
	X (Rs.)	*Z (Rs.)*	*W (Rs.)*	*(Rs.)*
Sales	50,000	8,000	1,00,000	2,30,000
Less: Variable costs	– 16,000	– 26,000	60,000	–1,02,000
Marginal contribution				1,28,000
Less: Fixed costs				– 68,000
Net profit				60,000

(iii) Decisions on Product Priorities

It often happens that a firm has to decide on the relative importance to be attached to various products; in other words, the priorities for various products are to be fixed. If the output of only single product can be increased, which product should be chosen? If the production of one of the products is to be curtailed, again which product should suffer the curtailment?

Normally, on the assumption that fixed expenses will remain unaffected, the question posed above is answered on the basis of contribution per unit of each product. The product which produces the highest contribution should be accorded the highest priority and that whose contribution is the least should come at the bottom of the list. Of course, if product produces no or minus contribution, its production and sale should be immediately given, up unless there are other advantages.

(iv) Scarcity of Factor of Production

Though nohnally priorities for various products cart be decided on the basis of contribution of each product, the principle has to be modified when a particular factor is in short supply and it is necessary that the available supplies should be put to the best use. In such a case, the proper thing to do is to work out the contribution of per unit of scarce factor and accord the highest priority to that product which produces the highest contribution. Consider the following figures of cost and profit:

	A	*B*
	Rs.	*Rs.*
Materials	10.00	15.00
Labour	6.00	8.00
Overheads-Variable	3.00	5.00
Fixed	5.00	7.00
Total cost	24.00	35.00
Profit	3.00	4.00
Selling price	27.00	39.00
Contribution	8.00	11.00

On the basis of contribution shown above B will be more profitable than A. But suppose both products use imported raw materials and that the foreign exchange allotment is limited to Rs. 9000 per period. In that case one can either produce 900 units of A or 600 units of B and one can see that the total contribution thus will be Rs. 7,200 (*i.e.*, 900 × Rs. 8) if all the materials used for production of A and Rs. 6,600 in the other case. Thus A becomes more profitable than B. This conclusion could also be arrived at by ascertaining the contribution per rupee spent on materials. The figures are:

A Re. 0.80, *i.e.*, Rs. 8.00 ÷ 10

B Re. 0.73, *i.e.*, Rs.11.00 ÷ 15

Thus one of the principles to remember, when relative product priorities are being fixed, is that contribution per unit of scarce factor or production should be the highest for products selected for preferential treatment.

Selection of an Optimum Sales Mix

When a factory produces more than one product, a problem is faced by the management as to which product-mix will give the maximum profits. The best product mix is that which yields the maximum contribution. For example, A company produces X and Y. The following are the facts regarding costs:

Products	*X*	*Y*
Contribution per unit	Rs. 2	Rs. 3
Required production hours per unit	1	2
Sales potential (in units)	1,500	800
Available Production hours	2,000 hours	

Determine the optimum product mix.

Solution.

	Products	
	X	*Y*
Contribution per unit	Rs. 2	Rs. 3
Required hours per unit	1	2
Contribution per hour (Contribution/Key factor)	Rs. 2	Rs. 1.50

Since product X has the greatest contribution per hour, the optimum solution would be to produce all the X that can be sold and then if there are any hours left over, product Y. As such 1,500 units of X (1,500 hours) and 250 units of Y (500 hours) is the optimum product mix.

Sales Mix With No Input Constraint

The management of a hypothetical company is considering the sales budget for the next budget period. The sales manager of the company has made the following sales forecasts;

(i) 2,250 units of A and 1,500 units of B.

(ii) 4,500 units of A only.

(iii) 3,000 units of B only.

(iv) 3,000 units of A and 1,000 units of B.

The costing department has provided the relevant information shown in this Table relating to products on a per unit basis:

TABLE

	Product A	*Product B*
	(Rs.)	(Rs.)
Selling price	300	500
Direct materials (DM)	100	125
Direct Labour (DL)	50	75
Variable overheads (VO)	50	75
Fixed costs	Rs. 2,00,000 per annum	

Problem. Recommend the optimal sales mix.

Decision. The sales alternative which yields the highest marginal contribution leading to the highest profit will be recommended. The marginal contributions for products A and B are Rs. 100 and Rs. 225 respectively as shown in their Table A B.

TABLE

Mariginal Contrinution Per Unit

Product A and B

	Product A	*Product B*
	(Rs.)	*(Rs.)*
Selling price	300	500
Less : Variable costs :		
DM	– 100	– 125
DL	– 50	– 75
VD	– 50	– 75
Marginal contribution	100	225

TABLE

NET INCOME IN VARIOUS ALTERNATIVE

	Product A (Rs.)	*Product B* (Rs.)	*Total* (Rs.)
Sales alternatives:			
(i) 2,250 units of A and 1,500 units of B			
Marginal contribution	2,25,000	3,37,500	5,62,000
Less: Fixed costs			– 2,00,000
Net income			3,62,000
(ii) 4,500 units of A only			
Marginal contribution	4,50,000		4,50,000
Less: Fixed costs			– 2,00,000
Net income			2,50,000
(iii) 3,000 units of B only			
Marginal contribution	—	6,75,000	6,75,000
Less: Fixed costs	—		– 2,00,000
Net income			4,75,000
(iv) 3,000 units of A and 1,000 units of B			
Marginal contribution	3,00,000	2,25,000	5,25,000
Less: Fixed costs			–2,00,000
Net income			3,25,000

Thus, a sales mix consisting of selling only 3,000 units of B is the best as it yields the highest profit.

❐

9

Ratio Analysis

Ratio analysis is a technique of analysis and interpretation of financial statements. It is the process of establishing and interpreting various ratios for helping in making certain decisions. It involves four steps:

(i) Selection of relevant data from the financial statements depending upon the objectives of the analysis.

(ii) Calculation of appropriate ratios from the above data.

(iii) Comparison of the calculated ratios with the ratios of the same firm in the past or the ratios developed from projected finanacial statements or the ratios of some other firms.

(iv) Interpretation of the ratios.

Ratio is one figure expressed in terms of another; it is an expression of rationship between one figure and the other figure which are mutually interdependent. Absolute figures are valuable but they standing alone, convey no meaning unless compared with another. For example; Profit Rs. 6,00,000, Stock Rs. 12,00,000 or Fixed Assets Rs. 36,00,000 are not helpful. But these single figures become important when studied in relation to other figures either in the same statement like the amount of profit and the amount of capital employed. Such relationship of accounting information given in terms of money are commonly referred to as financial ratio. For example if the current assets of a firm are Rs. 5,00,000 and the current liabilities are Rs. 2,50,000 then the ratio of current assets for current liabilities will work out to be $\frac{5,00,000}{2,00,000}$ or 2. Such a ratio is called simple or pure ratio. A ratio can also be expressed as percentage by simply multiplying the ratio by 100. As in the above example the ratio is 2 × 100 or 200%. It can also be expressed in proportion for example rate of current assets to current liabilities is 5,00,000 : 2,50,000 or 2 : 1. Some analysts also express ratio as a rate or time.

For example the ratio of stock turnover is say, $\frac{50,000}{10,000} = 5$ times which simply conveys that stock has been turned over 5 times.

USE AND SIGNIFICANCE OF RATIO ANALYSIS

The ratio analysis is the most powerful tool of financial analysis. It is used as a device to analyse and interpret the financial health of enterprise. Just like a doctor examines his patient by recording his body temperature, blood pressure etc. before making his conclusion regarding illness and before giving his treatement, a financial analyst analyses the financial statements with various tools of analysis before commenting upon the financial health or weakness of an enterprise. A ratio is known as a symptom like blood pressure, the pulse rate or the temperature of an individual. It is with the help of ratios that the financial statement can be analysed more clearly and decision made from such analysis.

Ratio analysis is an important technique of financial analysis. It means for judging the financial health of the concern. Following are the advantages:

(i) Accounting ratios are essential for understanding the affairs of a firm, specially its operating efficiency. Accounting ratios are also useful for diagnosis of the financial health of a business concern. This is done by evaluating liquidity, solvency, profitability etc. Such an evaluation enables management to assess financial requirements and capabilities of various business units.

(ii) A firm would like to compare its performance with that of other firms and of industry in general. The comparison is called 'inter-firm comparison'. In the performance of different units belonging to the same firm is to be compared it is called intra-firm comparison. Such comparison is almost impossible without proper accounting. Progress of the firm is measured year to year with the help of ratios.

(iii) Accounting ratio simplifies, summaries and systematises a long array of accounting figures to make them understandable. Its main contribution lies in bringing into bold relief the inter-relationship which exists between various segments of business as expressed through accounting statements. The importance of accounting ratios, that is, relationship worked out among various accounting data which are mutually dependent and which influence each other in a significant manner, arises from the fact that often absolute figures standing alone convey no meaning. They become significant only when considered along with other futures. In the words of Biramn and Dribin. "Financial Ratio are useful because they summaries briefly the results of detailed and complicated computation."

(iv) Ratio analysis helps in making decision from the information provided in these financial statements. Financial statements are prepared for decision making.

(v) Accounting ratios are useful for understanding the financial position of the concern. One may quickly perceive the relationships without working out the ratio, but that merely means that the ratio has been roughly worked out in the mind—for example, when we see that a small business firm has earned a rather large profit. Thus, accounting ratios are an extremely useful device for analysing the financial statements—the balance sheet and profit and loss account. Bankers, investors, creditors, etc., all analyse balance sheets and profit and loss accounts by means of ratios.

(vi) The financial strength and weakenss of a firm are communicated in a more easy and understandable manner by the use of ratios. The information contained in the financial statements is conveyed in a meaningful manner to the one for whom it is meant. Thus, the ratio helps in communicating and enhances the value of the financial statements.

(vii) Ratio analysis also helps making effective control of the business. Standard ratios can be based upon proforma financial statements and variances or deviations, if any, can be found by comparing the actuals with the standards so as to take a corrective action at right time.

(viii) Ratio Analysis is of much help in financial forecasting and planning. Planning is looking ahead and the ratios calculated for a number of years work as a guide for the future. Meaningful conclusions can be drawn for future from these ratios.

(ix) Accounting ratios are of great assitance in locating the weak spots in the business even though the overall performance may by quite good. Management can then pay attention to the weakness and take remedial action. For example, if the firm finds that the increase in distribution expenses is more than proportionate to the results achieved, these can be examined in detail and depth to remove any wastage that may be there.

LIMITATIONS OF RATIO ANALYSIS

Except in few cases, accounting ratios by themselves are not significant—they assume significance only when compared with the relevant ratios of others firms (or of the industry in general) or of previous periods. The profit of a firm to sales is 5% : whether this is satisfactory or not will depend upon the figure for previous years or figures for another firms. If other firms earn 6%, this firm is doing not as well as it should; if the firm earned 4.5% of sales on profit in the previous year, it must be considered tohave done better this year by earning 5%; if other firms earn 6%, this firm is not doing as well as it should. Thus to get the true message from the ratios relating to a firm, they must be set against ratio of the previous period or of other firms. Ratio analysis is very fashionable these days and is useful but one should be aware of its limitations also. These limitations should be kept in mind while making use of ratio analysis for interpreting the financial statements. The following are the main limitations of accounting ratios:

(i) Changes in price level often make comparison of figures for various years difficult. For example, the ratio of sales to fixed assets in 1989 would be much higher than in 1979 due to rising prices. It should, however, be noted in this connection that the sales will be expressed in terms of current prices whereas the fixed assets would be expressed still on the basis of cost which is incurred in the past. Hence, figures of the past years must be adjusted in the light of price level changes before comparing the ratios of these years.

(ii) Another point to remember is that people put different meanings on different terms. A firm may work out ratio on the basis of profit after interest and income tax; another firm may consider profits to be before interest but after tax; a third firm may take profits before interest and tax. Obviously, the ratio that will be worked out will be different and will not be comparable. Before comparison is made, one must see that the ratio have been worked out on the same basis.

(iii) Another important point to keep in mind is that there is almost no single standard ratio against which the actual ratio is measurable. Circumstances differ from firm to firm and the nature of each industry is different. Therefore, the standard will differ for each industry and the circumstances of each firm will have to be kept in mind. For instance, one industry may have to invest heavily in fixed assets and another industry may have to keep large stocks of raw materials and finished goods. For these reasons, the performance of the one industry may not be properly comparable with that of another. For each industry, standard ratios will have to be worked out separately, mostly on the basis of actuals for a few represnetative companies which may be considered as reasonably sound and competent. The performance of industry may then be compared, remembering the circumstances of each firm.

(iv) When two firms' results are being compared, it should be kept in mind that the firms may follow different accounting policies. For example, one firm may charge depreciation on the straight line basis and the other on diminishing value. Such differences will not make some of the accounting ratios strictly uncomparable unless adjustment for different accounting policies followed is made.

(v) Accounting ratios are, as a matter of fact, tools of quantitative analysis only. But sometimes it is quite possible that the qualitative factors may over-ride the quantitative factors may over-ride the quantitative aspects. The conclusions derived from the ratio analysis under such circumstances may get distortecd. For example in reality, credit may be granted to a customer on the basis of information regarding the financial position of his business as disclosed by certain ratios but the grant of credit ultimately depends upon the character and managerial ability of the customer. Under such circumstances, the conclusions derived from ratio analysis would be misleading.

(vi) Accounting ratios are worked out on the basis of past facts and figures. Thus, the ratios cannot reflect current conditions. Hence, it is not desirable to use them for forecasting current and future events because past events are quite different from future events. In the modern business, it is more important to have an idea of the probable happenings in future, rather than those in the past. From this point of view, the management is more interested in the forecasting of future events than in the analysis of the past events. Thus, ratios would be significant only if they throw light on the probable happenings in future. In other words, predictive analysis is more significance than historical analysis.

(vii) Accounting ratios may be worked out for any two figures even if they are not significantly related. For example, a ratio may be worked out for sales and investment in government securities. Such ratios will only be misleading. Care should be exercised to work out ratios between only such figures as have cause and effect relationship. One should also be reasonably clear as to what is cause and what is effect.

(viii) Ratios, sometimes, give a misleading picture in the absence of absolute data from which such ratios are derived. For example, one firm produces 1,000 units in one year and 2,000 units next year; the progress is 100%. Another firm raises production from 6,000 units to 8,000 units—the progress is only $33\frac{1}{2}\%$. The second firm will appear to be less active than the first firm if only the rate of increase is compared. It is, therefore, useful if along with ratios absolute figures are also studied—unless the firms being studied are equal in all respects. In fact, one should be extremely careful while comparing the results of one firm with those of another if the two firms differ in any significant manner, say, in size, location, degree of automation or mechanisation, etc.

(ix) Accounting ratios are based on accounting data. Therefore, they can be only as correct as the accounting data on which they are based. They suffer from all the inherent weakness of the accounting system itself. For example, if inventory values are inflated, not only will one have an exaggerated view of profitability of the concern, but also of its financial position. Take another example: suppose the ratio of profit to capital employed for a firm is very good but it is found later that the profit was improperly computed. ignoring some vital provision. To put reliance on the ratio then would be risky. Therefore, unless the balance sheet and the profit and loss account are reliable, the ratios based on them would not be reliable. Thus, the basic data must be absolutely reliable, if the ratios worked out on its basis are to be relied upon.

EARNING POWER OR OVERALL PROFITABILITY

The overall efficiency of a firm can be evaluated on the basis of combination of net profit margin ratio and investment turnover. The combined profitability is known as earning power and return on investment. The earning power of a business organisation may be defined as the over all profitability of an enterprise. This ratio has two components *(i)* net profit margin is net profit to sales, *(ii)* profitability of investments which is reflected by investment assets turnover. The earning power (ROI ratio) of a particular firm can be calculated in the following manner:

Earning power = Net profit margin × Investment Turnover

where,

$$\text{(i) Net Profit Margin} = \frac{\text{Net Profit after tax}}{\text{Sales}} \times 100$$

$$\text{(ii) Investment Turnover} = \frac{\text{Sales}}{\text{Average total investments}}$$

"Investment" may refer to (i) total assets, (ii) capital employed, and (iii) shareholders, equity. For the purpose of Investment Turnover, we use the term "assets". The earning power may be computed as follows—

$$\text{Earning power} = \frac{\text{Net Profit after tax}}{\text{Sales}} \times \frac{\text{Sales}}{\text{Total Assets}}$$

$$= \frac{\text{Net Profit After Tax (NPAT)}}{\text{Sales}}$$

The basic elements of earning of a business firm are portrayed in the following chart known as Du Pont Chart.

Du Pont Chart

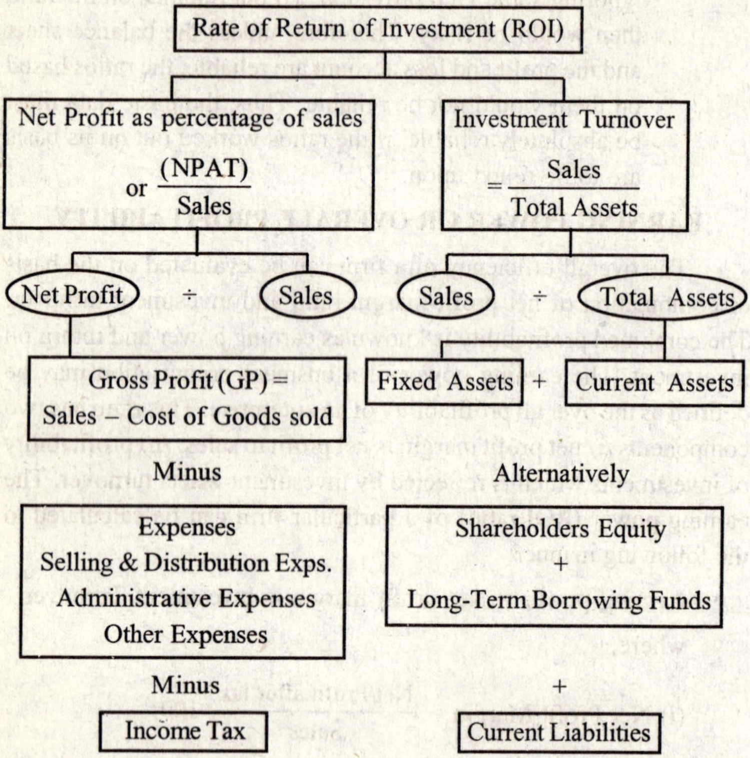

The earning power or the ROI ratios is the main criterion of measure the profitability and operational efficiency of a firm. It shows the interaction of the profitability and activity ratios. It implies that the performance of a business organisation can be improved either by generating more sales volume per rupee of investment or increasing the profit margin per rupee of sales.

Example.

Determine Earning Power Ratio

	Firm X	*Firm Y*
	Rs.	*Rs.*
1. Net Sales	8,00,000	80,00,000
2. Net profit	80,000	80,000

3. Total assets	8,00,000	8,00,000
4. Profit margin (2 ÷ 1)	10%	1%
5. Investment turnover (1 ÷ 3)	1 time	10 times
6. ROI ratio (4) × (5)	10%	10%

It is evident that the earning power of the firms X and Y is the same. But firm X has higher profit margin and the firm Y has a higher investment turnover. The usefulness of DU Pont analysis lies in the fact that it depicts the overall picture of the performance of a firm as also enable the management to identify the factors which have a bearing on profitability. In the aforesaid example, if firm Y improves its profits margin from 1% to 2% its earning power will be doubled-assuming sales remain constant. Similarly, firm X can double its earning power simply by a marginal increase in its investment turnover, as it indicates that the assets are used more efficiently and effectively *i.e.*, more sales per rupee of investments. Thus, the ROI (earning power) ratio is a very important ratio. It can be used to asess the profitability of a firm a period of time, of its various departments of division, as also inter-firm and inter-industry comparisons.

VARIOUS LIQUIDITY

Adequate liquidity makes the firm to be able to meet its obligations as they become due. In fact analysis of liquidity needs the preparation of cash flow statement and cash budgets. Liquidity ratios establish the relationship between cash and other current assets to current liabilities. They provide quick measurement of liquidity. The failure of a company to meet its obligations, due to lack of sufficient liquidity, will result in bad credit image, loss of creditors confidence, or even in facing law suits which may cause closure of the company.

A very high degree of liquidity is also not good. Idle assets do not earn anything else. The firm's fund will be unnecessarily tied up in current assets. Therefore, there is a need to make a proper balance between liquidity and lack of liquidity.

The most common ratios to judge liquidity are—

(i) Current Ratio, (ii) Quick Ratio.

(i) Current Ratio

Current Ratio (CR), is also called Working Capital Ratio. It is the most widely used analytical device based on balance sheet. It shows ability of a company to meet its maturing current obligations. In other words, it shows the relation between the current assets and current liabilities.

$$\text{Formula of Current Raito} = \frac{\text{Current Assets}}{\text{Current Liabilities}}$$

(a) Current Assets include cash in hand, cash at bank, debtors, bills receivable, prepaid expenses, inventories, closing stock of work-in-progress, and short-term liquid investment.

(b) Current Liabilities include sundry creditors, bills payable, bank overdraft, outstanding or accrued expenses and income tax payable.

Example.

Current Assets	**Rs.**	**Rs.**
Cash in Hand	20,000	
Cash at Bank	40,000	
Inventories at end	60,000	
Bills Receivable	20,000	
Debtors	20,000	
Prepaid Expenses	10,000	
Government Securities	10,000	1,80,000
Current Liabilities	**Rs.**	
Creditors	10,000	
Bills Payable	10,000	
Outstanding Expenses	20,000	
Provision for Taxation	15,000	
Bank Overdrafts	5,000	60,000

$$\therefore \text{ Current Ratio} = \frac{\text{Rs. } 1{,}80{,}000}{\text{Rs. } 60{,}000} = 3:1$$

Standard. Generally 2 : 1 (two to one) ratio is referred to as a standard of liquidity for business. However, this proportion may be treated as general trend. The standard proportion may differ from one compnay to another compnay. Therefore, standard of liquidity for a particular business should be determined from the nature of business. It can be less than 2 : 1 if the business have all cash transactions like Indian Railways. On the other hand, it will be more than 2 : 1 in a company having credit transactions as a State Electricity Board.

Significance. From the aforesaid example, the ratio indicates that for every Re. 1.00 of current liabilities there are Rs. 3 of current assets. The current ratio indicates roughly the liquidity of assets or ability of a business to meet its maturing current obligations. The great popularity of the current ratio reflects the facts that almost every body, who has occasion to analyse the balance sheet, whether he is primarily interesed or has a long-term perspective, knows that prospects can only be bleak for firms if they are not in a position to pay their obligations currently due or to be due. Cash need not be immediately available to meet all current liabilities appearing in the balance sheet but there should be Cash equivalent current assets in the business. Higher current ratio provides higher margin of safety to creditors etc.

(ii) Acid Test or Quick Ratio or Liquid Ratio

Current ratio fails to convey information on the composition of the current assets of a firm. Secondly, current ratio is a very old concept. Acid test or liquid ratio or quick ratio is a measure of liquidity designed to overcome the defect of current ratio. It is also referred to as quick ratio as it is a measurement of the firm's ability to convert its current assets quickly into cash in order to pay its current liabilities.

$$\text{Formula of Acid Test Ratio} = \frac{\text{Quick Assets}}{\text{Liquid Liabilities}}$$

$$\text{(or) Quick Ratio} = \frac{\text{Quick Assets}}{\text{Current Liabilities}}$$

Quick Assets are assets which can be converted into cash immediately or at a short notice without diminution of value.

Quick Assets = current assets – inventory – closing stock of work-in-progress – prepaid expenses.
= cash in hand + cash at bank + debtors + Govt. securities + B/R etc.

Why Inventory or Prepaid Expenses are not Included into Quick Assets? The answer is that these assets are not easily or readily convertible into cash. Prepaid expenses by their very nature are not available to pay off current debts.

Liquid liabilities = Creditors + B/P + outstanding expenses + Provision.

Notes. Bank overdraft is not included into liquid liabilities because it tends to become some sort of a permanent mode of financing.

e.g. refer current ratio example.

Quick assets = Rs. 10,000 (*i.e.* not including prepaid expenses and inventory in the total current assets)

Quick liabilities = Rs.55,000 (*i.e.* not including Bank overdraft).

$$\text{Quick Assets Ratio or Acid Test Ratio} = \frac{1,10,000}{55,000} = 2:1$$

Standard. Generally Acid Test Ratio 1 : 1 is considered satisfactory as a firm can easily meet all current claims.

The Liquid or Quick Ratio is more rigorous and penetrating test of liquidity position of a firm. Yet it is not a final or conclusive test. Both current as well as Quick Ratios should be simultaneously used and considered in relation to the industry average to infer whether short-term financial position of the firm is satisfactory or not. In other words, determination of the rate at which various short-term assets are converted into cash is another important dimension of liquidity. And, therefore, it is concomitant of the analysis of short-term financial position. Other ratios included in this category are—

Inventory Turnover Ratio

The aforesaid Liquidity Ratios relate to the liquidity of a firm as a whole. Another way to finding out liquidity is to determine how quickly certain current assets are converted into cash. These ratios are called as turnover ratios. The three turnover ratios that are relevant are:

(i) Inventory Trunover Ratio

(ii) Debtors Turnover Ratio

(iii) Creditors Turnover Ratio

Defensive-Interval Ratio

The liquidity ratio shows the ability of a firm to pay its current liabilities. Besides it, the liquidity position of a business undertaking can also be examined in terms of its ability to pay projected daily expenditure from operations. The Defensive-Interval Ratio provides such a measure of liquidity.

Formula

$$\text{Defensive – Interval ratio} = \frac{\text{Liquid Assets}}{\text{Projected daily cash requirements}}$$

and, Projected Daily Cash

$$\text{Requirement} = \frac{\text{Projected Cash Operating Expenditure}}{\text{No. of days in a year (365)}}$$

The Projected Cash Operating Expenditure is based on past expenditures and future plans. It is equivalent to cost of goods sold excluding depreciation, plus selling and administrative expenditure and other ordinary cash expenditure, Alternatively,

Projected Cash Operating Expenditure = Total expenses – non-cash expenses like depreciation and amortisation.

Example.

The projected cash operating expenditure of M/s Divya and Co. Ltd. for the next year is Rs. 3,65,000/-. It has liquid assets amounting to Rs. 80,000.00 The Defensive Interval Ratio will be:

$$\text{Defensive linterval Ratio} = \frac{\text{Rs. } 80{,}000}{\text{Rs. } 1{,}000} = 80 \text{ days}$$

$$\text{Projected daily cash requirement} = \frac{\text{Rs. } 3{,}65{,}000}{365} = \text{Rs. } 1{,}000$$

Interpretation. The figure of 80 days depicts that the business has liquid assets which can meet the operating cash requirements of the business for 80 days without resorting to future revenues.

Standard. A higher ratio will be better as it reflects the ability of a firm to meet cash requirements for a longer period of time. It provides a safety margin to the firm in determining its ability to meet basic operational costs.

The Liquidity Ratios are, undoubtedly, primarily relevant from creditors' point of view. Higher the liquid ratio better it is. But high Current and Acid Test Ratios would imply that funds have unnecessarily accumulated and are not being profitably utilised. Similary, an unnecessarily high rate of inventory turnover may indicate that a firm is losing business by failing to maintain an adequate level of inventory to serve the needs of customers. A rapid turnover of debtors may depict server of credit policies that hold revenue below levels that could be obtained by granting more liaberal credit terms.

While interpreting the short-term solvency position of the business firm by creditors, it should be kept in mind that sometimes management may be tempted to indulge in "window-dressing". This tactics can present a favourable Current Ratio position. This may be done by manipulating the value of inventory, recording in advance the cash receipts applicable to the next accounting period's sale of merchandise, ommission of liability for merchandise included in inventory and treating a short-term obligation as long-term debt. Similarly, a balance sheet may be "window dressed" when the business defers the replenishment of, or has numerous special sales to reduce, its inventory at the close of the accounting period. In such a case, an analysis of current financial position based on year end data will tend to overstate a firm's average liquidity position.

TYPES OF RATIO ANALYSIS

In view of various users of ratios, there are many types of ratios which can be calculated from the information given in the financial statements. The particular purpose of the user determines the particular ratios that might be used for financial analysis. For example, a supplier of goods to a firm on credit or a banker advancing a short-term loan to a firm is interested primarily in the short-run paying capacity of the firm or say in its liquidity. On the other hand, a financial institution advancing a long term credit to a firm will be primarily interested in the solvency or long term financial position of the concern. In reality classification depends upon the objectives and available data on the basis of figures contained in the financial statements and therefore may be classified as follows:

(i) **Income Statement Ratios.** These ratios are calculated on the basis of the items of income statement only, *e.g.*, current ratio, debt-equity ratio, etc.

(ii) **Position Statement Ratios.** These ratios are calculated on the basis of the figures of position statement only, *e.g.*, current ratio, debt-equity ratio, etc.

(iii) **Inter-statement Ratios or Composite Ratios.** These ratios are based on figures of income statement as well as position statement, *e.g.*, fixed assets turnover ratio, net profit to capital employed, etc.

The above classification, however, is rather crude and unsuitable because analysis of position statement and income statement cannot be carried out in isolation. They have to be studied together to determine the profitability and the financial position of the business. Any one, including the management, which is interested in acquiring knowledge about the business, is concerned with these two aspects. Ratios, as tools for establishing true profitability and financial position of a company, may be classified as:

1. Profitability ratios,

2. Turnover ratios,

3. Financial ratios, and

4. Leverage Ratios.

To say the same thing in different words, some ratios will protray the financial position while others will portray the causes that lead to a change in it.

1. Profitability Ratios

The main object of a business concern is to earn profit. In general terms, efficieny in business is measured by profitability. Profit as compared to the capital employed indicates profitability of the concern. Thus, profitability is of the utmost importance for a concern. If a concern goes on losing, its financial condition will definitely be bad sooner or later. Profits enable a firm to improve its financial strength; therefore, ratios based on profitability are termed 'casual' ratios, indicating the causes of the present or expected financial position. These ratio, are designed to highlight the end result of business activities which is the sole criterion of the overall efficiency of a business concern. Thus, a measure of 'profitability' is the overall measure of efficiency. The following are the important 'profitability' ratios:

(i) Gross Profit Ratio. This ratio shows the relationship of sales with the direct costs such as purchase, manufacturing cost etc. and, thus, is important. Its formula is:

$$\text{Gross Profit Ratio} = \frac{\text{Gross Profit}}{\text{Net Sales}} \times 100$$

Any fluctuation in this gross profit is the result of a change either in 'sales' or the 'cost of goods sold' or both. Thus, this ratio shows the average margin on goods sold.

The gross profit is what is revealed by the Trading Account. It results from the difference between net sales and cost of goods sold without taking into account expenses generally charged to the Profit and Loss Account. A decline in gross profit is a serious matter and should be investigated carefully. It may be due to the following:

(i) The prices of materials may have gone up or wages may have increased and the selling price may not have increased in proportion to it;

(ii) The selling price may have fallen without there being a relative fall in the prices of materials or wages;

(iii) The closing stock may have been taken wrongly or wrongly valued. The gross profit and the gross profit ratio will fall if the stock is undervalued;

(iv) Conversely, if the closing stock is overvalued in last year, the gross profit and gross profit ratio will fall since the opening stock will be shown at a higher figure;

(v) Misappropriation of goods, so that the firm pays for them but someone also takes them away;

(vi) Wastages and losses, etc.; and

(vii) Failure to record sales arising from goods despatched towards the close of the period.

There will be higher gross profit and gross prófit ratio if the above causes reverse.

Objective and Significance. Gross Profit Ratio is a reliable guide to the adequecy of selling prices and efficiency of stock control. This ratio should be adequate to cover the operating expenses and to provide for fixed charges, dividends and building up of reserves. The ratio is compared to earlier year's ratios or with ratios of other firms. In such cases it has to be ensured that the method of calculating gross profit should not change and when compared with other firms, the firms should follow the same accounting system and practices. Of course, higher the gross profit ratio, the better it is. The objectives of working Gross Profit Ratio are:

(i) To determine the selling price so that there is adequate gross profit to cover the operating expenses, fixed charges, dividends and building up reserves:

(ii) To determine, how much the selling price per unit may decline without resulting in losses on operations of the firms; and

(iii) Gross Profit Ratio, when compared to earlier years, if significantly different, is a reason for the management to investigate the change.

Illustration.

From the following calculate gross profit ratio:

	Rs.
Gross Profit	42,000
Net Sales	3,00,000

Solution.

Calculation of Gross Profit Ratio

$$\text{Gross Profit Ratio} = \frac{\text{Gross Profit}}{\text{Net Sales}} \times 100$$

$$= \frac{42,000}{33,00,000} \times 100 = 14\%.$$

(ii) Net Profit Ratio or Margin. This ratio measures the rate of net profit earned as sales; hence may be called as 'Return on sales'. This ratio is very useful to proprietors and prospective investors because it reveals the overall efficiency and profitability of the concern. This ratio differs from the operating ratio in-as-much as it is calculated after deducting non-operating expenses *e.g.* loss on sale of fixed assets etc. from operating profit and adding non-operating incomes like interest or dividends on investment (non-trading), profit on sale of fixed assets etc. to such profit. It is calculated as:

$$\frac{\text{Net Operating Profit}}{\text{Net Sales}} \times 100.$$

Illustration.

	Rs.
Sales less Returns	1,00,000
Gross Profit	40,000
Admn. Expenses	10,000

Selling Expenses	10,000
Income from Investment	5,000
Loss on account of fire	3,000

From above calculate Net Profit Ratio.

Solution.

$$\text{Net Profit Ratio} = \frac{\text{Net Operating Profit}}{\text{Net Sales}} \times 100$$

$$= \frac{20,000}{1,00,000} \times 100 = 10\%.$$

(iii) Return on Investment (ROI). The net result of operation of a business is profit or loss. The sources used by the business to attain this (profit or loss) consists of both proprietor's (shareholders) funds and loans. The overall performance, and the most important, therefore, can be judged by working out a ratio between profit earned and capital employed. The resultant ratio, usually expressed as a percentage, is called Rate to Return or Net Profit to Capital Employed or more common by Return on Investment (ROI). Yield on Capital is another term employed to express the idea. The purpose is to ascertain how much income the use of Rs. 100 of capital generates. This ratio is calculated normally in the case of companies as:

$$\text{ROI} = \frac{\text{Net Profit}}{\text{Capital Employed}} \times 100$$

Net profit = Net trading profit after depreciation but before interest on fixed liabilities *e.g.* interest on debentures, dividend on shares and taxation.

Capital Employed = Equity Share Capital + Preference Share Capital +Undistributed profit + Reserve & Surplus + Fixed liabilities – Fictitious Assets.

Capital Employed = Fixed Assets + Current Assets – Current Liabilities.

Illustration.

Following is the Balance Sheet of M/s ABC Ltd.

Liabilities	*Rs.*	*Assets*	*Rs.*
Share Capital	20,00,000	Fixed Assets Net	29,00,000
Reserves	5,00,000	Current Assets	25,00,000
10% Loans	10,00,000	Underwriting Commission	1,00,000
Current Liabilities	15,00,000		
Profit for the year	5,00,000		
	55,00,000		55,00,000

Find out the Return on Investment.

Solution.

	Rs.
Profit before interest : Profit as stated	5,00,000
Interest	1,00,000
	6,00,000
Capital employed : Shares Capital	20,00,000
Reserves	10,00,000
Loans	10,00,000
	40,00,000
Less : Underwriting Commission	1,00,000
Capital Employed	39,00,000
or Fixed Assets, net	29,00,000
Working Capital (Rs. 25,00,000 – Rs. 15,00,000)	10,00,000
	39,00,000

$$\text{Return on Investment} = \frac{\text{Profit before Interest}}{\text{Capital Employment}}$$

$$\text{Return on Investment} = \frac{\text{Rs. } 6,00,000}{\text{Rs. } 39,00,000} \times 100 = 15.4\%$$

(iv) Return on Equity. The shareholders of any company are more interested in knowing how much their investment has earned. In other words, profits available to Equity shareholders. Profit that is available to the Equity Shareholders is not profit after interest, taxes and dividends payable on preference share capital. This ratio is known as Return on Equity. It is calculated as under:

$$\text{Return of Equity} = \frac{\text{Net Profit}}{\text{Equity Shareholder's Funds}}$$

Illustration.

	Rs.
10% Preference Share Capital (fully paid)	1,00,000
16,000 Equity shares of Rs. 10 each (fully paid)	1,60,000
Reserves and Surplus	6,40,000
Net Profit after tax	2,37,500

Calculate Return on Equity (ROE).

Solution.

	Rs.
Dividend on Preference Shares Capital:	
10% on Rs. 1,00,000	10,000
Equity Shareholders' funds:	
Paid-up amount of Equity Share Capital	1,60,000
Add : Reserves and Surplus	6,40,000
Total	8,00,000

$$\text{Return on Equity or ROE} = \frac{\text{Net Profit} - \text{Preference Dividend}}{\text{Equity Shareholders' Funds}} \times 100$$

$$= \frac{\text{Rs. } 2,37,500 - \text{Rs. } 10,000}{\text{Rs. } 8,00,000} \times 100$$

$$= \frac{\text{Rs. } 2,27,500}{\text{Rs. } 8,00,000} \times 100 = 28.44\%$$

(v) Operating Ratio. This ratio establishes the relationship between cost of goods sold and other operating expenses on the one hand and the sales on the other. It measures the cost of operation per rupee of sales. The ratio is calculated by dividing operating cost with the net sales and is generally represented as a percentage.

$$\text{Operating Ratio} = \frac{\text{Operating cost}}{\text{Net Sales}} \times 100$$

$$= \frac{\text{Cost of goods sold} + \text{Operating expenses}}{\text{Net Sales}} \times 100$$

The two basic elements of the ratio are operating cost and net sales.

Illustration.

	Rs.
Cost of Goods sold	3,50,000
Selling & Distribution expenses	20,000
Net Sales	5,00,000
Admn. & Office Expenses	30,000

Solution.

$$\text{Operating Ratio} = \frac{\text{Cost of goods sold} + \text{Operating expenses}}{\text{Net Sales}} \times 100$$

$$= \frac{3,50,000 + 20,000 + 30,000}{5,00,000} \times 100$$

$$= \frac{4,00,000}{5,00,000} \times 100 = 80\%.$$

(vi) Expenses Ratios. Expenses ratio is calculated by dividing each item of expenses or group of expenses with the net sales to analyse the cause of variation of the operating ratio. The ratio can be calculated for each individual item of expense or a group of items of a particular types of expenses like cost of sales ratio, Admn. expenses ratio, Selling expense ratio, material consumed ratio etc.

$$\text{Expense Ratio} = \frac{\text{Particular Expense}}{\text{Net Sales}} \times 100$$

Individual expense ratio may be calculated as:

(i) Cost of goods sold ratio $= \dfrac{\text{Cost of goods sold}}{\text{Sales}} \times 100$

(ii) Admn. & Office expense Ratio $= \dfrac{\text{Admn. \& Office Expenses}}{\text{Sales}} \times 100$

(iii) Selling & Distributive Expenses Ratio

$$= \frac{\text{Selling \& Distributive Expenses}}{\text{Sales}} \times 100$$

(iv) Non operating expenses Ratio $= \dfrac{\text{Non - operating Expenses}}{\text{Sales}} \times 100$

(vii) Earning Per Share (EPS). Earnings per share is a small variation of return on equity capital and is calculated by dividing the net profit after taxes and preference divided by the total number of equity shares.

$$\text{E.P.S.} = \frac{\text{Net profit after tax} - \text{Preference Dividend}}{\text{No. of Equity Shares}}$$

The earnings per share is a good measure of profitability and when compared with EPS of similar other companies, it gives a view of the comparative earnings or earning power of a firm. E.P.S. calculated for a number of years indicates whether or not earning power of the company has increased.

(viii) Dividend Yield Ratio. Shareholders are the real owners of a company and they are interested in real sense in the eanrings distributed and paid to them as dividends. Therefore, dividend yield ratio is calculated to evaluate the relationship between dividend per share paid and the market value of the share.

$$\text{Dividend Yield Ratio} = \frac{\text{Dividend per share}}{\text{Market Value per Shares}}$$

$$\text{Dividend per share} = \frac{\text{Dividend paid to Shareholders}}{\text{Number of shares}}$$

(ix) Dividend Payout Ratio or Payout Ratio. Dividend pay out ratio is calculated to find the extent to which earnings per share have been used for paying dividend and to know what portion of earnings has been retained in the business. It is is important ratio because ploughing back of profits enables a company to grow and pay more dividends in future.

$$\text{Dividend Pay out Ratio} = \frac{\text{Dividend Per Equity Share}}{\text{Earnings per share}}$$

(x) Price-Earning Ratio. This is the ratio between market price per equity share and earning per share. The ratio is calculated to make an estimate of appreciation in the value of a share of a company and is widely used by investors to decide whether or not to buy shares in a particular company. This ratio is calculated as:

$$\text{Price Earning Ratio} = \frac{\text{Market price per equity Share}}{\text{Earning per Share}}$$

Illustration.

The capital of Sun Co. Ltd. is as follows :

	Rs.
80,000 Equity Shares of Rs. 10 each	8,00,000
9% 30,000 preferene share of Rs. 10 each	3,00,000
	11,00,000

The following information has been obtained from the books of the company:

	Rs.
Profit after tax at 60%	2,70,000
Depreciation	60,000
Equity Dividend Paid	20%
Market price of Equity Share	40

You are required to calculate:

(a) Dividend yield on equity share,

(b) Earning per share,

(c) Price Earning Ratio.

(a) Dividend yield on Equity Share

$$= \frac{\text{Dividend per share}}{\text{Market price per Share}}$$

$$= \frac{2 \text{ (i.e. } 20\% \text{ of Rs. } 10)}{40} = .05 \text{ or say } 5\%.$$

$$\text{(b) Earning Per Share} = \frac{\text{Profit after tax \& Preference dividend}}{\text{Number of Equity Shares}}$$

$$= \frac{2{,}43{,}000 \text{ (i.e. } 2{,}70{,}000 - 27{,}000)}{80{,}000} = 3.04$$

$$\text{(c) Price Earning Ratio} = \frac{\text{Market Price Per Share}}{\text{Earnings per share}}$$

$$= \frac{40}{3.04} = 13.1:1$$

(1) Creditor Turnover Ratio. The analysis of creditor turnover ratio is basically the same as that of dєbtors turn over ratio except that in place of trade debtors. the trade creditors are taken as one of the components of the ratio and in place of average daily sales, average daily purchases are taken as the other component of the ratio. This can be calculated as :

$$\text{Creditor Turnover Ratio} = \frac{\text{Net Credit Annual Purchases}}{\text{Average Trade Creditors}}$$

If there is no information about credit purchase available, the figure of total purchase may be taken as the numerator and the trade creditors include sundry creditors and bills payables. If opening and closing balances of creditors are not known, the balance of creditors given may be taken to find out the ratio.

Illustration.

Following is the information about M/s ABC Ltd. for the year ending Dec. 1995 : Calculate credit turnover Ratio.

		Rs.
(i)	Sales for 1995	3,00,000
	Closing stock is Rs. 10,000 more than the opening stock.	
	Opening creditors	20,000
	Closing creditors	30,000
	Trade debtors at the end	60,000
	Net working capital	50,000

Solution.

$$\text{Creditors Turnover Ratio} = \frac{\text{Net Annual Credit purchase}}{\text{Average Trade Creditors}}$$

All purchases are taken as credit purchases.

$$\text{Credit Turnover Ratio} = \frac{2,50,000}{\left(\frac{20,000+30,000}{2}\right)}$$

$$= \frac{2,50,000}{25,000} = 10 \text{ times.}$$

(2) Activity Ratios (Turnover or Performance). Activity or performance or turnover ratios judge how well the facilities at the disposal of the concern are being used. The ratios are usually calculated on the basis of sales (cost of sales). These ratios are also knwon as turnover ratios as they express the rapidity with which is unit of stock/working capital or capital invested, etc., produces sales. These ratios indicate the efficiency with which the resources available to the business undertaking are utilised. Some important ratios are as below :

(i) Capital Turnover Ratio. This ratio shows the efficiency of capital employed in the business by computing how many times capital is turned over in a stated period.

The ratio is calculated as :

$$\frac{\text{Sales or cost of sales}}{\text{Capital Employed}}$$

Capital Employed = Shareholder's Fund + Long Term Liabilities

Higher the ratio the better it is. However, too high a ratio may indicate overtrading resulting in paucity of funds.

Illsutration.

Calculate the Capital Turnover Ratio from the following:

Sales	Rs. 1,61,000
Capital Employed	Rs. 2,30,000

Solution.

$$\text{Capital Turnover Ratio} = \frac{\text{Sales}}{\text{Capital Employed}}$$

$$= \frac{1,61,000}{2,30,000} = 0.70$$

(ii) Sales to Fixed Assets of Fixed Assets Turnover Ratio. This ratio shows how well the fixed assets are being utilised. If compared with a previous period, it indicates whether the investment in fixed assets has been judicious or not. The ratio is calculated as follows:

$$\text{Fixed Assets Turnover Ratio} = \frac{\text{Sales}}{\text{Fixed Assets}}$$

In computing Fixed Assets Turnover Ratio, the fixed assets are generally taken at written-down value at the end of year. However, there is no rigidity about it. It may be taken at original cost or at present market value depending on the object of the comparison. In fact, the ratio will have automatic improvement if the written-down value is used. It would be better if the ratio is worked out on the basis of the original cost of fixed asset. We will take fixed assets at cost less depreciation while working this ratio.

Illustration.

The following details have been given to you for Exe. Ltd. for two years. You are required to find out the Fixed Assets Turnover Ratio and comment on it.

	1988	*1989*
	Rs.	*Rs.*
Fixed Assets (at written-down value)	1,50,000	3,00,000
Sales	6,00,000	9,00,000

Solution.

$$\text{Fixed Assets Turnover Ratio} = \frac{\text{Sales}}{\text{Fixed Assets}}$$

$$= \frac{\text{Rs. } 60,00,000}{\text{Rs. } 1,50,000} \qquad \frac{\text{Rs. } 9,00,000}{\text{Rs. } 3,00,000}$$

$$= 4 \text{ times} \qquad 3 \text{ times}$$

The decline in fixed assets turnover ratio indicates that fixed assets have not been used as efficiently as, they had been used in the previous year. The management should investigate further and determine the reason for the fall.

(iii) Sales to working capital or Net Working Capital Turnover Ratio. The ratio express the number of times a unit invested in working capital produce sales. It is calculated as follows:

$$\frac{\text{Cost of Sales (or Sales)}}{\text{Net Working Capital}}$$

Net working capital = Current Assets – Current Liabilities.

The higher is the ratio, the lower is the investment in working capital and the greater are the profits. However, a very high turnover of working capital is a sign of over-trading and may put the concern in financial difficulties, the other hand, a low working capital turnover ratio indicates the working capital is not efficiency utilised.

Illustration.

Calculate the working capital turnover ratio from the following

Sales	Rs. 1,50,000
Current Assets	Rs. 1,00,000
Current Liabilities	Rs. 75,000

Solution.

Net Working Capital = Current Assets – Current Liabilities

$$= 1,00,000 - 75,000 = 25,000$$

$$\text{Net working capital turnover ratio} = \frac{\text{Sales}}{\text{Net Working Capital}}$$

$$= \frac{1,50,000}{25,000} = 6 \text{ times.}$$

(iv) Stock Tunrover Ratio or Inventory Turnover Ratio. This ratio establishes relationship between the cost of goods sold during a given period and the average amount of inventory carried during that period. It indicates whether stock has been efficiently used or not, the purpose being to check up whether only the required minimum has been locked up in stocks. It is usually considered better to work out the turnover against cost of sales since sales include an element of profit, whereas stock is usually at cost. The ratio is calculated as follows:

$$\text{Stock Turnover Ratio} = \frac{\text{Cost of Goods Sold}}{\text{Average Stock or Inventory}}$$

Cost of goods is calculated as follows:

$$\text{Cost of Goods Sold} = \text{Opening Stock} + \text{Purchase} + \text{Direct Expenses} - \text{Closing Stock}$$

Or

Cost of Goods Sold = Sales – Gross Profit.

$$\text{Average Stock} = \frac{\text{Opening Stock} + \text{Closing Stock}}{2}$$

Illustration.

The following details have been given to you for Exe. Ltd. for two years. You are required to find out the Fixed Assets Turnover Ratio and comment on it.

	1988	*1989*
	Rs.	*Rs.*
Fixed Assets (at written-down value)	1,50,000	3,00,000
Sales	6,00,000	9,00,000

Solution.

$$\text{Fixed Assets Turnover Ratio} = \frac{\text{Sales}}{\text{Fixed Assets}}$$

$$= \frac{\text{Rs. } 60,00,000}{\text{Rs. } 1,50,000} \qquad \frac{\text{Rs. } 9,00,000}{\text{Rs. } 3,00,000}$$

$$= 4 \text{ times} \qquad 3 \text{ times}$$

The decline in fixed assets turnover ratio indicates that fixed assets have not been used as efficiently as, they had been used in the previous year. The management should investigate further and determine the reason for the fall.

(iii) Sales to working capital or Net Working Capital Turnover Ratio. The ratio express the number of times a unit invested in working capital produce sales. It is calculated as follows:

$$\frac{\text{Cost of Sales (or Sales)}}{\text{Net Working Capital}}$$

Net working capital = Current Assets – Current Liabilities.

The higher is the ratio, the lower is the investment in working capital and the greater are the profits. However, a very high turnover of working capital is a sign of over-trading and may put the concern in financial difficulties, the other hand, a low working capital turnover ratio indicates the working capital is not efficiency utilised.

Illustration.

Calculate the working capital turnover ratio from the following

Sales	Rs. 1,50,000
Current Assets	Rs. 1,00,000
Current Liabilities	Rs. 75,000

Solution.

Net Working Capital = Current Assets – Current Liabilities

$$= 1,00,000 - 75,000 = 25,000$$

$$\text{Net working capital turnover ratio} = \frac{\text{Sales}}{\text{Net Working Capital}}$$

$$= \frac{1,50,000}{25,000} = 6 \text{ times.}$$

(iv) Stock Tunrover Ratio or Inventory Turnover Ratio. This ratio establishes relationship between the cost of goods sold during a given period and the average amount of inventory carried during that period. It indicates whether stock has been efficiently used or not, the purpose being to check up whether only the required minimum has been locked up in stocks. It is usually considered better to work out the turnover against cost of sales since sales include an element of profit, whereas stock is usually at cost. The ratio is calculated as follows:

$$\text{Stock Turnover Ratio} = \frac{\text{Cost of Goods Sold}}{\text{Average Stock or Inventory}}$$

Cost of goods is calculated as follows:

Cost of Goods Sold = Opening Stock + Purchase + Direct Expenses – Closing Stock

Or

Cost of Goods Sold = Sales – Gross Profit.

$$\text{Average Stock} = \frac{\text{Opening Stock} + \text{Closing Stock}}{2}$$

Illustration.

Calculate the stock turnover ratio from the following:

	Rs.
Opening stock	19,000
Closing stock	21,000
Sales	2,00,000

Gross Profit on sale is 25%.

Solution.

$$\text{Stock Turnover Ratio} = \frac{\text{Cost of Goods Sold}}{\text{Average Stock}}$$

$$= \frac{2,00,000-(25\%\times 2,00,000)}{20,000}$$

$$= \frac{1,50,000}{20,000} = 7.5 \text{ times.}$$

(v) Debtors Turnover Ratio or Receivable Turnover Ratio. This ratio is known as ratio of Net Sales to Gross Receivables. The main aim of this ratio is to ascertain after how much time the debtors of the firm make payment. The ratio is calculated by the formula.

$$\frac{\text{Net Credit Sales}}{\text{Average Accounts Receivables (Drs.} + \text{B/R)}}$$

(The term Accounts Receivable include 'Trade Debtors' and 'Bills Receivable') If this ratio is high, it indicates economy and efficiency in collection of amount due. The reverse is also true, while calculating debtors turnover, it is important to remember that doubtful debts are not deducted from total debtors. In case details regarding opening and closing receivables and credit sales are not given. The ratio may be worked out as follows:

$$\text{Debtor's Turnover Ratio} = \frac{\text{Total Sales}}{\text{Accounts Receivable}}$$

Illustration.

Calculate the Debtors Turnover Ratio from the following:

	Rs.
Total Sales for 1991	2,00,000
Cash Sales for 1991	40,000
Debtors as on 1.1.1991	35,000
Debtors as on 31.12.1991	55,000

Solution.

$$\text{Debtors Turnover Ratio} = \frac{\text{Credit Sales}}{\text{Average Debtors}}$$

$$= \frac{1,60,000}{45,000} = 3.56 \text{ times.}$$

This ratio indicates upto what extent the debts have been collected in the ratio is helpful to the moneylenders because average debt collections period can be found out easily. The higher average collection period will result in the blockage of funds with debtors.

(a) For calculating Average collection period in days

$$\text{Debtors Turnover Ratio} = \frac{\text{Total Debtors} \times \text{No. of working days}}{\text{Net Sales}}$$

or $$= \frac{\text{Debtors + B/R}}{\text{Credit Sales}} \times 365 \text{ days}$$

(b) Formula of calculating average collection period in months:

$$= \frac{\text{Debtors + B/R}}{\text{Credit Sales}} \times 12 \text{ months}$$

(c) Formula of calculating average collection period in weeks:

$$= \frac{\text{Debtors + B/R}}{\text{Credit Sales}} \times 52 \text{ weeks.}$$

(3) Financial Position Ratios. Financial position ratios show up the financial position of the business concern. A sound business concern is one which has good profitability and a sound financial position in the sense that it should be able to carry on its work smoothly and meet all the obligations both long term and short term without strain.

Most of the ratios to judge the soundness of financial position are based on the balance sheet. Basically, two ratios, *viz.*, the debt-equity ratio, showing the long-term financial policy followed by the concern, and the current ratio, showing the short-term financial policy, should throw enough light on the financial position of the concern. We discuss below these and other connected ratios.

Liquidity Ratios (Short-term solvency). Liquidity ratios measure the short-term solvency, *i.e.*, the firm's ability to pay off currernt dues. They comprise *(i)* current ratio, and *(ii)* quick ratio.

(i) Current Ratio or Working Capital Ratio. This ratio is used to assess the short-term financial position of the business cocnern. In other words, it is an indicator of the firm's ability to meet its short-term obligations. It matches the total current assets of the firm against its Current Liabilities. "Current Assets" means assets convertible and meant to be converted into cash within a year's time and "Current Liabilities" means liabilities repayable in a years time. This ratio is calculated as follows:

$$\text{Current Ratio} = \frac{\text{Current Assets}}{\text{Current Liabilities}}$$

It is generally accepted that currrent assets should be 2 times the current liabilities; then only will realisation from current liabilities; then only will realisation from current assets be sufficient to pay the current liabilities on time and enable the firm to meet other day-to-day expenses. Debtors outstanding for more than six months should not be normally included in current assets. Prepaid expenses should be treated as current assets. One must always ' ' careful about window dressing and, therefore, the various assets should be carefully scrutinised

Illustration.

From the following calculate current ratio :

	Rs.
Current Assets :	
Sundry Debtors	40,000
Inventories	60,000
Cash in hand	1,00,000
Current Liabilities :	
Sundry Creditors	80,000
Bills Payable	20,000

Solution.

$$\text{Current Ratio} = \frac{2,00,000}{1,00,000} = 2.$$

(ii) Quick Ratio, Liquid Ratio or Acid Test Ratio. This ratio explains the relationship between liquid assets and current liabilities. This ratio measures the firms ability to pay off claims of current creditors immediately. This is calculated as:

$$\text{Liquid Ratio} = \frac{\text{Liquid Assets}}{\text{Current Liabilities}}$$

Liquid Assets include cash in hand and cash at Bank, realisable securities and bills receivable (within a month), it does not include stock in hand and prepaid expenses. Since this ratio attempts to measure the firms capacity to pay off immediately its creditors the ideal ratio is said to be 1 : 1. If it is more, it is considered better.

Illustration.

From the following informatons calculate liquid ratios:

Current Assets:	*Rs.*
Cash	5,000
Debtors	29,000
Bills Receivable	5,000
Marketing Securities	15,000
Stock	52,000
Prepaid Expenses	2,000
	1,08,000
Current Liabilities :	
Sundry Criditors	30,000
Bills Payable	16,000
Outstanding Expenses	8,000
54,000	

Solution.

$$\text{Current Ratio} = \frac{\text{Current Assets}}{\text{Current Liabilities}}$$

$$= \frac{1,08,000}{54,000} = 2:1$$

$$\text{Liquid Ratio} = \frac{\text{Liquid Assets}}{\text{Current} + \text{Liabilities}}$$

$$= \frac{54,000}{54,000} = 1:1.$$

Solvency Ratio (Long Term Solvency)

Most of the ratio to judge the soundness of financial position and policies are based on the balance sheet. Basically, two ratios—the debt equity ratio showing the long term financial policy followed by the concern and the current ratio showing the short term financial policy should throw enough light on the financial policy of the concern. Current and quick ratios has already been discussed under the heading liquid ratios and other solvency ratios *e.g.* debt-equity ratio, interet coverage ratio, debt to total funds ratio etc. are being discussed below:

(i) Debt Equity Ratio. This is the ratio which is determined to ascertain the soundness of the long-term financial policies of the company. It is calculated as

$$\frac{\text{Long term debts}}{\text{Shareholders Funds + long term Debts}}$$

It portrays the proportion of total funds acquired by the firm by way of debts. The ratio considered appropriate goes on changing at one time it was thought that not more than half the long term requirements should be raised by way of long term lonas but now the proportion can be 2/3rds or even 3/4ths. In other words 67% to 75% of the long term funds required by an industrial concern may be raised by way of loans.

Shareholder's fund consists of preference share capital, equity share capital, capital reserves, revenue reserves, reserves representing marked surplus like reserve for contingencies, sinking fund for renewal of fixed assets or redemption of debentures etc. less fictitious assets like preliminary expenses, discount on issue of share/debentures etc.

Illustration.

From the following calculate the Debt Equity ratio.

	Rs.
10,000 Equity Shares of Rs. 10 each	1,00,000
General Reserves	45,000
Accumulated Profit	30,000
Debentures	75,000
Sundry trade creditors	40,000
Outstanding Expenses	10,000

Solution.

$$\text{Debt Equity Ratio} = \frac{\text{Debt (Total long term)}}{\text{Equity (Shareholders Fund)}}$$

$$= \frac{75,000}{1,75,000} = 3.7.$$

(ii) Interest Coverage Ratio. When a business borrows money, the lender is interested in finding out whether the business would earn sufficient profits to pay periodically the interest charges. A ratio which expresses this is called Interest Coverage Ratio or Debt Service Ratio or Fixed Charges Cover. This ratio is determined by debiting profit before interest charges. Thus, two variables involved in this ratio are fixed interest charges and net profit. Net profit before interest and income tax is to be taken in the computation of the ratio because we have to find how many times interest is covered by the profit and income-tax is paid after the deduction of interest. The ratio is calculated as:

Interest Coverage Ratio

$$= \frac{\text{Net profit before interest and tax}}{\text{Interest on fixed (long - term) loans or debentures}}$$

Interest being paid periodically, usually half yearly, it will take second place to other expenses which are paid monthly or weekly. This is the reason why the ratio is calculated using profit after other usual expenses. The ratio indicates how many times the profit covers the interest. It measures the margin of safety for the lenders. If profit just equals interest, it is a bad position for the company as nothing will be left for shareholders and an unsafe one for the lenders. The ratio should be 3 or more.

Illustration.

The operating profit of XLY Ltd. after charging interest on debentures and tax is Rs. 1,00,000. The amount of interest is Rs. 20,000 and the provision for tax has been made at Rs. 40,000. Calculate the interest coverage ratio.

Solution.

$$\text{Interest Coverage Ratio} = \frac{\text{Net profit before interest \& tax}}{\text{Interest charges}}$$

$$= \frac{\text{Rs. } 1,60,000}{\text{Rs. } 20,000} = 8 \text{ times.}$$

(iii) Debt to Total Funds Ratio. Just as it is normally sufficient to measure current assets against current liabilities for assessing the short-term financial soundness of a company the Debt to Total Funds Ratio is a measure for long-term financial soundness.

This is the ratio between long-term and total funds. It shows the proportion of total funds acquired by way of debt. It is worked out as:

$$\text{Debt to Total Funds Ratio} = \frac{\text{Debt}}{\text{Debt} + \text{Equity (or total long-term funds)}}$$

In India, this rato may be taken as acceptable if it is 0.67. A higher proportion would be riskly since loans with them obligation to pay interest at a fixed rate which may become difficult if profit is reduced. Hence, good concerns keep the debt to total funds ratio round acceptable norms only.

The debt-equity ratio and debt to total funds ratios indicate the way finances have been raised, the proper investment of funds is also important from the point of view of long term financial soundness. Hence, the ratio of long-term loans to fixed assets and proprietary Ratio are also important. They are explained below:

(i) Proprietary Ratio. This ratio establishes the relationship between proprietor's funds and total assets. Proprietor's funds mean share capital plus reserves and surplus, both of capital and revenue nature. Loss should be deducted. Funds payable to others should not be added. The difference between this ratio as % and 100 represents the ratio of total liabilities to total assets. It is woked out as follows:

$$\text{Proprietary Ratio} = \frac{\text{Proprietor's funds}}{\text{Total assets}}$$

$$\text{Proprietary Ratio} = \frac{\text{Proprietary funds or Capital Employed}}{\text{Short term and long term liabilities}}$$

$$\text{or} = \frac{\text{Owned Capital}}{\text{Total Capital}}$$

The higher the ratio, the more useful it is considered for the persons concerned with the company; as the company does not depend on outside sources for its working capital.

Illustration.

From the following calculate Proprietary ratio.

Liabilities	*Rs.*	*Assets*	*Rs.*
Preference share capital	1,00,000	Fixed Assets	2,00,000
Equity Share capital	2,00,000	Current Assets	1,50,000
Creditors	50,000	Goodwill	50,000
Reserves & Surplus	50,000		
	4,00,000		4,00,000

Solution.

$$\text{Proprietary Ratio} = \frac{\text{Shareholders Funds}}{\text{Total Tangible Assets}}$$

$$= \frac{(1,00,000+2,00,000+50,000)-50,000}{2,00,000+1,50,000}$$

$$= \frac{3,00,000}{3,50,000} = .86\% = 86\%.$$

(ii) Fixed Assets Ratio or Ratio of Capital and Long-term Funds to Fixed Asset. The ratio of long term loans to fixed assets is important and another aspect of long-term financial policy. This ratio is calculated as:

$$\text{Fixed Assets Ratio} = \frac{\text{Shareholders' Funds} + \text{Long - term loans}}{\text{Net Fixed Assets}}$$

It is well established that fixed assets should be financed only out of long-term funds. This ratio shows where this is so. This ratio will be 1 if long-term fund are equal to fixed assets. If this ratio is less than 1, it means that the firm has adopted the imprudent policy of using short-term funds for acquiring fixed assets. On the other hand, a very high ratio would indicate that long-term funds are being used for short-term purposes, *i.e.*, for financing working capital. It is not good from the firm's point of view because it is usually more difficult to raise long-term funds.

Fixed assets will mean cost less depreciation or net fixed assets. It will also include trade investments. Long-term funds will mean equity share capital, preference share capital, reserves, debentures and long-term loans.

Illustration.

From the following calculate the Fixed Asset Ratio.

	Rs.
Share capital	2,00,000
Reserves	50,000
9% Debentures	2,00,000
Trade Creditors	75,000
Plant & Machinery	2,00,000
Land & Building	2,00,000
Furniture	50,000
Trade Debtors	60,000
Cash Balance	40,000
Bills Payable	24,000
Stock	80,000

Solution.

$$\text{Fixed Assets Ratio} = \frac{\text{Long term Funds}}{\text{Fixed Assets}} = \frac{4,50,000}{4,50,000} = 1.$$

Absolute Liquid Ratio

All receivables *i.e.*, debtors and bills receivable are generally more liquid than inventories, yet there may be doubts regarding their realization into cash or in time. Absolute liquid ratio should also be calculated together with current ratio and acid test ratio so as to exclude even receivables from the current assets and find out the absolute liquid assets.

$$\text{Absolute Liquid Ratio} = \frac{\text{Absolute Liquid Assets}}{\text{Current Liabilities}}$$

Absolute Liquid Assets include cash in hand and at bank and marketable securities or temporary investments.

Illustration.

From the following balance sheet of M/s Indica Industries :

Calculate absolute liquid ratio.

Balance Sheet (as on 31 Dec.,' 1995)

Liabilities	Rs.	Assets	Rs.
Equity Share capital	5,00,000	Goodwill	50,000
8% Debentures	3,00,000	Plant & Machinery	4,00,000
Bank Creditors	75,000	Land & Building	1,50,000
Sundry Creditors	60,000	Trade Investments	2,00,000
Bills Payable	30,000	Marketable Securities	50,000
		Cash	45,000
		Bills Receivable	40,000
		Bank Balance	30,000
	9,65,000		9,65,000

Solution.

$$\text{Absolute Liquidity Ratio} = \frac{\text{Absolute Liquid Assets}}{\text{Current Liabilities}}$$

$$\text{Absolute assets} = 45{,}000 + 3000 + 5000$$
$$= 1{,}25{,}000$$

$$\text{Current Liabilities} = 75{,}000 + 60{,}000 + 30000$$
$$= 1{,}65{,}000$$

$$\text{Absolute Liquid Ratio} = \frac{1{,}25{,}000}{1{,}65{,}000} = 0.757$$

The ratio of 0.757 shows that the company has Rs. 0.75 as absolute liquid assets against every Rs. 1/- of current liability.

Capital Gearing Ratio

This ratio is used to describe the relationship between equity share capital including reserves and surpluses to preference share capital and other fixed interest bearing loans. If preference share capital and other fixed interest bearing loans exceed the equity share capital including reserves, the firm is said to be highly geared. The firm is said to be in low gear if preference share capital and other fixed interest bearing loans are less than equity capital and reserves.

Capital Gearing Ratio =

$$\frac{\text{Equity Share Capital} + \text{Reserve \& Surplus}}{\text{Preference Capital} + \text{Long term debts bearing fixed interest}}$$

Illustration.

	1991	1992
Rs.	Rs.	
Equity Share Capital	5,00,000	4,00,000
Reserve & Surplus	3,00,000	2,00,000
8% preference share capital	2,50,000	3,00,000
6% Debentures	2,50,000	4,00,000

Capital Gearing Ratio

$$= \frac{\text{Equity Share Capital + Reserve \& Surplus}}{\text{Preference Capital + Long term debts bearing fixed interest}}$$

$$1991 = \frac{5,00,000+3,00,000}{2,50,000+2,50,000} = 8.5 \text{ (Low Gear)}$$

$$1992 = \frac{4,00,000+2,00,000}{3,00,000+4,00,000} = 6.7 \text{ (High Gear)}$$

Ratio of Current Assets to Fixed Assets

This ratio will differ from industry to industry and therefore, no standard can be laid down. Any decrease in the ratio shows that trading is slack. Any increase in the ratio shows that inventories and debtors have unduly increased or fixed assets have been intensively used. An increase in the ratio, acompanied by increase in profit, indicates that business is expanding.

This ratio is worked out as : $\frac{\text{Current Assets}}{\text{Fixed Assets}}$

Ratio of inventory to Working Capital

The ratio of inventory to woking capital is worked out as :

$$\frac{\text{Inventory}}{\text{Working Capital}}$$

The working capital is the excess of current assets over current liabilities. Increase in the sale requires increase in size of inventory but from a sound financial point of view, inventory should not exceed amount of working capital. 1:1 is a desirable ratio.

(4) Leverge Ratios. In the financial management the leverage ratios refer to employment of funds to accelerate rate of return to owners. It may be favourable or unfavourable. When the earning are found excess over the fixed cost of the fund, it is favourable when the rate of return remains lower, it is unfavourable leverage may be classified as:

(a) Financial leverage

(b) Operating leverage

(a) Financial Leverage. The use of long-term fixed interest bearing debt and preference share capital along with share capital is called financial leverage or trading as equity. It is owners' equity which is used as a basis to raise loans and that is why it is called trading on equity. The long term fixed interest bearing debt is employed by a firm to earn more from the use of these sources than their cost so as to increase the return on owners equity. Leverage can operate adverse also if the rate of interest on long term loans is more than the expected rate of earnings of the firm. Therefore, it needs caution to plan the capital structure of a firm. Financial leverage can be calculated as:

Financial Leverage

$$= \frac{\text{Earnings before Interest \& Tax (EBIT)}}{\text{Earnings before Interest \& Tax - Interest \& Preference dividend}}$$

(b) Operating Leverage. It is obained by dividing contribution *i.e.*, sales minus variable cost by the EBIT *i.e.* earnings, before interest & tax.

$$\text{Operating Leverage} = \frac{\text{Contribution}}{\text{Earning Beofore Interest \& Tax}}$$

Illustration.

From the following calculate *(i)* operating leverage *(ii)* Financial leverage:

	Original	After an increase of 20% in Sales
	1	2
Sales (20,000 units @ Rs. 10)	2,00,000	2,40,000
Variable Cost (Rs. 6 per unit)	1,00,000	1,44,000
Fixed Cost	60,000	60,000

Contd.

	1	2
Earning before Interest & Tax (EBIT)	20,000	36,000
Less : Interest	5,000	5,000
Profit Before Tax (EBT)	15,000	31,000
Tax at 50%	7,500	15,500
	7,500	15,500

Solution.

Contribution = Sales – Variable Cost

	Original	*After an increse of 20% in Sales*
	= 2,00,000 – 1,20,000	= 2,40,000 – 1,44,200
Contribution	= 80,000	= 96,000

(i) Operating leverage :

$$= \frac{\text{Contribution}}{\text{EBIT}} \quad = \frac{80,000}{20,000} \quad = \frac{96,000}{36,000}$$

= 4 = 2.67

(ii) Financial leverage

$$= \frac{\text{EBIT}}{\text{EBIT} - \text{Interest}} \quad = \frac{20,000}{15,000} \quad = \frac{36,000}{31,000}$$

= 1.33 = 1.16

Illustration.

From the following details calculate the stock turnover ratio.

	Rs.
Cost of goods sold	4,50,000
Stock at the beginning of the year	1,25,000
Stock at the close of the year	1,75,000

Solution.

Computation of Stock Turnover Ratio

	Rs.
Cost of Goods Sold	4,50,000
Opening Stock	1,25,000
Closing Stock	1,75,000

$$\text{Average Stock} = \frac{1,25,000 + 1,75,000}{2} = 1,50,000$$

$$\text{Stock Turnover Ratio} = \frac{\text{Cost of Goods Sold}}{\text{Average Stock}}$$

$$= \frac{4,50,000}{1,50,000} = 3 \text{ times}$$

Illustration.

(a) Calculate Debtors Turnover Ratio from the following data:

	Rs.
Total sales for the year	2,00,000
Cash sales for the year	40,000
Debtors at the beginning of the year	20,000
Debtors at the end of the year	60,000

(b) Calculate stock turnover ratio from the data given below:

	Rs.
Stock at the beginning of the year	20,000
Stock at the end of the year	10,000
Purchases	50,000
Carriage inwards	5,000
Sales	1,00,000

Solution.

(a) Average Debtors $= \frac{20,000 + 60,000}{2} = 40,000$

Credit Sales = 2,00,000 – 40,000 = 1,60,000

$$\text{Debtors Turnover Ratio} = \frac{\text{Credit Sales}}{\text{Average Debtors}}$$

$$= \frac{1,60,000}{40,000} = 4$$

(b) Cost of Sales :

	Rs.
Purchases	50,000
Add : Carriage Inwards	5,000
Opening stock	20,000
	75,000
Less : Closing stock	10,000
	65,000

$$= \frac{\text{Average stock (Opening stock + Closing stock)}}{2}$$

$$= \frac{20,000 + 10,000}{2} = 15,000$$

$$\text{Stock Turnover Ratio} = \frac{\text{Cost of Sales}}{\text{Average stock}}$$

$$= \frac{65,000}{15,000} = 4.33$$

Illustration.

Following is the balance sheet of Media Prints Ltd. as on 31/03/1986.

	Rs.			Rs.
Creditors	6,000	Cash		5,000
Bills Payable	10,000	Investment (Govt. Security)		15,000
Outstanding Expenses	1,000	Sundry Debtors		20,000
Taxation Provision	13,000	Stock		30,000
Total Current Liabilities	30,000	Total Current Assets		70,000
6% Mortgage liabilities	70,000	Fixed Assets	1,80,000	
7% Pref. shares	10,000	*Less* Dep. Provision	1,50,000	1,30,000
Equity Shares	50,000			
Reserves & Surplus	40,000			
	2,00,000			2,00,000

Other Informations:

(i) Net sales 3,00,000/

(ii) Cost of Goods Sold 2,58,000.

(iii) Net income before taxation 20,000.

(iv) Net income after taxation 10,000.

You are to calculate:

(i) Liquidity ratio,

(ii) Current ratio,

(iii) Proprietary ratio,

(iv) Gross Profit ratio,

(v) Net Profit Ratio.

Solution.

(i) $\text{Liquidity Ratio} = \frac{\text{Liquid Assets}}{\text{Current Liabilities}} = \frac{\text{Rs.}40,000}{\text{Rs. }30,000} = 1.3:1$

(ii) $\text{Current Ratio} = \frac{\text{Current Assets}}{\text{Current Liabilities}} = \frac{\text{Rs. }70,000}{\text{Rs. }30,000} = 2.3:1$

(iii) Proprietary Ratio $= \frac{\text{Proprietor's Funds}}{\text{Total Assets}}$

$$= \frac{1,00,000}{2,00,000} = 5:1 \text{ or } 50\%.$$

(iv) Gross Profit Ratio $= \frac{\text{Gross Profit}}{\text{Net Sales}} \times 100$

$$= \frac{\text{Rs. } 42,000}{\text{Rs. } 3,00,000} \times 100 = 14\%$$

Working Notes:

Gross Profit= Net Sales – Cost of Godos sold

= Rs. 3,00,000 – Rs. 2,50,000 = Rs. 42,000

(v) Net Profit Ratio $= \frac{\text{Net profit after tax}}{\text{Net sales}} \times 100$

$$= \frac{\text{Rs. } 10,000}{\text{Rs. } 3,00,000} \times 100 = 3.3\% \text{ Approx.}$$

Illustration.

From the following calculate the proprietary Ratio

	Rs.
Equity Share Capital	1,00,000
Preference share capital	50,000
Reserve and surplus	25,000
Debentures	60,000
Creditors	15,000
	2,50,000
Fixed Assets	1,25,000
Current Assets	50,000
Investment	75,000
	2,50,000

Solution.

$$\text{Proprietary Ratio} = \frac{\text{Shareholder's Funds}}{\text{Total Assets}}$$

$$= \frac{\text{Rs. } 17{,}50{,}000}{\text{Rs. } 2{,}50{,}000} = 0.7 \textit{ Or } 70\%.$$

Illustration.

From the following summary of the final Accounts of M/s Sun Star Ltd. for the year 31st Dec. 1995:

Rs. ('000)

Trading and Profit & Loss A/c

Net Sales			800
Less :	Cost of Goods sold		
	Opening Stock	40	
	Purchases	600	
		640	
Less :	Closing stock	20	620
	Gross Profit		180
	Admn. Expenses	35	
	Selling Expenses	10	
	Interest on debentures	15	60
	Net Profit		120

Balance Sheet

Liabilities	Rs.	Assets	Rs.
Equity share capital	300	Fixed Assets	400
Debentures	100	Stock	24
Reserves	140	Debtors	100
Trade Creditors	40	Bank balance	56
	580		580

Calculate :

(i) Operating Ratio,

(ii) Stock Turnover Ratio,

(iii) Working Capital Turnover Ratio,

(iv) Debtors Turnover Ratio,

(v) Profitability Ratio.

Solution.

$$\text{(i) Operating Ratio} = \frac{\text{Cost of goods sold} + \text{Operating exp.}}{\text{Sales}} \times 100$$

$$= \frac{620 + 60}{800} \times 100 = 85\%.$$

[Cost of goods sold = Sales – gross Profit]

$$\text{(ii) Stock Turnover Ratio} = \frac{\text{Cost of goods sold}}{\text{Average stock}}$$

$$\left[\text{Average Stock} = \frac{40 + 20}{2}\right] = 30$$

$$\text{or} \quad = \frac{620}{30} = 20.67 \text{ times.}$$

$$\text{(iii) Working capital Turnover Ratio} = \frac{\text{Cost of Goods Sold}}{\text{Working Capital}}$$

[Working Capital = Current Assets — Current Liabilities]

$$= \frac{620}{140} = 4.43 \text{ times.}$$

$$\text{(iv) Debtors Turnover Ratio} = \frac{\text{Credit Sales}}{\text{Average debtors}}$$

$$= \frac{800}{100} = 8 \text{ times.}$$

(v) Gross Profit Ratio $= \frac{\text{Gross Profit}}{\text{Sales}} \times 100$

$= \frac{180}{800} \times 100 = 2.25\%.$

and Net Profit Ratio $= \frac{\text{Net Profit}}{\text{Sales}} \times 100$

$= \frac{120}{800} \times 100 = 15\%.$

Illustration.

Calculate the following ratios from the balance sheet given below:

(i) Debt Equity Ratio,

(ii) Liquidity Ratio.

(iii) Fixed Assets to Current Assets,

(iv) Fixed Assets Turnover.

Balance Sheet

Liabilities	*Rs.*	*Assets*	*Rs.*
Equity share of Rs. 10 each	1,00,000	Goodwill	60,000
Reserves	20,000	Fixed Assets (atleast)	1,40,000
Profit & Loss A/c	30,000	Stock	30,000
Secured loan	80,000	Sundry Debtors	30,000
Sundry Creditors	50,000	Advances	10,000
Provision for Taxation	20,000	Cash Balances	30,000
	3,00,000		3,00,000

The sales for the year were Rs. 5,60,000

Solution.

(i) Debt Equity Ratio $= \frac{\text{Long term Debts}}{\text{Shareholder's Funds}} = \frac{80,000}{1,50,000} = 0.53$

(ii) Liquidity Ratio $= \frac{\text{Liquid Assets}}{\text{Current Liabilities}} = \frac{70,000}{50,000} = 1.4$

(iii) Fixed Assets to Current Assets $= \frac{\text{Fixed Assets}}{\text{Current Assets}}$

$$= \frac{1,40,000}{1,00,000} = 1.4.$$

(iv) Fixed Assets Turnover Ratio $= \frac{\text{Sales}}{\text{Fixed Assets}}$

$$= \frac{5,60,000}{1,40,000} = 4.$$

Illustration.

From the following statement of Bose India Ltd. for the year ending 31st March, 1995, your are required to rearrange the items for the purposes of financial analysis and calculate the following ratios.

(i) Current Ratio
(ii) Quick Ratio
(iii) Operating Ratio
(iv) Stock Turnover Ratio
(v) Fixed Assets Turnover Ratio
(vi) Debtors Turnover Ratio
(vii) Net operating Profit to Capital employed

Balance Sheet as on 31st March, 1995

Liabilities	*Rs.*	*Assets*	*Rs.*
Share Capital issued and fully paid up 50,000 shares of Rs. 10 each	5,00,000	Land & Buildings	5,00,000
General Reserve	4,00,000	Plant & Machinery	20,00,000
Profit & Loss A/c	1,50,000	Stock	1,50,000
Sundry Creditors	2,00,000	Sundry Debtors	2,50,000
		Cash & Bank Balance	1,50,000
	12,50,000		12,50,000

Profit & Loss Account for the year ending 31st march, 1995

	Rs.		Rs.
To opening stock	2,50,000	By Sales	18,00,000
To Purchases	10,50,000	By closing stock	1,50,000
To Gross profit	6,50,000		
	19,50,000		19,50,000
To selling & Distribution Expenses	1,00,000	By Gross Profit	6,50,000
To Admn. Expenses	2,30,000	By Profit on sale of fixed Assets	50,000
To Finance Expenses	20,000		
To Net profit	3,50,000		
	7,00,000		7,00,000

Solution.

$$\text{(i) Current Ratio} = \frac{\text{Current Assets}}{\text{Current Liabilities}}$$

$$= \frac{\text{Stock + Sundry Debtors + Cash \& Bank}}{\text{Sundry Creditors}}$$

$$= \frac{5,50,000}{2,00,000} = 2.75.$$

$$\text{(ii) Quick Ratio} = \frac{\text{Liquid Assets}}{\text{Current Liabilities}}$$

$$= \frac{4,00,000}{2,00,000} = 2.$$

$$\text{(iii) Operating Ratio} = \frac{\text{Operating Cost}}{\text{Net Sales}}$$

Operating Costs = Cost of Goods + Selling & Distribution Expenses + Admn. Exp.

= 11,50,000 + 1,00,000 + 2,30,000

= 14,80,000.

Net Sales = 18,00,000

$$\text{Operating Ratio} = \frac{14,80,000}{18,00,000} = 0.82$$

(iv) Stock Turnover Ratio

$$= \frac{\text{Cost of Goods Sold during the year}}{\text{Average Inventory}}$$

$$= \frac{(\text{Opening Stock} + \text{Purchases}) - \text{Closing Stock}}{\dfrac{\text{Opening Stock} + \text{Closing Stock}}{2}}$$

$$= \frac{11,50,000}{2,00,000} = 5.75.$$

$$\text{(v) Fixed Assets Turnover Ratio} = \frac{\text{Net Sales}}{\text{Fixed Assets}}$$

$$= \frac{18,00,000}{7,00,000} = 2.57.$$

$$\text{(vi) Debtors Turnover Rato} = \frac{\text{Net Sales}}{\text{Debtors}}$$

$$= \frac{18,00,000}{2,50,000} = 7.2$$

(vii) Net Operation Profit to Capital Employed

$$= \frac{\text{Net Operating Profit}}{\text{Capital Employed}} \times 100$$

$$= \frac{3,50,000 + 20,000 - 50,000}{10,50,000} \times 100$$

$$= \frac{3,20,000}{10,50,000} \times 100 = 30.48\%.$$

Illustration.

Following is the Balance Sheet of Sheetal Enterprises for the year ended 31st Dec. 1994.

Balance Sheet

Liabilities	Rs.	Assets	Rs.
Equity share capital	4,00,000	Goodwill	2,40,000
Capital Reserve	80,000	Fixed Assets	5,60,000
12% Mortgage loan	2,00,000	Stock	1,20,000
Sundry Creditors	1,60,000	Investments (Short term)	40,000
Provision for Taxation	80,000	Cash	1,20,000
Profit & Loss A/c	1,20,000		
	10,80,000		10,80,000

Calculate the following ratios:

(i) Current Ratios,

(ii) Quick Ratio,

(iii) Proprietary Ratio,

(iv) Debt-Equity.

Solution.

(i) Current Ratio $= \dfrac{\text{Current Assets}}{\text{Current Liabilities}}$

$$= \frac{1,20,000 + 40,000 + 1,20,000}{1,60,000 + 40,000 + 80,0000}$$

$$= \frac{2,80,000}{2,80,000} = 1.$$

(ii) Quick Ratio $= \dfrac{\text{Quick Assets}}{\text{Current Liabilities}}$

$$= \frac{(40,000 + 1,20,000)}{2,80,000} = 0.57$$

(iii) Proprietary Ratio $= \dfrac{\text{Proprietor's Funds}}{\text{Net Tangible Assets}}$

$$= \frac{4,00,000 + 80,000 + 1,20,000}{10,80,000 - 2,40,000} = 0.71$$

(iv) Debt Equity Ratio $= \dfrac{\text{Long terms Debts}}{\text{Shareholders' Funds}}$

$$= \frac{2,00,000}{6,00,000} = 0.33$$

Illustration.

Following are the earning of last year of M/s New Deal Industries Ltd.

Profit before tax	Rs. 24,46 lakhs
Tax rate	60%
Proposed dividend	20%
Capital of the company is:	
9% preference shares	Rs. 10 lakhs
Equity Shares, 3,000 shares of Rs. 100 each	Rs. 30 lakhs
Reserve in the beginning of year	Rs. 22 lakhs

From the above calculate:

(i) Earning per share,

(ii) Price Earning ratio,

(iii) Earnings yield ratio,

(iv) Dividend payment ratio

The current market price of the equity share is Rs. 200.

Solution.

(i) Earning per Share:

	Rs.
Profit before tax	24,46,000
Less : Tax @ 60%	14,67,600
	9,78,400
Less : Preference dividend @ 9% on Rs. 10 lakh	90,000
Net profit available for equity shareholders	8,88,400

$$\text{Earning per share} = \frac{8,88,400}{30,000} = \text{Rs. } 29.61.$$

(ii) Price Earning Ratio :

$$\text{Price Earning Ratio} = \frac{\text{Earning per share}}{\text{Market price per share}} \times 100$$

$$= \frac{29.61}{200} \times 100 = 14.8\%.$$

(iii) Earning Yield Ratio :

$$\text{Earning Yield Ratio} = \frac{\text{Net profit available for equity shareholders}}{\text{Amount available for equity shareholders}} \times 100$$

$$= \frac{8,88,400}{54,88,400} \times 100 = 16.19\%.$$

(iv) Dividend Payment Ratio:

$$\text{Dividend Payment Ratio} = \frac{\text{Proposed Dividend}}{\text{Net profit}} \times 100$$

$$= \frac{6,00,000}{8,88,400} \times 100 = 67.54\%.$$

❐

10

Fund Flow and Cash Flow Analysis

The word fund here means net working capital. Working capital is ordinarily understood as excess of current assets over current liabilities, some persons call total of current assets as Gross Working Capital and current assets minus current liabilities as Net Working Capital or Net Current Assets. The word flow here means movements of this working capital *i.e.*, either increase in working capital or decrease in working capital in comparison to previous year. Fund really speaking is transfer of cost or cash equivalent *(A)* from one equity to another equity, or *(B)* from one assets to another assets, or *(C)* from assets to equity. Fund Flow Statement is a statement which shows changes in net working capital of an enterprise over a period of time which is mostly one year.

Fund Flow Statement shows sources and application of funds in a summary from over a period of time and indicates increase or decrease in net working capital of the enterprise during the period.

According to Smith and Brown, "A fund flow statement is prepared in a summary form to indicate charges (and trends if prepared regularly) occurring in items of financial condition between two balance sheet dates."

Fund Flow Statement is a Statement which shows sources of funds and their application during a prescribed period. Excess of sources over application indicates increase in working capital and excess of application of funds over sources indicates decrease in working capital. Here working capital and net working capital both are treated as the same. In whole of this chapter the word working capital has been used.

Ratio analysis and other analysis indicate the static aspects of financial statements, its dynamic aspect is shown by Fund Flow Statement. It indicates the comparative position of working capital of two balance sheets' dates.

In a business there is always inflow and outflow of funds. At the date of balance sheet both inflows and outflows of funds are stopped for a while. Therefore, on the basis of two balance sheets one tries to know the inflow and outflow of funds which are technically known as sources and application of funds.

This statement analyses the items which result in sources of funds and application of funds. Items resulting in non-flow of funds are not used in this balance sheet and if necessary some other particular are required to prepare their statements.

Various Names of Fund Flow Statement

(i) Sources and application of funds, *(ii)* Where got and where gone statements, *(iii)* Statement of inflow and outflow of funds, *(iv)* Statement of funds supplied and funds applied etc.

OBJECT AND USES OF FUND FLOW STATEMENT

The main object of this statement is to find out increase or decrease in working capital during a period by showing sources and uses of working capital.

Working Capital is most important for the business. It should be raised and used properly. Proper control of working capital is the keystone for the success of a business. This statement helps in achieving this purpose. Following are the uses of this statement which show its importance:

(i) It indicates the financing policies of the enterprise in respect of capital structure and expansion of assets.

(ii) It is used as basis for future planning.

(iii) It points out the sound or weak financial position of the enterprise.

(iv) Amounts of funds required for future develpment can be estimated on its basis.

(v) An idea about various sources of funds can be made by comparing these sources with the sources of previous years, it can be concluded whether the company is doing well or not.

(vi) Various uses of funds can be known and after comparing them with the uses of previous years, improvements or downfall in the company can be assessed.

(vii) It helps in improving the rate of income on assets.

(viii) It points out the causes for changes in working capital.

(ix) It explains the current area of business.

(x) Banks and other financial institutions get information regarding power of generating sources of funds and their uses with the help of this statement. These days this statement is regarded as a modern tool of assessing financial position of an enterprise.

(xi) Previous year's financial position can be compared on its basis.

(xii) It can also be found whether sources of funds are increasing or decreasing or are constant.

(xiii) It helps in knowing whether uses of fund are increasing or decreasing.

(xiv) It points out why income is more even when current assets have decreased.

(xv) It shows the method of financing of increase in working capital.

(xvi) It states income from operation and throws light on increase or decrease in dividends.

Whatever information regarding financial matters is not found out in other financial statements like Balance Sheet and Profit and Loss Account, is found out by this statement. During modern period everybody is flowing in some way or the other and is flowing very fast, why not funds too should flow. It is the flow of funds, that tells the current financial position of the enterprises and the standard of managerial policies and foresight.

LIMITATIONS OF FUNDS FLOW STATEMENT

1. It does not provide information about variations in cash position.
2. This statement lacks originality because it is only rearrangement of the matter of financial statement.
3. When both the aspects of a transaction are current, they are not included in this statement.
4. When both the aspects of a transaction are non-current, even then they are not inlcuded in this statement.
5. It does not show various changes which take place continuously. It only indicates fund flow in a summary form.
6. It indicates only past position and not future, through projects fund flow may serve this purpose but it is based only on estimates.
7. It gives some additional information only and cannot be regarded as an ideal tool for furnishing full financial position.
8. Possession of intensive and deep-rooted knowledge of accountancy and financial management is a prerequisite to make its intepretation.

WORKING CAPITAL

As the main aim of fund flow statement is to indicate changes in working capital, it is desirable to understand working capital.

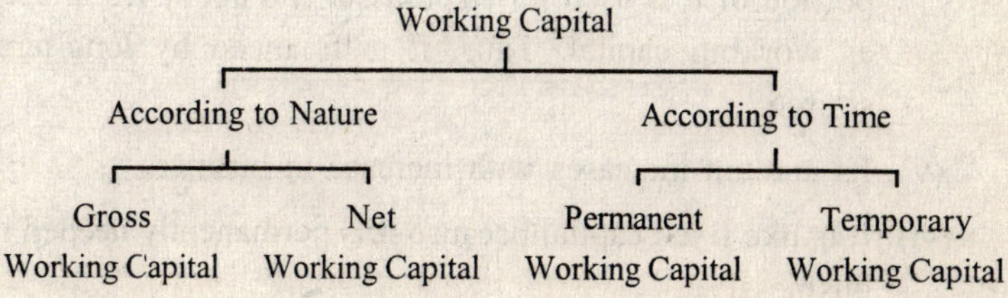

Working Capital According to Nature

Grass Working Capital. Working capital means funds invested in total current assets which are required in day-to-day running of the business. It is called Gross Working Capital. This capital is very important because fixed assets cannot work without it. For example, without raw material, machine is useless, and money invested in raw materials is working capital.

Net Working Capital. It is the excess of current asset over current liabilities.

Working Capital According to Time

Working capital is divided into two parts from the point of time, namely, permanent working capital and temporary working capital.

Permanent Working Capital. Minimum level of investment in current assets is called permanent working capital. To carry out minimum level of activity at all times, some minimum amount of captial is required which is permanent working capital.Characteristics of Permanent Working Capital are as follows:

(i) It always remains in the business in the one form or the other.

(ii) It constantly changes its form from cash to stock and from stock to debtors and from debtors to cash again and so on.

(iii) The suppliers of permanent working capital need not expect any return during the lifetime of the enterprise.

(iv) It is financed by long-term sources. It is the beginning when business is commenced with capital, nearly 2/3 portion of it is used for fixed asset and about 1/3 is used as working capital. Thus, it is financed by long-term source.

(v) Its amount increases with increase in business.

(vi) It is like fixed capital because it is permanently needed in business.

(vii) As it is financed by long-term finance, hence current ratio should always be more than one.

Temporary Working Capital. Capital required over minimum level of working capital is called temporary working capital. Its size is not fixed because it increases or decreases according to increase or decrease in business. In seasonal industries during season, temporary working capital required is too much. It is generally financed by short-term funds. Characteristics of Temporary Working Capital are as follows:

1. It is required in addition to permanent working capital.
2. It is needed for meeting additional day-to-day requirements due to increase in business.
3. It is financed by short-term debt.
4. In seasonal industries during season its requirements is abnormally hight.
5. It meets short period liquidity requirements of the enterprise.

Both permanent and temporary working capitals in adequate amount are required for smooth running of the enterprise. Changes in this working capital are measures through fund flow statement.

STEPS AND RULES RELATING TO PREPARATION OF FUND FLOW STATEMENT

1. Transactions Affecting Non-current Accounts Only. If there is a transaction which affects non-current accounts only it is not considered for flow of funds. Any account which is not current is treated as non-current as in the case of cloth business Building A/c, Machinery A/c, Furniture A/c and Vehicles A/c etc. are non-current.

When both aspects of transaction are non-current, no flow of fund takes place. Only that items can affect fund flow which either increases the working capital or decreases it and working capital is the excess of current assets over current liabilities. Therefore, the transaction must affect any one of the current assets or current liabilities in order to influence fund flow. The conclusion is that transactions affecting only non-current assets and non-current liabilities are ignored for the purpose of preparing fund flow statement.

2. Transactions Affecting Current Account Only. If both the aspects of a transaction are affecting current account only, no flow of fund takes palce. Flow of fund is related with working capital and working capital is the result of excess of current assets over current liabilities. Fund flow statement should either increase or decrease in working capital. It can happen only when current assets and current liabilities are disproportionately increases or decreases.

(A) Decreases in both Current Assets and Current Liabilities by the Same Amount. If current assets is decreased and current liabilities are also decreased by the same amount there is no changes in working capital.

(B) Increase and Decrease in Current Assets Only by the Same Amount. If one current assets decreases and other current assets increases by the same amount there is no working capital hence no effect on fund flow.

C. Increase in Current Assets and Current Liabilities by the Same Amount. This even does not effect the working capital therefore there will no flow of fund.

(D) Increase and Decrease in Current Liabilities Only by the Same Amount. In this situation working capital will not be effected or the amount of current liabilities will remain the same. There will be no flow of fund.

3. Transactions Affecting Current and Non-Current Liabilities. If a transaction is such that one aspect of it affects current account and its other aspect affects non-current account. There will be effect on working capital and fund will flow. Such transactions are considered for fund flow statement. The following situation may raise flow of funds:

(A) Increase in current assets and non-current liabilities.

(B) Decrease in non-current liabilities and current assets.

(C) Increase in non-current assets and decrease in current assets.

(C) Decrease in non-current and increase in current assets.

Steps and Rules

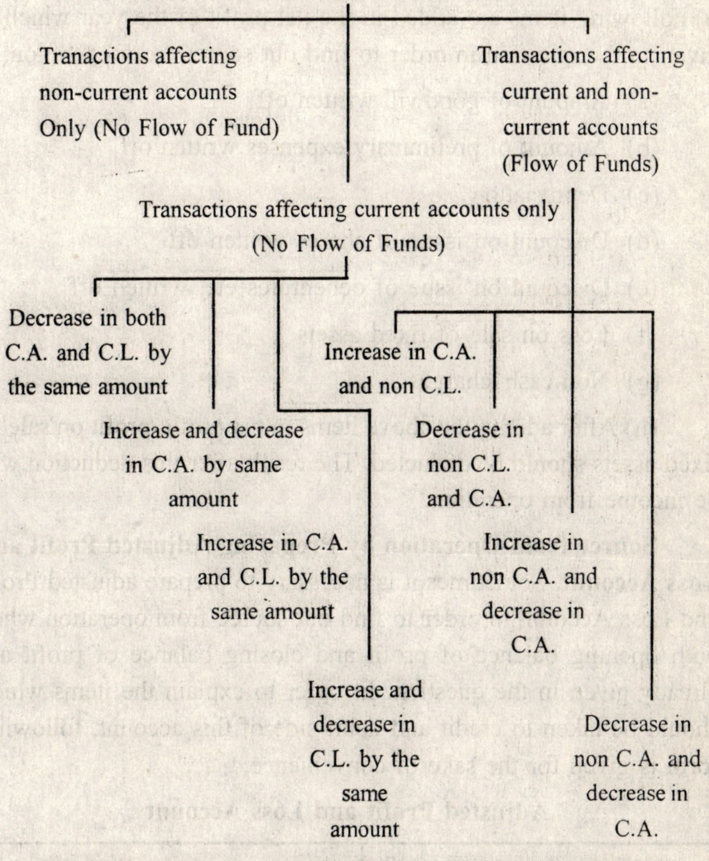

PROFIT AND LOSS ACCOUNT AND FUND FLOW

1. Sales and closing stock are treated as source.
2. Opening stock, purchases, and all expenses, and all expenses of revenue nature are treated as application of fund.
3. It is better to show the excess of sales and closing stock over opening stock, purchases and all revenue expenses as source of fund as it is net profit.

4. If total of sales and closing stock is less than total of opening stock, purchases and all revenue expenses, the deficiency is net loss. It is treated as application of fund.

Source from Operation by Preparing a Statement. (i) Following items are added in the net profit of the year which is given in the question in order to find out source from operation:

(a) Amount of goodwill written off
(b) Amount of preliminary expenses written off
(c) Depreciation
(d) Discount on issue of shares written off
(e) Discount on issue of debentures etc. written off
(f) Loss on sale of fixed assets
(g) Non-cash charges

(ii) After adding the above items in net profit, profit on sale of fixed assets should be deducted. The result after this deduction will be income from operation.

Source from Operation by Preparing Adjusted Profit and Loss Account. Sometimes it is necessary to prepare adjusted Profit and Loss Account in order to find out source from operation when both opening balance of profit and closing balance of profit are already given in the question. In order to explain the items which should be taken to credit and debit side of this account, following form is given for the sake of convenience:

Adjusted Profit and Loss Account

	Rs.		*Rs.*
To General Reserve (increase)		By Opening balance of profit (already given in the question)	
To Debenture Sinking Fund (increase)		By Decrease in revenue reserve	
To Other revenue reserve (increase)		By Profit of sale of fixed assets	

Contd.

	Rs.		*Rs.*
To Depreciation on various fixed assets		By Source from operation (excess of debit total over credit total)	
To Decrease in discount of issue of debentures			
To Decrease in discount of issue of shares			
To Loss on sale of fixed assets			
To Goodwill (amount written off)			
To Preliminary Exps. (amount written off)			
To Dividend Equalisation A/c (increase)			
To Proposed dividend during the year			
To Provision for tax during the year			
To Balance c/d (closing Balance of profit already given in the question) Rs.			Rs.

If credit total is more than debit total, excess of credit over debit is regarded as application from operation.

CURRENT AND NON-CURRENT ITEMS

Preparation of fund flow statement is based on the distinction of current and non-current itmes, hence following are some of the headings about which information regarding treating them as current or non-current is given:

1. Proposed Dividend. It may be treated both as current or non-current.

(a) ***As Current.*** If proposed dividend is treated as current liability, actual payment of this dividend is not treated as application of fund.

(b) *As Non-current.* If it is treated as non-current, its actual payment is treated as application of fund.

2. Depreciation. It is treated as non-current because it relates to non-current assets.

3. Dividend. Devidend is treated as non-current because it relates with non-current liability, *i.e.*, share capital.

4. Provision for Bad and Doubtful Debts. It is treated as current because it relates with current assets *i.e.*, debtors.

5. Relationship. It is a general rule that if an item relates to non-current, it should be treated as non-current and if an item relates to current, it should be treated as current.

6. Provision for Tax. It may be treated either as current or as non-current.

(a) *As Current.* If it is treated as current liability, tax payment is not regarded as an items of application of fund and provision for tax is not adjusted to profit or loss for finding out income from operation.

(b) *As Non-current.* If provision for tax is treated as non-current, payment of tax is treated as application of fund and it is treated for adjustment of profit or loss.

7. Capital. Capital of all types is non-current liability whether it is equity or preference.

8. Debentures. Debentures are non-current liabilities.

9. Share Premium. It is non-current liability because it relates with non-current item share capital.

10. Profit and Loss. It is non-current.

11. Forfeited Shares. It is non-current liability because it relates with non-current *i.e.*, shares.

12. Capital Reserve. It is non-current liability.

13. Transfer to Dividend Equalisation Fund. It is non-current.

14. Debentures Sinking Fund. Transfer to debentures sinking fund is non-current.

15. Transfer to General Reserve. It is treated as non-current.

16. Transfer to Compensation Fund. It is treated as non-current.

17. Long Period Loans. They are treated as non-current. If only loan is given, it is treated as long period loan.

NON-CURRENT ASSETS

Following are treated as non-current assets:

1. All fixed assets which are given in Schedue VI of the Companies Act, 1956, namely:

(i) Good will,

(ii) Land,

(iii) Buildings,

(iv) Leaseholds,

(v) Railway sidings,

(vi) Plant and machinery,

(vii) Furniture and fittings,

(viii) Development of property

(ix) Patents, Trade-marks and Designs,

(x) Live-Stock,

(xi) Vehicles etc.

2. All Deferred Expenditures like:

(a) Preliminary expenses.

(b) Abnormally heavy advertisement expenses.

(c) Discount on issue of Debentures.

(d) Discount on issue of shares.

(e) Commission and Brokerage on shares and debentures

(f) Interest paid out of capital during construction.

(g) Development expenditure not adjusted.

3. Profit and Loss Account debit balance which is treated as net loss.

CURRENT ASSETS

Following are generally treated as current assets:

1. Cash in Hand,
2. Cash at Bank,
3. Bills Receivable,
4. Closing Stock,
5. Debtors,
6. Income earned but not yet received,
7. Prepaid expenses,
8. Any other amount which is receivable within short period *i.e.*, a period of one year.

CURRENT LIABILITIES

Following items are treated as current liabilities:

1. Creditors,
2. Bills Payable,
3. Outstanding Expenses,
4. Instalment of long period loan falling due for payment during current year,
5. Provision for taxation (it may also be treated as non-current as has been explained earlier),
6. Provision from dividend (it may also be treated as non-current as has been explained earlier),
7. Bank overdraft if it is of casual nature (if it is of continuous nature, it is treated as non-current.)

Treatment of Current and Non-current in Fund Flow Statement at a Glance

	Particulars	*Use in Fund Flow Statement*
1.	Both aspects of a transaction are current.	No flow of fund, hence not used in Fund Flow Statement.
2.	Both aspects of a transaction are non-current.	No flow of fund, hence not used in Fund Flow Statement.
3.	One aspect of a transaction is current other aspect is non-current.	Fund flows, hence used in Fund Flow Statement.

Additional Information

If additional information is given in addition of balance sheets of two different dates, concerned account related with this information should be prepared. In case it is not necessary to prepare an account, treatement on the basis of source or application of fund should be made.

Hidden Information

With the help of above-mentioned additional information and balance sheets, hidden information is derived which is very essential for preparation of Fund Flow Statement. For this purpose concerned account is prepared and the balance of this account gives the hidden information which is used as source or application of fund as the case may be.

Example. Amount of machinery in Balance Sheet of December 31, 1985 is Rs. 1,80,000 and the amount of same machinery in Balance Sheet of December 31, 1984 is Rs. 1,50,000. Arrangement for depreciation on machinery has been made to the extent of Rs. 25,000 in 1985. Find out hidden information for Fund Flow Solution.

By preparing Machinery Account, hidden information can be found out.

Machinery Account

	Rs.		Rs.
To Balance b/d	1,50,000	By Depreciation A/c	25,000
To Purchase (Balancing figure)	55,000	By Balance c/d	1,80,000
	Rs. 2,05,000		Rs. 2,05,000

Above machinery Account indicates the balance of Rs. 55,000. This amount shows that a machinery of R. 55,000 has been purchased, hence it is application of fund.

PROVISION FOR TAXATION ACCOUNT

Missing figure about transfer to provision for Taxation Account can be found out by preparing Provision for Taxation Account.

Example.

Provision for taxation at the end of December 31, 1985 is Rs. 70,000 and at the end of December 31, 1984 is Rs. 56,000 Income-tax paid Rs. 40,000 during the year 1985. Prepare provision for taxation account and find out hidden figure for Fund Flow Statement.

Solution.

Provision for Taxaton Account

	Rs.		Rs.
To Bank A/c	40,000	By Balance b/d (Opening balance)	56,000
To Balance c/d (closing balance)	70,000	By Profit and Loss A/c (Balancing amount)	54,000
	Rs. 1,10,000		Rs. 1,10,000

Rs. 54,000 must have been transferred from Profit and Loss Account to Provision for Taxation Account.

PROJECTED PROFIT AND LOSS ACCOUNT V/S PROJECTED FUND FLOW STATEMENT

When Balance Sheet of current year and projected Profit and Loss Account of next year and some additional information are given, a projected Fund Flow Statement is prepared. For this purpose projected Balance Sheet of next year is prepared with the help of given information. Comparison of amounts of projected Balance Sheet is made with the Balance Sheet of current year which is already given, and on the basis of the comparsion and additional information, a Fund Flow Satement is prepared for the period for which projected Balance Sheet has been prepared. This Fund Flow Statement is called projected Fund Flow Statement.

Fund flow Statement may be prepared in any one of the following two methods:

1. Vertial Method.
2. Horizontal Method.

VERTICAL METHOD

Its specimen is given below:

Statement of Sources and Applications

Sources:	*Rs.*
Issue of Capital	....
Issue of Debentures	....
Long-term Borrowings	....
Fortfieited Shares	....
Provision for Taxation (if treated non-current)	....
Provision for Dividend (if treated non-current)	....
Sales of Fixed Assets	....
Non-trading Receipts	....
Capital Reserve	....
Sale of Investments	....
Share Premium	....
Source from Operation	....
Total of Sources or Total Fund Provided	....

Contd.

Application:	*Rs.*	
Purchase of Fixed Assets	....	
Purchase of Investments	....	
Repayment of Pref Shares Capital	....	
Repayment of Debentures	....	
Repayment of long period loans	....	
Payment of Dividend (if treated non-current)	....	
Payment of Tax (if treated non-current)	....	
Non-trading Expenses	....	
Loss from operations	....	
Total Applications	....	
Increase/Decrease in working capital		....

HORIZONTAL FORM

Fund Flow Statement can be prepared in horizontal form also. Its specimen is given below:

Fund Flow Statement

Or

Statement of Sources and Application of Funds

	Rs.		*Rs.*
Issue of Capital	....	Purchase of Fixed Assets	....
Issue of Debentures	....	Purchase of Investments	....
Long-term Borrowings	....	Repayment of Pref. Share	
Share Premium	....	Capital	....
Sale of Fixed Assets	....	Repayment of Debentures	....
Sale of Investment	....	Payment of Dividend	....
Forfeited Shares	....	(if treated non-current)	
Non-trading Receipts	....	Payment of Taxes	....
Provision for Taxation	....	(If treated non-current)	
(If treated non-current)		Non-trading Expenses	....

Contd.

	Rs.		Rs.
Provision for dividend (If treated non-current)	....	Loss from operations	....
Capital Reserve	....	Excess of Sources of Funds over Application of Funds (Increase Balances in Working Capital	
Source from Operation	....		
Excess of Application over Sources, if any (Decrease in Working Capital)	....		
Total	....	Total	....

SCHEDULE OF CHANGES IN WORKING CAPITAL

Schedule of changes in working capital is a schedule which shows increase or decrease in working capital in detail by indicating changes in individual items of working capital. It is also called Statement of Change in Working Capital.

It is mostly prepared on the basis of current assets and current liabilities but now items of non-current assets and non-current liabilities are also used for it. Thus, there are two methods of its preparation:

1. Use of Current Assets and current liabilities only.
2. Use of both current and non-current assets and liabilities.

USE OF CURRENT ASSETS AND CURRENT LIABILITIES

A Current Assets

(i) The amount of every current assets of the current year is compared with its amount of previous year. If the amount of current asset of the current year is more than its amount of previous year, the excess is recorded in debit column.

(ii) If the amount of current asset of the current year is less than its amount of the previous year, the deficiency is recorded in credit column.

(iii) It must be noted that the difference of each current assets are recorded separately.

(iv) If the amount of current liability of current year is less than its amount of previous year, the deficit is recorded in debit columns.

(v) The difference of each individual current liability is recorded separately.

(vi) If the amount of current liability of current year is more than its amount of previous year, the excess is recorded in the credit column.

(vii) Total of all debit amounts and all credit amounts which have been recorded on the basis of above are found out.

(viii) If debit of total of current is more than credit total the excess is called net increase in working capital.

(ix) Two additional columns for the purpose of writing above-mentioned accounts are made in the Schedule of changes in working capital. Its specimen form is given below :

(x) If credit total of current is more than debit total of current, the deficiency is called net decrease in working capital.

Schedule of Changes in Working Capital

Particulars	*Amount of the prev. year*	*Amounts of the current year*	*Changes in current assets and current liabilities*	
			Dr.	*Cr.*
	Rs.	Rs.		
Total	....	....		
Net Increase in working capital				

USE OF BOTH CURRENT AND NON-CURRENT ASSETS AND LIABILITIES

The form of this schedule is just like the above schedule with only one difference that two more columns *i.e.*, one for debit and other for credit are also made for writing increase or decrease in non-current assets and liabilities. Specimen form is given below:

Schedule of Changes in Working Capital

Particulars	*Amount of the prev. year*	*Amounts of the current year*	*Changes in current assets and current liabilities*		*Changes in non-current assets and non-current liabilities*	
			Dr.	*Cr.*	*Dr.*	*Cr.*
	Rs.	Rs.				
Total	....	....				
Net Income or decrease in working capital						

RULES FOR PREPARATION OF CHANGES IN WORKING CAPITAL SCHEDULE

The amounts of every current and non-current assets of the current year are compared with the amounts of such assets of the previous year and increases or decreases are recorded as per following particulars:

(i) Rules for recording ıncrease and decrease in current assets and current liabilities are the same as have been discussed earlier.

(ii) If the amount of non-ccurent asset of the current year is more than its amount of previous year the excess is recorded in debit column.

(iii) If the amount of non-current assets of the current year is less than its amount of previous year, the deficiency is recorded in credit column.

(iv) Differences of each non-current assets are recorded separately.

(v) If the amount of non-current liability of the current year is more than its amount of previous year, the excess is recorded in credit column.

(vi) If the amount of non-current liability of the current year is less than its amount of previous year, the deficiency is recorded in debit column.

(vii) Total of all debit and credit balances are made.

(viii) If the total of debit balances of non-current is less than total of credit balances of non-current, the excess is treated as decrease in working capital.

(ix) Depreciation is treated as non-current liability.

(x) Differences of each non-current liability are recorded separately.

(xi) If the total of debit balances of non-current is less than total of credit balances of non-current, the deficiency is treated as net increase in working capital.

Equal Balances. It is worth nothing that the difference in total of debit amounts and credit amounts of current assets and current liabilities will be the same as that of the balance of the total of debit and credit amounts of non-current assets and liabilities. If current assets and liabilities will show credit balance, then non-current assets and liabilities will show debit balance of the same amount and vice versa.

Record of debit and credit of current and non-current assets and liabilities for schedule of changes in Working Capital at a Glance

Assets	Treatment	
Increase in Current Assets	Debit	Increase in assets is recorded in debit column
Increase in Non-current Assets	Debit	
Decrease in Current Assets	Credit	Decrease in liabilities is recorded in credit column
Decrease in Non-current Assets	Credit	
Liabilities		
Increase in Current Liabilities	Debit	Increase in liabilities is recorded in debit column
Increase in Non-current Liabilities	Credit	
Decrease in Current Liabilities	Debit	Decrease in liabilities is recorded in credit column
Decrease in Non-current Liabilities	Debit	

Balance Equal

Total of debit of C.A. and C.L. — Total of credits of C.A. and C.L. = Total of credits of non C.A. and non C.L.—Total of debits of non C.A. and non C.L.

BASIS OF PREPARATION OF SCHEDULE OF CHANGES IN WORKING CAPITAL

This schedule is prepared only on the basis of two balance sheets, *i.e.*, amounts of the balance sheet of one year and the amounts of the balance sheet of other years. If any other information in addition to balance sheets is given, such informations are not made use of in preparing this schedule. It must be carefully noted that all such additional informations are ignored for the purpose of this schedule, but are used for preparing Fund Flow Statement . Answer of changes in working capital will be the same in this Schedule and Fund Flow Statement hence it is advisable to prepare schedule of changes in working capital to know the amount of changes in working capital without in the least incurring the labour of going in the complexities of additional information.

Example I.

Find out flow of fund from operation on the basis of the following:

Profit and Loss Account
(For the year ended on Dec. 31, 1985)

	Rs.		*Rs.*
To Opening Stock	8,000	By Sales	40,000
To Purchases	12,000	By Closing Stock	5,000
To Wages	5,000		
To Carriage inward	5,000		
To Gross Profit	15,000		
	Rs. 45,000		Rs. 45,000
To Salaries	5,000	By Gross Profit	15,000

Contd.

	Rs.		Rs.
To Depreciation on machinery	100	By gain on sale of Furniture	150
To Depreciation on Furniture	50		
To Preliaminary expenses	100		
To Goodwill (written off)	50		
To Loss on sale of Machinery	50		
To Net Profit	9,800		
Rs.	15,150	Rs.	15,150
To General Reserve	4,800	By Balance b/d	10,000
To Dividend Equalisation Fund	2,000	By Net Profit of current year	9,800
To Proposed Dividend	1,00		
To Interim Dividend	1,000		
To Debenture Redemption Fund	2,000		
To Balance c/d	9,000		
Rs.	19,800	Rs.	19,800

Solution.

First method

		Rs.
Balance of Profit and Loss Account		9,000
Add : Items not forming part of fund flow:	Rs.	
Depreciation on Machinery	100	
Depreiation on Furniture	50	
Preliminary Expenses	100	
Goodwill	50	
Loss on sale of Machinery	50	
General Reserve	4,800	
Dividend Equalisation Reserve	2,000	

	Proposed Dividend	1,000	
	Interim Dividend	1,000	
	Deb. Redemption Fund	2,000	11,150
			99,150
Less:	Items not forming part of fund flow :		
	Gain on sale of furniture		150
			20,000
Less:	Opening balance of Profit		10,000
	Source form Operation	Rs.	10,000

Second Method

Adjusted Profit and Loss Account

	Rs.		*Rs.*
Depreciation of machinery	100	Balance b/d (Jan. 1,1985)	10,000
Depreciation on Furniture	50	Profit and sale of Furniture	150
Preliminary Expenses	100	Source from Operation	10,000
Goodwill	50		
Loss on sale of Machinery	50		
General Reserve	4,800		
Dividend Equalisation Reserve	2,000		
Proposed Dividend	1,000		
Interim Dividend	1,000		
Debentures Redemption Fund	2,000		
Balance c/d (closing balance on Dec., 31, 1985)	9,000		
Rs.	20,150	Rs.	20,150

Example II.

The following are the summarised Trial Balances of a limited company as on 31st March, 1984 and 1985:

	1984 Dr.	1984 Cr.	1985 Dr.	1985 Cr.
	Rs.	Rs.	Rs.	Rs.
Fixed Assets	23,36,960	—	24,60,500	—
Current Assets	9,60.540	—	7.91,800	—
Debenture Discount	30,000	—	25,000	—
Issued Capital :				
Equity	—	15,00,000	—	15,00,000
Preference	—	3,00,000	—	4,00,000
Share Premium	—	30,000	—	40,000
Debentures	—	5,00,000	—	5,00,000
Current Liabilities	—	6,20,000	—	4,40,000
Provision for Depreciation	—	1,80,000	—	1,95,000
Dividend for 1983-84	—	—	1,50,000	
Provision for Doubtful Debts	—	6,000	—	5,000
Profit and Loss A/c:				
Previous year balance	—	24,400	—	1,91,500
Net Profit	—	1.67,100	—	1,55,800
Total Rs.	33.27.500	33.27.500	24,27,300	34.27.300

(a) During the year ended 31st March, 1985 machinery costing Rs. 2,00,000 (accumulated provision for depreciation Rs. 60,000) was sold for Rs. 1,50,000.

(b) Rs. 1,00,000 Preference Share Capital was issued during 1984-85 at a premium of Rs. 10,000.

(c) The net profit for 1984-85 has been arrived at after taking credit for the profit on sale of machinery, reduction in the provision for doubtful debts and writing off the discount on issue of debentures.

You are required to prepare:

(a) a statement showing the net increase in the working capital during the year 1984-85; and

(b) a statement showing the sources of the increase in the working capital and application therefore during the year.

Solution.

Statement of Sources and Application of Funds
(For the year 1984-85)

Sources of Funds	*Rs.*	*Application of Funds*	*Rs.*
Sale of Machinery	1,50,000	Purchase of Fixed Assets	3,23,540[8]
Issue of Pref. Shares	1,00,000	Dividend Paid (1983-84)	1,50,000
Premiumun on Pref. Share	10,000	Increase in Working Capital	12,260
Sources from Operation	2,25,800[1]		
Rs.	4,85,800	Rs.	4,85,800

[1]Profit and Loss Account
(Adjusted)

	Rs.		*Rs.*
To Discount on Debentures	5,000[4]	By Balance b/d	1,91,500[2]
To Provision for Depreciation	75,000[5]	By Profit on Sale of Machinery	1,0,000[3]
To Closing Profit	3,47,300[6]	By Sources from Operation	2,25,800[7]
Rs.	4,27,300	Rs.	4,27,300

[2] Rs. 24,400 + 1,67,100 = Rs. 1,91,500;

[3] Rs. 2,00,000 – 60,000 = Rs. 1,40,000; Rs. 1,50,000 – 1,40,000 = Rs. 10,000;

[4] Rs. 3,00,000 – 25,000 = Rs. 5,000;

[5] Rs. (60,000 + 1,95,000) – 1,80,000 = Rs. 75,000;

[6] Rs. 1,91,500 + 1,55,800 = Rs. 3,47,300;

[7] This amount is balancing figure.

[8] Fixed Assets Account

	Rs.		*Rs.*
To Balance b/d	23,36,960	By Provision for Depreciation	80,000
To Profit on Sale of Machinery	10,000	By Cash (Sale of Machinery)	1,50,000
To Cash (Purchase of Machinery)	3,23,540[9]	By Balance c/d	24,60,500
	Rs. 26,70,500		Rs. 26,70,500

[9] This amount is balancing figure.

Statement of Change in Working Capital

Particulars	*1983-84*	*1984-85*	*Effect on Working Capital*	
			Dr.	*Cr.*
	Rs.	Rs.	Rs.	Rs.
Current Assets	9,60,540	7,91,800		
Less : Provision for D. Debts	6,000	5,000		
	9,54,540	7,86,800		1,67,740
Current Liabilities	6,20,000	4,40,000	1,80,000	
Working Capital	3,34,540	3,46,800		
Increase in Working Capital	12,260			
Rs.	3,46,800	3,46,800	1,80,000	12,260

Example III.

From the following Balance Sheets of A Ltd. make out: (i) Statement of changes in the Working Capital, and (ii) Fund Flow Statement:

Balance Sheet of A Ltd.

	1984	*1985*		*1984*	*1985*
	Rs.	*Rs.*		*Rs.*	*Rs.*
Share capital	2,00,000	2,50,000	Land and Buildings	2,00,000	1,90,000
General Reserve	50,000	2,50,000	Machinery and Plant	1,50,000	1,69,000
Profit and Loss A/c	30,500	30,600	Stocks	1,00,00	74,000
Short Period Bank					
Loans	70,000	—	Debtors	80,000	64,200
Crditors	1,50,00	1,35,200	Cash	500	600
Provision for		Bank	—	8,000	
Taxation	30,000	35,000	Goodwill	—	5,000
	Rs. 5,30,500	5,10,800		Rs. 5,30,500	5,10,800

During the year ended 31st December, 1985:

(i) Dividend of Rs. 23,000 was paid;

(ii) Assets of another company were purchased for a consideration of Rs. 50,000 payable in shares. The following assets were purchased: Stocks Rs. 20,000; machinery Rs.25,000;

(iii) Machinery was purchased for Rs. 8,000;

(iv) The net profit of the year was Rs. 66;100;

(v) Depreciation written off : Building Rs. 10,000, Machinery Rs. 14,000;

(vi) Income-tax paid during the year was Rs. 28,000; Provision of Rs. 33,000 was made for taxation.

Solution.

Fund Flow Statement

Sources of Funds	*Rs.*	*Application of funds*	*Rs.*
Share Capital	20,000[1]	Purcahses of Machinery	8,000[6]
Source from Operation	90,100[2]	Dividend Paid	23,000
Income-tax-paid	28,000		
Increase in Working Capital	51,100		
Rs.	1,10,100	Rs.	1,10,100

[1] Closing Capital Rs. 2,50,000 - (Opening Capital Rs. 2,00,000 + Machinery Rs. 25,000 + Goodwill R. 5,000) = Rs. 20,000 Here Goodwill of Rs. 5,000 has been found out as : Rs. 50,000 - (20,000 + 25,000) = Rs. 5,000. Only that portion of capital has been treated as source here which represent current stock and that is Rs. 20,000.

[1] Profit and Loss Account
(Adjusted)

	Rs.		*Rs.*
To Depreciation on Machinery	14,000[3]	By Balance b/d	30,500
To Depreication on Building	10,000[4]	By Sources from Operation	90,100
To Dividend	23,000		
To Provision for Taxation	23,000		
To General Reserve	10,000[5]		
To Balance c/d	30,600		
Rs.	1,20,600	Rs.	1,20,600

[3] (Opening balance Rs. 1,50,000 + Cash purchases Rs. 8,000 + Purchase by shares Rs. 25,000) – Closing balance Rs. 1,69,000 = 14,000.

[4] Rs. 2,00,000 – Rs. 1,90,000 = Rs. 10,000;

[5] Rs. 60,000 – Rs. 50,000) = Rs. 10,000;

[6] Purchase of machinery in shares has not been considered because it affects current assets, *i.e.*, cash but purchase of machinery in shares has not been considered because it affects fixed liability, *i.e.*, capital.

Statement Showing Changes in Working Capital

Particulars	*1984*			*1985*	*Effect on Working Capital*	
					Dr.	*Cr.*
	Rs.	Rs.	Rs.	Rs.	Rs.	Rs.
Current Assets:						
Stock		1,00,000		74,000		26,000
Debtors		80,000		64,200		15,800

Cash		500		600	100	
Bank		—		8,000	8,000	
Total		1,80,500		1,46,800		
Current Liabilities :						
Bank Loans	70,000				70,000	
Creditors	1,50,000		1,35,200		14,800	
	2,20,000	2,20,000		1,35,2000		
		-39,500		+11,600		
Increase in Working Capital		+ 51,100[1]				51,100
		11,600		11,600	92,900	92,900

1 Rs. 39,500 + 11,600 = Rs. 51,100

Alternative Method

Statement Showing Changes in Working Capital

Partuiculars	*1984*	*1985*	*Changes in current assets and current ·liabilities*		*Changes in non-current assets and non-current liabilities*	
			Dr.	*Cr.*	*Dr.*	*Cr.*
	Rs.	*Rs.*	*Rs*	*Rs*	*Rs.*	*Rs.*
Land & Buildings	2,00,000	1,90,000	—	—	—	10.000
Machinery & Plant	1,50,000	1,69,000	—	—	19,000	—
Stocks	1,00,000	74,000	—	26,000	—	—
	1,00,000	74,000	—	26,000	—	—
Debtors	80,000	64,200	—	15,800	—	—
Cash	500	600	100	—	—	—
Bank	—	8,000	8,000	—	—	—
Goowill	—	5,000	—	—	5,000	—
	5,30,500	5,10,800				

Share Capital	2,00,000	2,50,000	—	—	—	50,000
General Reserve	50,000	60,000	—	—	—	10,000
P. & L. A/c	30,500	30,600	—	—	—	100
Bank Loan	70,000	—	70,0000	—	—	—
Creditors	1,50,000	1,35,200	14,800	—	—	—
Provision for Taxation	30,000	35,000	—	—	—	5,000
	5,30,500	5,10,800				
Net Increase in W.C.				51,100	51,100	
			92,900	92,900	75,100	75,100

Example IV.

From the following Balance Sheet of Sudhir Ltd. make schedule of changes in Working Capital and Funds Flow Statement :

Balance Sheet of A Ltd.

	1984	*1985*		*1984*	*1985*
	Rs.	*Rs.*		*Rs.*	*Rs.*
Share Capital	3,00,000	4,00,000	Goodwill	—	20,000
Reserve	50,000	50,000	Fixed Assets	3,75,000	3,94,000
Profit and Loss A/c	40,000	45,000	Stocks	1,20,000	1,12,00
Bank Overdraft	60,000	—	Advance	3,000	1,000
Creditors	50,000	52,000	Debtors	92,000	87,000
B/P	45,000	23,000	Cash at Bank	5,000	6,000
Provision for Tax	50,000	50,000			
Rs.	5,95,000	6,20,000	Rs.	5,95,000	6,20,000

Additional information obtained from the General Ledger is as follows:

During the year 1985 a dividend of Rs. 15,000 was paid. The assets of another company were purchased at Rs.1,00,000 payable in fully paid shares of the company. The assets consisted of Stock Rs. 45,000, fixed assets Rs. 35,000 and Goodwill Rs. 20,000.

Income-tax paid during the year was Rs. 35,000. The net profit for the year was Rs. 55,000 before charging tax.

Solution.

Fund Flow Statement

(For the Year 1985)

Sources of Funds	*Rs.*	*Application of funds*	*Rs.*
Share Capital	45,000[1]	Income-tax	35,000
Source from Operation	71,1000[2]	Dividend	15,000
		Increase in Working Capital	66,000
	Rs. 1,16,000		Rs. 1,16,000

[1] Rs. 4,00,000 – Rs. 3,00,000 = Increase in share capital Rs. 1,00,000. That portion of share capital which is equal to current assets = Rs. 1,00,000 - (Fixed assets Rs. 35,000 + Good will Rs. 20,000) = Rs. 45,000.

[2] Profit and Loss Account

(Adjusted)

	Rs.		*Rs.*
To Depreciation	16,000	By Balance b/d	40,000
To Dividend	15,000	By Source from Operation	71,000[2]
To Income-tax	35,000		
To Balance c/d	45,000		
	Rs. 1,11,000		Rs. 1,11,000

[1] (Opening balance of fixed assets Rs. 3,75,000 + Purchase of fixed assets Rs. 35,000) - Closing balance Rs. 3,94,000 = Rs. 16,000 depreciation.

[2] This amount is balancing figure.

Schedule of Changes in Working Capital

Particulars	*1984*		*1985*		*Effect on Working Capital* *Dr.*	*Cr.*
	Rs.	Rs.	Rs.	Rs.	Rs.	Rs.
Current Assets:						
Cash at Bank		5,000		6,000	1,000	—
Debetors		92,000		87,000	—	5,000
Advances		3,000		1,000	—	2,000
Stock	1,20,000		1,12,000	—	8,000	
Total	2.20,000		2,06,000			
Current Liabilities:						
Creditrors	50,000		52,000		—	2,000
B/P 45,000		23,000		22,000	—	
Bank Overdraft	60,000	-1,55,000	—	75,000	60,000	—
Net Working Capital	65,000		1,31,000			
Increase Working Capital		66,000				66,000
		1,31,000		1,31,000	83,000	83,000

Note : Provision for Taxation has not been treated as current liability here because additional information for payment of income-tax is given in it.

Example V.

Find out flow of fund from operations on the basis of following Profit and Loss Account:

Profit and Loss Account
(For the year ended on Dec. 31, 1985)

		Rs.			*Rs.*
To Opening Stock		10,000	By Sales	1,50,000	
To Purchases	80,000		Less : Returns	5,000	1,45,000
Less: Returns	10,000	70,000			
To Carriage		5,000	By Closing Stock		35,000
To Wages		10,000			
To Outstanding Wages		5,000			
To Gross Profit		80,000			
		Rs. 1,80,000			Rs. 1,80,000
To Salaries		18,000	By Gross Profit		80,000
To Insurance	1,800		By Gain on sale of machinery		2,250
Less : Prepaid	100	1,700			
To Depreciation on plant		700			
To Dep. on machinery		300			
To Dep. on furniture		50			
To Loss on sale of furntiture		100			
To Preliminary Exps.		400			
To Goodwill (written off)		1,000			
To Provision for Taxation		4,000			
To Net Profit		56,000			
		Rs. 82,250			Rs. 82,250

Solution.

First method (Statement Form)

		Rs.
Net Profit as per Profit and Loss Account		56,000
Add : Items not forming part of fund flow:	Rs.	
Depreciation on Plant	700	
Deprecation on Machinery	300	
Depreciation on Furniture	50	
Loss on sale of Furniture	100	
Preliminary Expenses	4,00	
Goodwill	1,000	
Provision for Taxation	4,000	6,550
Less:		62,550
Items not forming part of fund flow :		
Gain on sale of furniture		2,250
	Rs.	60,300

Alternative Method (Account Form)
Adjusted Profit and Loss Account

	Rs.		*Rs.*
Opening Stock	10,000	Sales (Net)	1,45,000
Purchases (Net)	70,000	Closing Stock	35,000
Carriage	5,000		
Wages	10,000		
Outstanding Wages	5,000		
Salaries	18,000		
Insurance	1,700		
Sources from Operation	60,300		
	Rs. 1,80,000		Rs. 1,80,000

Example VI.

A Ltd. has been in operation for several years but suffered a set back in its operations about three years back. It expects to show better results in future and has plans to expand rapidly. The summarised Balance Sheet and Profit and Loss Accounts of the company are given below:

Balance Sheet

(Rs. in lakhs)

	1984 *Rs.*	*1985* *Rs.*	*1986* *Rs.*
Fixed Assets (Gross)	365	350	360
Less: Depreciation to date	100	125	160
Net Fixed Assets	265	225	200
Debtors	325	335	380
Stock of Raw Materials	100	75	120
Stock of finished and semi-finished goods	280	250	350
Other Current Assets	10	10	15
Total Asset;	980	895	1,065
Share Capital	60	60	60
Reserves	1	3	90
Term Loans	—	—	155
Bank Overdraft	650	650	475
Current Liabilities and Provisions	269	182	285
Total Liabilities	980	895	1,065

Profit and Loss Account

(Rs. in lakhs)

	1984	*1985*	*1986*
Sales	880	1,000	1,225
Materials	50	725	850

Contd.

	1984	*1985*	*1986*
Salaries and Wages	125	130	140
Other Expenses	60	70	65
Depreciation	25	30	35
Interest	60	50	50
	920	1,005	1,140
Net Operating Profit (Loss)	(40)	(5)	85
Non-Operating Profit	Nil	7	2

Prepare a statement showing sources and uses of funds.

Solution.

Statement of Sources and Uses of Funds

(For the year ending on Dec. 31, 1984, 1985 & 1988)

	1985 (Rs.in lakhs)	*1988 Rs. in lakhs)*
Sources of Funds:		
Operating profits before depreciation	25[1]	120[2]
Not-Operating Profit	7	2
Loss on sale of fixed assets written off	10[3]	—
Term Loan	—	155
Total	42	277
Application of Funds:		
Purchase of Fixed Assets	—	10[4]
Increase in Working Capital	42	267

Statement of Changes in Working Capital

	1984 (Rs.in lakhs)	*1985 (Rs.in lakhs)*	*1986 Rs. in lakhs)*
Current Assets	715[1]	670[2]	865[7]
Current Liabilities including bank overdraft	919[8]	832[6]	760[10]
Net Working Capital	-204	-162	+105
Increase in Working Capital	—	42[11]	267[12]

[1] 1985 : Net loss Rs. 5 lakhs + Depreciation Rs. 30 lakhs = Profit Rs. 25 lakhs.

[2] 1986 : Net Profit Rs. 85 lakhs + Depreciation Rs. 35 lakhs = Rs. 120 lakhs.

[3] In 1984 Fixed Assets Rs. 385 lakhs - in 1985 Fixed Assets Rs. 350 lakhs = Reduction in Fixed Assets Rs. 15 lakhs

Depreciation in 1985 Rs. 30 lakh while cumulative depreciation increases by (Rs. 125 lakhs - Rs. 100 lakhs) - Rs. 25 lakhs only, hence Rs. 5 lakhs written off. Above-mentioned Rs. 15 lakhs - Rs. 5 lakhs = Rs. 10 lakhs loss.

[4] 1986 Fixed Assets Rs. 380 lakhs - 1985 Fixed Assets Rs. 350 lakhs = Rs. 10 lakhs.

[5] Rs. in lakhs 325 + 100 + 280 +10 = Rs. 715 lakhs.

[6] Rs. in lakhs 335 + 75 + 250 + 10 = Rs. 670 lakhs.

[7] Rs. in lakhs 380 + 120 + 350 + 15 = Rs. 865 lakhs.

[8] Rs. in lakhs 650 + 369 = Rs. 919 lakhs.

[9] Rs. in lakhs 650 + 182 = Rs. 832 lakhs.

[10] Rs. in lakhs 475 + 285 = Rs. 760 lakhs.

[11] Deficit of Rs. 204 lakhs is reduced to Rs. 162 lakhs hence 204 - 162 = 42 lakhs indicate increase in working capital.

[12] Deficit of Rs. 162 lakhs is wiped out and excess of Rs. 105 lakhs is there, hence total increase is Rs. 162 + 105 = Rs. 267 lakhs.

Example VII.

From the following Balance Sheet of A Ltd., make out (I) Statement of Changes in Working Capital, and (2) Funds Flow Statement.

Balance Sheet of A Ltd.

	1984 Rs.	1985 Rs.		1984 Rs.	1985 Rs.
Equity Share			Goodwill	1,10,000	80,000
Capital	3,00,000	4,00,000	Land and Buildings	2,00,000	17,000
8% Redeemable Pref.			Plant	80,000	2,00,000
Share Capital	1,50,000	1,00,000	Investment	20,000	30,000
Capital Reserve	—	20,000	Sunday Debtors	1,40,000	1,70,000
General Reserve	40,000	50,000	stock	77,000	1,09,000
P & L. A/c	30,000	48,000	Bills Receivable	20,000	30,000
Proposed Dividend	42,000	50,000	Cash in Hand	15,000	10,000
Sundry Creditors	25,000	47,000	Cash at Bank	10,000	8,000
Bils Payable	20,000	16,000	Preliminary .Expenses	15,000	10,000
Liabilities for Expenses	30,000	36,000			
Provisions for Taxation	40,000	50,000			
Rs.	6.77,000	8,17,0000	Rs.	6,77,000	8,17,000

(i) A piece of land has been sold out in 1985 and the profit on sale has been credited to capital reserve.

(ii) A machine has been sold for Rs. 10,000. The written down value of the machine was Rs. 12,000. Depreciation of Rs. 10,000 is charged on Plant Account in 1985.

(iii) The investments are trade investments. Rs. 3,000 by way of dividend is received including Rs. 1,000 from pre-acquisition profit has been credited to Investment Acccount.

(iv) An interim dividend of Rs. 20,000 has been paid in 1985.

Solution.

Fund Flow Statement
(For the Year 1985)

Sources of Funds	*Rs.*	*Application of funds*	*Rs.*
Issue of Equity Capital	1,00,000[1]	Purchase of Plant	1,42,000[10]
Sale of Machine	10,000	Investment	11,000[11]
Sale of Land	50,000[2]	Repayment of Preference Capital	50,000[12]
Dividend Received	3,000	Proposed Dividend Paid	42,000
Source from operation	1,43,000[3]	Interim Dividend Paid	20,000
		Increase in Working Capital	41,000
	Rs. 3,06,000		Rs. 3,06,000

[1] Rs. 4,00,000 - 3,00,000 = Rs. 1,00,000.

[2] Land and Buildings Account

	Rs.		*Rs.*
To Balance b/d	2,00,000	By Cash (Sale)	50,000*
To Profit transferred to capital Reserve	20,000	By Balance c/d	1,70,000
	Rs. 2,20,000		Rs. 2,20,000

This is balancing figure.

[3] Adjusted Profit and Loss Account

	Rs.		*Rs.*
To Proposed Dividend	50,000	By Balance b/d	30,000
To General Reserve	10,000[4]	By Dividend	2,000[9]
To Interim Dividend	20,000	By Source from Operation	1,43,000
To Goodwill	20,000[5]		
To Provision for Taxation	10,000[5]		
To Depreciation on Plant	10,000		

To Loss or Sale of Plant	2,000[7]		
To Preliminary Expenses	5,000[8]		
To Balance c/d	48,000		
Rs.	1,75,000	Rs.	1,75,000

[4] Rs. 50,000 – 40,000 = Rs. 10,000;

[5] Rs. 1,00,000 – 80,000 = Rs. 20,000;

[6] Rs. 50,000 – 40,000 = Rs. 10,000;

[7] Rs. 12,000 – 10,000 = Rs. 2,000;

[8] Rs. 15,000 – 10,000 = Rs. 5,000;

[9] Rs. 3,000 – 1,000 = Rs. 2,000.

[10] Plant Account

	Rs.		*Rs.*
To Balance b/d	80,000	By Depreciation	10,000
To Cash (Purchase)	1,42,000	By Cash (Sale)	10,000
		By Profit and Loss	2,000
		By Balance c/d	2,00,000*
Rs.	2,22,000	Rs.	2,22,000

* This is balancing amount.

[11] Investment Account

	Rs.		Rs.
To Balance b/d	20,000	By Depreciation A/c	1,000
To Cash (Purchase)	11,000*	By Balance c/d	30,000
Rs.	31,000	Rs.	31,000

* This is balancing amount.

[12] Rs. 1,50,000 – 1,00,000 = Rs. 50,000.

Note: Investments have been considered for Funds Flow Statement here because they are trade investments.

Statement Showing Changes in Working Capital

Particulars	*1984*		*1985*		*Effect on Working Capital*	
					Dr.	*Cr.*
	Rs.	Rs.	Rs.	Rs.	Rs.	Rs.
Current Assets:						
Debtors		1,40,000		1,70,000	30,000	
Stocks		77,000		1,09,000	32,000	
B/R		20,000		30,000	10,000	
Cash in Hand		15,000		10,000		5,000
Cash at Bank		10,000		8,000		2,000
Total		2,62,000		3,27,000		
Current Liabilities:						
Creditors	25,000		47,000			22,000
B/P	20,000		16,000		4,000	
Liability for Expenses	30,000		36,000			6,000
Total	75,000	-75,000	99,000	– 99,000		
Working Capital		1,87,000		2,28,000		
Increse in Working Capital		41,000				41,000
		2,28,000		2,28,000	76,000	76,000

CASH FLOW ANALYSIS

A cash flow statement shows the sources of cash receipt and the purposes for which payments are made thus explaining the changes in the cash balances of the business. This statement summarise the changes in cash position of the firm. The transactions which increase the cash position of the concern are treated as inflow of cash and which decreases the cash flow statement traces the various sources which bring in cash such as cash from operations, sale of current and fixed assets, issue of share capital and debentures etc. and applications which causes outflow of cash such as loss from operation, purchase of current and fixed assets; redemption of debentures and preference shares and other long term debts for cash. Cash statement shows the cash receipts and disbursement during the period. For example if the cash balance of a business concern shows by the balance sheet on 31st December, 1992 at Rs. 40,000 which the cash balance as per its balance sheet on 31 st December, 1993 is Rs. 55,000/-. It means that there has been an inflow of cash of Rs. 15,000/- in the year 1993 as compared to the year 1992. The cash flow statement explains the reasons for such inflows or outflows of cash, as the case may be. A cash flow statement is not very much different from a fund flow statement. During preparing the fund flow statement the sources and uses of all 'funds' (working capital) are taken into account while in preparation of cash flow statement, the sources and uses of cash alone are taken into account. The focus is on 'cash' rather than on 'net working capital'. Cash flow statement is prepared to show the impact of various transactions on the cash position of firm. It takes into account the transactions resulting in cash in flow only. A cash flow statement is a statement which summaries sources of cash inflows and uses of cash outflows of a firm during particular period of time, *i.e.*, months or a year.

Objectives of Cash Flow Statement

In cash flow there are number of objectives of financial management.

(a) The object of cash flow statement is to summarise the cause of changes in cash position between the two different years, months, dates of balance sheets. It shows the sources of and uses of cash. This statement analyses changes in non-current account as well as current accounts to determine the flow of cash.

(b) It indicates a comparison of the cash flow statement for the previous year with the budget for the year which indicate to what extent the resources of the concern were generated and applied to the plan. It is specially useful to management while preparing cash budget.

(c) A business concern may earn large profits yet it may run out of cash or when it suffered a loss and still has plenty of cash at bank. The cash flow analysis would unable the financial manager to account for such state of affair.

(d) This statement is useful in evaluating financial policies and current cash portion of a concern. Analysis of cash flow is useful for short-term planning. The fund flow statement is particularly useful for long term planning, cash flow statement provides information for planning the short range needs of the firm. It is very helpful to analyse the pattern of cash inflow and outflow. A business concern needs sufficient cash to pay debt maturing in the near future, to pay interest and other expenses, to pay dividends to the shareholders and to plan purchases of fixed assets. It may, thus, plan out the investment or surplus or meeting the deficit, if any.

The following are 'sources' and 'applications' of cash, as used for preparing a cash flow statement.

Sources of Cash. Cash from operations is the main internal source. The net profit shown by the Profit and Loss Account will have to be adjusted for non-cash items for finding out cash from operations. The items are as follows:

(a) Good will, preliminary expenses, etc. when written off against profits, reduce the net profits without affecting the cash balance. The amounts written off should, therefore, be added back to profits to find out cash from operations.

(b) Sale of fixed assets is taken as a separate source of cash, it should be deducted from the profits.

(c) If the profit for the year has been arrived at after charging transfers to reserves, such transfers should be added back to profits. In case operation shows a net loss, such net loss after making adjustments for non-cash items will be as an application of cash.

(d) Loss on sale of fixed assets does not result in outflow of cash and, therefore, should be added back to profits.

(e) Gains from sale of fixed assets is taken as a separate source of cash, it should be deducted from net profit.

(f) Depreciation does not result in outflow of cash and therefore, net profit will have to be increased by the amount of depreciation or development rebate charged, in order to find out the real cash generated from operations.

To find out real cash from operations, adjustments will have to be made for 'changes' in current assets and current liabilities arising out on account of operations *viz.*, trade debtors, trade creditors, bills receivable, bills payable etc. This may be done by applying the general rules:

Increase in current asset or decrease in current liability results in decrease in cash and decrease in a current asset or increase in a current liability results in increase in cash.

Applications of Cash. It may take any of the following terms:

(a) Payment of tax will result in decrease of cash, hence, it is as application of cash.

(b) The decrease in unsecured loans, deposits etc. denotes that they have been paid off to that extent. It results therefore in outflow of cash.

(c) Loss suffered on account of business operations will result in outflow of cash.

(d) The payment of long term loan such as loans from financial institutions or debentures results in decrease in cash. It is, therefore, application of cash.

(e) Cash may be utilised for purchase of additional fixed assets or renewals or replacement of existing fixed assets.

(f) Payments for plant and machinery purchased on deferred payment basis has to be made as per agreement. It is, therefore, an application of cash.

(g) Payment of dividend decreases the cash for business and hence it is application of cash.

CONSTRUCTION OF CASH FLOW STATEMENT

Cash Flow Statement (CFS) is prepared with the help of balance sheet, Profit and Loss Account and other additional information. The calculation and measurement of cash flow is primarily based on P & L A/c or Income Statement. It should be noted that items in an Income Statement are shown on accrual basis while items are shown on cash basis in Cash Flow Statement. Cash flow measurement depends primarily on determining cash receipts and cash payments over a given period, whereas income is determined by matching revenue and expenses in a given period. Therefore, a number of items appear on either the Cash Flow Statement or the Income Statement but not on both. For instance, depreciation and bad debts written off are recognised in determining the net income, hence they are debited to the Income Statement/P. & L. A./c, but they are excluded from the Cash Flow Satements as they don't require any cash outlay or in other words, they are non-cash items.

There are two parts of Cash Flow Statement *i.e.*, cash inflow and cash outflow. Cash inflow means sources of cash and cash outflow means uses of cash. The items of cash inflow and outflow are computed separately.

The main items of cash flow are as follows—

I. SOURCES OF CASH/CASH INFLOW

The following are the items of cash inflow:

1. Cash From Operation. There are two methods to calculate cash from operation—

(A) Cash Sales Methods. Cash from operation can be calculated on this method as—

Cash from operation (CFO) = Cash Sales (Cash purchase + Cash operating expenses)

Where, Cash Sales = Total Sales – Credit Sales

or, Cash Sales = total Sales – Increase in Debtors and B/R

Note. It should be noted that decrease in the amounts of debtors and bills receivable (B/R) should not be added to total sales. Such decreases should be shown separately as collections from debtors/bill receivable under sources of cash because it represents the amount collected from previous year's debtors or B/R.

Cash Purchase = Total Purchase – Credit Purchases

or Cash Purchase = Total Purchase – Increase in Trade Creditors and Bills payable (B/P)

Where, Total Purchases = Cost of Goods Sold + Increase in Stocks (or minus decrease in stock)

Cash Operating Expenses are determined as follows—

(Amount in Rs.)

Total operating expenses for the period		- - - -
Less : Non – Cash items (*e.g.* Depreciation)		- - - -
	Rs.	- - - -
Add : Decrease in outstanding expenses	- - - -	
Increase in prepaid expenses	- - - -	- - - -
		- - - -
Less : Increase in outstanding expenses	- - - -	
Decrease in prepaid expenses	- - - -	- - - -
Cash Operating Expenses	Rs.	- - -

Format of Determining Cash from Operations

(Amount in Rs.)

Total Sales		----
Less : Credit Sales		----
Cash Sales		----
Less : Cash Purcahses—		
Total Purchase	----	
Less : Credit Purchases	----	----
(or increase in Account Payable)	----	----
Less : Cash operating expenses (after adjusting non-cash items, accruals and pre-payments)		----
Cash From Operation		----

Note—Cash Sales method is the best method.

(B) Net Profit Method. Cash From Operation (CFO) can be determined by this second method *i.e.*, net profit method. In this method, in the amount of net profit depreciation, loss on the sale of fixed assets, intangible assets written off and other non-cash items are added. On the other hand, all non-business income, increase in receivables, stock-in-trade, prepaid expenses, reduction in deferred credit and decrease in payables should be deducted from it.

Format of Calculating Cash from Operation on the Basis of Net Profit Method

(Amount in Rs.)

Net profit as per Income Statement		----
Add: (A) Non-Cash items:		
(i) Depreciation	----	
(ii) Loss on the sale of fixed assets written off		
(iii) Goodwill written off	----	
(iv) Advertising Suspense a/c written off	----	

	(B) Non-business expenses Dividend paid	----	
	(C) Increase in Current Liabilities	----	
	(Account payable outstanding expenses etc.)		
	(D) Decrease in Current Assets	----	----
Less:	(A) Non-business Income		----
	Income from investment	----	
	(B) Decrease in current liabilities	----	
	(A/c payable outstanding expenses etc.)		
	(C) Increase in current assets	----	----
	(Prepaid expenses A/C Receivable etc.)		
	Cash From Operation	Rs.	----

Tutorial Notes About Treating Operating Profit as Cash From Operations (CFO)

Some authorities opine to show operating profit (as determined under FFS) instead of cash from operations. If this procedure is adopted, changes in Current Assets and Current Liabilities will not be adjusted in net profit (as in (A) and (B) methods) but will be shown directly in the Cash Flow Statement. Accordingly the increase in stock, debtors and B/R and decrease in creditors, B/P etc. will be shown as application of cash, and increase in creditors and B/P and decrease in stock, debtors and B/R as sources of cash.

2. Increase in Share Capital. If Equity share capital or Preference share capital is increased during the concerned period then it will be the part of cash inflow or sources of cash. The net effect (add premium on share and less discount on issue of share) of issue of share capital should be taken into account. However, an increase in share capital happens due to purchase of fixed assets (*i.e.*, shares are issued in consideration other than cash) or shares are issued in conversion of debentures or long-term loans, it would not be inflow of cash.

3. Issue of Debentures, Loans etc. If debentures are issued or loans are taken in cash, it will form a source of cash. However, if debentures are issued or loans raised for consideration other than cash, it will not constitute inflow of cash.

4. Reduction in or sale of assets. If fixed assets are sold and long term investments are reduced by receipt of cash, these proceeds will form part of the source of cash or cash inflow.

5. Other Receipts. There may also be some other sources of cash inflow such as sale proceeds of by-products or waste materials, cash receipts of dividend and interest, income tax refund, compensation received etc.

II. APPLICATION OR USES OF CASH OR CASH OUTFLOWS

The items are as follows—

1. Operating Loss. The procedure of calculation of operating loss is the same as Cash From Operation. Operating loss is shown under application of cash flow.

2. Redemption of Preference Shares/Debentures. Cash actually paid for redemption of share/debentures (*i.e.*, adding premium or deducting discount on the redemption of shares/debentures) constitutes outflow of cash. Arrears of dividend are also shown as outflow of cash. However, if equity shares are given for repayment of preference share capital or debentures, it will not constitute cash outflow.

3. Decrease in or Repayment of Loans. Decrease in loans or repayment of long-term or short-term loans, creditors or B/P, these will form outflow of cash.

4. Increase in or Purchase of Fixed Assets. The acquisition of fixed assets and investments constitutes cash outflow. However, if the acquisition is made on credit or by the issue of shares or debentures, it will not involve outflow of cash.

5. Other Payments. Payment of dividend (interim or final but not stock dividend), income tax, interest compensation etc., will constitute outflow of cash.

FORMS OF CASH FLOW STATEMENT (CFS)

CFS may be prepared in the following types:

(a) ***Reminder Type.*** Under this method, the Cash Flow Statement is divided into two parts—sources of cash and applications of cash. The difference of the total of both the sides shows the surplus deficiency of cash at the end of the year.

(b) ***Self-Balance Type.*** Under this method, the cash flow statement is prepared in the same manner—sources and uses of cash as the Reminder Type. But the short side of the statement is balanced with the figure of variation in the balance of cash and then both sides are closed.

(c) ***Reconciling Type.*** In this method one starts with the opening balance of cash. To the opening balance all items for the inflow of cash are added and outflows of cash are deducted; the net figure must be cash in hand *i.e.*, closing balance of cash at the end of the specific period. This method is more popular and widely used.

Specimen of Report Form Reconciling Type Cash Flow Statement

(Amount in Rs.)

Opening Cash Balance		- - - -
Add: Sources of Cach/Cash inflows		
1. Cash from operation	- - - -	
2. Collection from Debtors or Decrease in Debtors	- - - -	
3. Sale of Investments	- - - -	
4. Issue of Share Capital Debentures	- - - -	
5. Increase in Loans	- - - -	- - - -
Total Cash Available		- - - -

Less: Application of Cash/Cash Outflows

1. Purchase of Machinery	- - - -	
2. Dividend paid	- - - -	
3. Decrease in Accounts Payable	- - - -	
4. Repayment of Bank Loan	- - - -	
5. Redemption of Debentures	- - - -	- - - -
Cash balance at the end		- - - -

Account Form Reconciling Type Cash Flow Statement

Sources of Cash	Amount Rs.	Application of Cash	Amount Rs.
Opening Cash Balance	—	Loss from Operation	—
Other Sources of Cash:	—	Purchase of Machinery	—
Cash from Operation	—	Repayment of Bank Loans	—
Sale of Investment	—	Redemption of Preference	—
Issue of Shares/Debentures	—	Share Capital/Debentures	—
Loans	—	Decrease in Accounts Payable	—
Collection from Debtors	—	Closing balance of Cash	—
Total (Rs.)	—	Total (Rs.)	—

DIFFERENCE BETWEEN CASH FLOW AND FUND FLOW STATEMENT

Both the statements shows the changes in the financial position of concern yet there are many points which show the difference between Fund Flow and Cash Flow Statement. The following are the main points:

(a) Cash is the part of working capital and, therefore, an improvement in the cash position results in improvement in the funds position but the reserve is not true. So the inflow of cash results, the inflow of funds but inflow of funds may not necessarily results in flow of cash.

(b) Cash Flow Statement is merely a record of cash receipts and disbursement. It is valuable in its own way but it fails to bring to light many important changes involving the disposition of resources. While studying the short term solvency of a business one is interested not only in cash balance but also in the assets which may easily be converted into cash.

(c) Cash Flow Statement is useful for short terms financial planning where as Fund Flow Statement is useful for long term financial planning.

(d) In Cash Flow Statement an increase in a current liability or decrease in a current asset (other than cash) results in increase in cash or vice versa whereas in case of Fund Flow statement an increase in current liability or decrease in a current asset results in working capitals and vice versa.

(e) Funds from operations are calculated by making adjusted profit and loss account taking into consideration all adjustments which are made at the end of the accounting period. Cash Flow Statement deals with only actual receipts and payments of income and expenses. In order to calculate cash from operation further adjustments are required to be made for increase and decreases in current assets and current liabilities.

(f) Cash Flow Statement is more useful to the management as a tool of financial analysis in short period as compared to Fund Flow Statement. It has rightly been said that shorter the period covered by analysis, greater is the importance of cash flow statement. Example, if it is to be found out whether the business can meet its obligations maturing after 10 years from now, a good estimate can be made about firms capacity to meet its long term obligations if changes in working capital position on account of operations are observed.

Utility to Cash Flow Statement

A cash flow statement, is an important, financial tool for the management. Its utility can be discussed as follows:

(a) Cash flow statement discloses the complete story of cash movement. The increase in or decrease of, cash and the reason therefore can be known. It discloses the reasons for low cash balance inspite of heavy operating profits or for heavy cash balance inspite of low operating profits.

(b) The extent of success or failure of cash planning can be known by comparing the projected cash flow statement with the actual cash flow statement and necessary remedial measures can be taken.

(c) Cash flow analysis helps in evaluating financial policies and cash position. Cash in the basis for all operations and hence a projected cash flow statement will enable the management to plan and contribute the financial operations properly. The management can know how much cash is needed, from which source it will be derived, how much can be generated internally and how much could be obtained from outside.

(d) Cash flow statement provides information about funds which will be available from operations. This will help the management in determining policies regarding internal financial management *e.g.* possibility of repayment of long term debt, dividend policies, planning replacement of plant and machinery etc.

METHOD ADOPTED FOR CASH FLOW STATEMENT

Cash flow statement shows the impact of various transactions on cash position of a firm. It is prepared with the help of financial statement *i.e.* balance sheet and profit and loss account and some additional information. A cash flow statement starts with the opening balance of cash and balance at bank, all the inflows of cash are added to the opening balance and outflow of cash are deducted from total. The balance *i.e.* opening balance at bank, all the inflows of cash are added to the opening balance and outflow of cash are deducted from total. The balance *i.e.* opening balance of cash and bank balance plus inflow of cash minus outflows of cash is reconciled with the closing of cash. The cash flow statement involves the determining of:

(a) Inflows of Cash

(b) Outflows of Cash

(a) Sources of Cash Inflows

(i) Cash flow from operations

(ii) Increase in existing liabilities or creation of new liabilities

(iii) Reduction in or sale of Assets

(iv) Non-trading receipts

(b) Cash Outflows

(i) Cash lost in operation

(ii) Decrease in or discharge of liabilities

(iii) Increase in or purchase of assets

(iv) Non-trading payments

In order to prepare cash flow statement the following two methods are used:

(1) Statement Form

(2) Account Form

(1) Statement Form. Under this form cash statement begins with the opening cash and bank balances. The sources of cash are added to it and applications of cash deducted out of it. Proforma of the same is given below :

Cash Flow Statement

		Rs.
Cash balance in the beginning		
Add:	Cash inflows:	
	Cash from operations	
	Issue of share or bonds	
	Sale of fixed assets	
	Raising of Loans or accepting public deposits	
	Refund of Income-tax	
	Dividend received	
Less:	Outflows of Cash	
	Purchase of fixed assets	
	Repayment of Loans	
	Redemption of debentures bonds or preference shares	
	Payment of taxes	
	Payment of dividend	
	Purchase of long term investments	
	Drawings	
	Loss of Cash by embezzlement	
	Cash lost in operations	—

(2) Account Form or 'T' Form. Under this method, opening cash and bank balances are shown on the debit side; sources of cash are debited and applications of cash credited. The account is balanced by putting the closing balance on the credit side. A proforma of this form is given below:

	Rs.		Rs.
Cash Balance in the beginning		*Outflows of Cash:*	
Add: Cash inflows		Purchase of fixed assets	
Cash from operations		Payment of loans	
Issue of Shares		Redemption of debentures	
Issue of Debentures		and preference shares	
Sale of fixed assets		Payment of taxes	
Raising of Loans		Payment of dividends	
Refund of tax		Drawings	
Dividend received		Loss of cash by embezzlement	
		Cash lost in operations	
	——	Cash/bank balance at close	——

The major difference between a fund flow statement and cash flow statement lies in the amount shown as 'resources provided by business operations.' Most of the other items relating to non-current assets and liabilities appear in the cash flow statement with the same figure as they appear in the cash flow statement with the same figure as they appear in the funds flow statement. Therefore, funds from operations are to be adjusted so as to get the figure of cash from operations for preparing a cash flow statement.

CASH FROM OPERATIONS

'Funds From Operations' are based on Accrual Accounting system *i.e.*, sales, whether cash or credit and purchase, whether cash or credit are considered as cash items. Similarly, outstanding expenses are considered as the use of working capital and pre-payments of such expenses as source of working capital. But, under a cash concept of funds we are concerned with the 'cash basis of accounting.' Only cash sales and cash receipts from debtors against credit sales are recongnised as a source of cash. Similarly, cash purchases and cash payments to suppliers for credit purchases are regarded as the use of cash. The same holds true for other expenses and incomes. No consideration is to be given for outstanding and prepaid expenses and incomes.

Cash generated from trading operations will not be equal to the net profit as reported in the profit and loss account. It is so because of certain non-cash items (*e.g.*, depreciation on fixed assets, fictitious assets amortization) and non-operating items (*e.g.* loss or profit on sale of fixed assets, dividend received or paid, amount transferred to general reserve, provision for taxation and so on) changed to the profit and loss account. Non-cash and non-operating items are adjusted to the figure of profit or loss in the same way as these were adjusted for getting the figure of 'funds from operations' as we have already seen somewhere else.

Thus figure of profit is further adjusted for changes in current assets except cash and current liabilities except bank-overdraft to get the amount of 'cash from operations'. The following tables show the procedure for determining 'cash from operations.'

Format of Statement of Changes in Financial Position

	Amount (Rs.)
(A) Working capital from business operation *i.e.* : funds from operation (as per Funds Flow Statement)	....
(B) Adjustment to convert to cash basis:	
Add: Decrease in Current assets and increase in current liabilities (other than cash) 'itemwise'	....
Less: Increase in Current assets and decrease in current liabilities (other than cash) 'itemwise'	....
(C) Cash inflow from business operations	....

The same can be restated in the 'formula manner' as below:

Cash from operation	= Net profit (*i.e.*, funds from operations)	(+) Decrease in current assets and increase in current liabilties
		&
		(–) Increase in current assets and decrease in current liabilities

Cash is only one of the current assets and is part of net working capital. Therefore, the change in all of the other current assets and in the current liabilities must be analysed in relation to their effect in cash.

It may be remembered that changes in current assets and current liabilities only have been adjusted to the profit to get the figure of cash from operations. Changes in fixed assets and fixed liabilities have not been adjusted as these are shown separately in the cash flow statement. It is so because current assets (*i.e.*, debtors as a result of credit sales, inventories as a result of purchases and sales and prepaid expenses caused by operating expenses) and current liabilties (*i.e.* Creditors because of credit purchase and outstanding expenses caused by non-payment of some of the expenses of the current period) are directly related to operations.

CALCULATION OF OPERATING PROFIT

The figure of net profit shown in the Profit and Loss Account includes items which do not increase or decrease cash. Such items should be adjusted to net profit to determine the net increase in profit from operations. To ascertain profit from operations one should :

(a) take the profit as disclosed by P & L A/c,

(b) add those items that represent mere book entries without any payment or loss of cash.

(c) deduct profit arising out of special transactions such as sale of fixed asset or redemption of liability.

FORMULA FOR CASH FROM OPERATION

Cash from operation can be calculated with help of following formula.

	+ Decrease in stock
	+ Decrease in debtors
	+ Decrease in prepared expenses
	+ Decrease in accrued income
	+ Increase in debtors
	+ Increase in outstanding expenses
	+ Increase in income-in-advance
Cash from operation =	
Net Operating profit	*Or*
	– Increase in debtors
	– Increase in stock
	– Increase in prepaid expenses
	– Decrease in creditors
	– Decrease in outstanding expenses
	– Decrease in income-in-advance

Cash from operation =	+ Decrease in current Assets
Net Operating Profit	– Increase in current liabilities
	Or
	– Increase in current Assets
	– Decrease in current liabilities

Cash from operation may be calculated as follows:

	Rs.
Net profit for the period	....
Add: Non-cash items:	....
(individually be shown)	....

Less:	Net operating incomes		————
	Net operating profit		....
Add:	(Item-wise)	....	....
	Decrease in current Assets		
	(Except cash)		
	Increase in current liabilities	....	....
Less:	(Item-wise)	....	....
	Increase in current assets:		
	(Except cash)		
	Decrease in current liabilities:		
	Cash from operation	....	....

SOME ILLUSTRATIONS

Illustration.

Compute cash from operations from Profit and Loss Account

Profit and Loss Account

(year ending 31st Dec. 1991)

	Rs.		Rs.
To Rent	1,000	By Gross Profit	25,000
To Salaries	5,000	By Profit on sale of land	5,000
To Depreciation	2,000	By Income Tax Refurd	3,000
To Loss on Sale on plant	1,000		
To Goodwill written off	4,000		
To Proposed Dividends	5,000		
To Provision for Taxation	5,000		
To Net Profit	10,000		
	33,000		33,000

Solution.

Computation of Cash from operations
(year ending 31st Dec., 1991)

		Rs.	Rs.
Net profit as per P & L Account			10,000
Add:	Non-cash items (which do not result in outflow of cash)		
	Depreciation	2,000	
	Less on sale of plant	1,000	
	Goodwill written off	4,000	
	Proposed dividends	5,000	
	Provision for Tax	5,000	17,000
			27,000
Less:	Non-cash items (which do not result in flow of cash from operations)		
	Profit on sale of land	5,000	
	Refund of Tax	3,000	8,000
	Cash from operations		19,000

Illustration.

Prepare Cash Flow Statement from the following Balance Sheets as on 31st Dec. 1990 and 31st Dec. 1991.

Liabilities	*1990*	*1991*	*Assets*	*1990*	*1991*
Share Capital	1,00,000	1,50,000	Fixed Assets	1,00,000	1,50,000
Profit & Loss A/c	50,000	80,000	Goodwill	50,000	40,000
General Reserve	30,000	40,000	Inventories	50,000	80,000
12% Bonds	50,000	60,000	Debtors	50,000	80,000
Sundry Creditors	30,000	40,000	Bills Receivable	10,000	20,000
Outstanding Exps.	10,000	15,000	Bank	10,000	15,000
	2,70,000	3,85,000		2,70,000	3,85,000

Solution.

Cash Flow Statement
(year ending 31st Dec., 1991)

	Rs.	*Rs.*
Bank Balance as on 1.1.1990		10,000
Add: Sources		
Issue of shares	50,000	
Issue of bonds	10,000	60,000
Total Sources		70,000
Less: Applications	5,000	
Operations	50,000	55,000
Bank Balance as on 1991		15,000

Woking Notes : Adjusted Profit and Loss Account

	Rs.		Rs.
To Goodwill written off	10,000	By Balance c/d	50,000
To General Reserve	10,000	By Funds from operations	50,000
To Balance c/d	80,000		
	1,00,000		1,00,000

Cash From Operations

	Rs.	*Rs.*
Funds from operations		50,000
Add: Increase in creditors		10,000
Increase in outstanding expenses		5,000
		65,000
Less: Increase in inventories	30,000	
Increase in Debtors	30,000	
Increase in B/R	10,000	70,000
Cash outflow from operations		5,000

Illustration.

Following are the comparative balance sheets of M/s Golden Ind. Ltd.

Liabilities	*Dec. 31 1990*	*Dec. 31 1990*	*Assets*	*Dec. 31 1990*	*Dec. 31 1990*
	Rs.	*Rs.*		*Rs.*	*Rs.*
Share Capital	70,000	74,000	Cash	9,000	7,800
Debentures	12,000	6,000	Trade debtors (good)	14,900	17,700
Trade creditors	10,360	11,840	Stock in Trade	49,200	42,700
Provision for doubtful debts	700	800	Land	20,000	30,000
Prof & Loss A/c	10,040	10,560	Goodwill	10,000	5,000
	1,03,100	1,03,200		1,03,100	1,03,200

Additional Information:

(a) Dividends were paid totalling Rs. 3,500.

(b) Land was purchased for Rs. 10,000 and amount provided for the amortization of goodwill Rs. 5,000.

(c) Debentures loan was redeemed Rs. 6,000.

Prepare cash flow statement from the above balance sheet and additional information.

Solution.

Profit & Loss Appropriation A/c

	Rs.		*Rs.*
To provision for doubtful debt (800-700)	100	By Balance b/d	10,040
To Goodwill written off (10,000 – 5,000)	5,000	By Profit during the year (balance figure)	50,000
To Balance B/d	10,560		
	15,660		15,660

Cash From Operations

		Rs.
Profit during the year		5,620
Add:	Decrease in stock-in-Trade	6,500
	Increase in Trade Creditors	1,480
		13,600
Less:	Increase in Book-debts	2,800
	Cash from operations	10,800

Cash From Statement

		Rs.	Rs.
Cash balance in the beginning			9,000
Add:	Cash from operations		10,800
	Shares issued		4,000
			23,800
Less:	Debentures repaid	6,000	
	Land purchased	10,000	16,000
	Cash balance in the end		7,800

Illustration.

Prepare the cash flow from the Balance Sheets of M/s Lucky International Ltd.

Liabilities	*1991* Rs.	*1992* Rs.	*Assets*	*1991* Rs.	*1992* Rs.
1			*2*		
Equity share capital	3,00,000	4,00,000	Goodwill	1,15,000	90,000
10% Redeemable Pref. shares	1,50,000	1,00,000	Land & Building	2,00,000	1,70,000
General Reserves	40,000	70,000	Plant	80,000	2,00,000
Profit & Loss A/c	30,000	48,000	Debtors	1,60,000	2,00,000

Contd.

1			2		
Proposed Dividend	42,000	50,000	Stock	77,000	1,09,000
Creditors	55,000	83,000	Bills Receivable	20,000	30,000
Bills Payable	20,000	16,000	Cash in hand	15,000	10,000
Provision for taxation	40,000	50,000	Cash at bank	10,000	8,000
	6,77,000	8,17,000		6,77,000	8,17,000

Additional Information:

(i) Depreciation of Rs. 10,000 and Rs. 20,000 have been charged on plant account and land and building account respectively in 1992.

(ii) An interim dividend of Rs. 20,000 has been paid in 1992.

(iii) Income tax during the year in 1992 was paid Rs. 35,000.

Solution.

(i) Calculation of profit made during the year:

Adjusted Profit and Loss A/C

	Rs.		Rs.
To Goodwill	25,000	By Balance b/d	30,000
To Depr. plant	10,000	By Profit from operation	2,18,000
To Dep. Bldg.	20,000		
To Proposed dividend	50,000		
To Interim dividend	20,000		
To Provision for tax	45,000		
To General Reserve	30,000		
To Balance B/d	48,000		
	2,48,000		2,48,000

(ii) Calculation of cash from operation:

		Rs.	Rs.
Profit from operations			2,18,000
Add:	Increase in current liabilities	28,000	
	Creditors	Nil	
	Decrease in current assets		28,000
			2,46,000
Less:	Increase in current assets:		
	Debtors	40,000	
	Stock	32,000	
	Bill Receivable	10,000	
Less:	Decrease in current liabilities	4,000	
	Bills payable		86,000
	Cash from operation		1,60,000

Statement of Cash Flow

		Rs.	Rs.
Cash in hand and at bank as on Dec. 31, 1991			
	(Rs. 15,000 + 10,000)		25,000
Add:	Inflow of cash:		
	Cash from operations	1,60,000	
	Sale of land and building	10,000	
	Issue of Shares	1,00,000	2,70,000
	Total cash available for use		2,95,000
Less:	Outflow of cash:		
	Purchase of plant	1,30,000	
	Payment of Final dividend for the last year	42,000	
	Payment of interim dividend	20,000	
	Payment of tax	35,000	
	Redemption of Pref. shares	50,000	2,77,000
	Cash in hand and bank as on Dec. 1992		18,000

Illustration.

From the following information you are required to calculate Cash From Operation (CFO):

	31st March	
	1995	*1996*
	Rs.	*Rs.*
Debtors	50,000	47,000
Bills Receivable	10,000	12,500
Creditors	20,000	25,000
Bills Payable	8,000	6,000
Outstanding expenses	1,000	1,200
Prepaid expenses	800	700
Accrued Income	600	750
Income Received in advance	300	250
Profit made during the year	—	1,30,000

Solution.

Cash From Operation

		Rs.	*Rs.*
Profit made during the year			1,30,000
Add:	Decrease in Debtors	3,000	
	Increase in Creditors	5,000	
	Increase in Outstanding Expenses	200	
	Decrease in Prepaid Expenses	100	8,300
			1,38,300
Less:	Increase in Bills Receivable	2,500	
	Increase in Accrued Income	150	
	Decrease in Bills Payable	2,000	
	Decrease in Income received in advance	50	4,700
	CFO		1,33,600

Illustration.

The following information is in respect of M/s S.K.Y. Ltd. as on 1st Jan. 1996.

	Rs.
Fixed Assets	6,00,000
Less: Depreciation	2,10,000
	3,90,000
Bank balance	35,000
Current Assets other than Bank balance	2,50,000
Share Capital (Rs. 100 each)	3,00,000
Current Liabilities	1,00,000

The Company made the following estimate for 1996—

(a) The profit would be Rs. 55,000 after depreciation of Rs. 60,000.

(b) The company will acquire fixed assets costing Rs. 10,00,000 after selling one machine for Rs. 20,000 costing Rs. 50,000 and one on which depreciation provided amounted to Rs. 35,000.

(c) Current assets and current liabilities other than bank balance at the end of 1996 are expected to be Rs. 2,95,000 and Rs. 1,30,000 respectively.

(d) The Company will pay free of tax dividend of 10%, the rate of tax being 25%.

Ascertain the Bank balance (overdraft of SKY Ltd. at the end of 1996).

Solution.

Cash Flow Statement

Source of Cash	*Rs.*	*Application of Cash*	*Rs.*
Opening Cash Balance (1.1.96)	35,000	Purchase of Fixed Assets	1,00,000
Cash from Operation	95,000	Closing balance of Cash on	
Sale of Machinery	20,000	(31.12.96)	50,000
	1,50,000		1,50,000

Working Notes—

Cash From Operation

		Rs.	*Rs.*
Profit for the year			55,000
Add:	Depreciation	60,000	
	Increase in Current Liabilities	30,000	90,000
			1,45,000
Less:	Profit on sale of machinery	5,000	
	Increase in Current Assets	45,000	50,000
	Cash from Operation		95,000

Illustration.

The Statement of the Financial Position of M/s A.K.Y. Brothers for the year 1996 is given below. Prepare the firm's Cash Flow Statement.

Liabilities	1-1-96 Rs.	31-12-96 Rs.	Assets	1-1-96 Rs.	31-12-96 Rs.
Capital	14,78,000	12,30,000	Buildings and Other		
Bills Payable	58,000	50,000	Fixed Assets	2,00,000	1,60,000
			Cash	12,00,000	10,00,000
			Debtors	40,000	34,000
			Stock	16,000	26,000
	15,36,000	12,80,000		14,56,000	12,80,000

The additional information for the firm is-—

(i) There was no drawing.

(ii) There were no purchases or sales of either building or other fixed assets.

Solution.

Statement of Cash Flow

(for the year ended 31st December, 1996)

Sources of Cash	Amount Rs.	Application of Cash	Amount Rs.
Opening Cash Balance	80,000	Loss from Trading Operation	8,000
Add: Cash in flow		Addition of Stock	10,000
Decrease in Debtors	6,000	Decrease in Bills Payable	8,000
Sale of Machinery		Closing balance of Cash	60,000
	86,000		86,000

Working Notes—

1. Net loss for the year 1996		Rs.
Capital at the end		12,30,000
Capital at the beginning		14,78,000
		2,48,000

2. Cash lost in Operation/Trading loss from Operation

		Rs.
Net loss for 1996		2,48,000
Less: Non-Cash Charges	Rs.	
(i) Depreciation on Building (2,00,000 – 1,60,000)	40,000	
(ii) Depreciation on Other Fixed Assets (12,00,000 – 10,00,000)	2,00,000	2,40,000
		8,000

Illustration.

The following are two balance sheets relating to the years 1992 and 1993 and Profit and Loss Appropriation Account for 1993 of M/s Golden Jaipur Ltd. Prepare the Cash Flow Statement for the year ended 31st Dec. 1993.

Balance Sheet of Golden Jaipur as on 31st March

Liabilities	*1992 Rs.*	*1993 Rs.*	*Assets*	*1992 Rs.*	*1993 Rs.*
Share capital	5,00,000	6,00,000	Fixed Assets	10,00,000	11,20,000
Reserves	1,50,000	1,80,000	Less dep.	3,70,000	4,60,000
Profit & Loss A/c	40,000	65,000	Written off	6,30,000	6,60,000
Debentures	3,00,000	2,50,000	Stock in trade	2,40,000	3,70,000
Creditors for goods	1,70,000	1,60,000	Book Debts	2,50,000	3,30,000
Provision for Income-tax	60,000	80,000	Cash in hand and at bank	80,000	60,000
			Preliminary Exp.	20,000	15,000
	12,20,000	13,35,000		12,20,000	13,35,000

Profit & Loss Appropriation Account

	Rs.		Rs.
To Transfer to Reserves	30,000	By Balance b/d	40,000
To Dividend paid	80,000	By Net profit	1,35,000
To Balance c/d	65,000		
	1,75,000		1,75,000

Solution.

(i) Calculation of profit from operations:

	Rs.
Result of Trading operations	1,35,000
Add: Non cash changes:	
Depreciation written off during the year	90,000
Preliminary Expenses written off	5,000
Provision of tax	80,000
Profit from operations	3,10,000

(ii) Calculation of cash from opoerations:

	Rs.	*Rs.*
Profit from operations		3,10,000
Add: Decrease in current Assets:		
Sundry debtors		20,000
		3,30,000
Less: Decrease in current liabilities:		
Sundry creditors	10,000	
Less: Increase in current Assets:		
Stock-in-trade	1,30,000	1,40,000
Cash from Operation		1,90,000

Statement of Cash Flow

	Rs.	*Rs.*
Cash Balance, March 31, 1991		80,000
Add: Inflow of cash:		
Cash from operations	1,90,000	
Issue of shares	1,00,000	2,90,000
Total cash available for use		3,70,000
Less: Outflows of cash:		
Repayment of Debentures	50,000	
Fixed Assets acquired	1,20,000	
Dividend paid	80,000	
Income Tax paid	60,000	3,10,000
Cash Balance, March 31, 1993		60,000

Illustration.

The following are the Balance Sheets of M/s Usha Fibers Private Ltd. as on March 31, 1993 and 1994. Prepare a statement of cash flow.

Liabilities	*1993* *Rs.*	*1994* *Rs.*	*Assets*	*1993* *Rs.*	*1994* *Rs.*
12% Redeemable preference shares	—	1,000	Fixed Assets	4,100	4,000
Equity shares	4,000	4,000	*Less:* Depreciation	1,100	1,500
General Reserve	200	200		3,000	2,500
P & L A/c	100	120	Debtors	2,000	2,400
Debentures	600	700	Stock	3,000	3,500
Creditors	1,200	1,100	Prepaid Expenses	30	50
Provision for Taxation	300	420	Cash	120	350
Proposed Dividend	500	580			
Bank overdraft	1,250	680			
	8,150	8,800		8,150	8,800

Solution.

Cash Flow Statement

(year ending 31st March, 1994)

		Rs.	*Rs.*	*Rs.*
Opening Balance as on 1/1/1993			120	
Bank ovderdraft			(–) 1,250	(–) 1,130
Add:	Sources of Cash			
	Issue of Preference Shares			1,000
	Issue of Debentures			100
	Sale of Fixed Assets			100
	Cash from operations:			
Less:	Increase in Debtors	400	1,420	
	Increase in Stock	500		
	Increase in pre-paid expenses	20		

	Decrease in creditors	100	1,020	400
				470
Less:	Applications			
	Payments of tax	300		
	Payment of dividend	500		(–) 800
	Cash Balance			(–) 330
	Represented by:			
	Cash in Hand	350		
	Bank overdraft	(–) 680		(–) 330

Working Notes:

Dr. Adjusted P & L Account Cr.

	Rs.		*Rs.*
To Depreciation	400	By Balance b/d	100
To Proposed dividend	580	By Funds from operations	1,420
To Provision for Tax	420	(Balance Figure)	
To Balance c/d	120		
	1,5,200		1,5,200

Illustration.

From the following information you are required to prepare a cash flow statement of J.P. Cement Ltd. for the year ended 31st Dec. 1993:

Balance Sheet

Liabilities	*1992*	*1993*	*Assets*	*1992*	*1993*
	Rs.	*Rs.*		*Rs.*	*Rs.*
1			*2*		
Share Capital	70,000	70,000	Plant & Mach.	50,000	91,000
Secured loans	—	40,000	Inventory	15,000	40,000
(Repayable in 1997)					

Contd.

1			*2*		
Creditors	14,000	39,000	Debtors	5,000	20,000
Tax payable	1,000	3,000	Cash	20,000	7,000
P & L A/c	7,000	10,000	Prepaid Gen. Exps.	2,000	4,000
	92,000	1,62,000		92,000	1,62,000

Profit and Loss Account

(year ended 31st Dec. 1993)

	Rs.		*Rs.*
To opening Inventory	15,000	By closing inventory	40,000
To purchases	98,000	By Sales	1,00,000
To Gross profit c/d	27,000		
	1,40,000		1,40,000
To General Expenses	11,000	By Gross Profit b/d	27,000
To Depreciation	8,000		
To Taxes	4,000		
To Net profit c/d	4,000		
	27,000		27,000
To Dividend	1,000	By Balance b/d	7,000
To Balance c/d	10,000	By Net profit b/d	
	11,000		11,000

Solution.

Cash Flow Statement

	Rs.	*Rs.*
Cash Balance as on 1.1.1993		20,000
Add: Sources		
Raising of loans		40,000
Less: Applications:		
Plant & Machinery purchased	49,000	

Dividend paid	1,000	
Operations	1,000	
Tax paid	2,000	53,000
Cash Balance as on 31.12.1993		7,000

Working Notes:

(1) Cash From Operations

	Rs.	Rs.
Net profit as per P & L A/c		4,000
Add: Provision for Tax		4,000
Increase in creditors		25,000
Depreciation		8,000
		41,000
Less: Increase in inventory	25,000	
Increase in Debtors	15,000	
Increase in Prepaid Expenses	2,000	42,000
Cash outflow on account of operation		1,000

(2) Tax Payable Account

	Rs.		Rs.
To Bank	2,000	By Balance b/d	1,000
To Balance c/d	3,000	By P & L Account	4,000
	5,000		5,000

(3) Plant & Machinery Account

	Rs.		Rs.
To Balance b/d	50,000	By Depreciation	8,000
To Balance (Purchase)	3,000	By Balance c/d	91,000
	99,000		99,000

Illustration.

Following are the comparative balance sheets of M/s Gopal Ram Co. Ltd. on 31st Dec.

Liabilities	*1994* *Rs.*	*1995* *Rs.*	*Assets*	*1994* *Rs.*	*1995* *Rs.*
Share Capital	10,00,000	11,00,000	Goodwill	50,000	40,000
Debentures	5,00,000	3,00,000	Land & Building	4,20,000	6,60,000
General Reserves	2,00,000	2,00,000	Plant & Machinery	6,00,000	8,00,000
Profit & Loss A/c	1,10,000	1,90,000	Closing Stock	2,50,000	2,10,000
Trade creditors	50,000	49,000	Debtors	3,00,000	2,40,000
Bills Payable	20,000	30,000	Cash	3,00,000	24,000
Provisions for b/d	30,000	24,000	Preliminary Exps.	30,000	20,000
	19,50,000	19,94,000		19,50,000	19,94,000

Additional Information:

(a) During the year, a part of machinery costing Rs. 7,500 (accumulated depreciation thereon being Rs. 2,500) was sold for Rs. 3,000.

(b) Dividend of Rs. 1,00,000 was paid during the year ended 31st Dec. 1995.

(c) Income-tax Rs. 50,000 was paid during the year 1995.

(d) Depreciation for year 1995 was provided as follows:

Land and Building	Rs. 10,000
Plant & Machinery	Rs. 50,000

You have to prepare

(i) Schedule of changes in working capital,

(ii) Fund Flow Statement,

(iii) Cash Flow Statement.

Solution.

Schedule of Change in working capital

	1994	*1995*	*Increase in w.c.*	*Decrease in w.c.*
	Rs.	*Rs.*	*Rs.*	*Rs.*
Current Assets				
Debtors	3,00,000	2,40,000		60,000
Stock	2,50,000	2,10,000		40,000
Cash	3,00,000	24,000		2,76,000
Current Liabilities				
Trade creditors	50,000	40,000	10,000	
Bills payable	20,000	30,000		10,000
Prov. for Bad Debts	30,000	24,000	6,000	
			16,000	3,86,000
Decrease in W.C.			3,70,000	
			3,86,000	3,86,000

Profit & Loss A/c (Adjusted)

		Rs.		Rs.
To Loss on sale on machine		2,000	By Balance b/d	1,10,000
To Preliminary Expenses written off		3,000	By Profit during the year (Funds from operation)	3,82,000
To Goodwill written off		10,000		
To Dividends		1,00,000		
To Provision for tax*		1,20,000		
To Depreciation				
Land & Building	10,000			
Plant & Machinery	50,000	60,000		
To Balance c/d		1,90,000		
		4,92,000		4,92,000

Provision for Taxation A/c*

	Rs.		Rs.
To Tax paid	50,000	By Balance b/d	40,000
To Balance c/d	3,000	By P & L A/c	1,20,000
		(Balance of figure)	
	1,60,000		1,60,000

Plant & Machinery A/c

	Rs.		Rs.
To Balance b/d	6,00,000	By Cash A/c	3,000
To Cash A/c (Purchases	2,55,000	By P & L A/c	2,000
during the year)		By Depreciation A/c	50,000
		By Balance c/d	8,00,000
	8,55,000		8,55,000

Land & Building A/c

	Rs.		Rs.
To Balance b/d	4,20,000	By Depreciation A/c	10,000
To Cash A/c	2,50,000	By Balance A/c	6,60,000
(Purchases during the year)			
	6,70,000		6,70,000

Goodwill A/c

	Rs.		Rs.
To Balance b/d	50,000	By P & L A/c	10,000
		(Balancing figure)	
		By Balance c/d	40,000
	50,000		50,000

Fund Flow Statement

(Year ended 1st December, 1995)

Sources	*Rs.*	*Uses*	*Rs.*
Issue of Shares	1,00,000	Redemption of Debenture	2,00,000
Sale of Machinery	3,000	Income tax paid	50,000
Funds from operation	3,82,000	Dividend paid	1,00,000
Decrease in working capital	3,70,000	Purchase of Land & Building	2,50,000
		Purchase of Machines	2,55,000
	8,55,000		8,55,000

(c) For Cash Flow Statement, first calculate cash from operations.

Cash from Operations

	Rs.	*Rs.*
Profit during the year		3,82,000
Add: Decrease in current Assets & increase in current Liabilities:		
Closing stock	40,000	
Debtors	60,000	
Bills Payable	10,000	1,10,000
		4,92,000
Less: Increase in current Assets & decrease in current liabilities		
Provision for Bad Debts	6,000	
Trade Creditors	10,000	16,000
Cash from operations		4,76,000

Cash Flow Statement

	Rs.		*Rs.*
Cash Balance on 31.12.94	3,00,000	Payment of dividends	1,00,000
Add: Cash from operations	4,76,000	Payment of tax	50,000
Issue of shares	1,00,000	Repayment of Debentures	2,00,000
Sale of Machinery	3,000	Purchase of Land & Building	2,50,000
		Purcahse of Plant of Mach.	2,55,000
			8,55,000
		Closing balance on 31.12.95	24,000
	8,79,000		8,79,000

Illustration.

Balance sheets of M/c A and B as on 1st January, 1991 and on 31st December, 1991 are as follows:

Liabilities	*1.1.91*	*31.12.91*	*Assets*	*1.1.91*	*31.12.91*
	Rs.	*Rs.*		*Rs.*	*Rs.*
Capital	1,50,000	1,90,000	Cash	20,000	26,000
MRs B's Loan	30,000	—	Debtors	54,000	76,000
Loan from SBI	60,000	80,000	Stock	48,000	42,000
Sundry Creditors	50,000	56,000	Furniture	2,000	2,000
			Machinery	90,000	65,000
			Land	36,000	45,000
			Building	40,000	70,000
	2,90,000	3,26,000		2,90,000	3,26,000

During the year a machine costing Rs. 12,00 (accumulated deprecitation Rs. 4000) was sold for Rs. 5,500. The provision of depreciation against machinery as on 1st Jan. 1991 was Rs. 24,000 and on 31st Dec. 1991 Rs. 37,000. Net profit for the year 1991 amonuted to Rs. 60,000. You are required to prepare:

(i) Cash Flow Statement

(ii) Funds Flow Statements

Solution.

(a) Cash Flow Statement

(year ended 31st Dec. 1991)

	Rs.		Rs.
Opening Balance of Cash on 1.1.1991	20,000	Outflow of Cash:	
		Repayment of Mrs. B's loan	30,000
Sources of Cash in flow:			
Loan from SBI	20,000	Increase in Debtors	22,000
Increase in Sundry Creditors	6,000	Purchase of Land	9,000
Decrease in Stock	6,000	Purchase of building	30,000
Sale of machine	5,000	Drawings	20,000
Operating profit (including cash items)	79,500	Cash Balance 31.12.1991	26,000
	1,37,000		1,37,000

Workings Notes:

	Rs.
Operating Profit (including non-fund/cash items)	
Net profit for the year (as given)	60,000
Add: Non fund/Cash & non-operating items:	
Depreciation on machinery	17,000
Loss on sale of machinery	2,500
	79,500
Deprecation on Machinery	
Accumulated depreciation on 1.1.1991	24,000

Less: Depreciation on machinery		4,000
	Sold during year	20,000
	Accumulated depreciation at the end *i.e.* 31.12.1991	37,000
	Depreciation provided during the year	17,000
Drawings:		
	Capital on 1.1.1991	1,50,000
Add: Profit for the year		60,000
		2,10,000
Less: Capital at the end of the year 31.12.1991		1,90,000
	Drawings	20,000

(b) Schedule of Change in Working Capital

	1.1.91	*31.12.91*	*Increase in work cap.*	*Decrease in work cap.*
	Rs.	*Rs.*	*Rs.*	*Rs.*
Current Assets				
Cash	20,000	24,000	6,000	—
Debtors	54,000	76,000	22,000	—
Stock	48,00	42,000	—	6,000
	1,24,00	1,44,00		
Current Liabilities				
Sundry creditors	50,000	56,000		6,000
	50,000	56,000		
Working Capital	72,000	88,000		
Net increase in working capital	16,000			
	88,000	80,000	28,000	28,000

Fund Flow Statement

Sources	*Amount Rs.*	*Application*	*Amount Rs.*
Loan from SBI	20,000	Repayment of Mrs. B's loan	30,000
Sale of machine	5,500	Purchase of land	9,000
Funds from operation	79,500	Puchase of Building	30,000
		Drawings	21,000
		Net increase in W.C.	16,000
	1,05,000		1,05,000

❐

11

Reporting to Management

The success of a business depends on proper flow of information from lower levels to middle levels and from middle levels to higher levels of management. As a matter of fact, information is the life blood of business. The management would be able to function more efficiently and effectively in the information channel is so smooth and productive that it gets the desired information in time, for action. It is a matter of correct, timely, so to say prompt and to-the-point reporting which matters. In case the information in the form of reports is not submitted to management regularly, management find itself handicapped in taking follow-up actions. Besides, decisions can not be taken until and unless the past achievements are known and compared with the budgets and standards laid down. The variations reported to management provide significant material not only for corrective action but also for future decision accounting.

The increasing need for submitting information to management is stressed in NAA research series No.28 (NAA Bulletin, Volume-36).

> 'As an organisation grows, management must rely to a greater extent upon information complied, summarised and interpreted by the accounting department and other specialised functional groups in the company. Modern techniques for collecting, focusing and transmitting information to management have had an important place in making possible the efficient operation of large organizations needed to utilise the advances in scientific and engineering knowledge for producing better and less costly products. Even in small companies some systematic plan for collecting and presenting

> financial information is essential because management cannot personally observe and organise all the facts with respect to sales, costs and other aspects of a company's operations,"

Verbal communication in business is not of great use since one is likely to forget whatever is told to him. Even in small organisations oral reporting is not encouraged, though it cannot be avoided all through. Sometimes, when time is the essence of decision-making, oral communication is at once desired by top management which may be followed by written communication later reports are communications of such facts which are essential to be brought to the notice of management so as to enable it to take appropriate actions. A report can be called as a formal communication moving in the upwar direction. "Reporting", in the strict sense, is distinct from 'communication'. Communication is referred reporting. Reports submitted to management according to the responsibilities assigned will definitely be more useful in placing accountability by the management on different persons.

To as flow of orders from superiors to their subordinates. Reporting, generally, refers to the flow of information from subordinates to their superiors. Thus orders are 'communicated' while results are 'reported'.

The term 'reporting to management' refers to the formal system whereby relevant information is constantly fed to the management through reports. In large organisations, a separate management information division is established for the purpose. The management information system is founded on sound scientific principles so that proper functioning of the various departments is ensured. The reports may take the shape of statements, accounts, charts, graphs etc. The importance of reporting will be more and more, as and as the size of the business grows. Besides, the complexity of business operations also impel management to enforce a proper system of flow of information. The periodicity of reporting may, however, differ from concern to concern and even within a concern from one level to the other and from one department to the other.

Different levels of management need information of different types at different time intervals. The system of reporting should be such as to satisfy the informational needs of management fully. According to Lewis, "in a good and effective report, each reported fact is in some way related to the authority vested in a single individual or group of individuals. In other words, the reported fact relates to a specific action or a related series of actions which are regarded as the responsibility of a specific individual and the organisation reporting to him. Not only does the report show the present situation but it also reveals the trend or movement, favourable or unfivourable, over a period of time, By showing the projected future operation, which may be done as an extension of existing trends, the report reveals the potential development of unsatisfactory operations. In this way the need for corrective action is indicated before operations have actually turned seriously out of line. Corrective steps are then taken as a preventive measure. This is the essence of control through good reporting."

Hence reporting is a management tool for planning, coordination, control as well as decision making—all the functions which management has to perform are assisted by this significant tool. Reporting can be called as an important output of accounting function. Accountant is the custodian of factual data regarding cost, sales and profits therefore he provides a useful information service. Reporting, however, is a specialised function, for which a proper system is to be developed. Management reporting system is an organised method of providing each manager with all the data and only those data which he needs for his decisions, when he needs them and in a form which aids his understanding and stimulates he action. Effective reporting will take into account the requirements of different managerial personnel the concept of responsibility accounting may be used with advantage in a system of effective.

Objects of Reporting

The primary object of reporting to management is to reach sound judgments on the basis of operating results. Another object, which is closely allied to this and is important in terms of efficiency, morale and motivation, is to secure understanding and acceptance of the judgment by the people engaged in various aspects of the work of the enterprise. However, the latter purpose lies in the twilight zone between psychology, sociology, semantics, speech, language and graphic arts, as also newly evolving fields of organization theory, group dynamics and human relations. Though these disciplines are important for the purpose of reporting; they can only by touched briefly, wherever necessary, in the consideration of the subject in management.

GENERAL PRINCIPLES OF REPORTING

These principles are a series of generalizations to be applied to the different levels of administrative authority. Reporting should be prompt, it should present a comparison of actual facts with a norm of performance: it should be consistent; and, finally, it should be simple. Thus, the general characteristics of good reporting are:

1. Simplicity. Another requirement of reporting, simplicity, means the presentation of operating information in a clear manner by the elimination of extraneous data, the use of facts rather than quasi-interpretations and the use of graphs instead of statistical arrays whenever feasible. As is commonly understood, it does not mean the slurring over of details in much as details are necessary for proper management. Presentation of information in a clear manner requires exact and simple definitions of financial terms, precise use of technical terms and careful summarization of operating results. Simplicity of reporting especially for top-management, can be attained by ruthless elimination of extraneous data through the use of schedules, or through the preparation of separate reports, dealing with the extraneous matters. The use of graphic devices, specially makes it possible to indicate trends, or deviations from established goals, in a more striking form than is possible either by tabulation or narration though editorial comments also sometimes highlight the figures given in reports. The use of facts rather than quasi-interpretations, assists an operating executive by supplying him with hard facts based on books of accounts which can be used as guide to executive action.

There is another dimension to simplicity—readability—which is deemed to be of paramount importance. A non-accountant, and sometimes even an accountant, may overlook vital facts regarding operations if the figures are presented merely in a long column. The rounding off the figures to a significant point also aids in readability. Therefore, paisas are irrelevant and can be dropped off while, in large companies, even hundreds are approximated. The length of the report contributes much to readability. The report must, of course, be long enough to cover all significant points but not so long as it fails to sustain interest.

2. Consistency. Closely connected with the principle of comparison in reporting is the attribute of consistency because, without it, there cannot be any proper comparisons. Consistency envisages the presentation of the same information as between different reporting periods. It is also necessary to present information in a consistent manner to the various operating levels of management because, too often, the same statistical data are complied in different ways for the upper and lower management levels. In order to achieve consistency, information embodied in the report should emanate from a common source. Then, the person being reported on should have the same information as the executive to whom he reports. Thus, the upper levels of management need summaries of departmental performances which must agree with the details of the departmental reports.

3. Comparison. A report should enable some comparisons to be effected. This is possible only when the information contained in the report is placed in some perspective and time is by far the most important factor providing such a perspective. Thus comparisons are generally effected over time as well as with a norm of performance. Time comparisons, such as current month, last month and the same month last year disclose trends and highlight deviations needing attention. The determination of seasonal and secular trend, which is another aspect of the time perspective, permits prediction. Comparisons with the past, however, imply that past performance is being taken as the standard for judging the present but this is not necessarily true as objective, methods and business conditions never remain static.

4. Consideration of Cost. The cost of maintaining a system of reporting must be commensurate with the benefits derived therefrom so that the system may be able to earn its keep and may not become an unnecessary drag on the resources of an undertaking.

5. Dovetailing of Reporting and Responsibility. As every report must be directed to a control point in order that an appropriate response can be produced, it becomes necessary that it must be addressed to a responsibility centre and must contain a message about events controllable at that point. A serious problem of reporting lies in tailing the message content to a responsibility centre, at the same time permitting information pertaining to one level of responsibility to appear as details for a higher level of responsibility. Inasmuch as control reports are prepared periodically from routine procedures, the nature of the details must be preserved for special summaries, either in the underlying document evidencing the event recorded (pay roll summaries, sales slips, etc.) or by detailed entries in the ledgers, which can be extracted for particular reporting purposes. To illustrate, whereas total direct labour, direct material and burden cost may be accumulated in individual ledger accounts and combined for inventory valuation purposes, control reports for assembly department may reflect only the material, labour and burden costs controllable by the assembly department foremen.

6. Timing and Frequency of Presentation. The frequency of routine reports is dependent upon a number of factors which must be considered separately for each report. First, the frequency with which the information is needed by the recipient particularly having regard to the effective action which may result from it is important. Secondly, there is the natural time cycle of the basic data from which the report is prepared: invoices, for example, are frequently handled on a monthly basis. Lastly, the cost of preparing the report not only in terms of money but also the time of available staff must be weighed, against possible benefits. It will be a good idea if the person receiving the report is also told of the cost of preparing it.

The time required for preparation should be reduced to the minimum, for routine reports, the period should be known, agreed and adhered to rigidly. It is a waste of time and effort to prepare information which is too late to be of use and interest, of greater importance is the fact that the absence of information at the time when it is needed may mean either wrong decisions, or deferment of decision on matters which may be urgent, or even a complete failure to realise that action is necessary.

The need for speed cannot, however, be overstated. Statistics of actual performance, for example, are inevitably "history", no matter how promptly presented, and they would be too late to effect the performance. It must be remembered that the purpose of such information is often to supplement the personal qualities and facilities of management, never to replace them. Demands for unreasonable speed in presentation must never be allowed to cover up a failure to exercise proper care in supervision or to conceal absence of a normal degree of intelligence in anticipation.

Information collected and prepared in advance of action is of great value. Hence the importance of budgets. A great advantage of budgetary methods of control is that full and unhurried consideration of probable performance is made possible before the event.

As far as possible, on grounds of courtesy and diplomacy, copies should be presented simultaneously to all recipients.

7. Brevity. Reports should be so constituted as to require a minimum of time both in preparation and, more, particularly, in consideration. The complexities of present day management and the demands made on important executives are such that there is rarely time available for a detailed study of voluminous reports and statistics. Reports should, therefore, be as brief as is consistent with pertinence and clarity. The form should be such that salient points are immediately apparent—summary results should stand out to catch the eye first. The aim should be to produce a precise and concise statement, which leaves nothing unsaid that should be said, an nothing stated beyond that which is required to present a clear-cut picture of the mater being reported. "Padding" and verbose expressions must be avoided at all costs. Some executives have the rule that a report submitted to them must not exceeed one page—it may be supported by schedules but otherwise it must be complete.

The principle of exception-whereby reports are to a substantial degree limited to events which show variance from a predetermined plan by more than a given margin—enables consideration to be concentrated on those items most likely to require attention and action. Economy is effected in the amount of information presented.

It is sometimes recommended that information presented should be restricted to matters which are under the control of the recipient in each case, to allow concentration on essentials and to reduce the volume of reports and statistics to the minimum. It is considered, however, that this principle can be applied only to a limited extent. To allow each section of the undertaking to make its maximum contribution towards the common purpose to promote co-operation between departments and to preserve flexibility in organisation, it is essential that every person concerned in management should be provided not only with information bearing directly on his own department, but also with a certain amount of information on the work of related departments and of the undertaking as a whole.

8. Accuracy. Information should be as accurate as possible, subject to the following considerations:

(a) The purpose of there port may not require a high degree of accuracy. For example, it commonly happens that information is required on past performance for use only as a guide to the future. Under such circumstances, absolute accuracy at all points may be pointless.

(b) Clarity will be improved if unnecessary details (for example, paise when dealing with large sums) are suppressed.

(c) Accuracy should not involve an excessive cost of preparation, nor should it be achieved at the sacrifice of promptness in presentation.

9. Coordination of Statistics. It is important that all statistical information circulating in an organisation should have a sound basis, and that the figures used in and by different departments should be properly coordinated. Where unrelated or uncoordinated sets of figures are used, errors and misunderstand dings are bound to arise, confidence is lessened, and it is unlikely that full and effective use will be made of the information available.

For example, figures relating to orders on hand are frequently arrived at by accumulating quantities, weights or values of orders received and deducting those of orders despatched. Before the orders are executed, its exact quantity, weight or value may not be known and estimated figures may be used. If, on its subsequent despatch, actual quantity, weight or value is deducted from the orders on hand figures, the latter will contain a small error or difference. If such an error arises on every order; the total difference may eventually be considerable and may make the figures of orders on hand substantially inaccurate.

A problem such as this can be overcome by anyone of several methods. But if each department is left to find its own solution, it is unlikely that the same method will be used by all departments, and different treatments will result in different figures. The principle should be that figures and statistics used in all divisions and at all levels should be soundly based and perfectly related, and should appear in summary form in the reports rendered to general management. This will be achieved only if one person, preferably the accountant or budget officer, is made responsible for defining the detailed methods and principles by which the figures are to be prepared.

10. Elimination of Redundant Reports. A constant watch must be maintained with a view to eliminating reports which have become redundant, and to making revisions necessitated by changing conditions.

It is sometimes found that the submission at regular intervals of statistical reports in standardised forms results in a progressively declining interest on the part of recipients, and staleness develops. Where it is known that no use is being made of the information presented, the form, content, timing, and all other circumstances should be immediately investigated. Even to discontinue the report altogether may be useful.

11. Promptness. The importance of promptness in reporting cannot be over-stressed. It means that the report must be prepared and issued before it becomes ancient history. There are cases where promptness in presentation is more important than any other of the general principles of reporting. As business executives need quick reports to carry on day-to-day operations, very often the choice is between furnishing incomplete, and possibly incorrect data, in time or waiting until the veracity of information is verified. In cases where complete information is not required for indicating trends, reliability is sometime sacrificed for speed in reporting. In order to achieve promptness accounting executives can often improve their methods of collecting data thereby increasing the speed with which final information becomes available. Following are some of the ways in which accounting processes might be accelerated:

(a) Establishment of a record-keeping system tailored to the report requirements.

(b) Use of mechanical accounting devices to avoid clerical error and to increase productivity.

(c) Departmentalization of accounting work to prevent bottlenecks in reporting.

(d) Training of employees to report extraordinary conditions when they are first observed.

12. Adaptability. The form and content of the report should, as far as possible, be suited to the person using it, the purpose for which it is required, and the possible action which may ensue. The merit of reporting lies in varied presentations to suit the temperament and outlook of the different individuals who occupy managerial positions—though the subject-matter conveyed is in no way distorted. The contents of a report should be well planned. In this regard the following points have general application:

(a) a statement of the terms of reference for the report;

(b) the findings; and

(c) recommendation or action to be taken.

The general style, layout, the wording should be as simple as possible; effectiveness of a report is often dependent on the style, layout, etc. Graphic forms of presentation are deservedly popular. They are suited or the illustration of composition and trends, they allow a quick but broad appreciation of the facts which they portray. These advantages are well known: any textbook on statistics will deal with them.

Consideration should also be given to the manner in which the report will eventually be filled. Each routine report should have its standard size and shape. Where an unusual size or shape cannot be avoided, it may be helpful to present the report in or with a suitable file. Such measures, encourage recipients to keep the reports so that they are readily available for immediate reference.

USE OF REPORTS BY MANAGEMENT

The importance of the system of 'Reporting to Management' lies in the fact that it enables the management to 'feel the pulse of the undertaking' as it is sometimes called. There might be occasions when a particular report does not meet the requirements in a manner as is expected of it. Upon the emergence of such a situation, the report is either scrapped or readjusted to the needs. Thus the system of reporting is not static but is in a state of continuous development.

A good reporting system is a sensitive instrument in the hands of management keeping continuous record of the course of operations and giving instant warning in case anything untoward or unusual occurs. This makes the employees feel that their work is constantly brought to the attention of management which in its own turn, feels that it can rely on the reporting system to give notice of any need for its intervention. In this way high-level management is left free to devote its undivided attention to questions of over all policy and future development.

The usefulness of reporting system to management falls broadly into two categories—future planning and review of past performances. Reports dealing with forecast of conditions, under which planned operations would be carried opt, are of great use in deciding on future policy. This applies to budgets, estimates on the production of single products or product lines and forecast of business conditions in general. As regards the problem of capital outlay, the reporting system is relied on to provide estimates of savings or profits which serve as a guide for investments. Reports also provide a useful basis for deciding operating policy, volume of sales or production, sale prices, qualities, design, production methods, stock policy etc.

Current reports enable management at all levels to keep itself abreast of past performance as well as developments and it can keep a check on individual operating levels. These reports furnish the answers to questions which are frequently arising: 'What happened and where?' 'Who was responsible?' 'Why did things develop as they did?' The last question lies, by and large, outside the purview of accounting because it is affected by a number of factors not susceptible to accounting treatment. However, despite this deficiency of accounting technique, the report must include acceptable explanations for the people on the job. It is important to realize that reports and reporting methods are not in themselves, a control. They are intended to provide executives with a factual basis for the execution of their duties. The fact to be stressed is that it is not the writer of reports who establishes policy, the report writer establishes and interprets facts from which policies are developed by operating executives.

Reports classified on the basis of reporting can be routine reports or special reports.

(A) Routine Reports. This reports submitted to different levels management as per a fixed time schedule regularly are known as routine reports. These are not to be submitted on the happening of a particular event but are to be presented to the management as per a part of the system of everyday reporting.

A schedule may be prepared in advance indicating.

(i) Sources of data and the date by which the data should be ready at the respective sources.

(ii) The respective dates on which the manuscripts and the report are to be sent.

(iii) The recipients of the report and its copies.

(iv) The periodicity of reporting.

(v) Tilte of the report.

The preformation of such reports may be cyclostyled or printed as per the requirements of the business. The blank columns may be filed in on regular intervals as fixed beforehand.

(B) Special Reports. The reports submitted to management, not in periodic intervals regularly but, on specific occasions as per the requirements are known as special reports. They may be either called for by the management or may have become essential to be submitted on account of business exigencies. Special staff might have to be employed forpreparing such reports. Examples of some of the special reports are as under:

(i) A report on cost reduction scheme may be submitted by the cost accountant.

(ii) New product has come up in the market in competition—Board of Directors may call for a special report on the subject.

(iii) The market demand is receding—marketing manager may submit a report to this effect.

(iv) General Manager has received a complaint as regards theft of raw material from stores—he may call for a special report for the purpose from the stores department.

(v) A problem has cropped up in purchase of materials—purchase department may submit a special report for the purpose.

Industrial engineering, marketing, etc. Matters which may require treat men in special reports may be as follows:

(a) Reports by consultants and outside advisers on financial, commercial and management problems including recommendations by auditors.

(b) Reports by the secretary on company matters and legal obligations.

(c) Important matters revealed by the costing system and the results in terms of costs of contemplated alternative lines of action.

(d) Industrial relations.

(e) Trade association matters.

(f) Taxation.

(g) Wages and other cost connected with labour.

(h) Patent rights and changes in patent laws.

(i) Technological developments in the industries which may offer competition.

(j) Comparative performance and costs of existing production plan and more up-to-date equipments.

(k) Information about competitive products.

(l) Materials-reports by the purchase department on purchasing problems and by the cost accountant on the implications of price movement.

(m) Results of market analysis and sales research including methods of distribution, attitudes and possible moves by competitors.

(n) Political and economic developments at home and abroad.

The following illustration in respect of a special report would serve, *(a)* to understand the format of such reports, and *(b)* to familiarise to student with decisions of the sort discussed.

Illustration.

The Managing Director and majority shareholders of X Ltd. have asked your opinion as an accountant on a best course of action to be taken in the following circumstances:

The company has a fully owned subsidiary, Y Ltd. which is run efficiently and the shares were acquired in a boom period. The subsidiary supplies specialized components to the holding company at current rates. Owning to the fall inprices and the writing down of company's assets at market the rate of Rs. 7,00,000 a year the company has been showing losses recently at an average of Rs. 4,20,000 a year. As no foreseeable change in market conditions is likely, the position is expected to continue and closing down of the company has been contemplated.

Y Ltd. has now received the offer of a long-term contract for the supply of certain components to the value of Rs. 7,50,000 annually, the additional cost of production being estimated at Rs. 4,50,000. At the same time an outlay of Rs. 10,00,000 would be required for additional working capital and machinery. The offer of the contract is not considered by the board of the holding company to be acceptable since an estimated loss of Rs. 1 ,20,000 a year would still be incurred besides the capital outlay required; nevertheless, some hesitation is felt as in effect for Rs. 1 ,20,000 a year the delivery of the specialised components required by the holding company could be assured.

In view of the hesitation of Y Ltd., the company offering the contract has made a further offer to take over the subsidiary on a share exchange basis of Rs.20,00,000 in shares of Rs. 10 quoted at Rs. 34 which is considerably more than what would be obtained in the event of a closing down of the company. The Managing Director has intimated that for personal reasons he would not consider any proposal likely to exceed a period of eight years, he has suggested that cessation of business at the end of that time be assumed, when the assets at present held by Y Ltd., might be sold for Rs.5,00,000. If the company accepted the offer of the contract and acquired the additional assets, the total saleable value of the assets in eight years time would be about . Rs.11 ,00,000. Investments in other companies like Y Ltd., are expected to yield 10% per annum. Relevant figures obtainable from interest tables are:

Present value of Re. 1 in eight years	Re. 0.475
Present value of Re. 1 received annually for eight years	Re. 5.335

You are required to give a preliminary report according to the details supplied

Solution.

REPORT

Address

Date

The Managing Director,

X Limited,

....

Preliminary report on the proposed future policy for Y Limited In accordance with the information supplied in the letter dated have pleasure in submitting my preliminary report as follows:

Present Financial Position of the Company

(a) Losses. The company is at present sustaining average losses of Rs. 4,20,000 per annum with no foreseeable likelihood of improvement. This figure is arrived at after writing down losses on assets of Rs.7,00,000 per annum.

(b) Profit before Writing Down Assets. The profit before writing off losses on assets, *i.e.*, Rs. 2,80,000 (Rs. 7,00,000-Rs. 4,20,000) can be taken as the base. These profits are expected to continue for 8 years. The following courses are open:

(1) ***Sale on a Share Exchange Basis.*** As a sale on cessation of business would bring in considerably less than the offer for purchase as a going concern, the latter would be preferable. Sale would yield a present value of Rs.20,00,000.

(2) ***Continuing Present Operations.*** This is obviously a less profitable course than accepting the long-term contract but is worth considering.

Present value of an income of Rs.2,80,000 per annum	Rs.
for eight years at 10% (2,80,000 × 5.335)	14,93,000
Present worth of saleable value of assets at the end	
of eight years (Rs.5,00,000 × 0.467)	2,33,500
	17,26,500

(3) ***Acceptance of the Long-term Contract.*** If the long-term contract is accepted, the present loss figure might be adjusted as to:

		Rs.
Average annual net loss		4,20,000
Less: Depreciation charge written back:	7,00,000	
Additional net income from the contract	3,00,000	
		10,00,000
Actual income		5,80,000

The present value if this course were adopted would be:

	Rs.
Present value of an income of Rs.5,80,000 per annum for eight years at 10% (5,80,000 × 5.335)	30,94,300

Present worth of saleable value of assets at the end of eight years (Rs. 11,00,000 × 0.467)	5,13,700
	36,08,000
Less: Additional outlay	10,00,000
	26,08,000

Summary:

(a) Sale on share exchange basis	Rs. 20,00,000
(b) Continuance of present operations	Rs. 17,26,500
(c) Continuance of operations on acceptance of long-term contract	Rs. 26,08,000

Recommendation. The most profitable course of action seems to be the acceptance of the long-term contract and, provided the necessary finance can be raised, this course is recommended.

The next most profitable alternative would be the sale on a share exchange basis, but it would then be necessary to get a find assurance that supplies for X Limited would still be forthcoming. Despite the financial attraction of selling out, the company might deem it wiser to continue trading so as to ensure regular supplies.

....

Signature

The point to note is that the data available for the above report had to be specially collected and the report is only preliminary. The data cannot be completely obtained from the accounting system. Nor are such reports pre-pared periodically.

MODES OF REPORTING

Reports are prepared as statements, graphs and/or ratios and formulae.

So for as the statement are concerned, they may deal with anyone or more of the following:

(i) Actuals against budgeted figures.

(ii) Comparative statements for a period of time.

(iii) Statistical analysis of a particular type of expenditure over a period of time.

The information contained in the statements can also be presented by means of graphs which give a better visual view of the data than the long array of figures given in statements.

As regards the ratios, they may be part of a statement prepared for other purposes or may form part of a separate statement for a specific purpose. Ratios are sometimes expressed as percentages also. An illustrative list of different types of ratios and percentages used for the purpose of reporting is given below:

(a) Equity Ratio	Total Assets/Net Worth
(b) Liabilities-to Worth Ratio	Allliabilities/Net Worth or Long-term Debts/Net Worth
(c) Collection Ratio or Receivables Turnover Ratio	Net Credit Sales/Average Receivables
(d) Inventory Turnover Ratio	Cost of Sales/Average/Inventory at Cost or Net Sales/Average Inventory at cost
(e) Current Ratio	Current Assets/Current Liabilities
(f) Opening Ratio	Income Statement items/Net Sales: (i) Gross Profit analysis. (ii) Percentage profit after taxes on turnover. (iii) Precentage profit before taxes on turnover. (iv) Eamings per share. (v) Return on Investment (vi) Time-interest factor.
(g) Working Capital Turnover	Net Sales/working capital
(h) Equity Turnover Ratio	Net SaleslNet Worth

LABOUR COST EFFICIENCY REPORT FOR THE WEEK ENDING......

To Foreman....... Deptt......

Worker		Job Order No.	Operation		Std.	Hrs.		%	Total Cost	
No.	Name		No.	Description	Rate	Actual	Std.	Efficiency	Actual	Std.
Total										

Deptt. Efficiency : This Week........ Remarks by Foreman........

Last Week........

Last Month....... Remarks by Supdtt...........

Prepared by...............Date.............

Checked by...............Date.............

PRODUCTION AND COST STATEMENT FOR THE MONTH............

To : Works Manager

	This Month						Cumulative till date					
	Product A Qty. Produced.... Cost		Product B Qty. Produced.... Cost		Total Cost		Product A Qty. Produced.... Cost		Product B Qty. Produced.... Cost		Total Cost	
	Std. Rs.	Actual Rs.	Std. Rs.	Actual Rs.	Std. Rs.	Actual Rs.	Std. Rs.	Actual Rs.	Std. Rs.	Actual Rs.	Std. Rs.	Actual Rs.
Direct Material												
Direct Labour												
Overheads :												
Fixed												
Variable												
Total												

Variances:

Direct Materials	Rs.	Direct Labour :	Rs.	Overheads :	Rs.
Price	...	Rate	...	Fixed	...
Usgae	...	Efficiency	...	Variable	...
Total	—		—		—

Prepared by...........date.............Copies to 1..........

Checked by...........date...............Copies to 2..........

SALES AND PROFIT STATEMENT FOR THE MONTH OF.............

To : Managing Director

Area & Product	This Month						Cumulative		
	Budget			Actual			Variance		
	Qty.	Sales Amt.	Contribution Rs.	Qty.	Sales Amt.	Contribution Rs.	Qty.	Sales Amt.	Contribution Rs.
North Zone									
Product A									
Product B									
Product C									
Total									
South Zone									
Product A									
Product B									
Product C									
Total									
Total									
Product A									
Product B									
Total									

Total Contribution : Actual Rs.......Budgeted Rs......
Total Fixed Cost Actual Rs.......Budgeted Rs......
Profit Earned before Tax Actual Rs.......Budgeted Rs......

Prepared by...........Date..........Copies to 1
Checked by..........Date.......... 2

Sometimes, formulae are also used to throw light on some aspect of the operations of business, especially the following:

(a) Break-even point.

(b) Return on capital employed.

(c) Proft-volume ratio.

SPECIMEN FORMS OF MANAGEMENT REPORTS

Following are the specimen forms of some of the important management reports to be prepared and submitted regularly to the concerned authorities.

1. COMPARATIVE STATEMENT OF MANAGEMENT RATIOS FOR THE PERIOD ENDED......

Ratio	*Calculation*	*Unit*	*Actual*	*Budgeted*	*Variance (+) or (–)*
Return on Capital employed	$\frac{\text{Profit before tax}}{\text{Capital employed}}$ %				
Net Profit to Sales	$\frac{\text{Profit before tax}}{\text{Sales}}$ %				
Capital Turnover	$\frac{\text{Sales}}{\text{Capital employed}}$ times				
Operating Ratio	$\frac{\text{Operating Costs}}{\text{Sales}}$ %				
Current Ratio	$\frac{\text{Current Assets}}{\text{Current Liabilities}}$ times				
Stock Turnover	$\frac{\text{Cost of Sales}}{\text{Average Stock}}$ times				

DIFFERENT MANAGEMENT LEVELS

I. Reports of the Board of Directors

As the directors are not interested in the day to day management, their primary interest lies in the over-all working of the undertaking as highlignted by the profits. They are, therefore, interested in the profit and loss account as well as the balance sheet of the unit so much so that a monthly profit and loss account and balance sheet is usually given to the board. Over and above these, the following are also submitted to them for their perusal:

(i) The Board also likes to be enlightened in respect of return on capital employed which is very crucial for justifying the rationale of carrying on the business. Calculations are, therefore, made to disclose these figures. Coupled with this is the interest of the Board in certain ratios, like 'gross profit ratio' or 'ratio of overheads to sales', which throw light on the various aspects ofthe conduct of business. This might, in some cases, be carried to its farthest limit in the analysis of the individual heads of expense by placing them in relation to sales.

(ii) Statements giving details in respect of the items of profit and loss account and balance sheet which are, of course, prepared in a form that clearly brings out the comparison with the Master Budget as well as with the figures of the corresponding period in the previous year.

(iii) Statement are given to supplement the information contained in the profit and loss account and the balance sheet in its material particulars. Sometimes, these statements are quite numerous with the result that, in such cases, a small booklet containing a series of statements is prepared for the Board.

(iv) Unlike the prevailing general impression, the Board of Director does not consider cash reports of any special significance because it lies within the province of the Treasurer who carefully controls cash and securities. This centralization of cash management has helped in streamlining the system with the result that adequate finances are available whenever necessary. A study of a number of cases has revealed that the profit and loss account, balance sheet as well as other statistics furnished to the Board of

Directors reach their hands so that they remain of only academic importance because the period to which they refer already passes into history. Consequently, the Board cannot effectively use them as a basis of any action for reversing an unfavourable trend or for fully exploiting a favourable one. In view of this, it is considered expedient to sacrifice accuracy and precision for the sake of ensuring quick submission. Therefore, a certain element of estimation is bound to creep in the reports to the Board.

(v) A short report on the anticipated future results is also furnished to most of the Board of Directors. In case the Board is interested only in long-term plans, as happens in a number of cases, such are port is dispensed with.

(vi) A statement showing the general trend of costs is considered adequate for the Board because its interest in detailed costing is limited. This is done by pointing out the favourable and unfavourable variances from the budget which is based on predetermined costs.

(vii) As expenditure on development and research is generally undertaken under the direct responsibility of central management, and often the Board of Directors, separate reports on this item are sent to the Board.

(viii) Statistics showing the trend of production and sales are given to the Board as the working of an unit is dependent primarily on sales, production and raw materials. These would enable the Board to keep self well-informed of the position regarding availability of raw materials quantum of production, number and value of orders received as well as sales effected.

II. Reports to Top Management

In big companies, where the delegation of responsibility has been pushed to the farthest possible limits, top management acts as a clearing house between the operating divisions and Board of Directors. Generally speaking the reporting at this level is divided into reports for transmission to the Board of Directors and reports to be considered by the top management in respect of which no reference to the Board is necessary. As a number of persons at the central executive level are simultaneously on the Board, there is bound to be some overlapping, for the point of view of reporting, of the functions of central authority and the Board of Directors especially where the Board has more than half of its members from amongst those who belong to the top executive authority.

Being responsible for the performance of their own managerial functions, top executive managements are interested more in the operational side of the undertaking than in the purely financial side. They act as supervisors of and advisors to all divisional or departmental heads. Top management lives up to this role by receiving reports of variances from tile budgeted figures and these are very carefully studied and analysed.

Owing to the fact that the central executive authority is responsible for initiating policy, it has to be advised the Board as to what action should be taken on the reports submitted to it. In all this, greater emphasis is placed on the future than on the past, with the consequence that the report on this level must reflect this emphasis. Thus, budgetary control provides for the periodic ıevision of budgets for immediate future on the basis of past performances so that management may be able to exercise a more effective control. Reporting, in such cases, becomes a judicious blending of comments on past performance and the evaluation of the effect to such performance on future results.

III. Reports For Middle Level Management

Middle level management comprises of the different heads of departments, for example, production manager, sales manager, purchase manager, finance manager, general manager etc. There are a number of officers working under their charge. Middle level managers are accountable to the top management, therefore, they should receive regular information from their juniors as regards the progress of the work done. They are also responsible for taking day-to-day decisions and for the same, they need reports about the performance of their divisions. Thus, to plan, monitor, progress, measure, control and coordinate the different activities within their departments, such managers have to receive constant information.

A list of reports to the submitted to functional managers of the organisation has been presented below, together with the purpose and usual frequency of reporting.

Submitted to Whom	*Description of reports*	*Purpose*	*Frequency*
1. General Sales Manager	(i) Analysis of turnover by: – Products – geographical area – size of orders – distribution channels – salesmen – customer groups.	To compare current performance over time with budgets and/or standards. To identify changes in patterns of sales distribution & product mix.	Daily or Weekly and monthly
	(ii) Analysis of profit margins by products	To monitor actual margins aganist target margins.	Monthly
	(iii) Analysis of selling overheads, department-wise	To compare actuai and budgeted overheads and to exercise control over them.	Monthly
	(iv) Analysis of orders, enquiries and quotations.	To monitor progress of orher procurement.	Monthly
	(v) Summary of stock of finished goods.	To compare actual and budgeted levels of stock & to emamine levels in the light of anticipated demand.	Monthly

Contd.

Submitted to Whom	*Description of reports*	*Purpose*	*Frequency*
	(vi) Age profit of accounts receivable, together with details of bad debts.	To highlight customers requiring particular attention in view of defaults.	Monthly
	(vii) Analysis of customer complaints and sales returns.	To identity corrective action required.	Monthly
	(viii) Market price trends.	General appreciation of market.	Monthly or quarterly
	(ix) Special reports for new product development programmes.	To monitor the progress of new product development against plans.	Whenever needed
2. General Production Manager	(i) Departmental cost statements.	To compare actual performances over time, with budgets and or standards.	Monthly
	(ii) Lost production, by cause, department-wise.	To initiate or approve corrective action.	Daily or weekly and monthly
	(iii) Material usage statement, department wise.	To compare actual and budgeted usage.	Month
	(iv) Analysis of scrap, rectification and sales returns.	To identify significant causes and to effect necessary corrective action.	Monthly
	(v) Statement of pro duction orders and arrears.	To identify problems in scheduling production and the need for action.	Weekly

Contd.

Submitted to Whom		*Description of reports*	*Purpose*	*Frequency*
	(vi)	Statement of Quantity produced and despatched.	To compare actuals with targets.	Daily or weekly and monthly
	(vii)	Work-in-progress stock summary.	To compare actuals with budgets.	Monthly
	(viii)	Labour/plant utilisation report.	To minitor actual performmance against target.	Monthly
	(ix)	Special report for new product development programme.	To monitor the progress of new product development aginst plans.	Whenever needed
3. Research Development Manager	(a)	Departmental overhead cost summary	To compare actual and budgeted costs.	Monthly
	(b)	cost benefit analysis of projects	To provide upto-date evaluation of completed, in-progress and planned research projects.	Monthly
	(c)	Special report for new product development programme.	To monitor the progress of new product development against plans.	Whenever needed
4. Purchase manager	(a)	Material cost statements, departmentwise	To compare actual data over time, with budgets and/or standards.	Monthly
	(b)	Material Price variance report, departmentwise.	To examine the effect of planned purchasing policy and to highlight areas requiring control.	Daily or weekly and/or monthly

Contd.

Submitted to Whom	*Description of reports*	*Purpose*	*Frequency*
	(c) Summary of purchase commitments.	To have a forward approach.	Monthly
	(d) Sock summaries	To compare actual with budgets/standards.	Weekly or monthly
5. Administration Manager	(a) Departmental over hand cost summaries.	To compare actuals with budgets and to effect necessary corrective action.	Monthly
	(b) Responsibility centre staff performance	To compare actual performance against standards and to base control action.	Weekly, monthly or quarterly
	(c) Summary of employees, departmentwise.	To compare ,actual and budgeted data.	Monthly
	(d) Special reports for employees' strike.	To provide management with the reasons and assessment of prossible losses etc.	Whenever needed
	(e) Cost summaries, department-wise.	To identify variances between actual and budgeted data.	Monthly
	(f) Statement of changes in status of employees promotions, transfers, salary increases etc.	To compare actual and planned develoment.	Quarterly
	(g) Statement of employee efficiency-absenteeism labour turnover, productivity, idle time etc.	To monitor the efficiency of empolyes.	Monthly

IV. Operating Supervisors or Junior Management Level

This management level consists of foremen, superintendents, etc. who are interested more in physical performance than anything else.Then, operating supervisors would like to keep themselves abreast of day to day working of the operations under their charge-products manufactured from the material and with the help of labour and facilities under them.

In the context of their needs, specific and detailed reporting is required at the level of direct supervision. Operating supervisors should receive reports concerning the effectiveness of their operation showing planned performance, actual performance, and variations from the plans. In order that operating supervisors may be able to use their reports for the control of future operations, it is necessary that the reports give specific information about the department reported on. To illustrate, it is neither sufficient to tell the foreman of a manufacturing department that his direct labour cost is above the budgeted figure not is it adequate to tell him that his labour cost per unit was 20 per cent above the allowable rate because it throws the burden of analysis and investigation entirely upon the foreman, rather, if the reporting system is designed to show that defective work, rework and added operations caused a twenty per cent increase in direct labour cost, the reporting process has eminently served as a medium for investigation. Thus, reported facts supported by records of rework and scrapped material, provide both the supervising executive and his superior with a factual basis for taking corrective action. It is immaterial from the point of view of the operative executives whether the reports have been converted into money values or not. Apart from these, foreman or superintendent is interested in daily report and may even like to know the position shift by shift.

(A) External Reports

If the users of the report are the outsiders, *i.e.*, the shareholders, creditors, bankers, financial institutions, government etc., the reports are termed as external reports. Annual accounts of the companies are published together with the directors' reports and auditors' reports in the form of annual reports—these are external reports meant for outsiders. Such reports are prepared in accordance with the requirement of law. The provisions of Companies Act govern the preparation and presentation of such annual reports. Strictly speaking, such reports may not be termed as management reports.

(B) Internal Reports

If the users of the Information are the insiders, *i.e.*, managerial personnel at different levels including the board of directors, the reports are called internal reports. The management is free to decide about the size, nature, periodicity and requirements of such reports. It is actually the reporting to management at various levels, which is the point of our primary focus here.

Internal reports may be broadly classified into the following categories:

(i) Reports for top level management.

(ii) Reports for middle level management.

(iii) Reports for lower level management.

(c) Control Reports

If the performance of the person incharge of affairs is reported, it is known as reporting on the basis of responsibility accounting. The report which contains the performance in the manager of a profit centre is known as a control report. Since the top management can exercise control over the business by placing responsibility on the manager in-charge in case he does not perform the job assigned to the satisfaction of his superiors, the report is termed as a control report. A control report should have the following characteristics:

(i) There should be a direct relationship of reports with perssonal responsibility.

(ii) Actual performances must be compared with the available standards. Significant information must be highlighted; reasons for differences between actual and expected performance may also be given.

(D) Financial Reports

Reports which contain information about the financial position of the business may be technically called financial reports. Such reports may be classified as:

(i) ***Static Reports.*** Reports presenting the financial state of affairs of a business as on a particular date are termed as static reports. The balance sheet is a static report.

(ii) ***Dynamic Reports.*** Reports presenting the changes of financial state of affairs during a particular period of time are termed as dynam ic reports. Such reports are, for example, reports maintaining statement of changes in financial position (working capital or cash).

Steps for Effective Reporting

The following steps should be taken to make the reporting effective.

(i) ***Logical Outcome.*** Reporting should be the logical outcome of accounting routine; A detailed planning of flow of paper work and its analysis is required for the purpose.

(ii) ***Avoid Work Duplication.*** Duplication of work should be avoided. The formats of different accounting books should be designed in such a manner that control data is available without additional analysis.

(iii) ***Mechanisation.*** Use of codification and mechanisation would be made on an extensive scale. Reports are expedited on account of use of the system of mechanised accounting.

(iv) ***Timely Closure of Accounts.*** Accounts for a period should be closed well in advance of the end of the period. The point will be clear with the help of an example. Suppose the accounting period expires on 31st of December. The accounts relating total month of December may be closed, say, on 25th of December. The period from 26th of December to 31st of December may be used for data processing and reports may be submitted on 1st of January.

(v) ***Interim Estimates.*** Management may be provided with interim reports in case the actual data are not readily available, Such reports will contain estimates which should be logical and accurate as far as feasible.

ILLUSTRATIVE PROBLEMS

Taking into consideration the characteristics of good report and taking into account the different types of reports going to the different levels of management, the following illustrations of control reports in the foll of problems and solutions have been given.

Essentials of a Good System

The following are the essentials of a good management reporting or information system.

(i) Evaluation of Each Manager's Area of Responsibility. This system should yield information required for the evaluation of each manager's area of responsibility in relation to the goals of the organisation.

(ii) Proper Flow of Information. There should be a proper flow of information. It should flow from the right level of authority to the level of authority where the decisions are to be made. Moreover, complete and consistent information should flow in a systematic manner.

(iii) Proper Form. In order to facilitate decision-making, the information should be supplied in a proper form.

(iv) Proper Time. The system should ensure furnishing of the information at the proper time *i.e.* neither too late, nor too early.

(v) Cost Benefit Analysis. There should be a constant evaluation of the cost incurred in collecting and supplying the information and the benefit derived therefrom.

(vi) Flexibility. The system should be capable of being adjusted according to the requirements of the user.

Management reporting system has now become a specialised function. Large concerns these days have a separate Management

Information. Division. This division may be headed by the Accountant himself or the Management Cost Accountant or Information Manager, depending on the size of the business. However, whosoever may head this division, he must knew not only what information each level of management requires but also regarding the techniques to be employed for collecting, storing, processing and finally communicating the required information to the proper management levels.

QUARTERLY PROFIT MARGIN ESTIMATE.....20....to....20.....

Product	*% on Sales Final Revision*	*Actual realised last quarter*	*April-June*		*July-Sept.*		*Oct.-Dec.*		*Jan.-March*		*Total*
			Revised Forecast	*Actial*	*Revised Forecast*						*Final Revision*
Total											
Less : Overheads [as per 2]											
Less : Contingency											
Net profit before depreciation and development reserve											

Less : Depreciation & Development Reserve

Net Profit before appropation

Less : Loan Interest and Dividends

Taxes

Retained Profit

Prepared by ....

Submitted to ....

Date ....

QUARTERLY SALES ESTIMATE
ESTIMATE.....20....to....20.....

(in'000 rupees)

	April-June		*July-Sept.*		*Oct.-Dec.*		*Jan.-March*		*Total*
Product	*Estimate*	*Actual Deli-veries*	*Revised Estimate*	*Actual Deli-veries*	*Second Estimate*	*Actual Deli-veries*	*Final Revision*	*Actual Deli-veries*	*Final Estimate*

Prepared by ....

Submitted to ....

Date ....

QUARTERLY OVERHEAD EXPENSE
ESTIMATE.....20....to....20.....

(in'000 rupees)

	April-June		*July-Sept.*		*Oct.-Dec.*		*Jan.-March*		*Total*
Product	*Esti-mate*	*Actual paid and incurred*	*Revised Estimate*	*Actual paid and incurred*	*Second Estimate*	*Actual paid and incurred*	*Final Revision*	*Actual paid and incurred*	*Final Estimate*

Prepared by ....

Submitted to ....

Date ....

QUARTERLY ESTIMATED BALANCE SHEET

(in'000 rupees)

	Actual				Estimated		Actual				Estimated
Assets on	*1st Jan.*	*31st March incurred*	*30th June*	*30th Sept. incurred*	*31st Dec.*	*Liabilities as on incurred*	*1st Jan.*	*31th March incurred*	*30th June*	*30th Sept.*	*31st Dec.*
Cuttent Assets						Current Liabilities					
Fixed Assets						Other Liabilities					
Total Assets						Total Liabilities					

Prepared by ....

Submitted to ....

Date ....

❐

12

Contemporary Issues in Management Accounting

TECHNIQUES OF COSTING

Costing techniques refer the ways in which cost data is proccesed and related to cost centres and cost units. It relates the principles and rules governing ascertainment of cost of procedure and services. These techniques offer a guide as to which types of costs are charged to cost units or cost centres *e.g.* whether all costs are to be charged or only variable costs or the differential cost. The choice of costing techniques depends on the objectives of costing. Following are the techniques or types of costing:

(1) Absorption Costing or Full Costing. Absorption costing is also known as orthodox or conventional costing because this is the oldest costing technique and is followed even today. It is also called full costing or total costing because all chargeable costs whether fixed or variable, are charged to cost centres and cost units.

Under absorption costing both fixed and variable costs are treated as product cost, *i.e.*, both these costs are distributed over the output during the accounting period in which these costs have been incurred. Both cost of sales as well as unsold stocks are valued at variable cost plus proportionate fixed costs. Absorption costing is, thus, the process of charging all costs, both variable and fixed, to products, services, operations, jobs or processes. Technique of absorption costing is widely used for purposes of reporting.

(2) Marginal Costing or Variable Costing. Under marginal costing variable costs are treated as product cost but fixed costs are treated as period cost. Only variable costs, *i.e.*, direct material, direct labour, direct factory expenses and variable overheads, are charged to products, operations and processes. Fixed costs are wholly charged to the accounting period in which such costs are incurred, irrespective of quantity and value of goods produced and sold. Cost of sales as well as unsold stocks are valued at variable cost only.

According to C.I.M.A., marginal costing refers to "the accounting system in which variable costs are charged to cost units and fixed costs of the period are written off in full against the aggregate contribution. Its special value is in decision-making." Marginal costing is basically used for managerial decision-making and internal reporting. It helps in dumping decisions, make or buy, shut-down and product-mix decisions. It is more precise and offers a better yardstick for performance appraisal.

Direct costs are those which are conveniently and wholly identified with cost units. Therefore, it is said that under direct costing a unit is assigned only the direct cost. Indirect costs, including variable overheads, are disregarded for valuation of cost of sales and unsold stocks. It is said that marginal costing is based on variability of costs while direct costing is based on traceability of cost to cost units. Direct costs may include part of fixed costs which exclusively related to a particular product, and exclude variable overheads. The former are excluded under marginal costing and the latter are included.

However, in practice, the term marginal costing, variable costing and direct costing are used interchangeably, and they have been used as such in this text also.

(3) Uniform Costing. It is not a distinct form of costing. When a number of undertakings follow the same costing principles practices and procedures, it may be called uniform costing. According to C.I.M.A. Terminology it is "the use by several undertakings of the same costing system, *i.e.*, the same basic costing methods, principles and techniques." This involves standardisation of costing principles, methods and techniques by a number of undertakings, generally related in some way-being member of the same trade or industry association governed by the same regulatory agency. Standardisation may extend to defining costs and cost classifications, accounting, coding, depreciation methods, creation of cost centres, and methods of allocation and apportionment of cost.

Trade and industry associations, regulatory bodies or some such agencies may direct uniform costing to the undertakings under its control for purposes of cost comparision, common controls, establishment of common pricing policies, comparative performance evaluation, fixation of quotas, and collecting revenues in the form of duties, cess, etc.

(4) Differential Costing. As per C.I.M.A. Terminology, differential cost is "the difference in total cost between alternatives calculated to assist decision-making" Differential costing is the technique of comparing cost of two alternative for the purpose of deciding which alternative is the best.

The technqiues distinguishes between fixed and variable costs and also considers semi-variable costs. For example, if a producer is producing 10,000 units and he gets on order for 8,000 units more, he has to calculate cost of additional 8,000 units for comparing it with the price offered. The difference between the total cost of 18,000 unit and 10,000 units is the differential cost of 8,000 units and may involve semi-variable and fixed cost also, in addition to variable costs. It is a suitable technique for both short-run and long-run decision-making. Differential costing is a valuable technique for accept-reject decisions and for choice of alternatives.

DIFFERENT METHODS OF COSTING

The choice of a method of costing depends upon the nature of product, service and industry. Costs may be accumulated for a group of identical products, specific jobs, individual processes. Accordingly an appropriate method of costs collection is used.

Basic Methods

According to C.I.M.A. (Chartered Institute of Management Accountants) Terminology there are basically two methods of costing:

(i) Specific Order Costing. It includes job costing, batch costing and contract costing. Costing methods are applied to separate jobs, batches and contracts authorised by specific order. Each job, contract, etc. differs from the other and hence needs to be costed separately.

(ii) Operation Costing. It consists of costing methods applicable to standardised goods and services involving respective and continuous operations or processes. All costs are first charged to each individual operation or process. Cost of a product is ascertained by accumulating cost of its each process. Process costing and operating costing are examples of operation costing.

Many costing methods may not neatly fall into the category of either job costing or process costing. They may use some features of both the main costing systems. Such methods which combine the features of the basic costing methods may be called hybrid costing methods. Various variants of basic costing methods are discussed below?

(a) ***Job Costing.*** Under job costing costs are collected and accumulated for each job, project or work order separately. Each job is a separate cost unit. Each job is distinct, it is different from the other : and therefore, is to be separately costed.

Job costing is applicable to cases where the work is done according to customer's specification. In such cases a simple averaging of costs incurred during a period for different jobs does not give a meaningful value because costs vary markedly from job order to job order. Job costing is applicable to printing work, machine repair, machine installations, foundries, vehicle repair and servicing, engineering works, machine tools, etc.

(b) ***Contract Costing.*** A contract is a big job—big in terms of cost required and the time involved in completing a contract. Like jobs, each contract is different from the other. A contract is a cost unit. Costs are collected for each contract

separately. Large number of costs can be casily identified with specific contract because contracts are physically separate. Contract work is generally site-based. A separate account is maintained for each individual contract. A contract account is akin to mini Profit and Loss Account. It gives costs and profitability of each contract. This method is used in house building, engineering works, plant installations, ship-building, etc.

Job costing and contract costing are also known as 'Terminal Costing'

(c) ***Single, Unit or Output Costing.*** This method is applicable where an undertaking is producing standardised products in large number. Manufacture is continuous and the units produced are identical. The objective is to ascertain cost per unit of each product as well as the detailed components of costs. The cost per unit is determined by dividing the total cost incurred by the total number of units produced. Cost accountant periodically prepares cost sheet for each product giving full details regarding its cost.

Unit costing methods is applicable in industries like mining, oil drilling, cement works, brick works, breweries, steel production, etc. In all these cases there is a natural or standard unit of cost. The whole production cycle is costed as a single process.

(d) ***Process Costing.*** This method of costing is suitable for industries where manufacturing is carried on by distinct and well defined process. For example, in textile industry the three distinct processes are spinning, weaving and printing. Output of one processs becomes input for the next process, *e.g.*, output of spinning process is spun yarn which is input of weaving process, and output of weaving process is plane cloth which is input for printing process. Each procees produces identical units. Final output is obtained at the end of final process. There may be losses

and wastage at different processes. Some of the products may be produced jointly.

In process industries, make or buy decisions are involved before and after each process. Such decisons can be taken only if cost at each process is ascertained separately. Moreover, considerations of ascertaining efficiency at each process also require collection of cost at each process. This is done by preparing Process Account for each process. Total cost incurred at a process divided by total number units produced at the process gives cost per unit at the process. Due to this averaging, the method is called average costing. As the products are manufactured in continuous processes, particularly during modern times of mechanisation and automation, this is also called Continuous Costing. Process costing is suitable for textiles, chemicals, cement, breweries, paper, sugar industry, etc.

Conditions for use of process costing are:

(a) Continuous mass production;

(b) Production in distinct stages or processes;

(c) Output of one stage is input for the next stage;

(d) Units produced at each process are identical;

(e) Each stage or process produces saleable product; and

(f) Complete standardisation of products and processes.

(e) ***Operation Costing.*** Application of this method requires that production process of a product is separated in different operations. For example, production of a steel almirah is divided in operations, such as, cutting a steel sheet, welding the body, welding compartments, fixing the door and the handle, and polishing. Each operation is costed separately. The system is used when large quantities of standardised units are produced under repetitive conditions. Operation costing involves simultaneous production of different part of a product through use of different operations. Cost unit

may be a component or operation involved in production. Sum total of cost of all component or of all operations involved in obtaining the final product gives cost of the product.

Use of operation costing is very beneficial for cost control and achievement of high degree of efficiency where each production activity and process is divided into minute operations and a minute analysis of costs is done operation-wise. The system of operation costing is used where a repetitive production is carried out, production can be divided into distinct operations, or where components are to be stocked in semi-finished conditions for execution of special orders. The method is suitable for industries like leather products, toy-making, engineering, repair shops, etc.

(f) ***Composite or Multiple Costing.*** This method of costing is used where cost of a product cannot be ascertained by using any one of the above methods. It requires application of two or more of the methods of costing because the production is complex involving production of large number of parts of different types and sizes. The method is used in industries where a large number of components are produced separately and ten assembled into a final product. Cost of final product is obtained by adding cost of all components. Computation of cost of different components may be made by using different methods of costing due to varying nature of these components. Assembly of these components into final product may require use of still different method of costing. this type of costing is used in industries such as, automobiles, refrigerators, televisions and other electronics, computers, aeroplane, etc.

(g) ***Operating Costing.*** The method of operating costing is used for undertakings rendering service rather than producing tangile products. It is also used for service

departments of an undertaking. Examples of such services are passenger and freight transport, power generation, education, hospital, hotel, water works, gas supply, etc. An appropriate cost unit is to be selected to suit the nature of service. Operating costing, which is also called service costing, generally uses composite unit. The cost unit may be passenger-kilometre, ton-mile, kilowatt-hour, per lecture, per bed or per guest per day, etc.

(h) ***Cost-plus Costing.*** In case the payment of cost of work done to the contractor includes sum total of direct and indirect cost and also profit calculated as per agreed formula, the system is called cost-plus costing. The practice is prevalent in contracting business.

(i) ***Alternative-use Costing or Opportunity Costing.*** This is not strictly a method of cost ascertainment. It deals with the problem of demonstrating the most profitable course of action out of several available alternatives. The method involves comparison between not only costs and benefits from any particular project, but also from all available alternative. It is, therefore, more concerned with comparative rather than actual costs.

(j) ***Activity Based Costing (ABC).*** ABC is a new practice of assigning costs of jobs and process. As per ABC the cost are collected according to activities in business, such as, material ordering, material handling, quality testing, machine setups, soldering, insertion of parts, field demonstrations, after sale services, etc. Cost of each activity is ascertained separately. Jobs and processes for which cost is being determined are loaded with the cost of these activities depending on which job or process has made use of which activity to what extent. According to C.I.M.A. Terminology activity based costing refers to "cost attribution to cost units on the basis of benefits received from indirect activities, *i.e.*, ordering, setting-up, assuring quality, etc." ABC is also called 'activity accounting'.

ABC attempts to ascertain cost of units on the basis of cause and effect relationship. It emphasises inter-relationship between individual activities and the demand they make on the organisational resources. It also establishes a link between the activities required for producing products or services and their cost. ABC thus gives a clearer picture of revenues generated by products, brands, territories, clientage groups, facilities and distribution channels, and the resources consumed by them. ABC regards activity as a cost object and highlights inter-relationship between activities in different departments.

Under ABC overheads are not viewed merely as a burden which need to be minimised. Due importance is attached to overhead functions because a number of these functions, *e.g.*, production design, quality control, production planning and scheduling, attending to customer orders, after sale services etc., are as important as physical production process. All these overhead functions are separately costed under ABC.

ABC recognises that products, jobs and processes, etc. do not directly consume resources, but consume activities, which consume resources. The focus is on efficient management of activities-break them into parts, or combine them, or even do away with them if they are redundant or too expensive. Costs are brought down by managing the each activity well, *i.e.*, performing them most efficiently and economically. If the cost of activities is kept low, the cost of final product or service will also remain low.

ABC approach recognises a business as collection of activities—research and development, product design, product development, product introduction and promotion, and customer support activities. The business activities convert input from suppliers into output for consumers. The emphasis is on value addition and customer services.

(k) ***Life Cycle Costing.*** Product life cycle starts from the time of initial research and development till the time sale to the customers is completed. *i.e.*, after sale support is wihtdrawn. Various stages in the product life cycle are : research and development, product design manufacturing, marketing, distribution, and customer service including all after sale services.

Life cycle costing traces all types of capital costs and revenue costs to different stages in the product life cycle starting from initial research and development till the last stage of after sale customer services. It accumulates cost for all activities occurring over the entire life cycle of a product from its inception till it is finally abandoned.

Life cycle costing considers total cost—both capital cost and revenue cost, over the entire life of the product including all types of production office and administration, and marketing overheads. Since this costing considers the entire life span of the product it is also called 'cradle to grave' and 'womb to tomb' costing. As per C.I.M.A. Terminology life cycle costing is "the practice of obtaining over their life-times, the best use of physical assets at the lowest cost to the entity". The system is of great value for long-term decision-making and is especially usefull in capital budgeting.

VALUE CHAIN ANALYSIS

Value Chiain analysis is useful for the firms which manufacture any product and sell it or sender services. The concept of value chain was first of all sugested by Michael Porter in 1985. Porter described the value chain as "the internal processes or activities a company performs to design, produce, market, deliver and support its product. The further stated that a firms value chain and the way it performs individual activities are a reflection of its history, its strategy, its approach of implementing its strategy, and the underlying economies of the activities themselves." Porter has classified the business activities under two titles *e.g.* primary activities and secondary activities. Primary activities are concerned with converting the inputs directly into outports and delivery of products and after sale devices. In other words they include the following items:

(1) Movement and storage of materials

(2) Converting the inputs in to the end products.

(3) Getting orders and making their supply.

(4) Communication pricing and sales medium management.

(5) Establishment, repair and restoration of parts.

Secondary activities are those which are helpful for primary activities. These include the following items :

(1) Getting Materials. Supply of materials and purchase of consumable materials and assets.

(2) Technical Development. Technical know-how, processes and knowledge of technical input necessary for value chain activity.

(3) Human Resource Management. Recruitment, promotion, work place, evaluation, reward, management development and labour/employee relation.

(4) Basic Infrastructure. General management, planning, finance, accounting, legal, official work and quality management.

John Shank and V. Govindarajan have described the value chain in a comprehensive sense. According to them, "The value chain for any firm is the value-creating activitis all the way from basic raw material sources from components suppliers through to the ultimate end use product delivered into the final consumers hands." This statement shows the firm is a part of whole chain of the processes creating value of the firm.

The firms utilise the cost of internal processes and value chain concept in identifying the sources of profitability. Value chain analysis is not a proper science nor it is easier to understand. It is more an art in spite of being proper accounting report. There are a number of limitations in applying and interpreting the value chain analysis. It is, therefore not very practical.

ACTIVITY BASED COSTING

Activity based activity is a new search in the field of cost accounting in which overheads are absorbed in the cost of products on more practical basis. It is often argued by the supporters of this technique that a number of costs are located unnecessarily as common costs and they are absorbed on hypothetical basis. Number of firms have now adopted developed product technique resulting in overheads and labour cost hs now become a small part of the total cost. It is not relevant to absorb the overheads on the basis of direct labour in such an environment. The main basis of the activity based costing is that costs should be classified on the basis of their operation or reasons, then the cost drivers are utilised is a basis of absorption.

Coplan and Kooper of Harbard Business School who evolved this new concept for identifying the product cost in costing process. Stated that costs are to be classified into long term variable costs and short term variable costs. Traditionally short term variable costs are changing costs and long term variable costs are called fixed costs. Short term variable costs are related to product quantity and varies in proportion to the changes in product quantity. Long term variable costs varies in long run and not with production.

Coplan and Kooper further claims that this concept links the overhead costs with the forces inherent behind them commonly known as 'cost drivers'. Cost drivers may be defined as the activities or practices which are important cost determiner. In the method of activity based costing, product cost is identified keeping in new the better understanding of cost practices and the resources consumed through each product. Cost driver is an activity which creates cost. Activity based costing is dependent on this belong that activities create cost and therefore a relation between activities and products must be established.

Activity based costing follows this concept that all the activities of a company are in fact performed for the assistance and support to the product and delivery of materials and services. That is why they are to be treated as product cost. Almost all costs are separate as per factory and office overheads. They may be marked as individual products and product families as well. This is the concept of activity based costing under whch costs may be controlled more effectively by managing the forces causing such activities. We can understand the reasons of overhead costs with help of the report of cost consumed through major activities of the firm and their cost drivers. Thus the activity based costing provides more useful and suitable information for product mix decisions and controlling the performance activities.

Activity based costing is an accounting technique which emphasizes the cost of activities against the product and services. Due to this process the consumers of the product and services have to bear the burden of resources and overhead costs.

Step in Activity Based Costing

The following steps are needed for activity based costing :

(1) The major activities performed in firms are identified as product, collection etc.

(2) Identify the components effecting the cost of each activity cost drivers.

(3) Collect the correct datas regarding direct materials, direct labour and overhead costs.

(4) Determine the cost drivers for each activity relating the product with overhead costs.

(5) The subsidiary activities should be based on major activities.

(6) The cost of activities should be based on product as per the demand of product activities. For this the activity cost driver rate will be identified in the same way as overhead absorption rate in traditional system is identified:

$$\text{Activity Cost Driver Rate} = \frac{\text{Total Cost of Activity}}{\text{Activity Driver}}$$

Activity driving rate may be utilised for identifying the cost of product but it may also be used for identifying the cost of customer services and that of distribution means.

The whole process of activity based costing may easily be understood with the following:

Illustration.

A company produces three products A, B and C for which the standard costs and quantities per unit are as follows :

Products	*A*	*B*	*C*
Quntity produced	10,000	20,000	30,000
Direct materials/p.u. (Rs.)	50	40	30
Direct labour/p.u. (Rs.)	30	40	50
Labour hours/p.u.	3	4	5
Machine hours/p.u.	4	4	7
No. of Purchase requisitions	1,200	1,800	2,000
No. of set-ups	240	260	300

Production overhead split by departments

—Department 1 = Rs. 11,00,000

—Department 2 = Rs. 15,00,000

Department 1 is labour intensive and Department 2 is machine intensive

Total labour hours in Department 1 = 1,83,333

Total machine hours in Department 2 = 5,00,000

Production overhead split by activity

—Receiving/inspecting	Rs. 14,00,000
—Production scheduling/machine set-up	Rs. 12,00,000
	Rs. 26,00,000

Number of batches received/inspected = 5,000

Number of batches for scheduling and set-up = 800

You are required to :

(i) Prepare Product Cost Statement under traditional absorption costing and Activity Based Costing method.

(ii) Compare the results under two methods.

Solution.

Traditional Absorption Costing :

Absorption r ates :

$$\text{Department 1} = \frac{\text{Rs. } 11{,}00{,}000}{1{,}83{,}333 \text{ labour hours}} = \text{Rs. 6 per labour hour}$$

$$\text{Department 2} = \frac{\text{Rs. } 15{,}00{,}000}{5{,}00{,}000 \text{ machine hours}} = \text{Rs. 3 per machine hour}$$

Product Cost Statement :

Products	*A*	*B*	*C*
	Rs.	Rs.	Rs.
Direct materials	50	40	30
Direct labour	30	40	50
Overhead :			
Department 1	18	24	30
	(3 hrs. × Rs. 6)	(4 hrs. × Rs. 6)	(5 hrs. × Rs. 6)
Department 2	12	12	21
	(4 hrs. × Rs. 3)	(4 hrs. × Rs. 3)	(4 hrs. × Rs. 7)
	110	116	131

Activity Based Costing

Cost driver rates :

$$\text{Receiving/inspecting} = \frac{\text{Rs. } 14{,}00{,}000}{5{,}000 \text{ (No. of batches received / inspected)}}$$

$$= \text{Rs. 280 per requisition}$$

Production scheduling/Machine set-ups

$$= \frac{\text{Rs. } 12,00,000}{800 \text{ (No. of batches for scheduling)}}$$

= Rs. 1,500 per requisition

Product Cost Statement (per unit)

Products	*A*	*B*	*C*
	Rs.	Rs.	Rs.
Direct materials (Rs.)	50	40	30
Direct labour (Rs.)	30	40	50
Overhead :			
Receiving	34*	25	19
Production scheduling	36*	20	15
Total cost per unit	150	125	114

(Rs. 280 × 1,200) ÷ 10,000 units = Rs. 34*; similarly Rs. 25 and Rs. 19)

(Rs. 1,500 × 240) ÷ 10,000 units = Rs. 36**; similarly Rs. 20 and Rs. 15

The two absorption methods produce different results. Product C apears to be much more expensive using the traditional method than it does with ABC, while product A is the opposite. If it is assumed that ABC is more accuate, which it may or may not be, then product C would be overpriced on the traditional method and sales would presumably be poor as a consequence—assuming competitors supply more cheaply. Product A would be the opposite: sales would be high and it is possible that the company would unknowingly make a loss per unit on product A.

MATERIAL CONTROL

Material or inventory control involves systematic control and regulation of procurement, storage and usage of materials so as to maintain a smooth flow of production with optimum investment in inventories. Thus, basically material control is to be exercised at three stages:

(a) Control on policies, systems and procedures connected with the procurement of materials:

(b) Control of storage of materials; and

(c) Control on issue and usage of materials.

These controls primarily aims at ensuring that:

(i) Prodcution process is not hampered due to non-availability of materials at right time and of right quality; and

(ii) Investment in materials is kept at optimum level so that cost of materials per unit of output is kept at minimum.

Importance of Material Control

Material cost is a major element in total cost of production. Materials constitute more than 60 per cent of total cost in large variety of manufacture, such as, cotton yarn, cotton textile, earth moving equipment, small tools, sugar, woollen textile, jute products, bread and other confectionary items. In a modern competitive world, a small percentage of wastage in material handling and material use may push an organisation into losses.

There could be losses at the time of purchase of materials in a large number of ways:

(i) purchase of too large quantities resulting in larger storage costs;

(ii) purchases in too small lots resulting in larger ordering costs;

(iii) purchases at higher price either due to inefficient buying or involving manipulations;

(iv) delayed purchases;

(v) purchases of inappropriate quality, etc.

Lack of control on materials or loose control results in higher consumption of materials per units of output, wastage, spoilage, higher scrap and pilferage. All these result in higher cost of output.

In many cases overheads are also related to material cost. An economy in material consumpton also results in reduction in overhead cost per units of output.

Inefficiencies and frauds relating to materials have an impact on overall culture and environment in the organisation. These inefficiencies and frauds tend to penetrate deeper and spread wider. They tend to result in total collapse of the undertaking unless a costly surgery is undertaken at some stage.

Quantitative and Financial Controls

Material control involves control at two levels:

(i) Control on total quantity of materials purchased, stored and used, called quantity controls: and

(ii) Control on total monetary investment in materials, called financial controls.

There is no conflict between the two. In fact the two are complementary. A control on physical units of materials at the time of purchasing, storage and use in production will automatically result in lower investment in inventories.

CONFLICT IN DEPARTMENTAL OBJECTIVES

Purchase department is interested in reducing its work load and simultaneously demonstrating that purchases are made at lowest prices and at lowest overhead costs relating to purchasing function. Consequently they are interested in bulk purchases. This will mean larger investment in inventories. Production manager is cautious that production must never stop or slow down due to inadequate supplies of materials. He is also interested in longer production runs to minimise production cost. As a result he always wants abundant supplies of materials to take care of all production related contingencies. These considerations lead to larger investment in inventories.

Finance manager aims at pruning all unnecessary investment in inventories. His objective is to facilitate smooth production with minimum necessary investment in materials.

Material control reconciles these conflicts through encouraging efficiency in material procurement, efficieny in storage and efficiency in issue and usage of materials, the last largely falling within the domain of production function.

Aspects of Material Control

There are two aspects of material control: (a) Accounting and procedural aspect, and (b) Operational aspect:

(a) ***Accounting and Procedural Aspect.*** This is concerned with laying down detailed procedures for requisitioning, ordering, receiving, stocking, issuing, and paying for materials, This includes maintaining documentary evidence from the stage requirement of materials is initiated till the time materials are used in production.

(b) ***Operational Aspect.*** This deals with maintaining adeqaute supplies of all types of materials for smooth production operations; and also keeping investment in materials at lowest levels.

Objectives of Material Control

Two basic objectives of material control are; Continuous supply of materials for smooth production, and meeting material requirement at least cost. These can be further elaborated into the following objectives of material control:

1. **Continuous Availability of Materials.** Materials of all types should always be available for production. Situation of production stoppages due to materials running out of stocks, should be avoided. Such production stoppages are very costly in terms of loss of overheads and denial of sale. Panicky purchases should also be avoided.

2. **Optimum Investment in Materials.** Excessive investment in materials resulting from over stocking reduces profitability of the business. An important objective of material control is to ensure that the requirements of materials are met with minimum investment in materials.

Over stocking of materials locks up capital unproductively and increases storage cost. It is as bad as under stocking.

3. **Economy Purchasing.** Materials should be purchased at the lowest possible price without sacrificing quality, regularity and dependability of supplies.

4. **Regular and Dependable Information about Materials.** There should be up-to-date records of each type of material—the stock position, the minimum and the maximum level, special problems regarding certain types of materials and the list of dependable suppliers. This helps placing order of right size, at the right time and to the right supplier.

5. **Strict Quality Control.** There should be a strict system of quality control. The order for supplies of right quality of materials should be authorised. Materials should be tested at the time of their receipts and the person who has tested them should initial his work so that responsibility can be fixed if the quality has been compromised.

6. **Minimum Handling Cost and Time.** Materials should be stored at such a place and in such a manner that:

   (i) materials can be located at ease,

   (ii) there is minimum effort involved in making materials available to the user departments, and

   (iii) time consumed in tracing the materials and making them reach the user department should be least.

IMPORTANCE OF FIXED AND VARIABLE COST FOR DECISION-MAKING

Both fixed and variable costs are important for decision-making. However, their comparative importance differs at project stage and at operations stage.

Project stage or planning stage is one when the firm is in the process of deciding. What to produce? Which technology to deploy? How much capacity to create? And where to locate?

When the above basic decisions have been taken and implemented, and the firm is actually producing and selling, then it is said to be at the operations stage or operating stage.

At project stage both fixed and variable costs are relevant to decision-making process. The choice of product, technology, capacity size and location, and all governed by both these costs. The firm will not install a plant unless it hopes to recover both fixed variable costs fully and earn an adequate profit. It will choose that technology and location which result in least total of fixed and variable cost at the anticipated level of activity.

However, at project stage fixed cost acquires greater importance due to its various characteristics already mentioned. Decision regarding fixed costs involve large sum of money, are of irrevocable character, and affect operations of a firm for a long period of time. Hence these decisions attract greater attention.

At operations stage most of the fixed costs are sunk costs. They have been incurred and we can do nothing about them. Only way to recover them is to utilise them. The golden rule is let bygones be bygones. Let the dead remain buried in the grave. This approach holds true in all spheres in life. If we understand the rules of life deeply, the rules in spiriutal life and materialistic life are not so much different as they apparently appear. Whatever has happened, has happened. Our current decisions should be based on current costs. Therefore most decisions at operations stage are guided by variable costs.

Fixed costs become irrelevant for a number of decisions at operations stage. There is no point crying over costs which have already been incurred and we can do nothing in respect of them. Let our present decisions be not distorted by past costs. Certain fixed costs, such as, cash fixed costs, avoidable fixed and discretionary fixed costs have a role to play in certain decisions at operations state. Understanding the distinction between fixed and variable costs and their role in different types of decisions at different stages, is the crux of decision-making-budgeting, cost analysis, cost control, price fixation, make or buy, shut down, acceptance or rejection of a proposal, profit planning, etc.

CONTRACT COSTING PROCEDURE

The basic procedure for recording costs of contracts is as follows:

Contract Number. Each contract is assigned a distinct contract number for the purpose of identifying contracts and costs associated with contracts.

Contract Ledger. A Contract ledger is maintained in which a separate ledger account is opened for each contract for recording complete details of costs incurred, work-in-progress, revenues and profits or losses from each contract. Specimen of contract ledger is as follows:

Contract Ledger

Contract Account

Contract No........................	Contract Price.....................
Site Location......................	Terms of Payment...............
Date of Commencement......	Work Certified....................
Date of Completion............	Date................Rs...............
Remarks............................	Date................Rs...............

Dr. Cr.

Date	Particulars	Materials	Wages	Direct Expenses	Overheads	Sub-Contract Costs	Other exp.	Total	Date	Particulars	Materials	Wages	Direct Expenses	Overheads	Sub-Contract Costs	Other exp.	Total
Total																	

COST OF PRODUCTION

Sum total of prime cost, production overheads and office and administration overheads is known as 'cost of production'.

Selling and Distribution Overheads

All cost incurred in making the finished product reach upto the customer are grouped as 'selling and distribution overheads'. These costs can be categorised as: *(i)* selling costs, *(ii)* publicity costs, and *(iii)* distribution costs.

(i) Selling costs refer to all those incurred on maintaining the sales office and sales staff *e.g.*, sales office rent, expenses relating to sales office-telephohe, stationery, light, etc., sales salaries, sales commision, marketing research, etc.

(ii) Publicity costs include expenditure incurred on advertisments and sales promotion, such as, publicity through television, radio, sign boards, neon signs, posters, hand bills, etc.

(iii) Distribution expenses include all expenses incurred in transporting the product from producer's premises to the customer's place, *e.g.*, carriage outward, expenses relating to delivery van, etc.

Cost of Sales

Total of prime cost, production overheads, office and administration overheads and selling and distribution overheads is known as 'cost of sales'.

Cost Sheet or Cost Statement

Cost sheet is prepared periodically to present details of cost incurred during a particular period on producing a particular cost unit. It gives details regarding total cost as well as different components of the total cost and cost per unit. Following are the components of cost:

1. Prime Cost = Direct Maerials + Direct Labour + Direct Factory Expenses.

2. Production Cost or Works Cost = Prime Cost + Factory Overheads.
3. Cost of Production = Production Cost + Office and Administration Overheads
4. Cost of Sales = Cost of Production + Selling and Distribution Overheads.
5. Sales = Cost of Sales ± Profit/Loss.

The build-up of cost and the details of cost components are given in the form of a chart also.

Functional Classification of Cost and Cost Build-up

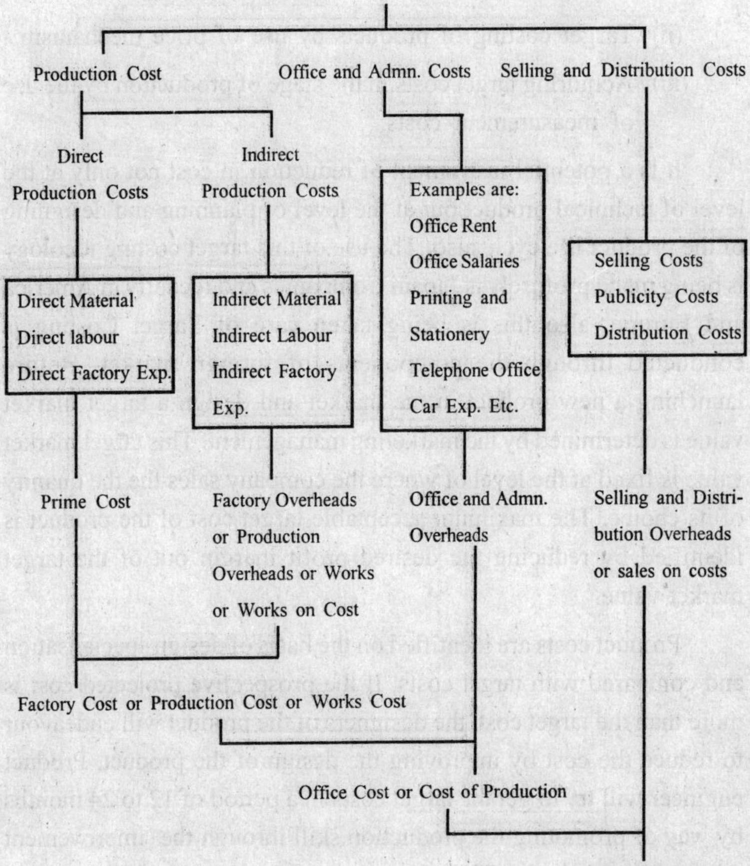

TARGET COSTING

Target costing was evolved in 1970's in Japan. Target costing may be defined as an instrument of cost management utilised in reduction of the total cost of product with the help of production, engineering, research and development etc. in its life cycle. Target cost is the projected cost of a product that enables a company to persist and compete in the market for a long time.

Shakugai has stated the process of target costing as under:

(i) Designing and planning of products of high quality which would satisfy the needs of customers.

(ii) Target costing of products by use of price mechanism.

(iii) Acquiring target costs in the stage of production by the use of measurement costs.

It is a potential instrument of reduction in cost not only at the level of technical product but at the level of planning and designing of the product life cycle also. The use of this target costing ideology is being made profusely is Japani Companies and recently in America and Europe, also this is being taken care of Target Costing is conducted through the components of foreign market. Before launching a new product in the market and design a target market value is determined by the marketing management. This target market value is fixed at the level of where the company sales the the quanity of its choice. The maximum acceptable target cost of the product is identified by reducing the desired profit margin out of the target market value.

Product costs are identified on the basis of design specialisation and compared with target costs. If the prospective projected cost is more than the target cost, the designers of the product will endeavour to reduce the cost by improving the design of the product. Product engineer will try to get the target costs in a period of 12 to 24 months by way of promoting the production skill through the improvement of product methods. This the team of designers, engineers and market managers will concentrate on the necessity of getting the target cost in the production along with cost accountant.

This concept is also used for reduction in the existing product cost. Where the target costing concept is used, the cost of the product is determined by market value and cost pricing is not utilised for the purpose. The cost of a new product may be more than the target cost yet the target cost is the only base of the product decisions. It is expected to equalise the product target cost at a particular demand level with product management like target competetive price. Ultimately it becomes the target of the company.

Steps in the Target Costing Process

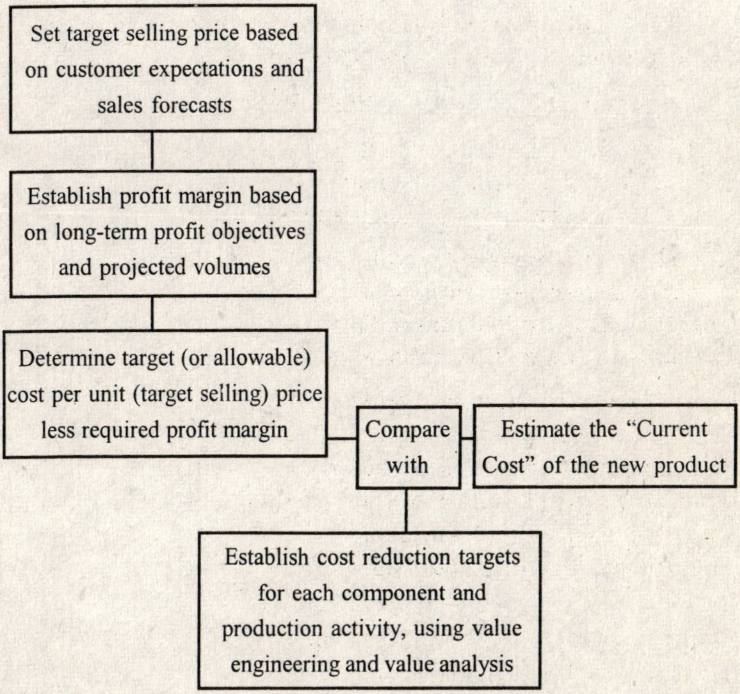

Component costs, involving reverse engineering [illegible]